Risks and Returns

Risks and Returns
Managing Financial Trade-Offs for Inclusive Growth in Europe and Central Asia

David Michael Gould and Martin Melecky

 WORLD BANK GROUP

Contents

Figures

Tables

About the Authors and Contributors

Authors

David Michael Gould is Lead Economist in the Europe and Central Asia (ECA) Region of the World Bank. David is the author of several books and peer-reviewed journal articles on international trade and finance, migration, and economic policy. Currently, he is leading ECA regional flagship studies on networks and connectivity and financial market development. During his 13 years at the World Bank, he has led teams to deliver country development strategies and analytical and lending operations in Europe, Latin America, and South Asia. Before coming to the World Bank, David served as the Director of Global Economic Analysis at the Institute of International Finance and as Senior Economist and Policy Adviser at the U.S. Federal Reserve. He has held visiting research positions at the Central Banks of Mexico and Chile. He holds a PhD in international economics from UCLA and is a Chartered Financial Analyst (CFA) charter holder.

Martin Melecky is Lead Economist in the Office of the Chief Economist for South Asia at the World Bank. Currently, he leads two regional flagships: *Economic Corridors of South Asia* and *Finance for Shared Prosperity in Europe and Central Asia*. Recently, he has led financial sector assessment programs, development policy operations, and investment and technical assistance projects in Kazakhstan, Maldives, Moldova, Montenegro, Sri Lanka, and Tajikistan. He is the lead author of the chapter in the 2014 *World Development Report* on the role of the financial system in risk management. His country experience with the World Bank also covers Albania, Armenia, Bulgaria, the Arab Republic of Egypt, the former Yugoslav Republic of Macedonia, Romania, the Russian Federation, and Turkey. Before coming to the World Bank, Martin worked as an Economist at the Dutch Central Bank, as a Consultant at the European Central Bank, and as a Consultant for the Czech National Bank. His research has focused on financial stability and financial inclusion, monetary policy and macroeconomic modeling, public debt management and fiscal policy, and currency substitution and exchange rate dynamics. He has coauthored two books and published more than 30 papers in professional journals. A Czech national, Martin received a PhD in economics from the University of New South Wales, Australia.

Contributors

Elisabeth Beckmann is an Economist in the Foreign Research Division of the Austrian Central Bank, where her main responsibility is the OeNB Euro Survey of households in Central, Eastern, and Southeastern Europe. She has published in peer-reviewed journals and is Country Economist for Croatia, contributing to the regular economic forecast. She wrote the contribution to this report while on secondment in the Office of the Chief Economist for Europe and Central Asia at the World Bank. Elisabeth studied at University College London, Ludwig Maximilian University of Munich, and the University of Glasgow; she holds a PhD in economics from the Vienna University of Economics and Business.

Leora Klapper is a Lead Economist in the Finance and Private Sector Research Team of the Development Research Group at the World Bank. Her publications focus on corporate and household finance, entrepreneurship, and risk management. Her current research studies the impact of digital financial services, especially for women. She is a founder of the Global Findex database, which measures how adults around the world save, borrow, make payments, and manage risk. Previously, she worked at the Board of Governors of the Federal Reserve System and at Salomon Smith Barney. She holds a PhD in financial economics from New York University Stern School of Business.

Davide Salvatore Mare is a Lecturer in business economics at the University of Edinburgh Business School and Research Fellow of the Institute for Competitiveness (I-Com). He collaborates with the World Bank on several research projects, including the Bank Regulation and Supervision Survey. Before joining the University of Edinburgh Business School, Davide gained extensive professional experience in risk management practices as a management consultant for top European banks in Italy, Spain, and the United Kingdom. He is an expert in the assessment of individual banks' risk of default and in applied financial valuation. His main research interests lie in banking, focusing on bankruptcy prediction, credit risk, and efficiency.

Georgi Panterov is a Research Analyst in the World Bank's Office of the Chief Economist for Europe and Central Asia. His research interests focus on financial markets, exchange rates, and econometrics. During his time at the World Bank, he has worked on the *Golden Aging* report and the ECA economic updates. Before joining the World Bank, he worked with Google, the U.S. Department of Agriculture, and American University. He is a PhD candidate in economics at American University in Washington, DC.

Anca Maria Podpiera is a Consultant for the World Bank in the areas of finance and macroeconomics. Her recent research focuses on macro and macroprudential supervision, stress-testing practices in Central and Southeastern Europe, consumer protection, and the role of financial sector strategies in developing financial sectors. She participated in Financial Sector Assessment Programs, covering issues of competition and efficiency of the financial sector. Before coming to the World Bank, she was an Economist in the Monetary and Statistics Department of the Czech National Bank. She is a Romanian national and holds a PhD in economics from the Center for Economic Research and Graduate Education, Prague.

Siddharth Sharma is an Economist at the World Bank, specializing in issues of firm-level productivity growth and innovation, business regulation, and the functioning of labor markets in low- and middle-income countries. His research has been published in peer-reviewed economics journals, and he has contributed chapters to a number of World Bank policy reports, including regional flagship reports on youth employment in Africa and population aging in Europe and Central Asia. Siddharth has an MA in economics from the Delhi School of Economics and a PhD in economics from Yale University.

Hernan Winkler is an Economist at the Office of the Chief Economist for the Europe and Central Asia Region of the World Bank. He specializes in applied microeconomics, with a particular focus on issues related to labor markets, and the sources and consequences of poverty and inequality. His research has been published in peer-reviewed journals, including the *Review of Economics and Statistics* and the *Journal of Development Economics*. He is currently leading a World Bank regional report on the effects of the Internet in Europe and Central Asia. He holds a PhD in economics from the University of California at Los Angeles.

Foreword

When the countries in the Emerging Europe and Central Asia (ECA) region began their quest to open up from centrally planned economies toward market-based systems some 25 years ago, I was a young financial analyst at the World Bank. I saw firsthand the infectious excitement among people, entrepreneurs, and policy makers for the expected new opportunities that greater economic freedom and access to finance offered. A banker in Estonia confidently told me the whole region was going from the "third world to the first world, without stopping at second." It was a chance to build economies from the bottom up, avoiding the mistakes more advanced countries had made in the past. Although there was much optimism at the time in the region, for many countries the transition was not the straightforward upward path they had anticipated. In fact, there were many bumps in the road; and it is easy to forget that it was excruciatingly painful at times, particularly during the early years, when economies and financial systems were being turned upside down.

Since the early stages of ECA's transition and recovery, the financial sector has played a crucial, but widely misunderstood, role in the region's development trajectory, particularly for the middle- and lower-income groups. It is cast as either the hero or the villain.

As the hero in the transition story, ECA financial systems' role in allocating credit helped entrepreneurs willing to take risks to transform old firms into new companies and provided financing for new industries that had never before existed in the region. It also helped modernize risk management systems, allowed for imports of new technology, and created more transparency in financial accounts as foreign banks flocked to the region demanding more harmonized financial information.

As the villain, the financial sector contributed to two costly crises in the late 1990s and post-2008. It went overboard in supplying credit during the booms because banks and authorities overlooked serious gaps in governance and prudential supervision. In the busts, credit may have contracted too much because authorities lacked the tools and legal frameworks to restructure bad debt, a situation that persists today, tying up money that could otherwise be used for productive investments.

While the hero-villain analogy is dramatic, it represents the core theme of this report and is relevant not just for Emerging ECA but also for many countries around the world—advanced and emerging. There are "risks and returns" in financial sector development, and the opportunities as well as trade-offs should be understood and incorporated into financial sector policy making. The development and transformation of ECA's financial sector has been one of the most critical aspects of transition to market-based economies in the past quarter-century, and in many ways this transition is still ongoing.

This topic is perhaps more important today than at any time since the 2008 financial crisis. Stagnating income growth, particularly of middle- to lower-income earners, has led to increasing dissatisfaction with the limited opportunities provided by the status quo. This frustration provides the impetus for reshaping financial policies. A healthy and balanced financial sector could strengthen structural adjustment in ECA's eastern, oil-dependent economies and innovation in its western countries.

Our report, *Risks and Returns: Managing Financial Trade-Offs for Inclusive Growth in Europe and Central Asia,* argues for reaching beyond increasing access to credit. ECA countries must build integrated (bank and nonbank) financial systems, enabling prudent inclusion in a region significantly lagging in the use of saving products. Striking the right balance across all dimensions of financial development (stability, efficiency, inclusion, and overall depth) is crucial for achieving and sustaining inclusive growth.

Redesigning financial policy involves addressing trade-offs often overlooked in the past. Too much credit and imprudent financial inclusion have led to banking crises. Overly stringent regulation has hindered inclusion and efficiency gains. Both shortfalls have had negative consequences for shared prosperity.

The report draws inspiration and its title from the fundamental principal of investing, which requires that undertaking the risk of an investment today be adequately guided by its future expected returns. Today's financial policy decisions involve an element of risk but should be guided by the prudent evaluation of trade-offs and analysis of expected development returns. The mutual aspiration of the people of Europe and Central Asia for inclusive financial development has been successful, even if some policy and institutional changes could further improve outcomes. The lessons learned from Emerging ECA's past and future success can be a guide to other regions around the world.

Cyril Muller
Vice President, Europe and Central Asia Region
The World Bank Group

Acknowledgments

This report was written by a team led by David Michael Gould, Lead Economist in the Office of the Chief Economist for Europe and Central Asia at the World Bank, and Martin Melecky, Lead Economist in the Office of the Chief Economist for South Asia at the World Bank (and formally Senior Financial Sector Specialist in Europe and Central Asia). The core team members were Davide Salvatore Mare, Georgi Panterov, Anca Maria Podpiera, and Hernan Winkler. The work was carried out under the overall supervision of Hans Timmer, Chief Economist for the Europe and Central Asia Region.

Thorsten Beck, Professor of Banking and Finance, Cass Business School, London, and Research Fellow, Centre for Economic Policy Research; Ross Levine, Professor and Willis H. Booth Chair in Banking and Finance, Haas School of Business, University of California at Berkeley; Ugo Panizza, Professor of Economics and Department Head, Pictet Chair in Finance and Development, The Graduate Institute of International and Development Studies; and Nicolas Véron, Senior Fellow at Bruegel and a Visiting Fellow at the Peterson Institute for International Economics provided their insights, encouragement, and guidance at all stages of this project. Many thanks go to Aurora Ferrari, Practice Manager, Financial Systems and Markets (GFM1A; World Bank); Maria Soledad Martinez Peria, Division Chief of the Macro-Financial Division, International Monetary Fund (IMF); Ceyla Pazarbasioglu, Senior Adviser, GFM1A; and Erik Feyen, Lead Financial Sector Economist, GFM1B, for their support and guidance during the writing of this project.

Many people participated in the writing of the report. The main authors and contributors were:

- Overview: David Michael Gould and Martin Melecky
- Chapter 1: Davide Salvatore Mare (with contributions by David Michael Gould and Georgi Panterov)
- Chapter 2: David Michael Gould, Martin Melecky, and Georgi Panterov
- Chapter 3: Hernan Winkler and Siddharth Sharma (with contributions by Thea Yde-Jensen)
- Chapter 4: Elisabeth Beckmann (visiting from the Austrian Central Bank) and Leora Klapper (with contributions by Jake Hess)
- Chapter 5: Martin Melecky and Davide Salvatore Mare
- Chapter 6: Martin Melecky and Anca Maria Podpiera.

Main authors on special topics were:

- Understanding the role and governance of state-owned banks: Ilias Skamnelos
- Problems confronting growth and financial systems in Central Asia: David Michael Gould and Konstantin Dorofeyev
- Tackling the high and persistent level of nonperforming loans in ECA: Carl Chastenay
- Achieving equilibrium credit provision in ECA countries with the help of cross-border supervision: Thorsten Beck and Katia D'Hulster
- Weighing different strategies for developing capital markets in ECA: Ana Carvajal with inputs from Georgi Panterov
- Developing private pension schemes in ECA: John Pollner
- Increasing the use of electronic payments: Lois Estelle Quinn
- Setting up the framework for macroprudential policy in ECA countries: Attila Csajbok
- Promoting the use of insurance for increased risks from climate change: Eugene Gurenko
- Learning from crisis simulation exercises in ECA: Aquiles Almansi and Attila Csajbok.

Ekaterina Ushakova oversaw the production of the report, and Rhodora Mendoza Paynor provided support. Content editing was done by William Shaw.

Many thanks go to commentators and reviewers at the initial stages of the report, including, at the World Bank, Laura Tuck, Vice President, Sustainable Development Practice Group; Martin Raiser, Country Director, Brazil; Samuel Munzele Maimbo, Practice Manager, Finance for Development; Saroj Kumar Jha, Senior Director, Fragility, Conflict, and Violence Cross-Cutting Solutions; Mamta Murthi, Director of Strategy and Operations, Africa Region; Ellen Goldstein, Country Director, South East Europe Country Management Unit; Qimiao Fan, Country Director, Bangladesh, Bhutan, and Nepal Country Management Unit; Rolf Behrndt, Practice Manager, Finance and Markets, Europe and Central Asia; and Martin Čihák, Adviser, IMF.

This report would not have been timely or relevant without the insights and inputs of the Austrian Central Bank; Polish Central Bank and Financial Supervision Authority; Polish Company for the Management of the Obligatory Pension Fund; Polish Confederation Lewiatan; Energa Group, Poland; Regional Pomeranian Chamber of Commerce, Gdansk, Poland; Central Bank of Uzbekistan; Central Bank of Romania; Central Bank of Tajikistan; Banking Association of Kazakhstan; Croatian Central Bank and Financial Services Supervisory Agency; European Bank for Reconstruction and Development; European Commission; Raiffeisen Bank; ERSTE Bank; UniCredit Bank; and Finance Watch, Brussels, as well as various private sector individuals and firms in the Emerging ECA region.

Abbreviations

ADB	Asian Development Bank
AMC	asset management company
B40	bottom 40 percent of the income distribution
BIS	Bank for International Settlements
BRSS	Bank Regulation and Supervision Survey
CAR	Capital Adequacy Ratio
CCB	countercyclical capital buffer
CRD IV	Capital Requirements Directive
CRR	Capital Requirements Regulation
CSE	crisis simulation exercise
DGF	deposit guarantee fund
DTF	distance to frontier
EAP	East Asia and Pacific
EBRD	European Bank for Reconstruction and Development
ECA	Europe and Central Asia
EU	European Union
Europa Re	Europe Reinsurance Facility Ltd.
FAS	Financial Access Survey (International Monetary Fund)
FIRST	Financial Sector Reform and Strengthening Initiative
FSAP	Financial Sector Assessment Program
FSC	financial stability council
FX	foreign exchange
GDP	gross domestic product
GEF	Global Environmental Fund
GFDD	Global Financial Development Database (World Bank)
IFC	international financial center
IFI	international financial institution
IMF	International Monetary Fund
LAC	Latin America and the Caribbean
LITS	Life in Transition Survey
LMIC	lower-middle-income country
MENA	Middle East and North Africa
NPL	nonperforming loan
NUTS	Nomenclature of Territorial Units for Statistics

OECD	Organisation for Economic Co-operation and Development
ROA	return on assets
SAR	special administrative region
SECO	State Secretariat for Economic Affairs (Switzerland)
SEE	Southeastern Europe
SEE CRIF	Southeastern Europe Catastrophe Risk Insurance Facility
SME	small and medium enterprise
SSA	Sub-Saharan Africa
TFP	total factor productivity
T60	top 60 percent of the income distribution
UMIC	upper-middle-income country
VOOC	voluntary out-of-court

Country and Economy Codes

AFG	Afghanistan
AGO	Angola
ARE	United Arab Emirates
ARG	Argentina
ARM	Armenia
AZE	Azerbaijan
BDI	Burundi
BEL	Belgium
BEN	Benin
BFA	Burkina Faso
BGD	Bangladesh
BGR	Bulgaria
BIH	Bosnia and Herzegovina
BLR	Belarus
BLZ	Belize
BOL	Bolivia
BTN	Bhutan
CAF	Central African Republic
CHE	Switzerland
CHL	Chile
CHN	China
CIV	Côte d'Ivoire
CMR	Cameroon
COD	Congo, Dem. Rep.
COG	Congo, Rep.
CRI	Costa Rica
CZE	Czech Republic
DJI	Djibouti
DNK	Denmark
DOM	Dominican Republic

ECU	Ecuador
EGY	Egypt, Arab Rep.
ESP	Spain
EST	Estonia
ETH	Ethiopia
FRA	France
GBR	United Kingdom
GEO	Georgia
GHA	Ghana
GIN	Guinea
GRC	Greece
GRD	Grenada
GTM	Guatemala
HKG	Hong Kong SAR, China
HND	Honduras
HRV	Croatia
HTI	Haiti
HUN	Hungary
IND	India
IRN	Iran, Islamic Rep.
IRQ	Iraq
ISR	Israel
JAM	Jamaica
JOR	Jordan
JPN	Japan
KAZ	Kazakhstan
KEN	Kenya
KGZ	Kyrgyz Republic
KHM	Cambodia
KOR	Korea, Rep.
KSV	Kosovo
KWT	Kuwait
LAO	Lao PDR
LKA	Sri Lanka
LTU	Lithuania
LUX	Luxembourg
LVA	Latvia
MAR	Morocco
MDG	Madagascar
MEX	Mexico
MKD	Macedonia, FYR
MLT	Malta
MMR	Myanmar
MNE	Montenegro
MNG	Mongolia
MOZ	Mozambique

MRT	Mauritania
MWI	Malawi
MYS	Malaysia
NAM	Namibia
NER	Niger
NGA	Nigeria
NLD	Netherlands
NOR	Norway
NPL	Nepal
NZL	New Zealand
PAN	Panama
PHL	Philippines
POL	Poland
PRT	Portugal
PRY	Paraguay
ROM	Romania
RUS	Russian Federation
RWA	Rwanda
SDN	Sudan
SEN	Senegal
SGP	Singapore
SLE	Sierra Leone
SLV	El Salvador
SRB	Serbia
SVK	Slovak Republic
SVN	Slovenia
TGO	Togo
THA	Thailand
TJK	Tajikistan
TKM	Turkmenistan
TTO	Trinidad and Tobago
TUR	Turkey
TZA	Tanzania
UGA	Uganda
UKR	Ukraine
URY	Uruguay
USA	United States
VCT	St. Vincent and the Grenadines
VEN	Venezuela, RB
VNM	Vietnam
WSM	Samoa
YEM	Yemen, Rep.
ZAF	South Africa
ZMB	Zambia
ZWE	Zimbabwe

Note: All dollar amounts are U.S. dollars ($) unless otherwise indicated.

Regional Classifications Used in This Report

Europe and Central Asia (ECA)

Central Asia

Central Europe

Other Eastern Europe

Russian Federation

South Caucasus

Turkey

Western Balkans

Central Asia	Central Europe	Other Eastern Europe	South Caucasus	Western Balkans
Kazakhstan	Bulgaria	Belarus	Armenia	Albania
Kyrgyz Republic	Croatia	Moldova	Azerbaijan	Bosnia and Herzegovina
Tajikistan	Czech Republic	Ukraine	Georgia	Kosovo
Turkmenistan	Hungary			FYR Macedonia
Uzbekistan	Poland			Montenegro
	Romania			Serbia
	Slovak Republic			
	Slovenia			

Benchmarking regional groups

Northern Europe	Southern Europe	Western Europe
Denmark	Cyprus	Austria
Estonia	Greece	Belgium
Finland	Italy	France
Latvia	Malta	Germany
Lithuania	Portugal	Ireland
Sweden	Spain	Luxembourg
		Netherlands
		United Kingdom

Overview

Main Findings of the Report

- Over the last 25 years financial sectors in Emerging Europe and Central Asia (ECA) developed unevenly. In the western part of the region, finance has been dominated by large foreign banks with rapid credit deepening, but at the cost of financial booms and busts. In the eastern part of the region, finance has been characterized by large, politically connected banks with high inefficiencies and exposure to domestic economic and political shocks, including the recent collapse in oil prices.

- To boost growth and shared prosperity, finance in ECA must become more balanced and account for trade-offs between financial inclusion and stability. ECA should strive to enhance financial efficiency, broaden finance beyond banking, and focus on inclusion through domestic saving rather than simply through credit expansion.

- Overall, a more balanced approach to financial development is necessary to underpin sustained inclusive growth and the ability of countries to better cope with current and future challenges—such as the need for structural economic shifts in the resource-rich eastern part of the region and further innovation and technological progress in the western part of the region.

Emerging ECA, perhaps now more than ever, faces the urgent need for financial sector reforms. Reforms are needed not only to make the region more resilient

1

to financial shocks but also to support efforts to strengthen income growth, particularly that of the middle- to lower-income earners, many of whom since the global financial crisis have questioned the benefits of greater economic and financial integration. Over the last 20 years, the region has confronted two major financial crises and is currently facing major banking stresses and currency pressures, if not full-blown crises, particularly in countries directly or indirectly dependent on oil exports. Moreover, the region now has to cope with greater policy uncertainty as Britain seeks a new relationship with the European Union (EU), the refugee crisis puts pressure on policy makers to slow migration, and many countries face new internal political dynamics.

> Reforms are needed not only to make the region more resilient to financial shocks but also to support efforts to strengthen income growth, particularly that of the middle- to lower-income earners.

The general sense of prolonged growth stagnation since the 2008 global financial crisis and lack of real (or perceived) improvement in standards of living of lower-income earners has led to an increasing level of dissatisfaction with the status quo, reflected in the changing regional political dynamics. Indeed, for the majority of lower- and middle-income households in Emerging ECA, real income levels have declined, or not increased appreciably, since they hit their peak in 2007.

Although improving financial sector development cannot solve all these problems, it can help support stability and inclusive growth. This, in turn, may help build a consensus for complementary policies that support inclusive sustainable growth, rather than a reflexive inward tug toward isolationism and away from the liberalization and integration policies that began during the early 1990s.

This report argues that financial development must go beyond improving the access to and pricing of credit. It should help build a broad-based and balanced financial system of both bank and nonbank markets, that enables responsible financial inclusion of firms and individuals and enhances financial efficiency and stability. Striking the right balance across these dimensions of financial development (stability, efficiency, inclusion, and broad depth) is crucial for finance to support inclusive and sustainable growth through improved transactions, savings mobilization, screening of projects, monitoring of firm managers, and risk management. Finding the right balance in financial development also involves trade-offs that are often overlooked, much to the peril of policy makers. Too much credit and overly generous support for financial inclusion (even if well-meaning) have led to financial bubbles and crises. Likewise, too much financial sector repression to achieve stability has generated financial exclusion and inefficiencies with negative consequences for economic opportunities and growth.

ECA Financial Systems Remain Vulnerable to Financial Shocks and Are Not Sufficiently Developed to Support Inclusive Growth

Despite some recovery since the 2008 crisis, ECA financial systems remain weak and vulnerable to further shocks. The share of nonperforming loans (NPLs) to total loans in ECA remains high at about 9 percent, ranging from about 30 percent in Ukraine to less than 1 percent in Uzbekistan; and several financial systems find it hard to reform and adjust. Financial policy makers are trying to boost the resilience of national financial systems and spur broad-based financial development.

Banks have faced considerable difficulties in adjusting to the more stringent regulatory standards introduced by the Financial Stability Board and Basel III, including the new Capital Requirements Regulation (CRR) and Directive (CRD IV) and the creation of a single supervisory mechanism in Europe. The adjustment process has been weaker in the eastern part of ECA in the least financially open economies. At the same time, Armenia, Belarus, the Kyrgyz Republic, the former Yugoslav Republic of Macedonia, the Russian Federation, Tajikistan, and Turkey joined the Alliance for Financial Inclusion by signing the Maya Declaration with important commitments to advance financial inclusion. Some ECA countries, such as Turkey, have already prepared financial inclusion strategies to implement policies and deliver on these commitments. A key element, however, is missing—the goal of supporting the resilience of financial systems is often at odds with making financial systems more inclusive, and this trade-off is rarely discussed among ECA's financial policy makers.

To understand ECA's financial development challenges, it is important to know the region's context. During the last 25 years, ECA's financial systems deepened from about 12 percent to about 55 percent of gross domestic product (GDP) on average. During the same period, ECA went through pronounced booms and busts in the credit cycle and experienced two waves of costly financial crises in the late 1990s and post-2008. As young institutions underpinning ECA's financial system developed, some countries learned to manage the financial cycle better than others, while the laggards on financial openness and liberalization have yet to feel the sting of large financial shocks. For instance, the Czech Republic and the Slovak Republic were hit hard by emerging market crises in the late 1990s but showed resilience during the 2008 global financial crisis. In contrast, Latvia and Russia were hit by both the emerging markets crises and the global financial crisis. Financially underdeveloped countries such as Turkmenistan and Uzbekistan were relatively shielded from the financial shocks because of their financial underdevelopment and still-low integration into global financial markets. To date, ECA's financial systems are only slowly recovering from the 2008 crisis, when financial deepening halted as the growth in both credit and GDP collapsed with an unclear path forward and urgent need for reform (figure O.1, panel a).

The roller coaster of ECA's financial development is reflected in the pattern of economic growth, as credit markets fed spending and growth exuberance during credit booms and starved depressed economies during credit busts (figure O.1, panel b). During boom times, access to credit eases and credit standards loosen, enabling risk-taking firms and individuals to overleverage and indulge in a spending frenzy. When market confidence plunges and credit intermediation freezes or contracts, both conservative and overleveraged creditors suffer and so does the economy. If the adjustment shock is really bad, the financial system and the economy can go into a crisis. To survive crises, banks often shrink loan portfolios and switch to the "risk-off" mode. This deprives some firms of necessary financing and delays economic recovery. The common policy response to crises has too often used taxpayers' money to bail out insolvent banks, and failed to adequately

FIGURE O.1 Booms and busts in ECA financial development affected economic growth

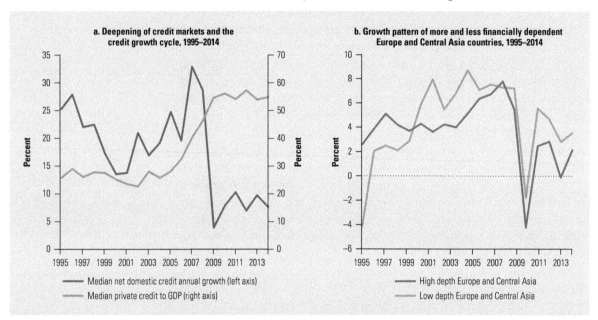

Sources: World Bank elaboration based on the Global Financial Development Database and World Development Indicators.
Note: The countries are divided into high and low depth if private credit to GDP is above or below the median for ECA.

address insolvencies of individuals. This response creates moral hazard and discourages saving as trust in the banking system falls.

As credit dependence of the economy increases, the effect of the booms and busts on the economy increases, too. Balancing broad financial development throughout the cycle becomes more and more important. Although the first wave of banking crises in ECA during the 1990s restrained economic growth in financially more dependent ECA countries, the second wave of crises after 2008 affected severely both more and less financially dependent countries in ECA—by 2008 both had reached higher levels of financial dependence (figure O.1, panel b). Today, the lack of trust in banks—demonstrated through high dollarization and low savings—combined with lagging financial efficiency render ECA financial systems unable to support economic growth.

The swing of policy from financial liberalization to regulatory tightening and back is one major factor behind the pronounced boom-and-bust pattern of ECA's financial cycles. Weak financial sector institutions and short-term populism in policy making often stand behind these switches in policy regimes. Financial liberalization often attracts risk-taking capital inflows that help the domestic financial system build leverage and economies of scale, but it comes also with greater aggregate liquidity risk exposure. Any sizable liquidity shock, be it domestic or foreign, is greatly amplified by this exposure and can distress the entire banking system. This dynamic can be observed in the increasing loan-to-deposit ratio of ECA's banking system before the two waves of banking crises (figure O.2, panel a). Countries such as FYR Macedonia or Armenia started with loan-to-deposit ratios greater than 250 percent in 1995. By 1998, Tajikistan's ratio stood at 505 percent,

FIGURE O.2 Financial liberalization and regulatory tightening can be added to the financial cycle

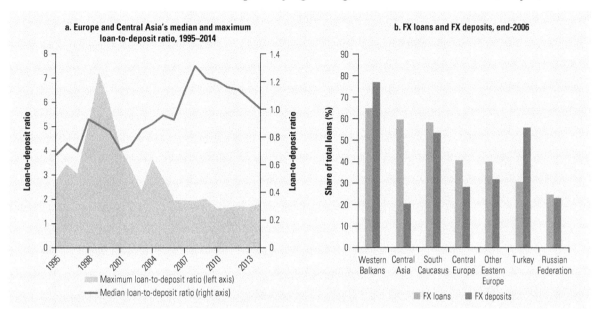

a. Europe and Central Asia's median and maximum loan-to-deposit ratio, 1995–2014

b. FX loans and FX deposits, end-2006

Maximum loan-to-deposit ratio (left axis)
Median loan-to-deposit ratio (right axis)

FX loans   FX deposits

Source: World Bank elaboration based on the Global Financial Development Database.
Note: FX = foreign exchange.

which was exceeded only by Bosnia and Herzegovina's ratio of 729 percent in 1999. Although these extremely high ratios in the 1990s could be ascribed to the economic transformation process, by 2007 the maximum loan-to-deposit ratios also reached unsustainable values. For instance, Kazakhstan, Ukraine, and Montenegro showed ratios of 197, 196, and 166 percent, respectively, in 2007.

When high exposure to aggregate liquidity risk is coupled with high exposure to aggregate foreign exchange (FX) risk, financial development becomes a house of cards (figure O.2, panel b). The aggregate hedging of lending in FX by deposits in FX is an illusion, as many countries, notably the Western Balkans, learned bitterly during the 2008 crisis. If all banks lend in FX to borrowers that do not earn FX, systemwide indirect exposure to credit risk can build up. If the local currency depreciates, the borrowers and banks run into big problems with insolvency. Croatia decided to tightly manage its currency relative to the Swiss franc to protect its retail borrowers in FX from continued stress, but this policy created other distortions, making the economy less competitive, and eventually had to be abandoned.

ECA policy makers face many challenges but possess only limited resources, including fragile political capital with pressure to deliver on sustained financial development that helps propel inclusive growth. Among the many challenges, ECA's policy makers will need to address the excessive focus on credit and its concentration in few economic sectors and income groups. Policy makers also need to encourage bank and nonbank credit institutions to supply credit to those in the economy who need it the most and can also manage it responsibly. Diversification could aid resilience, and ECA financial systems could take advantage of it. To this end, ECA can also develop a "spare tire" in its financial system—that is, the

FIGURE O.3 ECA is advanced on banking but lags on diversity in financial development

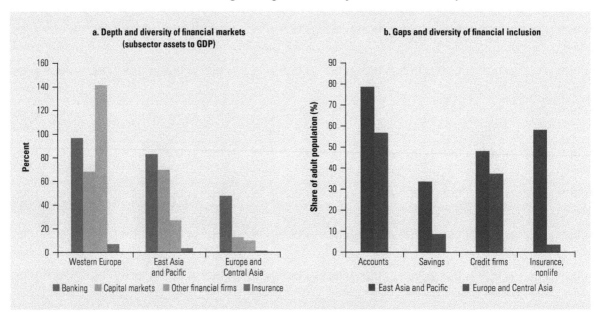

Sources: World Bank elaboration based on the Global Financial Development Database, Global Findex, and FinStats.

nonbank financial market including capital markets, the insurance sector, and other nonbank financial institutions. To date, Emerging ECA's financial system is significantly less developed and less diversified than the financial system of its closest benchmark, Western Europe, and its middle-income peer, East Asia and Pacific (EAP) (figure O.3, panel a).

Moreover, ECA policy makers need to focus on creating market incentives to improve the quality of financial sector deepening and diversification, ensuring that the financial system benefits more people and spreads across all income groups. ECA lags significantly behind EAP on the share of people with a bank account, those who formally save, firms that access credit lines, and people who can access (nonlife) insurance (figure O.3, panel b)—even though, on the use of e-payments, credit, and life insurance by individuals, ECA compares with EAP.

Setting Financial Policy Priorities

This report provides policy makers in ECA with a framework to set priorities for financial policies that incorporates universal cross-country experience but also provides a means to consider specific country context. It assumes that finance can be most useful for inclusive growth when people and firms can access and responsibly use finance; when finance is competitively priced; and when it is reliable and resilient—that is, when it does not propagate shocks back to people but helps them confront shocks. These desired attributes of finance correspond with measures of financial inclusion, efficiency, stability, and depth that are used to characterize the broad concept of financial development (box O.1). The four aspects together

BOX O.1 Financial Development: Dimensions and Selected Indicators

Stability. Nonperforming loans to total gross loans; balance sheet z-score (the sum of return on assets and the leverage ratio, all divided by the standard deviation of the return on assets); liquid assets to deposits and short-term funding; and bank capital to assets.

Efficiency. Net interest margin (percent of interest-bearing assets); overhead costs (percent of total assets); bank cost-to-income ratio; and stock market turnover ratio (percent of average market capitalization).

Inclusion. Number of branches per 100,000 adults; account at a financial institution (percent); borrowed from a financial institution (percent); debit card (percent); credit card (percent); saved at a financial institution (percent).

Depth (all indicators as percent of GDP). Private sector credit by financial intermediaries; domestic bank deposits; insurance premiums; stock market capitalization; and assets of nonbank financial intermediaries.

attempt to capture the ability of financial development to boost income growth and shared prosperity by mobilizing savings, evaluating projects, managing risks, monitoring managers, and facilitating transactions.

This report strives to capture the full concept of financial development and not focus on a single measure, such as financial depth. The report goes from the traditional summary measure of financial depth to the broader concept of financial development to get a more nuanced understanding of what matters for meaningful financial development that can support income growth and shared prosperity. We thus depart from the use of credit to GDP—which has proven an ambiguous measure of financial development (for instance Basel III now acknowledges the sustainable and unsustainable parts of the ratio)—as much as available data allow.

Through this framework, the report emphasizes three aspects to consider in decision making on financial policy: (a) the existing financial development gaps—that is, the distance to the financial development frontier the country should aim to close; (b) how much the closing of a particular gap—for financial stability, efficiency, inclusion, or depth—could advance growth and shared prosperity; and (c) whether the closing of one gap, such as the one for financial inclusion, can actually increase other gap(s), such as the one for financial stability, and pose a policy trade-off. Alternatively, is there a possibility that the closing of one gap can help close another gap and create synergies?

We use the chapters of the report to populate the framework for prioritizing financial policies in view of trade-offs (figure O.4). Chapter 1 benchmarks ECA and its subregions against its peers and the financial development frontier, performing the diagnostics of ECA's financial development. Chapters 2, 3, and 4 analyze which dimensions of financial development could support growth and shared prosperity the most; how the increasing financial dependence of firms could impact the creation and stability of jobs; and how the household saving behavior in ECA could be nudged toward better performance to help improve access to opportunities and economic resilience. Chapter 5 analyzes the potential interdependence

FIGURE O.4
The framework and logical flow of chapters for this report

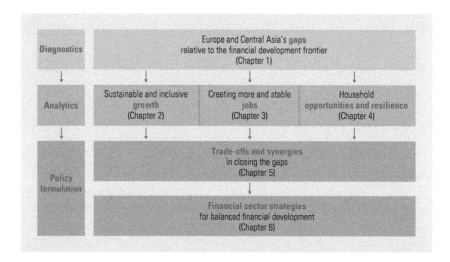

between two policy objectives that have been of major concern to policy makers in ECA: financial stability and inclusion. To implement the framework in specific country context, chapter 6 proposes a practical approach based on the international experience with using financial sector strategies to formulate comprehensive and balanced policies to achieve desired financial sector outcomes. Two countries that successfully used this approach are Malaysia and Switzerland. Chapter 6 also includes pointers for preparing financial sector strategies in individual ECA countries that bring together the main findings from the analyses of chapters 1–5.

ECA's Gaps in Relation to the Financial Development Frontier

A first-pass comparison with global financial indicators shows that ECA's financial sector performance has been mixed, with close to average levels of financial inclusion and efficiency but with underperformance on stability and financial depth, in particular of capital markets (figure O.5). Given the still-high NPL ratios, ECA's poor performance on financial stability is not a surprise. What could be surprising is ECA's average performance on financial efficiency compared with other regions, given its openness to foreign bank entry and competition from developed Europe. But Western Europe ranks even lower on this scale. Many ECA countries have relatively high net interest margins and overhead costs and low stock market turnover, indicating less financial efficiency compared to the global average.

In a more revealing approach, we develop the concept of a "financial development frontier" to give extra weight to indicators that matter the most for economic growth and actual country performance. The frontier is the median of the set for actual indicators of countries that are the top 20 percent of performers across all financial development indicators important for growth. So the frontier considers the trade-offs countries have faced, in practice, between financial sector outcomes. Within ECA, financial development varies markedly across countries (figure O.6). ECA lies below the frontier on almost every indicator, with ECA's performance on efficiency being the farthest from the frontier and firm inclusion being the closest.

FIGURE O.5 ECA performs at or below the average on financial development, particularly on financial depth and stability

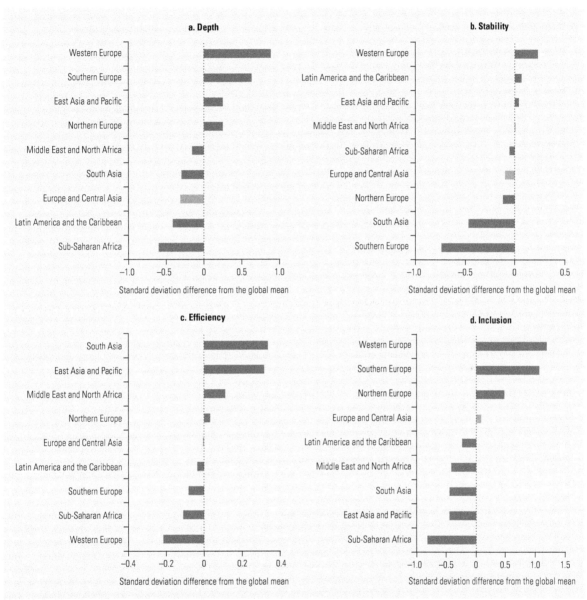

Sources: World Bank elaboration based on the Global Financial Development Database, Global Findex, and World Development Indicators.
Note: Each financial development index comprises subcomponent indicators described in chapter 1. The individual financial indicators are standardized before they are aggregated into the overall index.

There is also remarkable heterogeneity across the ECA region. Countries in the western side of the region, for example in Central Europe, perform better on firm inclusion and efficiency but underperform on stability. Countries in the eastern side of the region, such as in Central Asia, have traditionally overperformed on stability, but perhaps at the cost of efficiency, inclusion, and depth.

Behind these overall indexes, individual indicators tell an interesting story. As for financial depth, bank credit may be higher than the global experience given

FIGURE O.6 Overall, ECA performs well on financial inclusion of firms, but financial development varies markedly between the eastern and western halves of the ECA region

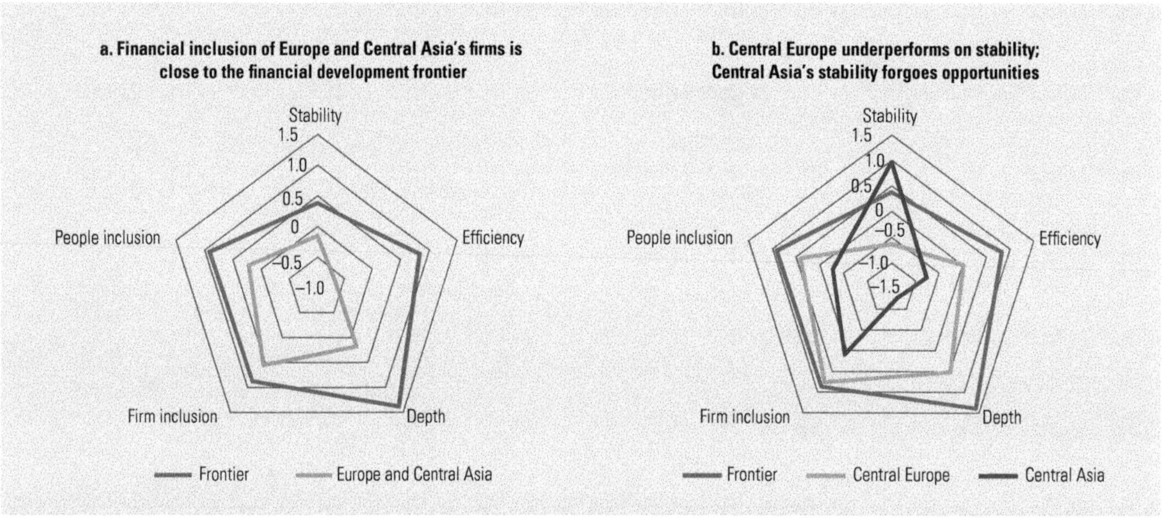

a. Financial inclusion of Europe and Central Asia's firms is close to the financial development frontier

b. Central Europe underperforms on stability; Central Asia's stability forgoes opportunities

Sources: World Bank elaboration based on the Global Financial Development Database, Global Findex, FinStats, and World Development Indicators.
Note: The values for the *frontier* of financial development represent the median values of each index for the economies in the 20 percent of overall financial development. Overall financial development is estimated as the average value of all components (stability, efficiency, depth, firm inclusion, and people inclusion).

the high foreign funding (consolidated foreign claims) that has been an important financing source for Emerging ECA's financial systems, particularly in Central Europe and the Western Balkans. Although Central Europe underperforms on stability relative to the frontier, ECA subregions with shallower and less internationally integrated financial systems, such as Central Asia and South Caucasus, fared better on financial stability. Underdevelopment may have provided some protection from the negative foreign financial shocks during the 2008 crisis but may have provided less protection during the recent oil bust. The efficiency of banking systems in the eastern side of the region, as seen in Central Asia, is the most lagging. Other Eastern European countries and countries in the South Caucasus show particularly low capital market efficiency. Russia and Turkey have inefficient banking sectors but relatively efficient capital markets. ECA subregions with higher income levels have higher levels of financial inclusion compared with other ECA subregions (South Caucasus, Central Asia, and Other Eastern Europe), as shown by the share of people who save at a formal financial institution as well as the percentage of firms with access to credit.

In sum, despite considerable progress, overall financial development in ECA lags behind its comparators on several indicators. Since the early 1990s the region achieved a significant increase in financial depth, owing to the rapid growth in bank credit and cross-border banking. However, this credit boom was followed by credit busts and banking failures with the onset of the global financial crisis. The crisis marked the beginning of a period in which reliance on the traditional drivers of financial development, such as capital inflows and rapid growth in domestic credit, has had to recede. Going forward, appropriate economic and financial policy could play a crucial role in improving financial efficiency and inclusion, while addressing the possible trade-offs with stability.

The Contribution of Financial Development to Growth in ECA and the World

How could the individual dimensions of financial development support income growth in ECA? To gauge this, one first needs to understand the effects of financial development on growth. To this end, we ran a comprehensive statistical analysis for over 100 countries using available data over the last 50 years. The relationships between the indexes summarizing the dimensions of financial development and the measures of long-term growth of aggregate income and the income of the bottom 40 percent of earners are described in figure O.7. The estimated relationships control for other drivers of income growth, such as initial income level, education, macroeconomic stability, the size of government, and investment. The analysis shows, for example, that a 1 standard deviation increase in the financial efficiency index would translate into a 0.6 percentage point increase in annual growth over the long run.

Financial inclusion of firms is not only the biggest contributor to long-term aggregate growth, but together with the inclusion of people it could also be the only financial indicator that matters for advancing shared prosperity. For the bottom 40 percent of earners, only firm inclusion and household inclusion are strongly associated with long-term income growth. For overall growth, firm inclusion has the greatest association with growth, followed by efficiency, stability, and household inclusion and depth. Firm access to finance, particularly the share of firms opening to equity investment, has a strong relationship with growth. Raising investment through the sale of equity may also improve firm corporate governance and accountability, which in turn can further improve growth of firms.

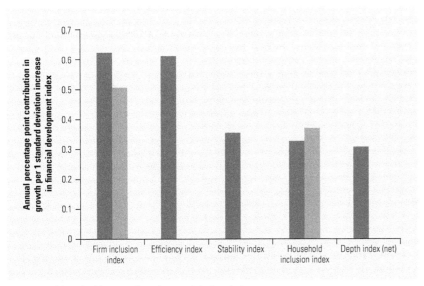

FIGURE O.7

Firm inclusion has the strongest relationship to aggregate growth and shared prosperity

- ■ Overall growth
- ■ Bottom 40 growth

Source: World Bank elaboration based on statistical analysis.
Note: Each column represents the coefficient on bivariate regression with the overall growth residual and the bottom 40 growth residual as the dependent variable. The growth residual is obtained from regressing the respective income growth on the core set of conditioning variables. See chapter 2 for a full description. The financial development indexes comprise the equally weighted sum of the standardized, significant indicators from each category.

Also, the number of firms with bank loans or lines of credit is significantly associated with both overall growth and the income growth of the bottom 40.

Stability is important for sustained income growth. Countries with lower volatility of credit (those less likely to experience boom-and-bust credit cycles) show higher growth rates, and the presence and severity of a banking crisis dampen long-term growth. Increasing NPL ratios are also negatively associated with aggregate growth and the growth of the income of the bottom 40 percent. Greater banking sector efficiency, as measured by low bank overhead costs, narrow lending-deposit spreads, and low bank net interest margins, is strongly associated with economic growth. Countries with more competition in the banking sector also tend to have higher rates of income growth for the bottom 40 percent. Greater competition can cause more efficient pricing of some financial services, and pressure financial intermediaries to diversify their client base by providing services to poorer households.

Consistent with other research, we find that the growth benefits of financial depth may diminish as depth becomes large or as deepening becomes too fast. Figure O.8 reports the net effect of this nonlinear result at the median of the sample. There is good reason to believe that the association between financial depth (particularly private credit) and growth is weaker as credit becomes ample. For instance, rapid deepening of credit markets without proper corporate governance and regulatory oversight can result in credit misallocation and soon-to-burst financial bubbles, as demonstrated by the 2008 crisis. However, separating financial depth by financial subsectors reveals growth benefits from the diversification of financial systems into the capital market and insurance sector.

Which dimensions of financial development should ECA countries prioritize in policy making? Combining the financial development gaps for ECA countries and

FIGURE O.8

Aggregate growth in ECA could benefit most from boosting financial efficiency—the bottom 40 percent could benefit most from greater financial inclusion

■ Efficiency
▨ Stability
▨ Firm inclusion
▨ People inclusion
■ Depth

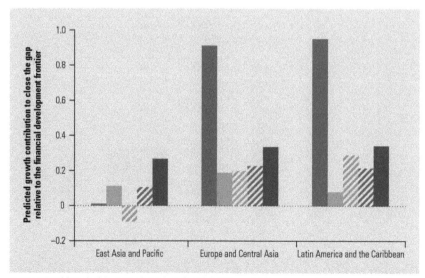

Sources: World Bank elaboration based on the Global Financial Development Database, Global Findex, FinStats, and World Development Indicators.
Note: The height of the bars represents the predicted growth contribution for moving to the frontier of financial development. The calculations are based on growth regressions with financial indicators and other growth determinants. The bars for firm and people inclusion are banded because they also impact bottom 40 growth. See chapter 2 for details.

the estimated growth effects of financial stability, efficiency, and inclusion reveals that Emerging ECA could benefit the most from implementing policies that improve financial efficiency (figure O.8). ECA has already achieved comparatively high levels, for instance, on firm and household access to finance. ECA's priorities are very similar to those of Latin America and the Caribbean (LAC), another middle- to high-income region. Disaggregated results for depth point to other significant benefits from diversifying ECA financial systems away from banking to capital and insurance markets.

Although efficiency is a key financial development dimension to improve growth across ECA, policy priorities vary across ECA subregions, particularly on stability and inclusion. For Central Asia, historically high stability may have been due to financial repression at the expense of inclusion and growth, and prevented the economies from pursuing certain development opportunities. In contrast, Turkey has much to gain by increasing stability compared to advancing financial inclusion of people and firms.

Despite the potential for financial dependence to exacerbate the economic downturn during a crisis, income growth in countries with more efficient, inclusive, and deeper financial markets does not suffer significantly more during a banking crisis (figure O.9). Moreover, greater financial inclusion of people and firms could mitigate the adverse consequences of a financial crisis. Thus, avoiding greater financial development to reduce the costs of a crisis is unlikely to pay long-term growth

FIGURE O.9 During crises, countries with more efficient and inclusive financial systems do not suffer significantly more

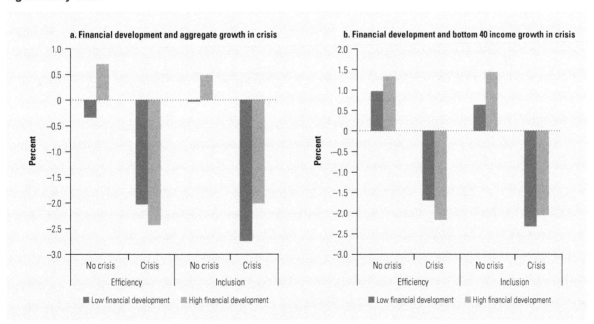

Sources: World Bank elaboration based on the Global Financial Development Database, Global Findex, FinStats, World Development Indicators, and the banking crisis database by Laeven and Valencia (2013).
Note: The height of each bar represents the average annual value of the growth residual (overall and bottom 40) in the absence of a banking crisis or during a banking crisis, for all countries in our sample. The definition of a crisis was taken from Laeven and Valencia (2013). The growth residuals are calculated from the baseline growth regressions of chapter 2. Each country is classified as having high (above median) or low (below median) financial development according to its score for each financial development index.

dividends. For example, policies focused solely on preventing banking crises at all costs may neglect the benefits of firm and household inclusion. A more efficient way of managing the risks and benefits from financial development would be through balanced policies that address trade-offs to avoid unintended consequences. These policies could involve developing institutional capacity for prudential oversight and complementary social assistance programs in the event of a crisis.

In summary, balanced financial market development in ECA can help boost inclusive growth through greater financial sector efficiency, inclusion, and broad-based depth. In formulating objectives of financial policy, policy makers should focus on all aspects of financial development as well as consider trade-offs—not simply base policy on the traditional measure of financial depth, particularly credit, that may be an ambiguous determinant of income growth. Given this report's findings, ECA governments focused on advancing shared prosperity should prioritize financial inclusion of firms, particularly through their participation in stock markets via issuance of new equity.

ECA Jobs in Financially Dependent Firms Are Vulnerable to Changing Credit Conditions

The firm-level relationship between financial sector development and jobs growth provides valuable insights into how macrofinance relates to the microeconomics of firms and jobs. In ECA, the bottom 40 percent of the income distribution are not as likely to be employed in the formal sector and also depend less on labor income because of social assistance and other nonlabor sources of income. It could appear that they have less to gain in income growth when financial development advances. But that is not necessarily the case. Although the poorer segments of the population are less likely to be formally employed, when they are employed, they tend to be employed in smaller, and in some countries (Turkey, Central Asia, and Western Balkans) younger, firms. These firms are precisely the ones that could benefit the most from greater access to credit (figure O.10).

> In ECA, the bottom 40 percent of the income distribution are not as likely to be employed in the formal sector and also depend less on labor income because of social assistance and other nonlabor sources of income.

The 2008 global financial crisis rapidly changed the external financing conditions for firms from easy to tight. The abundance of finance before the shock may have contributed to rising employment and wages, especially of the bottom 40, whereas the tightening of credit conditions after the shock may have reduced wages and employment. We find that firm dependence on credit has a large influence on employment and wages in rapidly changing financing conditions for firms. The firm-level data show that employment in financially dependent firms took a big hit after the global financial crisis, and it was not just due to the general decline in demand (figure O.11).

The credit crunch had a larger negative direct effect (through the impact on wages and employment) on individuals in the top 60 than in the bottom 40 percent of the income distribution in Western and Central Europe. Whereas in Western Europe the effects were driven mostly by a decrease in the number of salaried jobs, in Central Europe they were driven by a decline in both the number of self-employed and salaried jobs. Firms in Central Europe also responded to the credit crunch by reducing the number of work hours. The shortage in finance also had a

FIGURE O.10 ECA's bottom 40 are more likely to work in smaller firms that use less credit but may need it the most

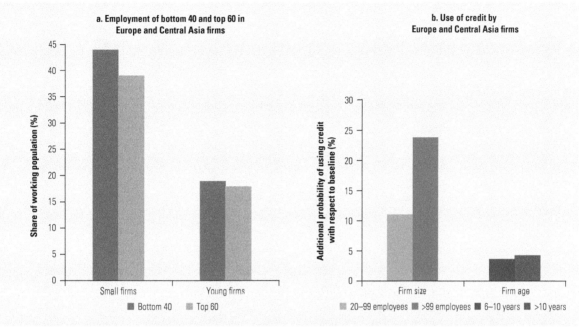

Sources: Panel a: Based on Life in Transition Survey (LITS) 2010; panel b: Elaboration based on World Bank Enterprise Surveys 2013.
Note: Panel b: These are the coefficients from ordinary least squares regressions controlling for country, sector, and area fixed effects. The dependent variable is a dummy variable equal to 1 if the firm has a line of credit. The omitted category is under 20 employees and younger than 6 years.

greater negative effect on the hourly earnings of the top 60 compared to the bottom 40, especially for the self-employed in both Central and Western Europe.

The crisis and the rapidly tightening credit conditions were also associated with a greater decline in the rate of firm entry and exit and the total number of firms in financially dependent sectors, relative to other sectors. This may imply that the crisis reduced the productivity gains from the entry of more productive firms and exit of less productive firms. Better external financing conditions allow more entrepreneurs with ideas to enter the market, grow, and challenge inefficient incumbents.

In sum, these results highlight trade-offs in improving external financing conditions for firms. Although the benefits of job creation and wage growth could be large as finance for firms improves, jobs in financially dependent firms are more sensitive to the business cycle—boosting them more in the upturn and hurting them more in the downturn. Moreover, firms that are already financially included and with larger shares of top 60 percent earners employed are likely to suffer the most. Given the existing state of firms' financing conditions in most of ECA, the trade-off between employment growth and greater financial shocks is less acute for households in the bottom 40. Because small firms that employ most bottom 40 workers use credit much less, households in the bottom 40 are currently less reliant than are households in the top 60 on jobs in financially dependent firms. There is scope to bring more opportunities to the bottom 40 by improving the external financing conditions for smaller firms throughout the financial cycle while mitigating the volatility of financial cycles.

FIGURE O.11 **More financially dependent firms in ECA experienced greater employment reduction after the 2008 financial crisis**

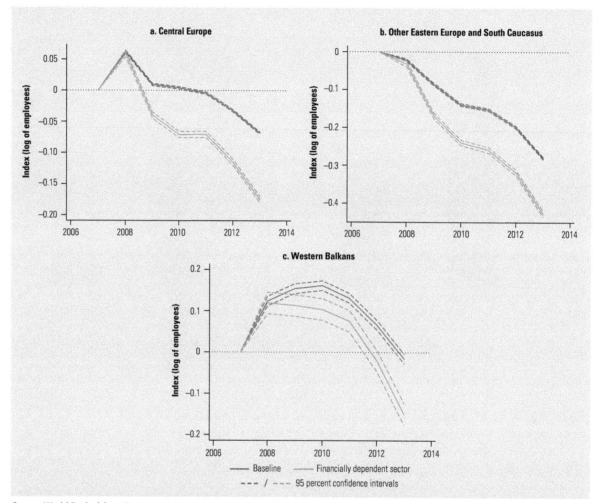

Source: World Bank elaboration.
Note: Each line shows the coefficients associated with year dummy variables for sectors highly dependent on external finance, or sectors in the top 25 percent of the index of financial dependence, and the rest. The coefficients were estimated using a balanced panel of firms from Orbis, a large database on firms. See appendix D for more details.

Lack of Trust in Banks Means that Few ECA Households Save

The importance of various factors in influencing household saving behavior varies across ECA countries and periods of time. However, there is one common outcome that can be observed across ECA. Despite ECA's relatively high level of income, the share of households in ECA that save is among the lowest of all world regions (figure O.12). More households in ECA may be saving than in the past, but much of their saving is informal, including in cash.

The experience of economic crises has had an important impact on saving decisions, keeping the region's propensity to save relatively low. The lack of trust in banks has a strong and significant impact on low participation in saving

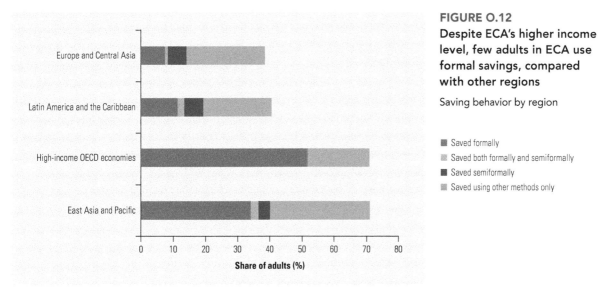

FIGURE O.12

Despite ECA's higher income level, few adults in ECA use formal savings, compared with other regions

Saving behavior by region

■ Saved formally
▨ Saved both formally and semiformally
■ Saved semiformally
▨ Saved using other methods only

Source: World Bank elaboration based on Global Findex database.
Note: OECD = Organisation for Economic Co-operation and Development.

FIGURE O.13 Trust in banks is generally low in Emerging ECA and is correlated with ECA's history of banking crises

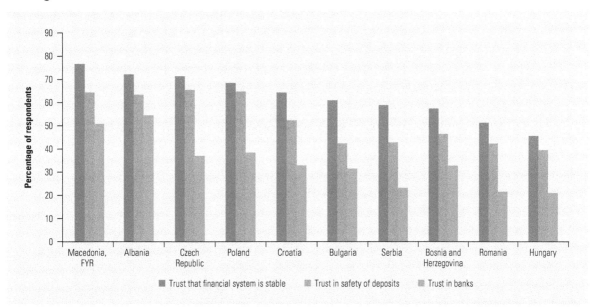

Source: World Bank elaboration based on OeNB Euro Survey, 2012–13.

instruments, even after controlling for risk aversion, expectations, and experience. The Euro Survey finds that trust in both foreign and domestic banks is low compared with that in nontransition economies and does not vary much with income level (figure O.13). However, trust in the safety of deposits and in the stability of the financial system is higher than trust in banks.

The safety of deposits and trust in the stability of the financial system have strong effects on savings and the choice of saving instruments. Taking into account numerous socioeconomic factors, individuals who trust deposit safety and the stability of the financial system are 5 percentage points more likely to have any type of savings (formal or informal), compared with the sample average of only 40 percent of adults who save. Conditional on having savings, trust in deposit safety increases the probability of holding formal savings by 4 percentage points and the probability of saving at banks by 5 percentage points—an effect similar in magnitude to having secondary education. Moreover, trust in the safety of deposits decreases the probability of saving in cash by 3 percentage points. Interestingly, those who trust that the financial system is stable are more likely to invest in life insurance or pension funds (4 percentage points more likely compared to the sample mean of 24 percent) and stocks, bonds, or mutual funds (2 percentage points more likely compared to the sample mean of 8 percent). Trust in the stability of the financial system is associated with diversification of saving instruments away from bank deposits by 6 percentage points, or a third of the sample mean.

In sum, the share of ECA households that save is low even when considering socioeconomic factors. To boost savings, trust in banks will need to improve. The percentage of savers in ECA is particularly low among bottom 40 households. Moreover, informal saving is widespread even among the top 60 percent of earners. Formal savings mainly include bank deposits; the share of those who save with nonbanks is very low. Policies could increase adoption and use of formal savings accounts. From international experience, promoting increased competition to lower account fees, providing incentives for opening an account, and paying wages and social benefits through bank accounts could nudge more people to start saving formally. Improving avenues for saving in the nonbank financial sector (mutual funds and private pensions) could also stimulate saving. Financial education programs can have uncertain impacts and have a better chance of working if targeted and tailored to country context.

The Trade-Offs between Financial Inclusion and Stability in ECA

Can ECA's policies to boost financial inclusion be designed to avoid adverse impacts on stability, or is instability just something ECA countries have to live with? To answer this question one must examine how financial inclusion and financial stability interact. As one might imagine, there is no simple formula for increasing stability and inclusion at the same time. Policy makers are likely to encounter trade-offs, as illustrated by the recent U.S. subprime crisis, India's microfinance crisis, and systemic defaults on foreign currency mortgages in Europe. But there are also possible synergies between inclusion and stability that could be exploited. For example, increasing inclusion in bank deposits by firms and individuals may increase stability by diversifying the deposit base. In contrast, increasing the use of credit by lowering credit standards can increase instability by lowering the quality of bank assets. This phenomenon was all too evident in the lead-up to the 2008 global financial crisis, including in Emerging ECA.

Ignoring important trade-offs and synergies between inclusion and stability can lead to poorly designed financial policies. When evaluating financial sector outcomes, and prioritizing the design and implementation of alternative financial policies, policy makers could miss important aspects by ignoring the interactions between financial stability and inclusion. To illustrate this point, it is useful to consider the following intuitive framework:

| Achieving joint financial stability and inclusion | = | Achieving financial stability | + | Achieving financial inclusion | + | Exploiting synergies and mitigating trade-offs between financial inclusion and stability |

Deploying policies to achieve financial stability and policies to achieve financial inclusion may not deliver the intended results if there are large trade-offs between the two outcomes. But, if the deployed policies can generate synergies between inclusion and stability, mutual reinforcement of the two goals can occur. The last element in the equation above highlights the possible interdependence between inclusion and stability, which can thus either add or subtract from the independent goals of stability and inclusion. While most studies and policies have typically focused on achieving the outcomes of either stable or inclusive financial systems independently, limited attention has been paid to the interdependence between the two outcomes.

Examining a wide array of measures of household and firm inclusion reveals an overall trade-off between financial inclusion and stability. Higher bank capitalization is negatively correlated with the use of financial services, particularly for individuals. Moreover, there is a trade-off between many inclusion indicators and the costs of banking crises. Greater financial inclusion (increase in account ownership or debit card penetration) is associated with more costly financial crises (output and fiscal costs, as well as the peak NPL ratios during crises). The median ratios of private credit to GDP in ECA had reached significantly higher levels than in similar economies by the mid-2000s, indicating that excessive inclusion may have contributed to the depth of the 2008 crisis.

Nonetheless, synergies between inclusion and stability are almost equally probable. Dissecting financial stability into resilience measures, volatility measures, and crisis measures reveals that financial inclusion can help mitigate volatility of growth in bank deposits and the volatility of bank deposit rates. While financial inclusion of individuals, such as account ownership, use of electronic payments, formal savings and credit, helps reduce the volatility of bank deposit growth and bank deposit rates, savings by firms can help enhance financial stability across all three dimensions: resilience, volatility, and low probability and cost of crises (figure O.14).

The relationship between inclusion and stability is systematically influenced by country characteristics, such as financial openness, tax rates, education, informality, and the depth of credit information systems. Whereas financial openness and formalization of the economy increase trade-offs between inclusion and stability, low tax rates, education, and credit information depth help generate synergies between the two goals (figure O.15).

Greater financial openness and movement of capital is particularly challenging in middle- and low-income countries, which tend to have a limited capacity to manage capital flows and ensure prudent and efficient allocation of the funding

FIGURE O.14

Although trade-offs between financial inclusion and stability dominate on average, synergies between the two outcomes could arise with almost equal probability

■ Trade-offs (most important include higher credit use by individuals and higher cost of crisis)

■ Synergies (most important include higher savings by firms and higher stability)

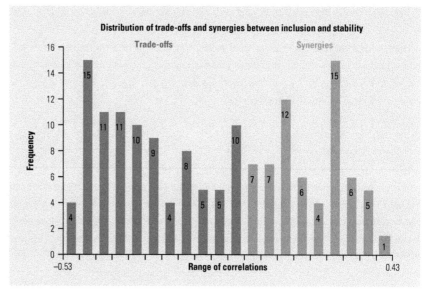

Source: World Bank elaboration.
Note: This figure represents the distribution of the frequency of pairwise correlation coefficients between financial stability and financial inclusion. It includes the values for the linear dependence of each individual financial stability indicator and each individual financial inclusion indicator.

FIGURE O.15 The inclusion-stability nexus is systematically influenced by country characteristics

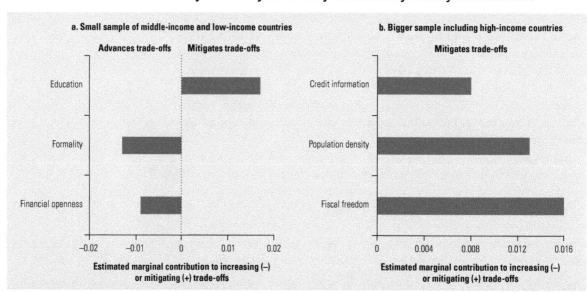

Source: World Bank elaboration.
Note: The figure shows significant determinants of the interplay (covariance) between financial inclusion and stability estimated in chapter 5 using a smaller country sample with a larger number of variables and a bigger country sample with a smaller number of variables due to limited data availability. A positive effect, for instance by "Education" in panel a, means that increasing education can help mitigate trade-offs (or promote synergies) between financial inclusion and stability.

to creditworthy firms and individuals. Countries with higher informality, as measured by the number of years firms operated without formal registration, experience a lower trade-off between financial inclusion and stability. A potential explanation is that previously informal firms that enter the formal sector tend to be greater risk-takers. Being higher risk-takers may have allowed these firms to earn higher returns to pay for more expensive informal credit. Because risk appetites are unlikely to change quickly after firms become formal, rapid increases in credit to previously informal firms that enter the formal sector should be monitored for potential threats to financial stability.

Low tax rates may generate synergies by stimulating precautionary savings due to smaller social safety nets and greater probability of unexpected increases in taxes. Education can generate a positive relationship between inclusion and stability by improving financial literacy and responsible financial inclusion that helps the financial system reap the benefits of economic scale and risk diversification. The depth of credit information systems generates synergies by improving screening of creditworthy customers, including new users of credit, and aids stability by, for example, improving the accuracy of estimations of expected losses. Finally, greater information depth also promotes competition in oligopolistic markets, decreases the cost of finance, and encourages more firms and people to start using a financial service or use more than one financial service. Particularly if financial policy focuses on advancing the financial inclusion of individuals, complementary policies to deepen credit information systems could help mitigate the estimated trade-offs with financial stability.

These findings have important policy implications. Because trade-offs and synergies between financial inclusion and financial stability are significant, they need to be addressed in policy making. As the next section documents, financial policy trade-offs are not adequately addressed by ECA countries, many of which have been undergoing rapid financial deepening that may restart after the recovery from the global financial crisis. In ECA and elsewhere, multiple government agencies (in many countries the central bank and other financial supervisors) and ministries (in many countries the ministry of finance, economic development, or strategic planning) are responsible for policy on both financial inclusion and financial stability. Therefore, the trade-offs and synergies must be addressed at a high enough policy-making level to ensure effective coordination. One important tool to formulate high-level policy for the financial sector is the financial sector strategy.

Using Financial Sector Strategies to Formulate Holistic and Balanced Financial Policy

A financial sector strategy should help the country build consensus on which aspects of financial development must be prioritized to support growth and shared prosperity going forward. A particular challenge faced by financial sector strategies is the need to address the systemic risk that advancing financial efficiency and inclusion can entail. In other words, while aiming to better satisfy the demand-side needs (people, firms, and governments) across multiple financial services (payments, saving instruments, credit, equity, and insurance), the strategy needs to find ways for public policy to ensure prudent management of systemic risk in the financial sector (banks, nonbank financial institutions, and capital markets). Evaluating the scope and quality of financial sector strategies in ECA and their impact on financial sector development can provide powerful insights into improving financial sector outcomes in the region.

Financial sector strategies started in the late 1980s. Some early strategy documents resulted from the collaboration between national governments or central banks with the help of international development organizations. Others were developed internally, or subsequent to evaluations from international financial institutions, such as the Financial Sector Assessment Programs conducted by the International Monetary Fund and the World Bank. As country institutions matured, country authorities such as the government and central bank took the initiative to conduct consultations and prepare the strategy for developing the financial sector. The global financial crisis prompted some countries to rethink the path for financial sector development. For instance, in Switzerland, the Federal Department of Finance, in collaboration with the Swiss Financial Market Supervisory Authority and the Swiss National Bank, formulated a set of objectives and strategic directions to strengthen the financial sector in the aftermath of the crisis.

ECA is a relative newcomer in developing formal financial sector strategies, the first being Turkey in 2001 (figure O.16). In 2006, ECA's interest in financial sector strategies grew (both Georgia and the Kyrgyz Republic, for example, initiated strategies in 2006) and by 2011–12 the number of strategies in ECA was on par with LAC but still behind EAP. ECA countries that adopted financial sector strategies more recently relied more on their own country authorities and less on international organizations when preparing the strategy. For instance, Turkey's 2001 and 2010 Strategic Plans were formulated by the Banking Regulation and Supervision Agency. In the Kyrgyz Republic, the 2006 and 2009 strategies were prepared

FIGURE O.16 ECA is a relative newcomer to using financial sector strategies for policy formulation

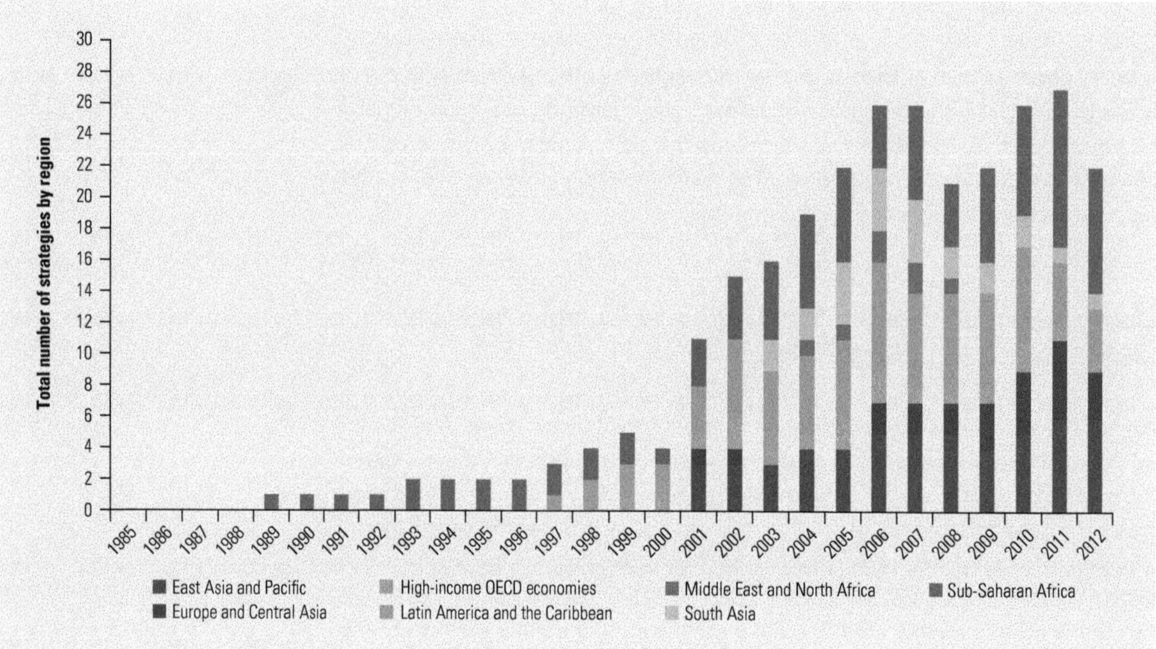

Source: Melecky and Podpiera, forthcoming.
Note: OECD = Organisation for Economic Co-operation and Development.

by the central bank. In Ukraine, a program of reforms was developed by the working groups of the Economic Reform Committee.

A key question is: Have strategies helped to improve financial sector outcomes in ECA and around the world? Taking into account underlying economic fundamentals, the report's analysis shows that financial sector strategies are associated with better financial sector outcomes. Good-quality financial sector strategies are found to support financial sector deepening, inclusion, and stability. This effect is weaker the lower the quality of the strategy or the shorter the implementation period. Furthermore, there does not seem to be any significant effect of the strategies on financial efficiency of banks. Nonetheless, the findings show that the strategies have a significant and positive association with the regulatory framework for getting credit, resolving insolvency, and enforcing contracts. The strategies' positive association with financial development is not limited to their role in improving the regulatory framework. Other ways in which strategies may improve financial development are through improving coordination of financial policy and reducing policy uncertainty for the private financial and real sectors.

In sum, the articulation of financial sector strategies has been positively associated in ECA and other countries with financial deepening, stability, and inclusion; and this relationship is greater for high-quality strategies. The strategies can affect financial outcomes not only by strengthening the regulatory framework but also by improving the coordination of policy within the government and across broader stakeholders of financial policy, including the private sector. More ECA countries could use financial sector strategies to help plan, communicate, and coordinate their financial sector policies. Although the existing ECA strategies rank favorably overall, they do not address trade-offs between financial development and systemic risk management and they fall behind EAP, LAC, and in particular Organisation for Economic Co-operation and Development economies in that respect (figure O.17). Only a few high-quality strategies can be found globally, such as those of Malaysia and Switzerland, which could serve as role models for ECA countries in their efforts to deploy financial strategies effectively.

Country Pointers to Focus Policy Efforts with the Help of Financial Sector Strategies

To summarize the overall findings of this report on addressing financial policy trade-offs for inclusive growth in Emerging ECA, we bring together in a quantitative way three aspects to consider in decision making on financial policy: (a) the existing financial development gaps—that is, the distance to the financial development frontier the country should aim to close; (b) how much the closing of a particular gap—for financial stability, efficiency, inclusion, or depth—could advance growth and shared prosperity; and (c) whether the closing of one gap, such as financial inclusion, can actually increase other gap(s), such as financial stability, and pose a policy trade-off or whether the closing of one gap can help close another gap and create synergies.

The findings of the report can be summarized visually by constructing the financial development frontier that maps the contribution of financial development to both aggregate growth and shared prosperity (figure O.18). We do so to illustrate

FIGURE O.17 ECA's few strategies rate well but fail to address policy trade-offs

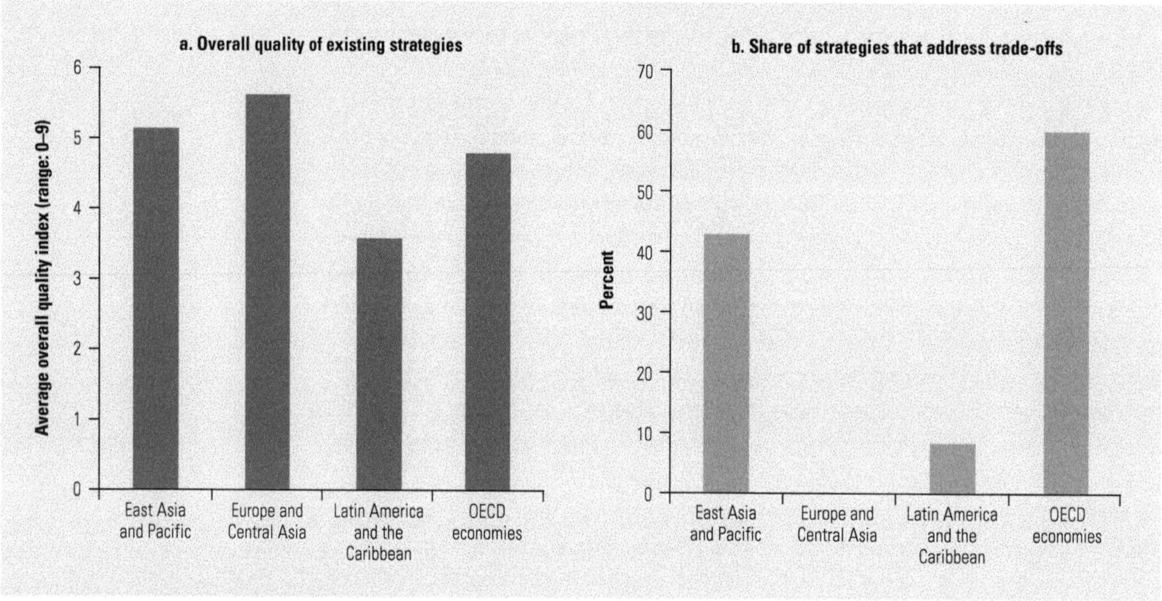

a. Overall quality of existing strategies
Average overall quality index (range: 0–9)
0
1
2
3
4
5
6
East Asia and Pacific
Europe and Central Asia
Latin America and the Caribbean
OECD economies
b. Share of strategies that address trade-offs
Percent
0
10
20
30
40
50
60
70
East Asia and Pacific
Europe and Central Asia
Latin America and the Caribbean
OECD economies

Source: Melecky and Podpiera, forthcoming.

FIGURE O.18
Advancing growth and shared prosperity in ECA subregions by moving to the financial development frontier

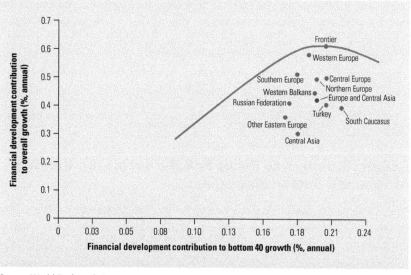

Financial development contribution to overall growth (%, annual)
0
0.1
0.2
0.3
0.4
0.5
0.6
0.7
0
0.03
0.05
0.08
0.10
0.13
0.16
0.18
0.21
0.24
Financial development contribution to bottom 40 growth (%, annual)
Frontier
Western Europe
Southern Europe
Central Europe
Northern Europe
Western Balkans
Europe and Central Asia
Russian Federation
Turkey
South Caucasus
Other Eastern Europe
Central Asia

Source: World Bank analysis.
Note: Values shown on the horizontal and vertical axes are calculated using the statistically significant financial development indicators and their growth regression coefficients from chapter 2, table 2.1. They represent the cumulative percentage point contribution to annual growth (overall and bottom 40 percent) of the financial sector. The frontier peak is the average growth contributions of the financial indicators of the top 20 percent of countries with the highest overall financial development in terms of depth, stability, efficiency, firm inclusion, and people inclusion.

the distance that an ECA country must cover to improve its financial development to enhance overall growth and shared prosperity and reach the potential of frontier countries. Figure O.18 depicts the current situation of Emerging ECA subregions compared to the benchmark subregions of Western, Northern, and Southern

Europe. The frontier line then represents the joint contributions of finance to the growth of aggregate income and the income of bottom 40 earners. The frontier peak represents the growth contributions of the average (median) financial indicators, important for income growth, for the top 20 percent of country performers on financial development.

Central Asia, Other Eastern Europe, and Russia are farthest from the financial development frontier and have the greatest potential to increase growth and shared prosperity through balanced financial development. The South Caucasus shows the highest growth of the bottom 40 percent growth due to financial inclusion, particularly in Armenia, but is still far away from the frontier in the direction of overall growth because other financial development dimensions are weak. Central Europe is the closest to the frontier, reflecting relatively strong financial development in most indicators in the Czech Republic, Poland, and the Slovak Republic.

Generally, the contribution of finance is weaker to bottom 40 growth (at about 0.17–0.22 percent of income growth a year) than it is to aggregate growth (at about 0.3–0.6 percent). Financial development's contribution to bottom 40 growth is primarily related to financial inclusion. If policy makers emphasize increasing bottom 40 growth through financial development, financial sector reforms will have to prioritize improving the financial inclusion of firms and households.

What are the policy focus areas that countries should consider when formulating financial sector strategies? Aside from the general guidelines articulated on what constitutes a good financial sector strategy (for example, improving coordination across financial policy stakeholders and in policy implementation while considering policy trade-offs), specific areas of focus can be identified for ECA subregions and countries. These focus areas are also determined by the potential trade-offs countries are likely to confront when trying to advance financial inclusion or stability. Table O.1 summarizes the findings of this report in a user-friendly manner. The rows of the table list Emerging ECA subregions, and the columns show financial outcome policy priority areas (efficiency, inclusion, stability, and depth)

TABLE O.1 Heat Map of Focus Areas for Financial Policy

ECA subregions	Focus areas for country-specific financial policy				
	Efficiency	Inclusion	Stability	Depth	Inclusion-stability trade-off
Central Europe					
Western Balkans					
Other Eastern Europe					
South Caucasus					
Turkey					
Russian Federation					
Central Asia					
Legend					
Policy priorities	Strong priority		Moderate priority		Modest priority
Trade-offs	Strong	Moderate	Modest	Intermediate	Weak

to improve growth and shared prosperity. The last column alerts financial policy makers to the likelihood of strong or weak trade-offs between improving financial inclusion and stability in ECA subregions.

Countries in the Western Balkans, for example, can better advance inclusive growth by focusing more on improving financial efficiency and inclusion than on increasing stability and financial sector depth. Moreover, although efficiency and inclusion may pay the highest growth dividends, prioritizing efficiency over inclusion is likely to be the best policy because general financial inclusion efforts are likely to impair financial stability as indicated by the strong trade-off between inclusion and stability for the Western Balkans. Therefore, for the Western Balkans, prioritizing efficiency and being selective in financial inclusion efforts that have low trade-offs with stability (firm and individual savings accounts) could pay off. Similarly, Turkey's policy priority should be on increasing stability because the country has experienced high financial volatility, and the country faces a strong trade-off between inclusion and stability. Thus, Turkey should use macroprudential policies that improve stability, which still leaves room for maintaining financial inclusion. In contrast, Russia's financial policy priorities should focus on advancing both financial inclusion and efficiency, and the increase in inclusion is unlikely to encounter a major trade-off with financial stability.

Because our analysis is based on long-term historical data, a word of caution is needed concerning short-term financial sector vulnerabilities and threats to financial stability. There are several countries—including in the subregions of Central Asia, South Caucasus, and Other Eastern Europe—now confronting financial stability issues that need to be resolved in the short term. Such issues and recommendations to address them should arise from ongoing monitoring and assessment reports of the country authorities, international financial institutions (IFIs), and market participants.

Overall, greater awareness of potential trade-offs in policy formulation is critical. Considering that there is a trade-off between household use of credit and financial stability, but a synergy between higher firm savings and stability, countries with currently lower levels of stability, such as Turkey or those in Central Europe, Other Eastern Europe, and the Western Balkans, may wish to prioritize reducing barriers to firm savings while monitoring closely the growth of household credit.

To advance financial stability, efficiency, and inclusion as well as to diversify financial systems, policy makers in ECA have put forward an agenda of policies. Table O.2 provides a list of the top policy options on the agenda of Emerging ECA countries and our assessment of their potential direct and indirect impacts on the four financial sector outcomes. These policy options encompass many dimensions of financial development and are fully discussed in the chapters, spotlights, and boxes in this report from the perspective of practical policy application within the ECA regional context.

TABLE O.2 List of Top Policy Options on the Agenda of Emerging ECA Countries

Policy options	Efficiency	Inclusion	Stability	Depth
Tackling the high and persistent level of nonperforming loans (NPLs) in ECA. Improving the framework for resolving bad loans, such as effectiveness of the judicial system, voluntary out-of-court restructuring, the insolvency regime, and tax treatment of NPLs can help improve financial stability while enabling credit institutions to better assess expected losses and more efficiently price loans. Indirectly, the freed-up capital for risk-taking can help encourage financial inclusion of people and small and medium enterprises and thus diversify the loan books of credit institutions.				
Achieving equilibrium credit provision in ECA countries with the help of cross-border supervision. Providing enough but not too much credit to an economy is a balancing act that the financial system has to perform, and financial supervisors manage to avoid booms and busts in the financial and real economic cycles. The equilibrium credit provisioning that strikes this balance is dependent on structural determinants such as the strength of legal rights and the depth of credit information and, in economies with a large presence of foreign banks, effective cross-border supervision. When the financial system adheres to the equilibrium level of credit provision, threats to stability abate and financial inclusion can continue in a responsible manner.				
Setting up the framework for macroprudential policy in ECA countries. Adopting financial stability as an explicit goal and assigning the responsibility and tools for macroprudential policy may not be enough for an effective macroprudential framework. Going the last mile requires setting up a robust internal structure and incentives to ensure timely and proportional responses to identified systemic vulnerabilities. Such responses ensure that contributions of financial firms to systemic risk are internalized and systemic risk is mitigated. This systemic discipline could also promote fairer competition and greater financial efficiency.				
Learning from crisis simulation exercises in ECA. The crisis simulations are realistic games to improve crisis preparedness and financial stability. They are stress tests of whether, in crisis times, the authorities will stick to their commitments to work cooperatively with each other or will revert to self-interest and ad hoc actions without broader evaluations of the situation. They explore the limits to information sharing and coordination, and the decision-making process, given the existing or proposed legal and operational frameworks. Analysis of the communication among authorities then reveals the needed reforms of the decision-making process as well as legal and operational frameworks.				
Understanding the role and governance of state-owned banks. Direct interventions of the state in the financial sector through bank ownership and operation could be motivated by market failures, social goals, or the countercyclical/safe haven role. The criticism of state banking stems from the potential for political capture, unfair competition, or the inherent tension between banking and social mandates. Reaping the benefits of state banking requires strong governance frameworks for state-owned banks and clear mandates driven by the rationale for direct state intervention.				

(Continued)

TABLE O.2 List of Top Policy Options on the Agenda of Emerging ECA Countries *(continued)*

Policy options	Efficiency	Inclusion	Stability	Depth
Weighing different strategies for developing capital markets in ECA. Developing capital markets can help diversify a country's financial system, increase efficiency of financial intermediation, and help build the "spare tire" in case of banking failures. However, capital markets are small in many developing regions, and ECA is no exception. In this context, two policy questions are usually posed in ECA countries: (a) whether a regional integration approach could help further develop ECA's capital markets and (b) whether a strategy to become an international financial center is worth pursuing for some ECA countries.				
Increasing the use of electronic payments. Electronic payments offer great potential to increase financial sector efficiency and integrate low-income households and communities, small-scale agriculture producers and vendors, and informal or marginalized economic segments into the financial system. The transition to greater use of electronic payments can be encouraged by focusing on existing transactions that are used by many households, including the delivery of government benefits, wage payments, utility bill payments, and remittances.				
Developing private pension schemes in ECA. Mandatory private pension systems (pillar 2—a funded system that recipients and employers pay into; this includes pension funds and defined-contribution accounts/plans) can help ensure that workers have adequate replacement income in retirement while reducing the future obligations of public pension programs and easing the fiscal strain from population aging. They can help diversify financial systems, increase their efficiency because of greater savings mobilization, and integrate more individuals and small firms in financial services. However, regulatory requirements and erroneous strategies for creating private pension schemes have impeded these objectives.				
Promoting the use of insurance for increased risks from climate change. Low-income households tend to depend on agriculture, which is particularly vulnerable to disasters. In Serbia, an estimated 125,000 people fell below the poverty line after the 2014 floods, with vulnerable groups and the rural population particularly affected. Despite the increased availability of high-quality flood and earthquake insurance packages that cost between US$15 and US$44 annually, the demand for catastrophe insurance products continues to be low. Moral hazard due to expectations of government support and lack of accurate assessment of risks by individuals and the public sector need to be addressed.				
Legend: degrees of the impact of the policy options	Major impact of the policy option	Moderate impact of the policy option	Minor impact of the policy option	Indirect impact of the policy option

References

Laeven, L., and F. Valencia. 2013. "Systemic Banking Crises Database." *IMF Economic Review* 61 (2): 225–70.

Melecky, M., and A. Podpiera. Forthcoming. "Financial Sector Strategies and Financial Sector Outcomes: Do the Strategies Perform?" Unpublished manuscript.

Europe and Central Asia Financial Systems in Historical and Cross-Country Contexts

In 2006, Central and Eastern Europe were booming. Laszlo Nagy, a suburban worker employed with a local service supplier to multinational firms near Budapest, considered taking a second mortgage to build a summer vacation house by Lake Balaton. Because the interest rate on mortgage loans in Swiss francs stood at 5.1 percent, less than half the rate in Hungarian forint (of 13.8 percent), he wanted to save with a good deal that a local bank keenly offered. Although he had no income in Swiss francs, the sweet deal was up for grabs—with no questions asked. From 159 forint per franc in January 2007, the forint-franc exchange rate depreciated sharply with the global financial crisis and touched 303 forint per franc in July 2015. Nearly 65 percent of Hungary's household mortgages were in Swiss francs (some 47 percent of gross domestic product [GDP]). Hungary's banking system trembled and halted when confronted with the systemwide failure in repayments. House prices plummeted and Laszlo, like hundreds of thousands of other Hungarians, was upside-down on his mortgage, struggling to make ends meet. The financial system failed him.[1] At that time, financial systems tumbled in many Europe and Central Asia (ECA) region countries. But some showed resilience.

This chapter examines financial development in ECA in historical and cross-country context as a means to gain insights into the gaps ECA faces. It provides the context for subsequent chapters that examine where ECA's financial development might be improved to enhance sustainable long-term growth (chapter 2), jobs (chapter 3), and household opportunity and resilience through saving (chapter 4). It looks at ECA's financial development from three perspectives: (a) in comparison to other World Bank regions, (b) across time and ECA subregions, and

(c) focusing on the dynamics before and after the global financial crisis. Furthermore, it examines the development along four areas: financial depth, stability, efficiency, and inclusion.

Main messages:

- By the early 1990s, ECA showed nascent financial systems. Rapid financial deepening over the last two decades helped ECA advance financial inclusion, but it also made ECA confront two waves of banking crises—that of the late 1990s and that associated with the 2008 global financial crisis. Balancing financial development and stability remains a challenge for the region.

- Overall the financial development in ECA is still low given the region's middle-income status. Although ECA has deep banking systems and shows progress on financial inclusion, financial stability and efficiency remain weak and capital markets are shallow.

- ECA has been the developing region most affected by the global financial crisis. While credit growth slowed down in the crisis, financial inclusion remained high compared with other regions—but is still very uneven across ECA subregions. The impact on banking efficiency was mixed.

How Do ECA Financial Systems Differ from Those in Other Regions?

Financial sectors in Emerging ECA have developed at different speeds and under often abrupt financial liberalization as the region transitioned from centrally planned to market economies.[2] The development has been shaped by several forces that have affected countries in multiple ways, including the proximity to the European Union (EU), international financial integration, and financial sector liberalization.

The process of financial integration in the EU has affected member, candidate, and neighboring countries. It has contributed to the strengthening of policies and institutions, along with spurring capital flows among countries, particularly from richer to poorer economies (Gill and Raiser 2012). More recently, initiatives such as the Banking Union[3] and the Capital Markets Union[4] could further increase the speed of institutional integration and influence the structure of countries' financial systems. They are also likely to elicit further harmonization in the regulatory and supervisory approaches. Box 1.1 discusses regulation and supervision in ECA.

Countries in the eastern part of the ECA region have been less affected by the development in the EU project but have been influenced by developments on the international markets. Resource-rich countries in Central Asia and South Caucasus have benefitted from highly liquid global markets. The possibility to tap wholesale funding and the ability to borrow in foreign currency have further increased the dollarization of the economies. Many have thus been dependent on external financing to bridge the gap between domestic savings and demand for credit.

A unique feature in ECA is the high presence of foreign-owned banks, instrumental for the financing of domestic investment through both foreign direct

BOX 1.1 Banking Regulation and Supervision in ECA

Financial systems in Europe and Central Asia (ECA) are predominantly bank-based, eliciting a prominent role for well-functioning regulatory and supervisory practices. Effective bank regulation and supervision are designed to protect bank charter value and avoid excessive (systemic) risk-seeking behavior, particularly when private sector monitoring is weak.[a] The regulatory environment in developing ECA countries has been influenced by the European Union accession of countries in central and southeastern Europe and by the international regulatory initiatives proposed by the Basel Committee on Banking Supervision. These have aligned ECA subregions to the practices observed in the benchmarking regional groups.

Data from the World Bank's Bank Regulation and Supervision Survey (BRSS) and the Deposit Insurance Database allow the measure of different features of banking regulatory environment in ECA, such as the degree of independence of supervision authorities, the freedom in engaging in a wide range of intermediation activities, explicit protection of depositors, and effective private monitoring.[b] In general, these measures should be combined with information on political institutions

to provide an accurate indicator on the efficacy of the banking regulatory environment in a specific country. Moreover, these indicators should be analyzed in conjunction to ascertain the impact on various policy outcomes.[c]

The **Independence of Supervisory Authory Index**[d] measures the degree of independence between politicians and banks. It reflects the form of appointment of banking officials, their accountability, and their length of term in office. Supervisory authorities are a key line of defense against unsound and unsafe banking practices. As a result, independence from short-term political gyrations and undue pressure from banks is paramount to grant an effective supervisory action. Higher values of the index indicate greater independence.

Across the majority of ECA subregions we notice a general increase in the degree of independence of banking supervisory authorities, particularly since 2007 (figure B1.1.1). Noticeable exceptions are the South Caucasus and Western Balkans, where the bank supervisors faced lower independence in 2011 than in 2007.

The **Activity Stringency Index**[e] indicates whether national regulatory authorities allow banks

FIGURE B1.1.1 Independence of banking supervisory authorities has generally increased in ECA since 2000

Median independence of supervision

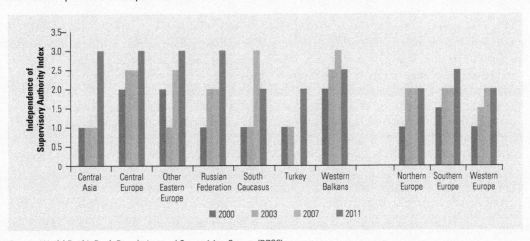

Source: World Bank's Bank Regulation and Supervision Survey (BRSS).

(Continued)

Banking Regulation and Supervision in ECA (continued)

FIGURE B1.1.2 Regulatory restrictiveness has generally fallen across ECA since 2000

Median activity stringency

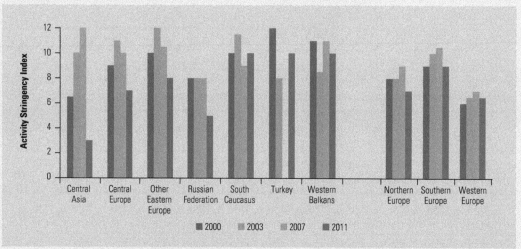

Source: World Bank's Bank Regulation and Supervision Survey (BRSS).

to engage in a wide spectrum of intermediation activities, namely securities, insurance, real estate, and ownership of financial firms. Regulatory restrictiveness can entail both benefits (for example, in terms of avoiding potential conflict of interests in the brokering of securities) and costs,[f] calling for targeted policies to strike a beneficial balance for the wider economy. Higher values of the index indicate greater restrictiveness.

Across all ECA subregions, except for Western Europe, we observe a lower value in 2011 than in 2000, meaning lower restrictiveness for banks in engaging in a wider range of intermediation activities (figure B1.1.2). Interestingly, several subregions had a more restrictive approach coming into the crisis (that is, 2007 figures for Central Asia, Western Balkans, Northern Europe, Southern Europe, and Western Europe) and have eased restrictions on banks since then. Particularly noteworthy is the change in the Central Asia subregion between 2007 and 2011, pointing to potential issues related to an abrupt financial liberalization.

The **Private Monitoring Index**[g] captures the extent to which private monitoring exists and

influences bank behavior. It includes information on the independent assessment of financial information made available to the public, the existence of deposit insurance—which reduces private monitoring incentives—and specific features associated with the publication of financial statement information. Effective private monitoring exerts pressure on and influences bank behavior. Higher values of the index denote stronger private monitoring.

ECA subregions show an average improvement in private monitoring since 2000 (figure B1.1.3). The ECA regional benchmarking group (Northern, Southern, and Western Europe) shows a general improvement over the period as do Emerging ECA subregions, except for Central Asia and the Western Balkans. Nonetheless, improvement has, in many cases, taken a bumpy path over time.

Overall the latest values on the three indexes give a mixed picture on the extent of change in the regulatory environment in ECA countries. Most regions show improved independence of supervision, but in some cases (Central Asia and the Western Balkans) there has been a deterioration in private monitoring (figures B1.1.1 and B1.1.3). In Central

(Continued)

BOX 1.1 *(continued)*

FIGURE B1.1.3 ECA subregions show general improvement in private monitoring since 2000

Median private monitoring

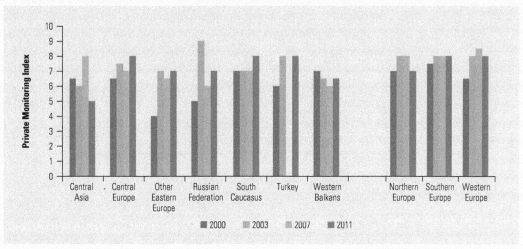

Source: World Bank's Bank Regulation and Supervision Survey (BRSS).

Asia and the Western Balkans, banks are allowed to engage in a wider set of activities with weaker private monitoring than in 2000, calling for caution for potential unchecked bank moral hazard behavior (figures B1.1.2 and B1.1.3). Central Asia, Central Europe, and the Russian Federation show the greatest increase in flexibility in engaging in intermediation activities (figure B1.1.2) and have an average level of private monitoring (figure B1.1.3), while the South Caucasus shows less flexibility but higher private monitoring. Turkey has increased the independence of supervision (figure B1.1.1), increased the flexibility in performing a diverse set of activities (figure B1.1.2), and significantly improved private monitoring since 2000 (figure B1.1.3). (See Melecky and Podpiera 2013, 2015, 2016.)

a. Čihák et al. 2012b.
b. Data on four BRSS waves (2001, 2003, 2007, and 2011) are available at http://go.worldbank.org/SNUSW978P0.
c. For example, official supervisory power, enhancement of private monitoring, and a reduction in restrictions of bank activities may be related to overall banking system stability.
d. See Barth, Caprio, and Levine (2006), appendix 2, for an in-depth explanation of the construction of the index.
e. See Beck, De Jonghe, and Schepens (2013) for an in-depth explanation of the construction of the index.
f. Barth, Caprio, and Levine (2008) suggest that tightened restrictions on bank activities may entail higher bank instability, lower bank development, and a reduction in the efficiency of financial intermediation.
g. See Barth, Caprio, and Levine (2006), appendix 2, for an in-depth explanation of the construction of the index.

investment and lending. Western European banks, attracted by higher return to equity, established a strong presence in Central and Eastern Europe, dominating the banking markets in several countries (for example, in 2013, Croatia, the Czech Republic, Montenegro, and the Slovak Republic) where foreign bank assets as a percentage of total banking assets averaged more than 85 percent. In some countries, regulators allowed ratios of loans to domestic deposits to become substantially greater than one, implying greater vulnerability to sudden capital outflows. The sources of external financing would often depend on membership in the

European Union or the intention to join. For other countries, such as Kazakhstan and the Russian Federation, the funding gap was filled through wholesale funding favored by highly liquid global international markets and booming oil prices. Following the 2008 financial crisis, the capital inflows dried out, forcing an external adjustment in many countries in the ECA region. The imbalances have been managed well by some countries (for example, Poland and Turkey), but less so by others (for example, Romania and Ukraine) where the excesses were left unmanaged and strong decline in investment ensued.

The fast credit growth in ECA countries preceding the global financial crisis was made possible through large external inflows intermediated by banks. Banks and shrinking external funding also constituted the main channel through which credit in ECA contracted after 2008. The median credit growth peaked at about 30 percent in 2007 and then declined sharply with the outbreak of the global financial crisis in 2008. Credit provision fell in several countries until very recently. For instance, Slovenia, battered by its banking crisis, posted a 17 percent decline in net domestic credit in 2014. In some countries, the slowdown was driven by close economic and financial links with Western Europe (Feyen et al. 2014), which has experienced repeated episodes of financial stress and volatility since 2007 (figure 1.1).

Credit provided by financial intermediaries to the private sector has been an important indicator of financial development. However, it is only one of many measures to gauge how well financial sectors operate and deliver on all the functions expected of a modern financial system. The range of financial outcomes that can more holistically describe a well-functioning financial system includes (a) depth, or the size and diversity of financial institutions and markets; (b) stability;

FIGURE 1.1 The volatility of credit is high in ECA

Median net domestic credit annual growth

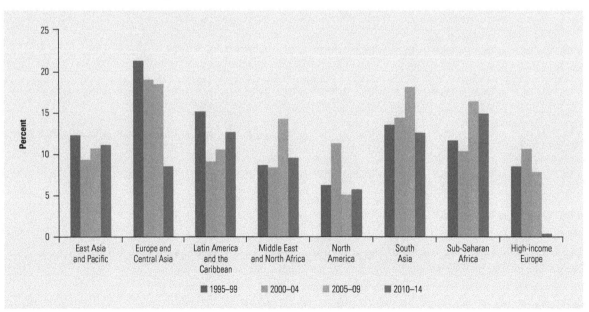

Source: World Development Indicators.
Note: Data do not include offshore financial centers (e.g., Luxembourg) as defined in Zoromé 2007 and FinStats.

(c) efficiency in the provision of financial services; and (d) inclusion, or the access and use of financial services and products.[5] The indicators of the four financial outcomes used to assess ECA financial systems are as follows:

a. *Depth* (all indicators as percent of GDP): private sector credit by financial intermediaries; domestic bank deposits; consolidated foreign claims of banks reporting to the Bank for International Settlements (BIS);[6] stock market capitalization; and nonbank financial intermediaries' assets

b. *Stability:* nonperforming loans to total gross loans; balance-sheet *z*-score;[7] liquid assets to deposits and short-term funding; and bank capital to assets

c. *Efficiency:* net interest margin (percent of interest-bearing assets); overhead costs (percent of total assets); ratio of bank cost to income; and stock market turnover ratio (percent of average market capitalization)

d. *Inclusion:* number of branches per 100,000 adults; percent of adults who have an account at a financial institution, have borrowed from a financial institution, use a debit or credit card, or have saved at a financial institution.

This set of indicators is chosen to maximize the distinct information conveyed by each variable, considering also lessons learned from existing research and time-series availability.[8]

ECA ranks below the global average compared to other regions on depth and stability and about average when it comes to efficiency and inclusion (figure 1.2). Interestingly, some higher-income European countries also rank below the average on stability and efficiency, indicating that the strength of individual financial development indicators is not necessarily related to the level of income. Thus, while income levels may play a role in financial sector development, other structural factors and policy choices also are important.

ECA financial systems are dominated by banks. More than half of ECA countries have higher credit and cross-border banking than other countries, but pension fund assets, stock market capitalization, and insurance in ECA are lower than in half of all countries (table 1.1). This also may reflect recent policies governing the organization of the pension system in some countries (for example, Croatia and Hungary).

ECA countries score poorly in terms of financial stability. Levels of nonperforming loans are considerably higher (see spotlight 2), and indicators of bank solvency and liquidity lower, than the global median. Bank capitalization is the only indicator that exceeds the global median.

Banking sector efficiency is relatively high in ECA: more than half of ECA countries have lower net interest margins, cost-to-income ratios, and overhead costs than the global median. However, the stock market turnover ratio is significantly lower, indicating greater reliance on banking compared to the nonbank sector.

Most indicators of financial inclusion in ECA, including the share of adults with a bank account, a loan, a credit card, and likely proximity to a bank, are higher than in more than half of the countries in the world. However, the share of the population saving formally is low (more on the reasons for this are investigated in chapter 4).

More than half of ECA countries have higher credit and cross-border banking than other countries, but pension fund assets, stock market capitalization, and insurance in ECA are lower than in half of all countries.

FIGURE 1.2 ECA performs at or below the average on financial development, particularly on financial depth and stability

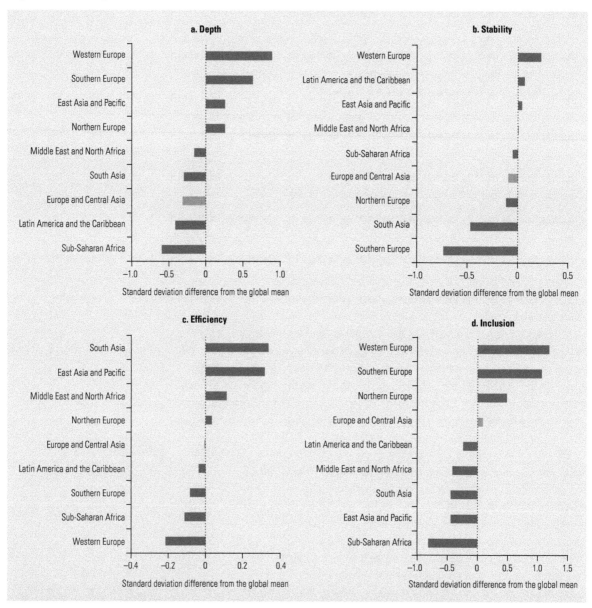

Sources: World Bank calculations using World Development Indicators, Global Findex, and Financial Access Survey.
Note: Regions at the top of each panel show the highest value in that category. The lower is the value of the individual index, the worse is the performance in the specific financial outcome. The individual financial indicators are standardized before they are aggregated into the overall index. The variables are standardized to have a mean of zero and standard deviation of 1. For each region the average value of the standardized variables is then subtracted from the global average standardized value. Data are based on the latest year, given the availability of information for all the indicators.

TABLE 1.1 Benchmarked ECA Financial Development Indicators

Indicator	ECA median value	Global median value	Percent difference
Depth (% GDP)			
Private sector credit	57.3	41.9	26.9
Domestic bank deposits	45.1	48.8	−8.2
Consolidated BIS claims	30.6	20.2	33.9
Stock market capitalization	13.0	28.1	−116.5
Insurance company assets	4.0	5.3	−34.5
Mutual fund assets	2.9	11.9	−312.4
Pension fund assets	4.0	9.7	−145.1
Stability			
Nonperforming loans (%, higher = less stable)	11.3	4.3	61.8
Z–score[a] (%, lower = less stable)	11.1	13.4	−20.8
Liquid assets to short-term funding (%, lower = less stable)	25.8	28.0	−8.7
Bank capital to assets (%, higher = more stable)	13.5	9.6	29.1
Efficiency (%)			
Net interest margin	4.2	3.8	8.4
Overhead costs	3.2	2.8	9.7
Bank cost-to-income ratio	59.0	56.1	4.8
Stock market turnover ratio	5.2	13.2	−154.0
Inclusion			
Account at a financial institution	56.5	45.1	20.2
Borrowed from financial institution	13.2	9.7	26.1
Debit card	39.7	28.5	28.3
Saved at a financial institution	8.7	14.9	−70.6
Credit card	13.5	10.1	24.9
Number of branches	24.3	12.3	49.4
Firms financially constrained (% of firms answering yes)	16.3	25.3	−55.2

Sources: World Bank calculations using World Development Indicators, FinStats, Financial Access Survey, and Global Findex.
Note: Depth and efficiency indicators are as per 2012, stability indicators as per 2013, and financial inclusion indicators as per 2014. Differences that indicate lower financial development appear in red type. BIS = Bank for International Settlements.
a. The z-score is an overall measure of bank solvency.

How Different Are Financial Systems within ECA?

Overall, the level of financial development differs greatly among ECA subregions and by indicator (figure 1.3). Indicators with a value greater than zero indicate financial outcomes that are greater than the global median values. Although several methods are available for comparing financial development indicators across countries, in this section we take a simple, easy-to-understand approach and compare to global median values (see box 1.2).

The median level of financial depth is lower than the global median in many developing ECA subregions except Central Europe, Turkey, and Western Balkans. Financial stability also differs greatly among ECA subregions. Countries in Central Asia, Russia, and South Caucasus have historically had more stability, whereas Eastern and Central Europe, Turkey, and Western Balkans have experienced less stability. The global financial crisis, banking crises, and the sovereign debt crisis have had a profound impact on the financial soundness of credit institutions in the latter group. In recent years, stability has declined for most of the ECA subregions, particularly Central Europe and the Western Balkans.

Although banking sector efficiency is relatively high in most ECA subregions, overall financial sector efficiency, which includes capital markets, is below the

FIGURE 1.3 Differences with benchmark levels of financial development vary across ECA subregions

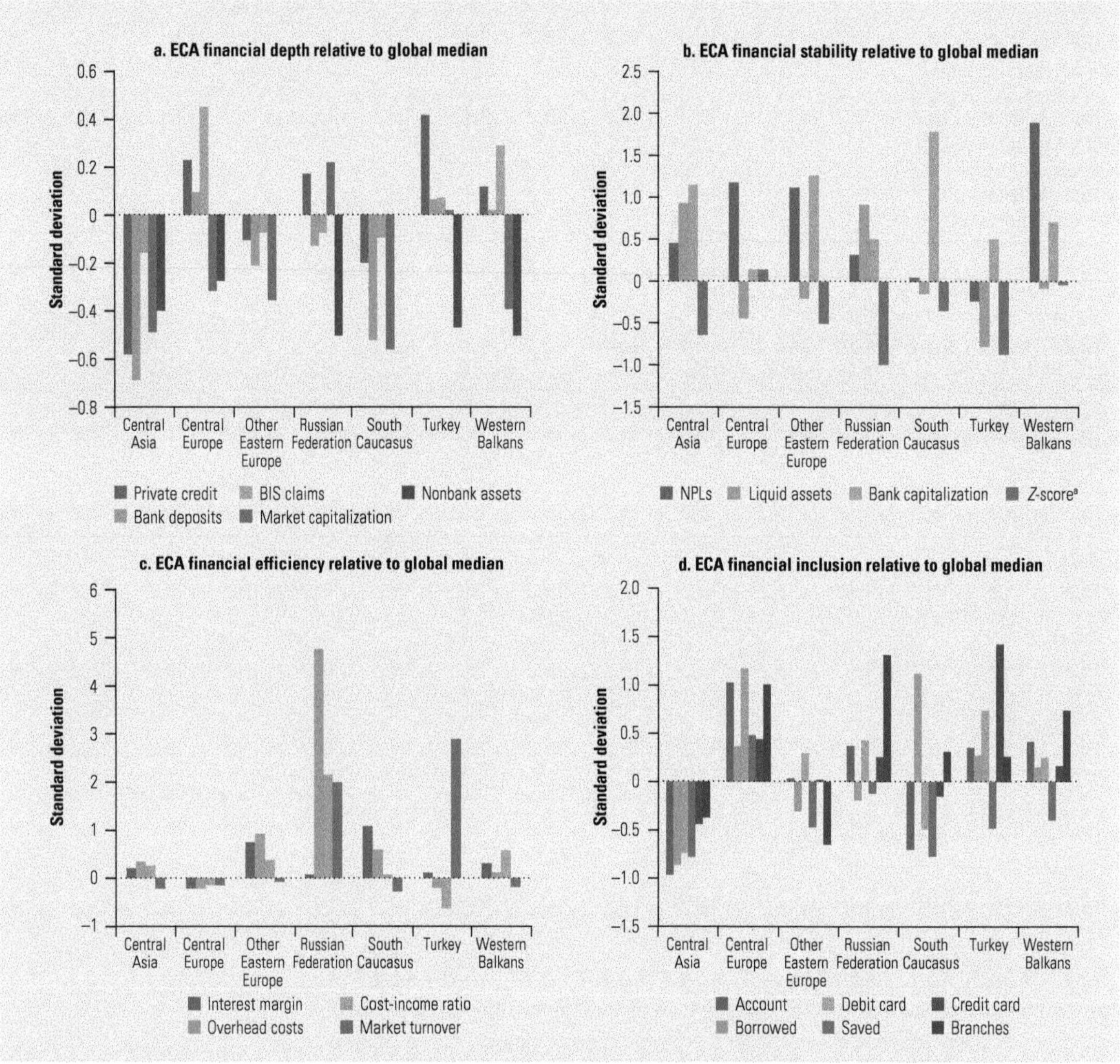

a. ECA financial depth relative to global median

Legend: Private credit | BIS claims | Nonbank assets | Bank deposits | Market capitalization

b. ECA financial stability relative to global median

Legend: NPLs | Liquid assets | Bank capitalization | Z-score[a]

c. ECA financial efficiency relative to global median

Legend: Interest margin | Cost-income ratio | Overhead costs | Market turnover

d. ECA financial inclusion relative to global median

Legend: Account | Debit card | Credit card | Borrowed | Saved | Branches

Sources: World Bank calculations using World Development Indicators, FinStats, Financial Access Survey, and Global Findex.
Note: Indicators are latest date available. Values are standardized with a median of zero and standard deviation of 1. Values shown are the indicator standard deviation from the global median value. BIS = Bank for International Settlements; NPLs = nonperforming loans.
a. The z-score is an overall measure of bank solvency.

global median (higher interest rate margins and cost ratios reflect lower efficiency, whereas high capital market turnover reflects greater efficiency). Russia stands out as having the lowest measure of overall efficiency, while Turkey has one of the highest, which is primarily due to capital market turnover. In recent years, most ECA subregions have experienced improvements in efficiency relative to the global median. However, Other Eastern European countries and Western Balkans have seen a relative decrease in efficiency.

Financial inclusion for the median country in Central Asia, South Caucasus, and Other Eastern Europe was lower than the global median, although these subregions achieved some improvement in recent years. At the other end of the

BOX 1.2 Methods of Comparing Financial Development among Countries

Two methods have typically been used to compare financial sector development between countries. The first, used in this chapter, involves a simple comparison of regional performance across various indicators of financial sector development. Using the selected characteristics, we provide a snapshot of the current level of financial development of the different World Bank regions relative to the global median level.

A second approach has also been used in the financial development literature, which is to compare financial sector development while controlling for nonpolicy determinants of performance. This is done by computing the estimated value for each indicator of financial sector development as a function of per capita income and structural economic characteristics over time.[a] The difference between the estimated and actual value is assumed to capture the quality of financial policies above what would be expected based on the level of overall development.[b] Although this procedure is informative, it assumes that higher income levels are good predictors of financial policies. However, financial policies are not always uniform for countries with the same level of economic development. In other words, balanced financial policy choices may not always be related to higher income levels, and country preferences and risk aversion may play an important role in determining policy.

Our simple approach to benchmarking Europe and Central Asia (ECA) in relation to the rest of the world is used to get a snapshot of how ECA compares in financial development. Complementing this approach, chapter 2 looks at benchmarking ECA financial sector development using the concept of the "financial development frontier" using all indicators and ranking countries' outcomes based on long-run growth outcomes. In this manner, we benchmark the quality of ECA's overall set of financial development indicators jointly using the set of actual financial development indicators of the top 20 percent of country performers and their overall and bottom 40 percent growth outcomes.

a. For many indicators, this information on the estimated value is available on FinStats, http://globalpractices.worldbank.org/finance/Documents/Finstats_user_manual%202016.pdf.
b. For more information on the technique, see Beck et al. (2008) and Čihák et al. (2012a).

spectrum, although Central Europe has a higher level of financial inclusion than the global median, it has experienced a relative decline in recent years.

Financial sector depth and diversification: Private credit by financial intermediaries and bank deposits are at or slightly higher than the global median benchmark, for all subregions except Central Asia, South Caucasus, and Other Eastern Europe. This casts doubt on the view that in several subregions there is an insufficient accumulation of deposits. However, it does not address the question of whether there is an investment gap (EBRD 2015) or if there is an imbalance between credit provision and local funding (Feyen et al. 2014). Interestingly, the high relative level of consolidated foreign claims in Central Europe and the Western Balkans suggests that cross-border capital flows are still important for financial development in emerging Europe (EBRD 2015). Countries tend to show similar patterns by subregion. For example, Central Asian economies generally had low financial depth and have seen little change since the 2008 crisis.

Foreign-owned banks may have helped increase lending in some parts of the region. In particular, countries in Eastern Europe that became members of the EU in the 2000s have seen a steady increase in the number of affiliates—either branches or subsidiaries—especially from Western European parent banks.

Although cross-border bank claims are lower compared to the precrisis period in a few countries, particularly in Central Asia, this subregion had relatively low levels of foreign financing to begin with. In more recent years (not captured by these figures), net capital outflows due to the economic uncertainty arising from the fall in oil prices, increasing fiscal deficits, fragile macro policy frameworks, large corporate tax liabilities, and acute political uncertainties have likely further reduced cross-border financing for Russia and countries in Central Asia and South Caucasus.

Stock market capitalization and insurance premiums relative to GDP remain low for most subregions. Whereas some countries have seen an increase in stock market capitalization as a percent of GDP since the crisis, most have seen a decline. Similarly, the level of insurance premiums changed little between the pre- and postcrisis periods.[9]

Efficiency: Efficiency measures vary greatly across the region. Banking overhead costs and cost-to-income ratios are high across the region compared to the global median, but most noticeably in Russia. A distinguishing feature is the efficiency of capital markets in the region, as measured by stock market turnover. Russia and Turkey have large market turnover rates, reflecting their unique ease of capital market transactions compared to other ECA subregions.

Following the financial crisis, the net interest margin fell in most ECA countries, indicating some increase in the efficiency of credit intermediation. With the notable exception of Russia, ECA countries also saw overhead banking costs decline in the postcrisis period because banks have tried to become more cost conscious. However, revenues declined even faster than costs, so that several countries experienced higher costs compared to revenues in the postcrisis period. The indicator of nonbank financial market efficiency (stock market turnover) deteriorated during the postcrisis period in most countries, with the exception of Central Europe—although it remains below the global median. Unlike depth and stability indicators, efficiency indicators are highly idiosyncratic and are less likely to show common trends within subregions.

Financial stability: In the regions where nonperforming loans are close to the global median (that is, Central Asia, Russia, the South Caucasus, and Turkey), the z-score, an overall measure of bank solvency, tends to be lower than the global median. It may be that low levels of nonperforming loans are associated with low risk-taking, which results in low bank profits. But low profits, in turn, raise riskiness and offset (to some degree) the desire to reduce risk by maintaining an overly conservative portfolio. Of the other stability indicators, the ratio of liquid assets to short-term funding is lower than the global median in just over half the subregions including Central Europe, Other Eastern Europe, South Caucasus, Turkey, and the Western Balkans, whereas bank capitalization is higher than the global median level for all subregions.

It is not surprising that indicators of financial stability fell following the financial crisis. Many countries, particularly in the Western Balkans, experienced an increase in the level of nonperforming loans. Moreover, the level of liquidity and bank capitalization fell in most of the countries. It also appears that the volatility of credit growth and deposit growth increased in the postcrisis period.

Financial inclusion: Indicators of financial inclusion exceed the global median in many ECA countries with the notable exception of Central Asia and on several indicators in the South Caucasus and Other Eastern Europe. Although ECA countries have made substantial progress in increasing financial inclusion, saving remains relatively low across the region. In addition, the pace of progress has been uneven, and the level of financial inclusion across the region remains diverse. Countries in Central Europe have relatively high levels of inclusion, with widespread account ownership and use of financial services. At the other end of the spectrum, however, countries in Central Asia show very low levels of financial inclusion. For example, almost all adults in Slovenia have a bank account, whereas the level of account ownership in Turkmenistan is very low and improved only marginally from 2011 to 2014 (from 0.4 percent to 1.8 percent). The share of adults that have borrowed from a financial institution also is low in Central Asia. The use of debit cards is widespread in Central Europe but low in some countries in Central Asia and South Caucasus. In addition, saving at a financial institution is higher in Central Europe. The level of financial inclusion among firms is even more heterogeneous. The number of financially constrained firms increased during the postcrisis period in several countries, and a lower share of firms received bank financing or raised funds on the stock market in 2013 compared to 2009.

Conclusion

Financial development in ECA lags behind its comparators on several indicators, particularly in financial depth (nonbank financial services), stability (high nonperforming loans), and efficiency (low capital market turnover). Inclusion tends to be relatively high, with the exception of Central Asia and the low use of formal saving accounts in other parts of the region. However, despite some setbacks with the onset of the global financial crisis, ECA has seen some improvement in financial sector outcomes, although the progress achieved over the past 20 years varies considerably.

Since the early 1990s the region has achieved a significant increase in financial depth, owing to the rapid growth in bank credit and cross-border banking. But this has come with a trade-off: many ECA countries saw this credit boom followed by credit busts and banking failures with the onset of the global financial crisis. The crisis marked the beginning of a period in which reliance on the traditional drivers of financial development, such as capital inflows and rapid growth in domestic credit, has had to decline. This highlights the role of policy in improving financial efficiency and inclusion, while addressing the possible trade-offs with stability (the potential for both trade-offs and synergies between inclusion and stability is the focus of chapter 5).

In the following chapter we delve into how ECA's characteristics and financial sector gaps translate into overall and bottom 40 percent growth impacts. Although ECA may lack nonbanking services compared to global norms and has experienced greater volatility, making gains in these areas may not provide as much "bang for the buck" as, for example, making progress on efficiency and inclusion. Chapter 2 will attempt to determine these financial development growth impacts and suggest areas on which ECA policy makers should focus to guide policy reforms.

Notes

1. A composite story. http://www.npr.org/2012/01/31/146140750/for-hungarian -borrowers-a-mortgage-nightmare.
2. Emerging ECA includes **Central Asia** (Kazakhstan, the Kyrgyz Republic, Tajikistan, Turk-menistan, Uzbekistan); **Central Europe** (Bulgaria, Croatia, the Czech Republic, Hungary, Poland, Romania, the Slovak Republic, Slovenia); **Other Eastern Europe** (Belarus, Mol-dova, Ukraine); **the Russian Federation; South Caucasus** (Armenia, Azerbaijan, Geor-gia); **Turkey; Western Balkans** (Albania, Bosnia and Herzegovina, Kosovo, the former Yugoslav Republic of Macedonia, Montenegro, Serbia).
3. For more information about the Banking Union, see the European Council's website at http://www.consilium.europa.eu/en/policies/banking-union/.
4. For more information about the Capital Markets Union, see the European Commission's website at http://ec.europa.eu/finance/capital-markets-union/index_en.htm.
5. See Levine (2005) and Zingales (2015) for a discussion of the various functions per-formed by financial institutions and financial markets to improve economic growth and development.
6. Examples of these claims are deposits and balances placed with banks and loans and advances.
7. The balance-sheet z-score is a measure of solvency built as the sum of return on assets and the leverage ratio, all divided by the standard deviation of the return on assets. See Mare, Moreira, and Rossi (2015) for a more in-depth explanation.
8. See for instance Beck et al. (2008), Čihák et al. (2012a), and World Bank (2013).
9. Although all indicators are shown as a percentage of GDP, we are considering several years of data and median values for each separate period and country. Short-term devel-opments, such as temporary drops in GDP, are therefore of limited importance.

References

Barth, James R., Gerard Caprio Jr., and Ross Levine. 2006. *Rethinking Bank Regulation: Till Angels Govern*. New York: Cambridge University Press.

———. 2008. "Bank Regulations Are Changing: For Better or Worse?" *Comparative Eco-nomic Studies* 50 (4): 537–63.

Beck, T., O. De Jonghe, and G. Schepens. 2013. "Bank Competition and Stability: Cross-Country Heterogeneity." *Journal of Financial Intermediation* 22 (2): 218–44.

Beck, T., E. Feyen, A. Ize, and F. Moizeszowicz. 2008. "Benchmarking Financial Develop-ment." Policy Research Working Paper Series 4638, World Bank, Washington, DC.

Čihák, M., A. Demirgüç-Kunt, E. Feyen, and R. Levine. 2012a. "Benchmarking Financial Systems around the World." Policy Research Working Paper 6175, World Bank, Wash-ington, DC.

Čihák, Martin, Asli Demirgüç-Kunt, María Soledad Martínez Pería, and Amin Mohseni-Cheraghlou. 2012b. "Bank Regulation and Supervision around the World: A Crisis Update." Policy Research Working Paper 6286, World Bank, Washington, DC.

EBRD (European Bank for Reconstruction and Development). 2015. "Rebalancing Finance." Transition Report 2015-16, EBRD, London.

Feyen, E., R. Letelier, I. Love, S. M. Maimbo, R. D. R. Rocha. 2014. "The Impact of Funding Models and Foreign Bank Ownership on Bank Credit Growth: Is Central and Eastern Europe Different?" Policy Research Working Paper 6783, World Bank, Washington, DC.

Gill, Indermit S., and Martin Raiser. 2012. *Golden Growth: Restoring the Lustre of the European Economic Model*. Europe and Central Asia Studies. Washington, DC: World Bank.

Levine, R. 2005. "Finance and Growth: Theory and Evidence." Chapter 12 in *Handbook of Economic Growth*, edited by P. Aghion and S. Durlauf. Amsterdam: Elsevier.

Mare, D. S., F. Moreira, and R. Rossi. 2015. "Nonstationary *z*-score Measures" (November 10). Available at SSRN: http://ssrn.com/abstract=2688367.

Melecky, M., and A. M. Podpiera. 2013. "Institutional Structures of Financial Sector Supervision: Their Drivers and Historical Benchmarks." *Journal of Financial Stability* 9 (3): 428–44.

———. 2015. "Placing Bank Supervision in the Central Bank: Implications for Financial Stability Based on Evidence from the Global Crisis." Policy Research Working Paper 7320, World Bank, Washington, DC.

———. 2016. "Central Bank Design and Banking Supervision." BAFFI CAREFIN Centre Research Paper No. 2016-30. Available at SSRN: http://ssrn.com/abstract=2815822.

World Bank. 2013. *World Development Report 2014: Risk and Opportunity: Managing Risk for Development*. Washington, DC: World Bank.

Zingales, I. 2015. "Presidential Address: Does Finance Benefit Society?" *Journal of Finance* 70 (4): 1327–63.

Zoromé, A. 2007. "Concept of Offshore Financial Centers: In Search of an Operational Definition." IMF Working Paper 07/87, International Monetary Fund, Washington, DC.

SPOTLIGHT 1
Understanding the Role and Governance of State-Owned Banks

The 2008 global financial crisis prompted a reconsideration of the role of state-owned banks in Europe and Central Asia (ECA). Massive privatization programs during the transition to market economies sharply reduced the state-owned banks' share of banking assets in the 1990s and early 2000s. A number of countries in western ECA encouraged a high degree of foreign entry in their banking sectors to strengthen competition (for example, through the introduction of new products and modern technologies), increase access to finance based on funding from foreign parents, improve stability and overall banking efficiency through spillovers to domestic banks, and prepare for joining the European Union. These policies indirectly limited the role of domestic players, including state-owned banks. By contrast, a number of eastern ECA countries did not attract foreign investors, or encouraged a higher degree of domestic and, often, state ownership in their financial systems. This more gradualist approach to financial sector reform, which for these countries tended to be more challenging than the privatization of state-owned enterprises, trade and foreign exchange reforms, and price liberalization, in part reflected the high prevalence of nonperforming loans and unsuccessful privatizations leading to the emergence of strong domestic interests (Roaf et al. 2014; World Bank 2005). In addition, the belief that a degree of national control over the banking system was important for national security limited political support for reform.

The 2008 global financial crisis resulted in an increased use of state-owned banks to ramp up financing to the private sector. Private sector banks with high levels of foreign funding and subsidiaries with weak parents experienced large funding reductions, dramatically changing bank business models (with foreign bank branches ring-fenced into subsidiaries) and funding patterns (with domestic deposits substituting for cross-border flows). Financial systems in western ECA with high participation of foreign banks suffered a collapse of credit growth, deposits fled to safe havens, and failed banks had to be resolved—all events with serious political consequences. Although the benefits of foreign participation continued to be recognized, foreign banks were suddenly perceived as a source of risk. State bank ownership was seen as a possible tool to jump-start credit flows, retain formal savings, and help resolve failed banks. For example, Poland's state-owned bank, PKO BP, expanded credit at a faster pace than private banks did following the crisis.

The rationale for state intervention through State Commercial and Development Financial Institutions (SCDFIs) is based mainly on the presence of market failures (for example, externalities), social goals, and more recently the countercyclical/safe haven role (table S1.1). With quantitative easing appearing to have little impact on economic growth, and many countries facing tightening fiscal constraints, policy makers have increasingly explored SCDFIs as potential countercyclical instruments. Less frequently quoted arguments for SCDFIs concern promoting competition, promoting trust, or providing a financial return to the state.

Criticisms of state commercial banking activities focus on the potential for political capture, unfair competition, or the "Sisyphus syndrome" (inherent contradictions between a banking and social policy mandate). Criticisms of state development banking activities emphasize the need to resolve the underlying market failure. For example, credit or collateral information weaknesses should be addressed by strengthening the country's financial infrastructure, and long-term finance should be promoted by reforms related to capital markets and institutional investors. However, it can be argued that such

TABLE S1.1 State Intervention Rationale as It Relates to SCDFIs

State intervention rationale	Intervention focus example	Alternatives
Market failures. Financing financially profitable projects that do not get financed because of market failures (for example, asymmetric information).	SMEs, agriculture, R&D, and capital-intensive sectors. International trade. Long-term finance (including infrastructure).	Develop financial infrastructure and capital markets (however, this takes time).
Social goals. Financing financially unprofitable projects that are socially valuable.	Rural and isolated areas.	Address through subsidies.
Countercyclical/safe haven. Financing financially profitable projects that do not get financed when private bank risk appetite overreacts to recessions. Reduce employment volatility. Provide safe haven for depositor flight and contagion circuit breaker during crisis. Note: guarantees and subsidies may take time to materialize, compared to direct lending.	Labor-intensive sectors. Wide geographic branch presence.	Use monetary policy (however, lenders may underreact to policy). Use foreign banks as safe haven (but can also be source of uncertainty). If lending growth continues after economic recovery, misallocations are possible.
Competition. Guaranteeing competitive behavior in a collusive banking sector.	Broader commercial banking.	Fix regulation and monitoring (however, this may be nonbinding).
Trust. Promoting intermediation in a context of a general mistrust of private banks.	Broader commercial banking.	Develop institutions and regulation (however, this takes time).
Return. Provide returns to the state as shareholder.	Broader commercial banking.	Not an appropriate use of public funds.

Note: Table does not show prudential regulation. R&D = research and development; SCDFIs = State Commercial and Development Financial Institutions; SMEs = small and medium enterprises.

reforms tend to be a long-term process, with direct state intervention providing a bridge until the constraints are lifted.

Addressing the shortcomings of SCDFIs will require an analysis of why state intervention is necessary, an analysis of whether the SCDFI effectively addresses the problem identified, and reforms to resolve the underlying market failure. Such reforms may cover a wide spectrum, including macroeconomic policies, financial regulation and supervision, and financial infrastructure and capital markets, and may require a long time to be fully effective. It is often difficult to justify a pure state commercial bank, particularly if the financial system enjoys broad competition and trust by depositors. State

development–oriented institutions may be useful to address social goals but may require reforms along three key dimensions: their mandate, the instruments deployed, and their governance structure.

State development–oriented institutions should have clear mandates driven by the rationale for state intervention. These institutions should target sectors that are directly affected by the market failure the state aims to address, and should complement the activities of private banks rather than creating a new market distortion. The concept of "gap-filling" is essential. For example, small and medium enterprises (SMEs) may be too large for microfinance institutions and too small for corporate banking models because they are considered too

SPOTLIGHT 1 *(continued)*

risky or too costly to service; trade financing may be hampered by risks associated with the complexity of international trade; remote areas may be too expensive to service; or agriculture financing may be too complex because of risks associated with crop yields. When more than one state institution is present in a country, strong coordination and clear mandates are essential to avoid overlaps. The institution should generate enough resources to be sustainable over time, so as not to be a financial burden to the state. However, the objective of state-owned banks should not be to maximize profits, because this may exacerbate the market failure that the institution is trying to address.

The countercyclical role of the SCDFIs does not need to be explicitly defined in the mandate, yet governance mechanisms should address its timing and duration. Such mechanisms may include a protocol to communicate a change in the authorities' priorities. In order to avoid compromising the financial stability of the institution, the shareholder should be willing to support these additional risks with capital. And the activities and balance sheet of the SCDFI should contract as overall financial sector activity recovers.

The selection of instruments by SCDFIs should depend on the intervention rationale, with a preference for indirect, market-friendly structures. Table S1.2 offers a range of SCDFI instruments. The structure and degree of institutional development of the country's financial system should be taken into account. Overall, direct lending by state development–oriented institutions should be undertaken in market segments (for example, client type, maturity, and security offered) not covered by the private sector. Importantly, direct lending requires highly specialized risk management, strong credit underwriting skills, and operational efficiency. On-lending by state development–oriented institutions to other financial intermediaries, on the other hand, limits the scope for political interference and distorting competition, and enables the channeling of a higher volume of resources at lower costs by leveraging the infrastructure of other institutions. Risk-sharing facilities are another indirect and market-friendly means of state intervention, with the

TABLE S1.2 Typology of SCDFI Instruments

Typology	Benefits
Direct lending (first-tier, retail). SCDFI direct provision of finance to the ultimate beneficiary. Finance can be a regular loan, leasing, or factoring.	Targeted approach, when ultimate beneficiary or location is too expensive for private financial intermediaries to serve.
On-lending (second-tier, wholesale). SCDFI on-lending to financial intermediaries for their direct provision of finance to the ultimate beneficiary. Finance can be a regular loan, leasing, or factoring.	Lower cost and risk management burden for the SCDFI. Limited scope for political interference and market distortion. Higher demonstration effect.
Risk-sharing facilities. SCDFI offering of credit guarantees partially offsets loan losses by private financial intermediaries upon the ultimate beneficiary's default.	Leverage public resources. Alleviate enterprise collateral constraints and financial intermediary risk aversion.
Grants. SCDFI direct or indirect (through third parties) provision of grants.	Achieve socially desired objectives. Ensure equitable income distribution.
Nonlending products. SCDFIs offering advisory services, capacity building, and training programs to financial intermediaries or ultimate beneficiaries.	Strengthen financial intermediaries or ultimate beneficiaries, typically complemented by financing.

Note: SCDFI = State Commercial and Development Financial Institution.

additional benefit of facilitating the leverage of public resources. Capacity-building and training programs for existing and prospective clients (financial intermediaries and ultimate beneficiaries) can increase the sustainability of state financing (Gutiérrez et al. 2011).

Finally, the capacity of the SCDFI to identify, measure, and manage its risks is a critical element for adequate governance and overall performance. In this regard, an SCDFI subject to bank regulation is more likely to develop proper systems of risk management that may increase efficiency.

There is a wide variety of SCDFIs in the EU-15[1] and ECA countries. A desk research undertaken for 25 countries in the EU-15 and ECA countries found more than 62 SCDFIs with state ownership above 50 percent and market share above 0.75 percent (excluding takeovers from the recent crisis). State commercial banks accounted for 56 percent of all SCDFIs, with the highest market share in Slovenia (where 5 banks hold 45 percent of bank assets), the Russian Federation (4 banks with 58 percent), Turkey (3 banks with 29 percent), and Belarus (3 banks with 52 percent). State development banks, which accounted for 34 percent of institutions in the sample, were present in 15 out of 25 countries. The six state hybrid banks, which have a policy mandate and accept some form of retail deposits, are relatively small and are located in Austria, Bulgaria, Croatia, France, the Kyrgyz Republic, and Sweden. State narrow financial institutions were not observed in the sample, perhaps because of their very small size.

These SCDFIs offer a wide diversity of mandates, instruments, and governance arrangements. For at least 28 SCDFIs (mostly state hybrid banks or state development banks) out of the total 62 SCDFIs reviewed, policy mandates were established by law. Those policy mandates include a variety of areas for financing, with the top three being SMEs, real estate, and agriculture. SCDFIs provide financing through a wide range of instruments, including on-lending, direct lending, insurance, and guarantees.

For example, the Polish BGK (State Development Bank of Poland) administers several state funds and EU structural funds programs, and services government-sponsored programs providing guarantees to SMEs and mid-size corporations. Export-import banks, a number of which are present in the sample countries, focus on direct lending or providing guarantees to exporters or their clients. Most SCDFIs are supervised by the country's central bank or by the equivalent supervisory authority. However, some state development–oriented institutions are supervised by the ministry of finance, a line ministry, or, as in the case with the Russian Vnesheconombank, by its own supervisory board.

State banks require a strong legal framework and governance structure to avoid the potential for government interference in credit decisions, unfair competition, or the build-up of bad loans. State development–oriented institutions should have clear mandates driven by the rationale for state intervention, and should target sectors that are directly affected by the market failure the state aims to address. The institution should generate enough resources to be financially sustainable over time so as not to be a financial burden to the state. However, the objective of state-owned banks should not be to maximize profits, because this may exacerbate the market failure that the institution is trying to address.

Effective governance mechanisms are critical. In performing a countercyclical role, provisions should be worked out ahead of time to ensure that the balance sheet declines as overall financial sector activity recovers. A clear differentiation between the rights and responsibilities of the bank's different stakeholders—including the shareholders, the board of directors, and the management—should be defined in legislation. In addition, the law needs to specify a supervisory and regulatory function that is independent of the shareholders, directors, and management. The board of directors should establish performance indicators and benchmarks to

SPOTLIGHT 1 *(continued)*

ensure the accomplishment of policy objectives and financial soundness, and also should have the authority to appoint and dismiss the chief executive officer and the head of internal audit.

Note

1. The EU-15 comprises the 15 member countries before expansion: Austria, Belgium, Denmark, Finland, France, Germany, Greece, Ireland, Italy, Luxembourg, the Netherlands, Portugal, Spain, Sweden, and the United Kingdom.

References

Gutiérrez, Eva, Heinz P. Rudolph, Theodore Homa, and Enrique Blanco Beneit. 2011. "Development Banks: Role and Mechanisms to Increase Their Efficiency," Policy Research Working Paper 5729, World Bank, Washington, DC.

Roaf, James, Ruben Atoyan, Bikas Joshi, Krzysztof Krogulski, and an IMF staff team. 2014. *25 Years of Transition: Post-Communist Europe and the IMF.* Washington, DC: International Monetary Fund.

World Bank. 2005. *Economic Growth in the 1990s: Learning from a Decade of Reform.* Washington, DC: World Bank.

2

Finance for Growth and Shared Prosperity

In 2016, *Forbes* reported that Poland is starting to gain traction as an incubator for new tech start-ups (Coleman 2016). Firms such as DocPlanner, a health care appointment-booking platform, closed a $10 million international bond offering, bringing total outside funding for the company to $14 million. It is now operational in 25 markets in Africa, Asia, and Europe. Still, although there are an increasing number of start-up firms accessing international financial markets to fund their operations, 60 percent of firms still get their start from self-financing, outside of formal financial markets (Goldman 2015). A precondition for creating private sector growth is a good business climate, and Poland has consistently shown improvement in the World Bank's Doing Business Indicators, ranked 25 out of 189 countries globally in 2016. However, whereas underlying economic fundamentals are critical to starting a business, financial markets can provide the necessary "leg up" to expand beyond borders and can be a significant driver of export-led growth. Without sufficient financial sector development—broadly defined—firms and individuals can't reach their full potential. For firms, this may mean maximizing sales and growth potential; for individuals it may mean job opportunities, investing in education, or saving for retirement.

This chapter aims to provide new evidence on how financial development affects the growth of aggregate income and the income of the bottom 40 percent of earners. It studies the effect of finance on growth, given the gaps identified in chapter 1 in the four dimensions of depth, stability, efficiency, and inclusion in the use of various financial services. Where the Europe and Central Asia (ECA) region[1] stands in each of these four dimensions captures the ability of financial

development to boost income growth by mobilizing savings, evaluating projects, managing risks, monitoring managers, and facilitating transactions (Levine 2005). The chapter uses the most comprehensive set of financial development indicators to date. When relating finance to income growth, it uses well-established control variables from the literature on finance and economic growth, poverty, and inequality to properly isolate the growth effect of finance. The analysis then points to areas where ECA's financial sector development stands to benefit inclusive growth the most.

Main messages:

- Finance affects growth through several dimensions, not just the depth of credit. For aggregate growth, the most economically important dimensions are financial efficiency, firm inclusion, and stability. However, for inclusive growth, the most important dimension of finance is the access to finance by firms, in particular to equity financing. Finance could affect income growth mostly by boosting allocative efficiency rather than mobilizing savings for investment.

- Given its stage of financial development, Emerging ECA could benefit most by implementing policies that improve financial efficiency because it has already achieved comparatively high access to finance by firms. Also, policies to foster financial stability remain important for some parts of Emerging ECA.

- Banking crises dampened medium-term growth in both the advanced European Union (EU) countries and Emerging ECA. Surprisingly, countries with more developed financial systems do not seem to suffer more in crisis times. On the contrary, we find that greater financial inclusion of individuals (and firms) can help cushion the busts in aggregate growth during banking crises. However, the cushioning effect is insignificant for the income growth of the bottom 40.

What Has Been the Growth Performance of Countries in ECA Excluding the Impact of Finance?

Although it may seem counterintuitive given ECA's slow growth following the global financial sector crisis, over a longer-run 15 years, aggregate growth and shared prosperity in ECA have been higher than would be expected—accounting for basic growth determinants but excluding the impact of financial sector development. The baseline expected level of growth is based on a simple regression of income growth on well-established growth fundamentals, following the existing literature but excluding the potential effects of finance.[2] Our basic question is how much of this higher-than-expected long-term growth might be explained by financial sector factors.

Excluding the impact of financial sector development, the median annual gross domestic product (GDP) growth in the region, for the period 2000–14, is 1.8 percent higher than indicated by the growth fundamentals. This is the highest unexplained growth among the developing regions, and is even greater than the unexpected growth in the developed European countries. Similarly, growth of the

FIGURE 2.1 Unexplained GDP and incomes of the bottom 40 percent increased much more rapidly in ECA than in other regions, 2000–14

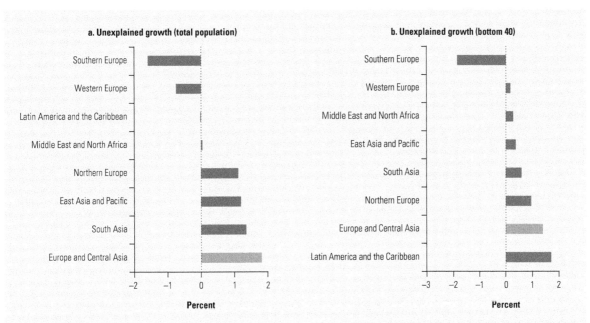

incomes of the bottom 40 percent in ECA is 1.38 percent higher than the benchmark model, the highest unexplained performance among all regions except Latin America and the Caribbean (LAC) (figure 2.1). This unexplained part of income growth may be correlated with financial development, as characterized by financial systems' depth, stability, efficiency, and inclusion, and is the key question investigated in this chapter.

Although finance may be the missing piece of the puzzle, other factors may be important, too. For example, since 2000, many of the Central Asian economies have grown considerably faster than other countries with similar macroeconomic situations (figure 2.2). This enviable growth performance is likely due to the fact that these resource-rich economies benefitted from the energy price boom that started around 2001. The commodity price boom also may have benefitted countries that are not energy exporters (for example, Armenia) through higher remittances, trade, and foreign direct investment. However, the 2014 plunge in oil and commodity prices adversely affected the region, and recovery will likely hinge on how quickly the region can adjust to this change.

Overall growth and shared prosperity in ECA were highly correlated over 2000–14 (figure 2.3). Most economies that outperform their benchmark for overall growth also outperform in terms of growth of the bottom 40 percent. This suggests that many of the factors that influence overall growth in ECA may also influence income growth of the bottom 40 percent. There are exceptions, however. For example, Bulgaria had an average annual GDP per capita growth rate that was about 2 percent higher than expected, but income growth of the bottom 40 percent did not outperform expectations.

FIGURE 2.2 Unexplained GDP and incomes of the bottom 40 percent increased much more rapidly in Central Asia, compared to the benchmarks, 2000–most recent year data are available

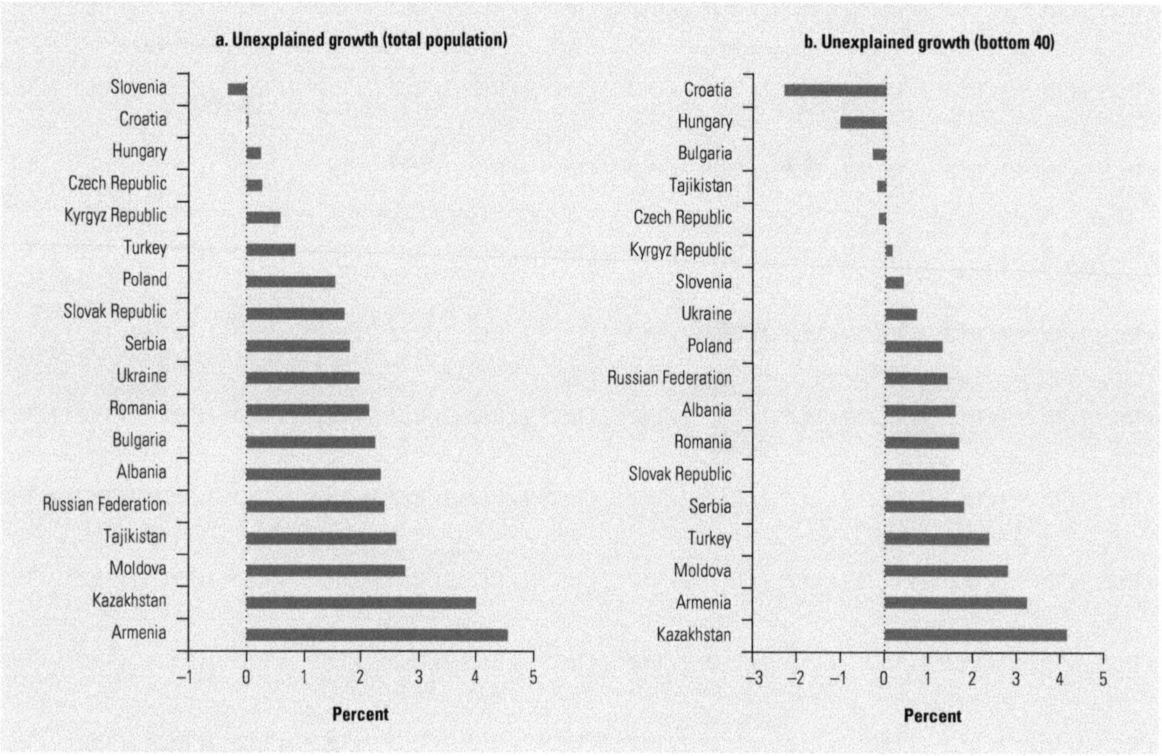

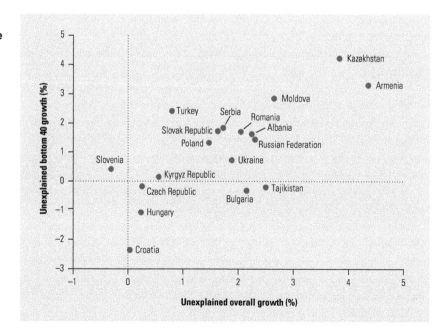

FIGURE 2.3

Unexplained overall income growth is correlated with the growth of incomes of the bottom 40 percent in ECA

Growth and shared prosperity, 2000–14

What Is the Relationship between Financial Development and Growth in ECA?

Empirical research shows that financial development can support economic growth, including the income growth of people in the bottom part of the income distribution. The seminal work of King and Levine (1993), and subsequent studies by Levine, Loayza, and Beck (2000); Beck, Levine, and Loayza (2000); and others, showed that financial sector deepening, as measured by credit to GDP, is associated with higher long-run growth due to both greater investment and increased total factor productivity. Moreover, further studies showed that financial development may help reduce poverty (Beck, Demirgüç-Kunt, and Levine 2007) and inequality (Beck, Demirgüç-Kunt, and Levine 2007; Demirgüç-Kunt and Levine 2009).

Financial development is positively associated with economic growth in ECA. Higher-than-expected growth of aggregate income and in the income of the bottom 40 percent is significantly associated with indicators of financial development, categorized by depth, stability, efficiency, and inclusion. Table 2.1 lists all indicators, out of the more than 60 indicators examined, where this relationship is positive and significant (see appendix C for a comprehensive list of all variables), controlling for the standard long-run growth determinants.[3] Each coefficient represents the marginal contribution above the traditional long-term growth determinants to the annual growth rate of GDP and of the income of the bottom 40 percent (see box 2.1 on the methodology used).

On the basis of cross-country experience only, the findings suggest that countries could boost their economic performance by focusing on a few key areas of financial development. Namely, the average country could gain the most by improving financial efficiency (such as the lending-deposit rate spread) and firm inclusion (for example, the number of firms with a bank loan). ECA already scores relatively high on financial inclusion and access (frequency and ease of interaction with the financial system by firms and individuals), so the benefits to further enhancements may be smaller than through greater efficiency. Nevertheless, the region may still increase growth by adopting policies designed to improve financial access. Based on cross-country data, further gains through improving stability may be smaller because its association with longer-term growth is lower than other dimensions of financial development. However, there is great heterogeneity among ECA countries, suggesting that some may still benefit a good deal from improving stability. The historical bar of good performance on financial stability has naturally dropped because of the global financial crisis. Therefore, our results may be understating the priority policy makers in ECA should give to fostering financial stability going forward relative to the focus on financial efficiency and inclusion.

The average country could gain the most by improving financial efficiency (such as the lending-deposit rate spread) and firm inclusion (for example, the number of firms with a bank loan).

Depth

The economic literature finds that the level of private credit as a share of GDP is positively associated with long-run economic growth, and this appears to be true in ECA. Some other measures of depth also have a significant relationship with growth, including stock market capitalization as a share of GDP, liquid liabilities as

TABLE 2.1 Financial Development and Its Association with Growth

		Overall growth residual	Bottom 40 growth residual
Financial depth	Private credit by deposit money banks to GDP (%)	.00402***	..
	Liquid liabilities (M3) to GDP (%)	.00521***	..
	Stock market capitalization to GDP (%)	.00203*	..
	Deposits to GDP	.00395***	..
	Depth index	**.00445***	..
	Depth index (squared)	*–.00138*	..
Financial stability[a]	Average output loss during banking crisis	–.00129***	..
	Average number of years in a financial crisis	–.00173***	..
	Average fiscal cost of a financial crisis	–.00074***	..
	Bank credit to bank deposits (%)	..	.01275**
	Credit/GDP volatility	–.00350 **	..
	Credit volatility	–.00253*	..
	Increase in NPLs	–.00955**	–.02240***
	Stability index[a]	**.00354***[a]**	..
Financial efficiency[a]	Bank lending-deposit spread (%)	–.00861***	..
	H-statistic	..	.00540**
	Bank overhead costs to total assets (%)	–.00553**	..
	Bank net interest margin (%)	–.00525**	..
	Efficiency index[a]	**.00611***[a]**	..
Financial access (firms and households)	Investments financed by equity or stock sales (%)	.00497***	..
	Firms using banks to finance working capital (%)	.00470*	..
	Firms identifying access to finance as a major constraint (%)	.00830***	..
	Firms with a bank loan or line of credit (%)	.00573**	.00799*
	Firm inclusion index	**.00622***	**.00505*
	Borrowed from a financial institution (% age 15+)	.00484**	.00362*
	Purchased agriculture insurance (% working in agriculture, age 15+)	.00865*	..
	Household inclusion index	**.00326**	**.00369**

Source: Gould, Melecky, and Panterov 2016.
Note: Each row represents a bivariate regression with the overall growth residual and the bottom 40 growth residual as the dependent variable. The growth residual is obtained from regressing the respective income growth on the core set of conditioning variables outlined in the methodology section. All finance indicators are transformed in logarithms. See appendix C for a brief description of each indicator. The financial development indexes comprise the equally weighted sum of the standardized, significant indicators from each category. The standardization procedure is done by subtracting the mean and dividing by the standard deviation of each series. The indexes are standardized after the aggregation procedure so each index has a mean of zero and standard deviation of 1. The regression coefficient on the index represents the growth contribution of an increase in the value of the index equal to 1 percent of its standard deviation. M3 = broad money; NPLs = nonperforming loans; .. = relationship was not significantly different from zero.
a. Signs are reversed to indicate the positive relationship of stability and efficiency with growth (the underlying variables are associated with instability and inefficiency).
* $p < 0.1$, ** $p < 0.05$, *** $p < 0.01$.

a share of GDP, and deposits as a share of GDP. However, none of the depth variables is significantly associated with the growth of the income of the poorest 40 percent of the income distribution.

The positive relationship between depth and growth is smaller in countries that already have high levels of financial depth (the square of depth has a negative and significant coefficient in table 2.1). There is good reason to believe that the association between financial depth (particularly private credit) and growth is weaker as financing becomes more plentiful and perhaps too complex. Based on our estimates, the highest marginal impact of depth on growth is reached at a depth index

BOX 2.1 Methodology for Financial Development Benchmarking

The methodology is based on estimating a global long-run growth model that includes proxies for financial development and controls for the standard macroeconomic fundamentals important for economic growth—like education, government size, and macroeconomic stability (for more background information on this literature see Beck 2008 and Panizza 2014). We use approximately 10-year period averages of data for more than 100 countries over 1960–2014 to estimate the impact of financial market development on growth.

The methodology is divided in two steps. First, we estimate the residuals from the standard long-run growth model for the bottom 40 percent and for overall growth. We can interpret these residuals as the "unexplained portion of economic growth." We then use the residuals as the dependent variable in a series of bivariate regressions where the independent variables are the logarithms of the various financial indicators. This econometric approach can be shown to be equivalent to estimating the model in one step with tight Bayesian priors on the coefficients of the long-term growth determinants (for an in-depth treatment of our econometric methodology please see appendix A; we investigate the issues pertaining to causality and correlation in appendix B). We choose this two-step methodology so as to maximize the number of observations and estimate a robust growth model. Moreover, with this methodology the structural parameters on the growth model are not subject to change with varying sample sizes of the financial sector indicators.

value similar to that of Portugal in the period between 2000 and 2014. Increasing depth beyond this point could generate decreasing returns to growth. Countries such as Canada, Cyprus, Luxembourg, Switzerland, and the United Kingdom, among others, have overall levels of financial depth that are above this peak impact.

Stability

Several financial stability outcomes are correlated with economic growth. Countries with higher volatility of credit (boom-and-bust credit cycles) tend to have lower growth rates. The presence and severity of a banking crisis is also negatively associated with long-term growth, as one would expect. Not surprisingly, an increase in the nonperforming loan ratio is negatively associated with overall long-run economic growth as well as with the growth of the income of the bottom 40 percent.

Efficiency

Three indicators of efficiency—bank overhead costs, the lending-deposit spread, and the bank net interest margin—are negatively correlated with economic growth. Countries with more competition in the banking sector, as measured by the H-statistic, tend to have higher rates of income growth for the bottom 40 percent. More competition can cause more efficient pricing of some financial services and pressure financial intermediaries to diversify their client base by providing services to poorer households.

Inclusion

The financial firm inclusion variables are significantly correlated with growth, and many of these coefficients are large. The share of firms opening to equity investment has a major impact on growth. Raising investment through the sale of equity may also improve firm corporate governance and accountability, which are also likely to improve growth. The number of firms with bank loans or lines of credit is significantly and positively associated with both overall growth and the income growth of the bottom 40 percent.

> **The greater the percentage of firms that use formal finance (such as firms with bank loans or firms that finance their investment through equity issuance), the higher the long-term growth rate.**

In general, the greater the percentage of firms that use formal finance (such as firms with bank loans or firms that finance their investment through equity issuance), the higher the long-term growth rate. Readily available credit may allow entrepreneurs to take advantage of business opportunities and weather economic downturns. Greater firm inclusion also may encourage firms to move out of the informal sector in order to use financial and banking services. These findings are consistent with Beck, Levine, and Loayza (2000), who show how increasing financial inclusion can improve competition, the demand for labor, and the dynamism of the labor market.

Financial inclusion of households is also positively associated with economic growth. The greatest effect may come from loans and insurance products. Credit could be a binding constraint on households that are looking to invest in human capital, so greater household inclusion can raise income growth rates. However, the number of household inclusion indicators that are significantly associated with growth is small compared to the number of significant firm inclusion indicators, perhaps because households also use financial services for nonpecuniary reasons, such as consumption smoothing.

Summary and Discussion of Findings

In general, the strongest associations between financial development and overall growth, in order of size, come from firm inclusion (0.622 index coefficient), efficiency (0.611 index coefficient), depth (0.445 index coefficient and –0.138 index squared coefficient), stability (0.354 index coefficient), and household inclusion (0.326 index coefficient). For the bottom 40 percent, only firm inclusion and household inclusion are significantly associated with income growth (index coefficients of 0.505 and 0.369, with firm inclusion having a larger impact).

Financial efficiency and stability are positively associated with aggregate growth but not with the income growth of the bottom 40 percent. In contrast, financial inclusion of firms and households is associated with both higher aggregate growth and higher income growth of the bottom 40 percent. The importance of firm inclusion in explaining aggregate growth remains even if we account for financial depth. These results may be biased because the uneven availability of data requires that the estimations controlling for depth use a different sample (the inclusion data are available only from 2002 onward). As a robustness check, we restricted the sample to the period of 2000–14 and found no change in the number of significant depth and efficiency indicators. Some of the stability variables, however, were not robust and changed signs. Most likely this was due to the particular time period because the unusually high growth in the lead-up to the 2008 financial crisis was not completely offset in the postcrisis period of contraction and slower growth.

The weak association between financial depth, efficiency, and stability and the income growth of the bottom 40 percent may be due to their primary reliance on wages paid in cash, meaning that they lack significant interactions with the formal financial system. Thus, traditional measures of depth and efficiency likely affect the income of the bottom 40 percent only indirectly, by affecting their wages and ability to find a job. Moreover, even if the direct effects of depth and efficiency are economically important for the incomes of the bottom 40 percent, incomplete and possibly noisier data on the growth of incomes in the bottom 40 percent may obscure this relationship. Although we attempt to control for the key underlying determinants of growth, other factors, particularly for lower-income countries such as in Central Asia, may lead to noisier data and obscure the marginal influence of financial sector development on growth (see box 2.2).

BOX 2.2 Problems Confronting Growth and Financial Systems in Central Asia

Recent discussions with financial sector participants highlight the poor business climates in Central Asia that severely constrain financial sector development. Weak law enforcement, burdensome regulations, high tax rates and arbitrary tax enforcement, corrupt and fraudulent practices, and excessive state involvement have boosted informality, dollarization, and interest rates; reduced the supply of long-term financial instruments; and led to underdeveloped banking, insurance, pension, and capital markets. Total credit to GDP equaled only 21.5 percent of GDP in Tajikistan (in 2014) and 41.5 percent of GDP in the Kyrgyz Republic.

Banking. Poor business climates, and in particular limited trust in formal financial systems, have resulted in a large share of transactions occurring outside the formal economy. Substantial savings are held in cash or invested directly in real estate or durable goods, thus reducing the finance intermediated by banks. In the Kyrgyz Republic, for example, banking assets equal only 34.5 percent of GDP, and in Uzbekistan bank deposits are only 23.6 percent of GDP. In Uzbekistan, restrictive regulations, including provisions that loan officers can be held criminally

liable for losses, have contributed to very conservative lending practices. These regulations have severely limited lending, although they also have maintained low levels of nonperforming loans (only 1 percent of loans according to the government, 6 percent according to Moody's).

Inadequate financial infrastructure also has constrained development. The effectiveness of registries that are essential to support the use of movable property as collateral is uneven. For example, in the Kyrgyz Republic the quality of services provided by the movable collateral registry (CCRO), although improving in 2006, has remained weak. By contrast, Uzbekistan has launched a collateral registry, an Internet-based platform that is publicly accessible. Financial statement reporting tends to be unreliable, for example in Tajikistan. Credit history monitoring in some countries is strong—Kazakhstan's private credit bureau covered 51.7 percent of the adult population and Tajikistan's 95 percent, which is higher than the Europe and Central Asia (ECA) average of 33.4 percent—but is mixed for the region overall.

Low levels of financial literacy, particularly in rural areas, tend to restrain the demand for credit

(Continued)

BOX 2.2 **Problems Confronting Growth and Financial Systems in Central Asia** *(continued)*

by low- and middle-income households. Many individuals have relatively little understanding of basic financial products, their benefits, and how to judge their value. For example, a survey showed that 80 percent of respondents in Tajikistan were not even familiar with basic banking terms.

Lending is mostly short term, in part because deposits tend to be short term. In Tajikistan the majority of credits are between 12 and 18 months, with a typical maximum for large firms of only 36 months. Even the more sophisticated banking system of Kazakhstan is dominated by short-term loans, as most bank deposits are held for less than a year (also, the consolidation of the pension assets into one state-managed plan has reduced long-term deposits in the banking system).

Fears over currency instability and a history of highly managed exchange rates and periodic large discrete devaluations, coupled with dependence on dollar- or ruble-denominated economic transactions (remittances from the Russian Federation and oil and other commodity exports), have encouraged individuals and firms to hold dollars rather than local currency. In turn, the limited supply of local currency deposits, banks' need to avoid large currency mismatches on their balance sheets (hedges against foreign exchange exposure in the region are limited and high cost), and the importance of foreign currency lending by microcredit organizations supported by international financial institutions means that most lending is denominated in U.S. dollars. In Tajikistan, loans denominated in foreign currency represented nearly 60 percent of the total credit portfolio of banks and microfinance institutions in early 2015. The share of foreign currency deposits in total deposits reached 61 percent in Kyrgyz banks and 55 percent in Kazakhstani banks in early 2015. Local currency loans to individuals and small and medium enterprises tend to be expensive and short term, except where government-supported programs are in place.

Insurance. Nonmandatory insurance products are little used in Central Asia, and in some cases

state-owned insurance companies enjoy a monopoly on compulsory insurance (auto insurance in Tajikistan, for example). Insurance premiums equal only 0.27 percent of GDP in Uzbekistan and 0.69 percent of GDP in Kazakhstan, both well below the ECA average of 1.6 percent (in 2012). Low incomes limit the demand for insurance, given more pressing short-term financial needs. Households tend to rely on government or family and friends to provide support in case of an adverse event, which often reflects rational behavior. For example, after recent floods in Kazakhstan, the government provided compensation for uninsured damaged properties. For idiosyncratic shocks that do not affect a large number of people, families typically pool resources to help those affected. Moreover, trust in insurance products is low, given examples of companies' failure to pay claims, the difficult and time-consuming process often involved in making a claim, lack of confidence in the courts' ability to fairly adjudicate disputes, weak consumer protection laws and institutions, and in some cases lack of confidence in companies' long-term viability. In Kazakhstan, even people employed in the insurance industry tend to rely little on insurance (in one insurance company, only 28 of about 500 employees bought property insurance for their houses or flats). The limited demand for insurance, while understandable, means that people forgo the lower costs and more assured payouts that could be provided by efficient, reliable commercial insurance products with a large pool of participants.

Pensions. Most state-provided pensions cover only 10–25 percent of preretirement income, and participation in government pension schemes is low because of high rates of informality. However, most individuals do not save additional amounts beyond the compulsory pension contributions; instead, they rely on extended families to provide support when they are no longer capable of participating in the workforce, or they expect to continue working after the official retirement age. There is little provision of private pensions in the region.

(Continued)

BOX 2.2 *(continued)*

Capital markets. Capital markets in Central Asian countries remain largely underdeveloped or even nonexistent (Tajikistan). Where capital markets do exist, the size and turnover are limited and participation of individual investors remains marginal. In Uzbekistan, the total volume of deals was only $7.6 million (at the official exchange rate), and individual investors accounted for only 2.8 percent of transactions. The limited development of capital markets in part reflects (as in the Kyrgyz Republic) poor enforcement of rules and regulations. Kazakhstan is an exception, with one stock exchange, "KASE" (owned by the National Bank of Kazakhstan), that provides a platform for trading debt, equity, currencies, and derivative instruments, with a total market capitalization of 14.7 percent of GDP in 2014.

Firm inclusion has a strong impact on the incomes of the bottom 40 percent. Growing and more productive sole proprietorships and microenterprises may benefit directly from greater access to credit. In addition, greater access to credit by small and medium enterprises and corporations could boost their employment and productivity. If these firms' financial inclusion contributes greatly to increasing wages and the number of jobs for the bottom 40 percent, then the indirect effect of the firms' inclusion on the income growth of the bottom 40 percent could be larger than the direct effect.

Which Dimensions of Financial Development Should ECA Countries Prioritize for Long-Term Growth and Shared Prosperity?

The relationship between financial development and growth often varies at different levels of financial development, for at least two reasons. First, for a given level of institutional development, if a region is close to the "frontier" of financial development, then further liberalization and increases in the supply of finance might reduce growth potential by increasing the likelihood of crises. For example, some have argued that the level of credit expansion prior to the global crisis was too high given institutional capacity and underlying fundamentals to support growth, so policy should have focused on building institutions and economic fundamentals, rather than on boosting financial depth. Second, some indicators of financial development have nonlinear associations with growth. Therefore, the same incremental change in a financial indicator may have a greater growth impact on an economy with a lower initial level of that indicator. For example, we find that, past a certain point of financial depth, further increases in depth can have a lower growth impact, most likely through its relationship with crises and overall economic instability.

Our global long-run analysis shows that the greatest returns to growth may come from policies focused on increasing financial inclusion of firms. However, given the fact that ECA already has relatively high levels of firm inclusion, this may not be the policy focus with the highest growth payoff. In fact, policies that are designed to improve financial efficiency may have greater overall returns.

In practice, the relationship between financial sector development and growth involves trade-offs. For example, a country may not be able to achieve high financial depth or inclusion without sacrificing some stability. This will be explored in more detail in this chapter (as well as in chapter 5). As a first pass, which should not be viewed as indicating a practical policy mix, we examine each indicator separately to get a sense of how ECA stands in relation to other regions and of how subregions in ECA compare to each other.

In contrast to the comparison of ECA financial development indicators with the global median values in chapter 1, we assess ECA's set of indicators relative to the set of countries that have achieved the highest growth outcomes associated with financial development. In other words, in this chapter we take the highest-ranked countries in terms of *overall* financial development associated with growth. We consider the benchmark or "frontier" to be the median of the set of actual countries that are the top 20 percent of performers across all four dimensions of financial development—depth, stability, efficiency, and inclusion. We then benchmark each country's financial development indicators against this frontier of financial development. In this way, the interpretation of the frontier is closer to the "financial feasibility frontier" of Beck and Feyen (2013).

The median country in ECA (which varies by indicator) is far from the frontier as far as efficiency, depth, and stability are concerned, but closer in terms of firm inclusion (table 2.2). These median indicators are multiplied by the financial indicator growth coefficients in table 2.1 to assess the growth impact of each indicator (figures 2.4 and 2.5).

Combining the actual level of ECA financial development indicators, their distance from the "financial sector frontier," and their impact on growth gives relative priorities for ECA's financial sector development strategy. The higher the bar in figure 2.5, the larger the potential growth impact. Emerging ECA could benefit most by implementing policies that improve financial efficiency and depth (particularly equity markets) because it has already achieved comparatively high levels on other important growth contributors, such as firm and household access to finance (figure 2.5).

ECA's priorities are very similar to those of LAC, another middle-to-high-income region. In contrast to Emerging ECA, in the advanced European regions, efficiency

TABLE 2.2 Financial Development Indicator Levels in ECA and the Financial Development Frontier

Indicator	ECA	Frontier	Distance from frontier
Depth	0.17	1.38	1.21
Efficiency	−0.67	0.83	1.49
Stability	−0.15	0.39	0.54
Firm inclusion	0.55	0.87	0.32
People inclusion	0.22	0.92	0.69

Note: The first column lists the median levels of each financial development indicator for the ECA region. As described in table 2.1, the indicators are standardized to have a mean of zero and standard deviation of 1. The second column lists the median value of each financial development indicator for the top 20 percent of all countries' experience over all indicators. All indicators are for the period 2000–14.

FIGURE 2.4 Increases in financial efficiency could generate the largest growth benefits for ECA countries relative to the financial development frontier

Potential contribution of financial development to growth, overall benchmarking

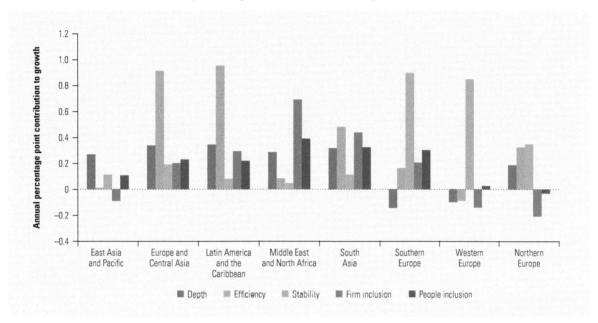

FIGURE 2.5

Within ECA subregions, financial efficiency generates the largest growth benefits

Potential contribution of financial development to growth, overall benchmarking

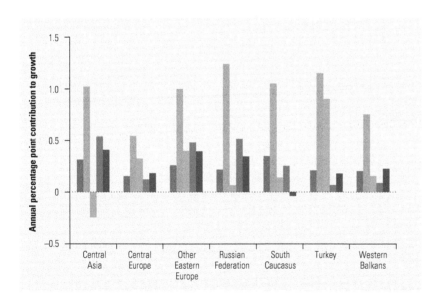

is already relatively high compared to the feasible frontier; consequently, the biggest boost to growth would be derived from a focus on greater stability.

In terms of stability, ECA (as well as several other emerging regions) may have traded greater stability for less depth and efficiency, at the expense of lower growth. In contrast, Southern Europe may have increased depth to the point of reducing stability, again at the expense of lower growth.

The analysis in table 2.1 suggests that only firm and people inclusion have a long-run positive correlation with the income growth of the bottom 40 percent

FIGURE 2.6

Of all financial indicators, only firm and people inclusion are significantly associated with B40 income growth in ECA

Potential contribution of financial development to B40 growth, overall benchmarking

■ Firm inclusion
■ People inclusion

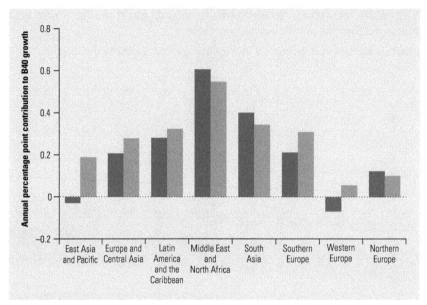

Note: B40 = bottom 40 percent of the income distribution.

(figure 2.6). Given the actual levels of inclusion, ECA would benefit from boosting household inclusion and firm inclusion. Increasing the financial access of the poorest households to the frontier would be associated with a somewhat higher impact on the income growth of the bottom 40 percent, compared to increasing firm inclusion for ECA.

Should Policy Priorities for Financial Development Be Modified Given the Possibility of Near-Term Financial Shocks?

The role of financial development and its importance to economic growth have been questioned in the aftermath of the 2008 global financial crisis. The common perception that the crisis was caused by the misbehavior of the financial sector and its use of complex financial instruments has caused many to worry about "too much" financial development. This is a legitimate concern. Having well-integrated financial markets in the global economy could potentially expose an economy to external shocks. Free capital flows can be a boon for a growing economy, especially if domestic savings do not increase rapidly enough to meet investment needs. However, external capital flows are also often the first to leave a country during a crisis. In addition, weakly supervised external and internal sources of finance (compounded by moral hazard because of explicit or implicit government insurance) may lead to the formation of asset bubbles that have overall deleterious effects on the economy. The supervision of foreign bank branches and subsidiaries, an important channel for external capital flows in ECA's economies before the crisis, raises particularly difficult challenges (see spotlight 3). On the other hand, financial development through better and more accessible insurance and hedging instruments that improve the management of risk may help mitigate the effect of large shocks during a financial crisis.

The findings in this chapter have so far shown that, over the long run, financial development appears to be positively associated with the growth of GDP and the incomes of the bottom 40 percent. In this section we ask the question: Should policy priorities for financial development be adjusted because of the possibility of near-term financial shocks?

In order to examine this question we adopt the following descriptive approach. We divide all countries into high and low development categories for each of the following financial development indexes: depth, efficiency, inclusion (firms), and inclusion (households). We then look at the growth performance of each group during banking crises. As before, we consider the residuals in growth equations that control for the typical long-term growth determinants (initial level of income, education, inflation, government size, and investment). The results are displayed in figure 2.7.

Overall growth appears to be faster in countries with better-developed financial markets than in those with less-developed ones in the absence of a banking crisis. Moreover, during a banking crisis, countries with deeper and more efficient financial markets don't seem to lose significantly more output than the less developed ones. Thus, the overall positive effects of developing deeper and more efficient financial sectors are not associated with a large cost that is realized as lost output during a banking crisis. In addition, countries with high inclusion experience higher growth during periods of no crisis, and suffer less income decline during crises. Regardless of which financial development indicator is chosen, the long-term benefits to financial development for all indicators outweigh the short-term costs of crises. This is indicated by the growth results that show the positive long-run impact of depth and efficiency. Consequently, avoiding financial sector development to reduce the costs of a crisis is unlikely to pay long-term growth dividends. Developing institutional capacity for supervision and regulation is perhaps the better strategy.

> Countries with high inclusion experience higher growth during periods of no crisis, and suffer less income decline during crises.

Although a similar pattern is observed in ECA and the EU, the decline during a crisis is much stronger. This is perhaps due to the sharp recession in advanced Europe during and after the 2008 financial crisis. Greater financial efficiency and depth appear to be more strongly associated with contractions during crisis periods. As with the global sample, financial inclusion of people can help mitigate the negative growth effect of crises also in ECA and the EU. The availability of data on the growth of the bottom 40 percent for ECA and the EU is too limited for meaningful results.

Conclusion

Financial market development in ECA coincides with overall economic development, and it can help the region mobilize domestic and foreign savings for greater domestic investment as well as improve economic efficiency through more effective resource allocation.

In formulating financial policy objectives, policy makers should focus on financial stability, efficiency, inclusion, and broadly defined measures of financial depth, because traditionally used measures of financial depth—particularly credit—could

FIGURE 2.7
During crises, countries with deeper and more efficient financial markets do not suffer significantly more

■ Low indicator
■ High indicator

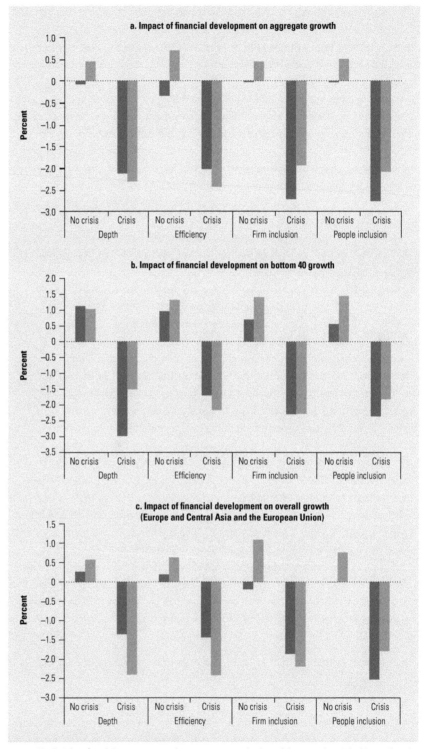

Note: The height of each bar represents the average annual value of the growth residual (overall and bottom 40) in the absence of a banking crisis or during a banking crisis, for all countries in our sample. The definition of a crisis was taken from Laeven and Valencia (2013). The growth residuals are calculated from the basic growth regressions described. Each country is classified as having high (above median) or low (below median) financial development according to its score for each financial development index.

be ambiguously related to income growth. If focusing on inclusive growth, countries should prioritize financial inclusion of firms in general. However, ECA could be in a specific situation because of its already high inclusion of firms in finance. Given ECA's stage of financial development, ECA policy makers should focus on advancing financial sector (bank) efficiency under stable financial conditions to boost aggregate growth. Income growth of the bottom 40 percent in ECA is much more sensitive to the financial inclusion of firms than the inclusion of individuals. However, levels of firm inclusion are already high in ECA, so that greater benefits for the bottom 40 could be achieved by increasing the inclusion of individuals.

During past crises growth fell slightly more for countries with high financial development than for those with low financial development. Moreover, the decline in growth during crises did not wipe out the benefits of financial development to long-term growth. Interestingly, financial inclusion of individuals could mitigate the negative growth effect of crises, but less so for the bottom 40 because they experience less financial inclusion.

These results highlight the importance of focusing on the trade-offs involved in financial development. Achieving the right balance in the many aspects of financial market development is likely to be more effective in increasing long-run growth than is emphasizing a single dimension at the expense of others. For example, policies focused solely on preventing banking crises at all costs may neglect the benefits of firm and household inclusion. A more efficient way of managing the risks and benefits to financial development would be through balanced policies as well as through complementary social assistance programs in the event of a crisis.

Notes

1. ECA includes Albania, Armenia, Azerbaijan, Belarus, Bosnia and Herzegovina, Bulgaria, Croatia, the Czech Republic, Georgia, Hungary, Kazakhstan, Kosovo, the Kyrgyz Republic, the former Yugoslav Republic of Macedonia, Moldova, Montenegro, Poland, Romania, the Russian Federation, Serbia, the Slovak Republic, Slovenia, Tajikistan, Turkey, Turkmenistan, Ukraine, and Uzbekistan.
2. Appendix A provides a formal presentation of the methodology used in these regressions.
3. As other studies that analyze the relationship between growth and financial development have shown, endogeneity is difficult to address completely. Methods such as instrumental variables have been used in prior studies, as have lagged variables. Using these methodologies, studies find that financial development still appears to be an important contributor to growth (Beck 2008). The empirical analysis in this study makes no definitive claim as to the causal relationship between growth and financial development but relies on prior literature that addresses this question.

References

Beck, Thorsten. 2008. "The Econometrics of Finance and Growth." Policy Research Working Paper 4608, World Bank, Washington, DC.

Beck, Thorsten, Asli Demirgüç-Kunt, and Ross Levine. 2007. "Finance, Inequality and the Poor." *Journal of Economic Growth* 12 (1): 27–49.

Beck, Thorsten, Asli Demirgüç-Kunt, and Ross Levine. 2010. "Financial Institutions and Markets across Countries and over Time: The Updated Financial Development and Structure Database." *World Bank Economic Review* 24 (1): 77–92.

Beck, Thorsten, and Erik Feyen. 2013. "Benchmarking Financial Systems: Introducing the Financial Possibility Frontier." Policy Research Working Paper 6614, World Bank, Washington, DC.

Beck, Thorsten, Ross Levine, and Norman Loayza. 2000. "Finance and the Sources of Growth." *Journal of Financial Economics* 58: 261–300.

Coleman, Alison. 2016. "Poland on Track to Becoming a Major European Tech Startup Hub." *Forbes*, May 20.

Demirgüç-Kunt, A., and R. Levine. 2009. "Finance and Inequality: Theory and Evidence." *Annual Review of Financial Economics* 1: 287–318.

Goldman, Stefania. 2015. "Polish Startups Note Steady Revenue." *ITKeyMedia*, November 26.

Gould, David M., Martin Melecky, and Georgi Panterov. 2016. "Finance, Growth and Shared Prosperity: Beyond Credit Deepening." *Journal of Policy Modeling* 38 (4): 737–58.

King, Robert G., and Ross Levine. 1993. "Finance and Growth: Schumpeter Might Be Right." *Quarterly Journal of Economics* 108 (3): 717–37.

Laeven, L., and F. Valencia. 2013. "Systemic Banking Crises Database." *IMF Economic Review* 61 (2): 225–70.

Levine, Ross. 2005. "Finance and Growth: Theory and Evidence." Chapter 12 in *Handbook of Economic Growth*, edited by Philippe Aghion and Steven Durlauf, 865–934. Amsterdam: Elsevier.

Levine, Ross, Norman Loayza, and Thorsten Beck. 2000. "Financial Intermediation and Growth: Causality and Causes." *Journal of Monetary Economics* 46 (1): 31–77.

Panizza, Ugo. 2014. "Financial Development and Economic Growth: Known Knowns, Known Unknowns, and Unknown Unknowns." *Revue d'économie du développement* 22 (HS02): 35–65.

SPOTLIGHT 2
Tackling the High and Persistent Level of Nonperforming Loans in Europe and Central Asia

Nonperforming loans (NPLs) in Europe and Central Asia (ECA) averaged over 12 percent of total loans in 2014, the highest ratio among global regions and significantly above the world average of 4 percent (figure S2.1).[1] Rapid credit growth prior to the global financial crisis was followed by a sharp rise in NPLs when the crisis hit. In some countries, the situation was made worse by the prevalence of loans denominated in foreign currency (often in euros or Swiss francs), which increased in value when the local currency depreciated. Worryingly, the NPL ratio continued to increase after the crisis, at first very rapidly between 2008 and 2010, and then more slowly from 2010 and 2013 as slow economic growth was accompanied by stagnation or even decline in the volume of loans, the denominator in the NPL ratio. In the euro area, by contrast, NPL ratios rose significantly immediately after the crisis, then stabilized at a high level after 2012 (figure S2.2).

FIGURE S2.1 NPLs in ECA are high, 2014

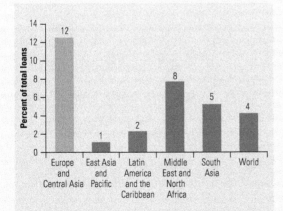

Source: FinStats.
Note: Developing countries only, except East Asia (all income levels). Aggregate NPL data are not available for Sub-Saharan Africa. NPLs = nonperforming loans.

FIGURE S2.2 NPLs in ECA increased sharply, 2008–14

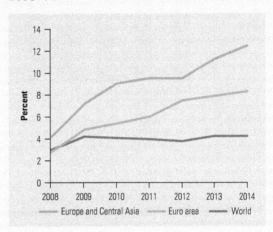

Source: FinStats.
Note: Developing countries only, except East Asia (all income levels). NPLs = nonperforming loans.

The dominant market share of foreign banks has impeded NPL resolution. Governments have little appetite to help the banks reduce their level of NPLs because foreign shareholders would reap the direct, immediate benefits, whereas the indirect benefits to the broader economy from a healthy banking system and increased lending are less immediately perceived. And parent banks, for which assets in ECA are small relative to the overall balance sheet, allocate few resources to resolving NPLs.

High levels of NPLs constrain lending to fundamentally viable but highly indebted companies, thus representing a drag on growth and employment opportunities for the poor. However, high NPL levels are not an immediate threat to the solvency of ECA banking systems, which remain adequately capitalized. The average capital-to-assets ratio in the region is 12 percent, the highest of all World Bank regions (figure S2.3).[2]

SPOTLIGHT 2 *(continued)*

FIGURE S2.3 The average bank capital-to-assets ratio is high in ECA, 2015

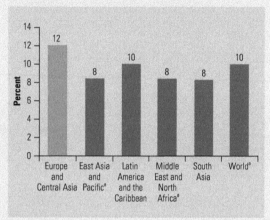

Source: FinStats.
a. 2014.

Reducing NPLs will require changes in the incentives framework. Banks have rescheduled NPLs to delay recognizing losses through write-offs or asset sales, particularly for collateralized loans where collateral values are kept optimistically high, resulting in low accounting provisions. Lax accounting and auditing standards, as well as inexperienced bank supervision, have enabled banks to delay recognition of losses. There is, in fact, doubt in some countries whether NPLs are even now fully recognized. At the same time, banks that wish to sell assets to resolve NPLs face serious difficulties.

Key recommendations for improving the incentives framework involve strengthening supervision; improving collateral tracking and valuation; removing tax disincentives for restructuring; reforming the insolvency regime to improve transparency and limit pro-debtor bias; improving the judicial system to achieve more rapid resolution of commercial disputes and reduce corruption; strengthening legal enforcement; promoting voluntary, out-of-court restructuring; establishing a secondary market for distressed assets; providing for asset management companies to handle systemwide NPLs; and

improving coordination among all stakeholders involved in NPL resolution.

Supervision. The tightening of supervisory standards, improved auditing and accounting norms, improved oversight of auditors, and mandatory increases in required provisions after a certain period of failure to service a loan (as was introduced in Croatia)[3] could improve incentives for NPL resolution.

Collateral tracking and valuation. Procedural delays, disputes over title, and the absence of a liquid market have plagued efforts to resolve NPLs. Many countries in ECA have inadequate collateral registries; in addition, cadastral and fiscal registries are often paper based and decentralized and contain obsolete, incorrect, or even contradictory information on land title and ownership. Most lending in ECA before the crisis was collateral based rather than cash-flow based, and an overvaluation of collateral commonly facilitated excess borrowing. Accurate collateral valuation will remain difficult until there is a significant increase in real estate transaction volume to form accurate evaluations. In the interim, the authorities can improve the situation by (a) clarifying legal title and allowing accelerated procedures for adjudicating title claims; (b) creating a centralized, automated land and collateral registry; (c) tracking real estate transactions; (d) improving the auction process to enable real price discovery; (e) reviewing and improving valuation standards; (f) tightening supervision and training of evaluators; and (g) imposing conservative measures in collateral evaluation for provisioning purposes.

Tax treatment of NPLs. Lack of clarity in the tax treatment of write-offs impedes NPL resolution. Banks can face difficulties in claiming a tax shield from the write-down of assets because they might be required, for example, to exhaust every opportunity for recovery. In some cases, the creditor must check decentralized, paper-based real estate registries in multiple locations to ensure that the debtor has no asset. This imposes a significant cost on banks, which usually expect no recovery from the debtor. Tax policy in some countries also creates a disincentive for loss recognition on the part of the debtor—for example, by viewing a loan write-off as a taxable donation to the debtor. Authorities can address these issues by reviewing the tax treatment of write-offs, on the one hand, and by mandating the write-off of "stale" NPLs after a certain period, as was introduced in Albania. These measures would encourage banks to rapidly process NPLs that have low expected recovery.

The insolvency regime. Issues with insolvency regimes vary by country but include confusion because of numerous amendments (six to seven in a decade in the case of Croatia); poor integration of the insolvency law (usually based on foreign best practice) with the local constitutional and legal framework (for example, Albania); and pro-debtor bias in the insolvency law, in consumer protection law, and in the broader judicial system (for example, Ukraine). There is a strong case for revamping the entire insolvency regime and connected laws (property law, tax code, consumer protection, and so on), but some stakeholders argue that it would be better to impose a moratorium on insolvency reform to enable creditors, debtors, courts, and the legal profession to make the current system work.

The judicial commercial system. Judicial systems across the region are often slow, ineffective, and open to significant procedural delays and appeals, a problem that is compounded, in the case of insolvency courts, by lack of experience and a significant increase in workload. Courts, moreover, often show a bias in favor of debtors. As a result, the judicial insolvency process often enables debtors to postpone payment and insolvency through evergreening and other dilatory tactics. In addition, judicial proceedings and enforcement in many countries remain subject to fraud and graft. These judicial issues reduce recovery in bankruptcy proceedings, and create a disincentive for debtors to collaborate

with their creditors in a voluntary restructuring because they do not face a credible threat of insolvency. Addressing these issues could involve (a) increasing the number of judges and judicial staff; (b) tracking workload and case flow to improve resource allocation; (c) providing extensive training; (d) improving case management information technology and infrastructure; (e) reviewing grounds for appeals and implementing measures to reduce frivolous claims; and (f) enforcing deadlines for judicial processes.

Enforcement procedures. Similar issues plague the enforcement of judicial decisions, as well as collateral and mortgages. Auction processes are slow, complicated, and cumbersome, and can make it impossible to have real price discovery. In Croatia, for example, no sale can take place below 50 percent of the (often inflated) appraisal value, so it is frequently impossible to sell through foreclosure proceedings. In addition, legal titles are open to numerous and lengthy challenges, while bailiffs and other insolvency professionals lack training and supervision and may face incentives that conflict with the interest of the creditor. For example, insolvency administrators in Serbia are paid on an hourly basis, creating an incentive to unnecessarily prolong the process. These issues can be addressed by reviewing and improving the auction process, clarifying legal title, and professionalizing judicial enforcement and bailiffs.

Voluntary out-of-court (VOOC) restructuring. VOOC restructurings are appropriate for NPLs arising from large corporations that are built around economically viable core operations, but where the company is unable to service its existing debt and is starved of new financing. With multiple banks exposed to different parts of the company, and different liens and security, there is often a lack of cooperation between creditors that results in a stalemate. Principles for VOOC restructuring have been codified in the INSOL principles for multicreditor workouts (INSOL Lenders Group Steering

SPOTLIGHT 2 *(continued)*

Committee 2000). The process can be further encouraged through sponsorship from the authorities and through tax and supervisory incentives.

Secondary markets. A viable secondary market in distressed assets is a key component of successful NPL resolution. Banks typically have neither the skills nor the financial incentives to manage large portfolios of NPLs and should therefore seek to sell NPLs or outsource their management. Although the sale of NPLs is usually legal in ECA countries, there are often country-specific impediments, such as restrictions on sale to nonbanks or to nonresident buyers, tightly construed rules on consumer data protection, and requirement of debtor consent to transfer a mortgage or pledged asset. These impediments should be reviewed and, where appropriate, removed. Authorities can also identify potential buyers and pools of liquidity for distressed assets, often with the help of international financial institutions such as the European Bank for Reconstruction and Development (EBRD) and the International Finance Corporation.

Asset management companies. A large volume of NPLs could be managed by pooling together all assets "at arms length" in an asset management company (AMC), under professional third-party management, whose aim is to maximize recovery value. A state guarantee—or the direct purchase of the distressed assets by a state entity—can help reassure markets about bank solvency. A state-sponsored AMC can represent a fiscal burden; even where the assets are transferred to the AMC at a discount to fair market value, the AMC—and therefore the state—implicitly assumes the potential downside risk. Given limited fiscal capacity in most ECA countries, it may be useful to explore a private sector alternative. In Italy, for example, two large banks agreed to pool their exposure to a subset of large defaulted companies and hand over management of these assets to a third-party restructuring firm. This approach may facilitate more skilled restructuring efforts and improve coordination among creditors, but it does not provide as strong a market signal about bank solvency as establishing a public sector AMC.

Coordination among stakeholders. The authorities in each country should convene a forum that brings together all relevant actors, from the public sector (national bank; ministries of finance, justice, and economy; tax authority; judiciary; consumer protection agency), the private sector (banks, investors, lawyers, insolvency practitioners, and corporate and individual debtors), and international organizations (the International Monetary Fund, the World Bank Group, and the EBRD are involved in NPL resolution in ECA; and the European Commission is involved in the area of judicial reform). The goals would be to (a) share information; (b) take stock of existing and planned initiatives; (c) agree on priorities, scope of work, and areas of responsibility; (d) ensure greater coordination; and (e) monitor progress. In a number of countries in Central and South Central Europe, the Vienna Initiative has provided a forum to initiate these discussions, which now need to be replicated and expanded at the country level.

Notes

1. Although definitional differences can distort the comparison of NPL levels between countries, the aggregate data are roughly consistent at the regional level.
2. Bank capital to assets is the ratio of bank capital and general reserves to total assets. It differs from the regulatory Capital Adequacy Ratio (CAR) in that capital and reserves are divided by *total assets* rather than by *risk-weighted assets* (RWA). In general, total assets are higher than RWA, so usually the CAR is higher than the bank capital-to-assets ratio. For comparison, the bank capital-to-assets ratio is 8.5 percent in East Asia and Pacific, 10.3 percent in Latin America and the Caribbean, 11.3 percent in Middle East and North Africa, and 7.8 percent in South Asia. Aggregate data are not available for Sub-Saharan Africa, but individual data are 7.8 percent for South Africa and 10.3 percent for Nigeria. The ratio in the euro area is 7.5 percent. CAR data are not available at the aggregate regional level; moreover, they are less directly comparable given differences in regulatory regimes.
3. Under the rules introduced by the Croatian National Bank, banks must increase their provision every six months by 5 percent of the nominal amount, irrespective of the level of collateral. This has led to an increase in the coverage ratio (provisions to nonperforming loans) from 46 percent at the end of 2013 to more than 50 percent by Q1 2015.

Reference

INSOL Lenders Group Steering Committee. 2000. *Statement of Principles for a Global Approach to Multi-Creditor Workouts*. London: INSOL International.

3

Jobs and Firms' External Financing Conditions

With the start of the second millennium, the access to finance in Romania was on the rise. Maria Cazacu, a tailor, saw this as an opportunity to scale up her business. She applied for an investment loan at a local bank to buy additional sewing machines and remodel her office. The loan agreement included a line of credit with standby liquidity to pay her staff's salaries and buy inputs in advance. Maria managed to hire additional employees, and her annual income grew fivefold. By 2007, she was confident to say she moved from being one of the poorest to one of the wealthiest people in her town.

Maria's fortunes, however, changed in late 2008 with the onset of the global financial crisis that spilled over to Romania. Her customers started to delay payments for the invoiced products, and she quickly became illiquid and was faced with insolvency problems. A few months later, she received a notice from her bank that her credit line was closed. Maria had no choice but to dismiss half of her employees and sell a number of sewing machines. Her income and capital returned to the levels that they were before she took the investment loan. Ironically, the bad times hit Maria's business harder than the risk-averse businesses that did not expand during the good times.[1]

Maria's story points to the risk associated with leveraging business through credit. On the one hand, access to credit opens the door to new business opportunities. On the other hand, it carries the danger of economic debacle when it is cut off, especially for entrepreneurs who directly depend on leveraging through credit to conduct businesses efficiently. For businesses without backup options

such as raising additional equity, financial volatility could mean losing one's shirt and livelihood.

This chapter studies how firms' use of credit can help boost shared prosperity by creating jobs in the Europe and Central Asia (ECA) region. Given ECA's context and potential growth trajectory described in chapters 1 and 2, it analyzes why firms' use of credit might have a different effect on the labor market outcomes of the bottom 40 and the top 60 percent of the income distribution. Finally, it estimates how the labor market effects of a credit crunch are different for these two groups in the region and looks at policies to improve prospects for both. Like Maria's story, the ECA region provides a good example of how firms' improved use of credit can help lift people out of poverty. Likewise, it shows how a sudden decline in the availability of credit can harm businesses, especially those that strongly depend on it.

Main messages:

- The bottom 40 percent of the income distribution (the bottom 40) are less likely to be formally employed, but when employed they are in firms that tend to benefit more from better external financing conditions. Improving firms' external financing conditions can increase the employment and income of individuals in the bottom 40 by allowing for firm entry, boosting firm growth and productivity and providing for a more efficient allocation of capital across the economy.

- When external financing conditions for firms tighten, higher income earners suffer the most because they tend to be employed in financially dependent firms. Greater financial dependence of industries in a country thus makes jobs more sensitive to the financial cycle and potentially more unstable.

- When a country's industry structure shows greater financial dependence and more firms get new access to credit, managing the volatility of the financial cycle gains importance. The trade-off between financial inclusion and greater leveraging of firms on the one side and financial stability on the other side becomes more pronounced.

Jobs and the Bottom 40 in ECA

If improved external financing conditions allow otherwise credit-constrained firms to enter the market and grow in ECA, it could potentially benefit the bottom 40 disproportionately because working-age individuals in the bottom 40 are less likely to be employed than their counterparts in the top 60. Individuals in the top 60 of the income distribution in ECA exhibit employment rates about 16 to 30 percentage points higher than those of their poorer counterparts. Even among the richer countries of Western Europe, labor market outcomes for the bottom 40 and the top 60 of the income distribution differ significantly (figure 3.1). The bottom 40 also tend to depend more on nonlabor sources of income than their counterparts in the top 60. Whereas individuals in the bottom 40 typically generate at most two-thirds of their total income by working, that figure for the top 60 is about 80 percent.

> Individuals in the top 60 of the income distribution in ECA exhibit employment rates about 16 to 30 percentage points higher than those of their poorer counterparts. Even among the richer countries of Western Europe, labor market outcomes for the bottom 40 and the top 60 of the income distribution differ significantly.

FIGURE 3.1 The bottom 40 are less likely to be employed and to depend on labor income

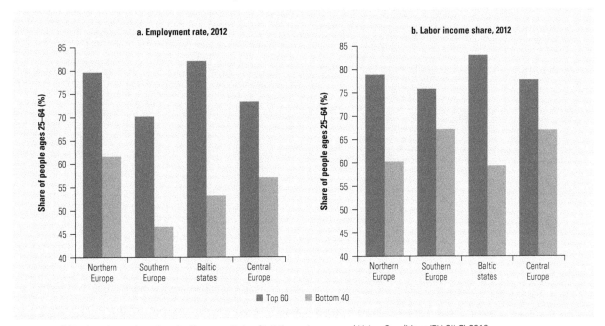

Source: World Bank estimates based on the European Union Statistics on Income and Living Conditions (EU-SILC) 2013.
Note: Other income sources include social assistance, pensions, and capital income. The Baltic states comprise Estonia, Latvia, and Lithuania.

Moreover, workers in the bottom 40 may benefit disproportionately from easier financing conditions because they are more likely to be employed in financially constrained firms than their counterparts in the top 60, reflecting two observations. First, smaller and younger firms have more limited financing options than larger and older firms. In every subregion within ECA except Turkey, larger firms are more likely to have a line of credit (see figure 3.2). This relationship seems to be stronger in the South Caucasus, Other Eastern Europe, the Western Balkans, and the Russian Federation, where firms with 100 employees or more are over 30 percent more likely than their smaller peers to have a credit line. Older firms are also more likely to have a credit line in the Western Balkans, Other Eastern Europe, and Russia. Second, workers in the bottom 40 are more likely to be employed in smaller and younger firms than workers in the top 60, although this is not true of all subregions (figure 3.3).

Can Improving Firms' External Financing Conditions Increase Employment and Income among Households in the Bottom 40 in ECA?

Increasing the availability of finance external to the firm can contribute to job creation by increasing the rates of firm growth and firm entry.[2] Empirical evidence shows that firm entry is lower in countries with lower financial inclusion and worse investor protection, because liquidity constraints may prevent entrepreneurs from starting a new business (Klapper, Laeven, and Rajan 2006). A more

FIGURE 3.2 Credit use is lower among smaller firms and younger firms in ECA

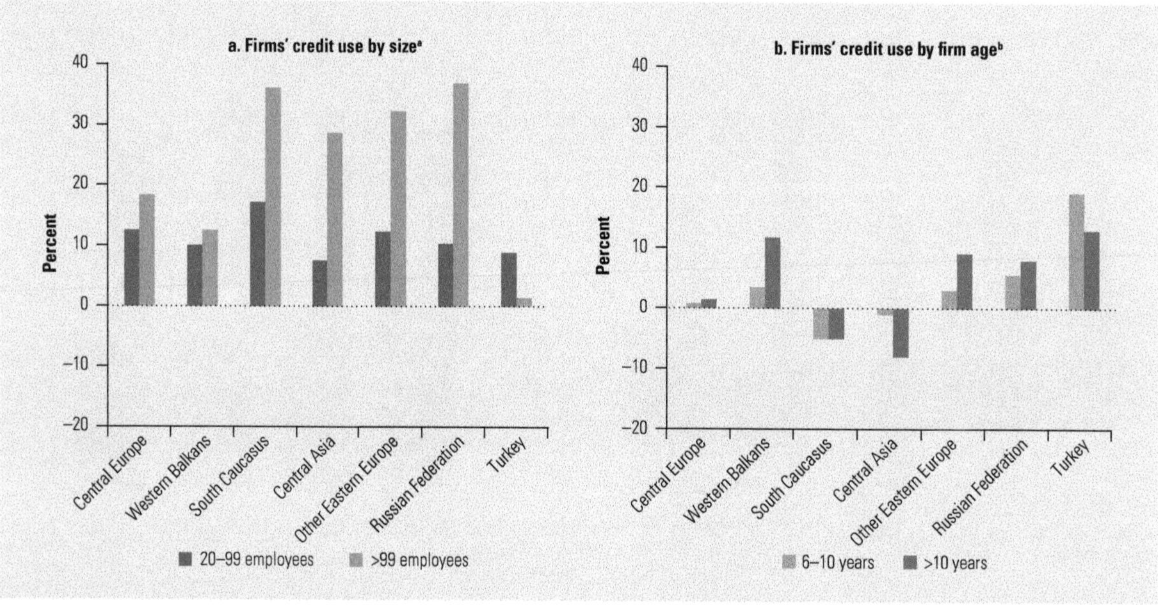

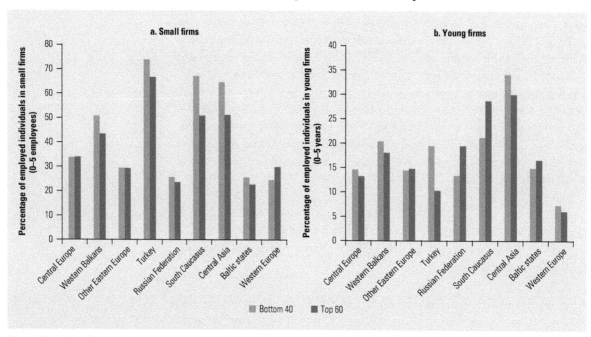

Source: Elaboration based on World Bank Enterprise Surveys 2013.
Note: These are the coefficients from ordinary least squares regressions controlling for country, sector, and area fixed effects. The dependent variable is a dummy variable equal to one if the firm has a line of credit. All data are significant at the 1 percent level except for the second category of Turkey (both panels).
a. Omitted category is under 20 employees.
b. Omitted category is younger than 6 years.

FIGURE 3.3 Workers in the bottom 40 are more likely to work in financially constrained firms

Source: Based on Life in Transition Survey (LITS) 2010.
Note: The green (blue) bars represent the percentage of workers in the bottom 40 (top 60) working in small and young firms. The Baltic states comprise Estonia, Latvia, and Lithuania.

business-friendly environment, including the ease of getting credit, and greater financial depth, as measured by the ratio of credit to gross domestic product (GDP), have been associated with higher rates of firm entry across the world (Klapper, Amit, and Guillén 2010). Furthermore, higher barriers to finance faced by firms can translate into slower firm growth, particularly among smaller firms (Beck, Demirgüç-Kunt, and Maksimovic 2005; Bloom and Van Reenen 2010).

Improving firms' external financing conditions may foster not only more jobs but also more productive and better-paid jobs. It can help firms become more efficient by enabling investment in research and development to improve products and production processes, as well as in better managerial practices. A healthier financial system can also increase aggregate productivity by improving the allocation of finance from less to more efficient businesses. There is evidence that improving firms' external financing conditions is linked with significant gains in terms of profits and return on investments (Bloom and Van Reenen 2010). Banking sector deregulation has also been linked with total factor productivity (TFP) gains at the firm level (Krishnan, Nandy, and Puri 2014). Moreover, financial sector reforms in ECA countries have been associated with large increases in TFP, especially by reducing capital misallocation between firms (Larrain and Stumpner 2015). Financial sector reforms in the region, such as improvements in collateral laws, have been linked with better external financial conditions for firms and with a reduction in distortions in the allocation of economic resources (Calomiris et al. 2015).

Improving firms' external financing conditions could have significant effects among the poorest households of ECA. Financial market imperfections, such as informational asymmetries, transaction costs, and contract enforcement costs, may be specially binding for the bottom 40, who are more likely to lack the resources required to start up a business or the collateral, credit history, and connections necessary to obtain finance (Beck, Demirgüç-Kunt, and Levine 2007). In Bosnia and Herzegovina, for example, even after controlling for the role of individual and social characteristics, richer households are more likely to become entrepreneurs and survive their first year of business, which emphasizes the importance of sources of internal finance in the region (Demirgüç-Kunt, Klapper, and Panos 2011).

At the same time, a large body of literature argues that, although better external financing for firms may initially benefit only a small group of latent entrepreneurs, it eventually reaches a much wider group of workers who also benefit from the associated increases in employment and wages (Demirgüç-Kunt and Levine 2009). General equilibrium models suggest that better external financing conditions reduce inequality mostly by increasing the demand for labor in the long term (Gine and Townsend 2004). Consistent with this finding, a quasi-natural experiment showed that bank deregulation increased disproportionately the demand for lower-skilled workers, who are more likely to be in the bottom 40 (Beck, Levine, and Levkov 2010).

Among countries in ECA, improved external financing conditions in the years leading to the crisis were accompanied by a higher rate of firm growth, particularly for microfirms (fewer than 10 employees). The rate of growth of

Among countries in ECA, improved external financing conditions in the years leading to the crisis were accompanied by a higher rate of firm growth, particularly for microfirms (fewer than 10 employees).

microfirms in sectors more dependent on finance was higher than for microfirms in less financially dependent sectors before the financial crisis hit the region (figure 3.4). By contrast, prior to the financial crisis, the growth rates of larger firms were substantially smaller, and similar between high and low finance-dependent sectors (for this analysis, sectoral financial dependence is defined on the basis of technological characteristics rather than on the observed level of finance—see box 3.1).

FIGURE 3.4
Better external financing conditions are associated with higher firm growth rates, particularly among smaller firms

■ Financially dependent sectors
■ Sectors not financially dependent

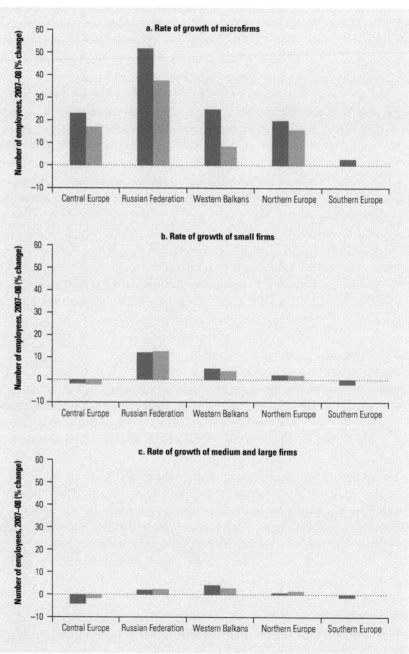

Source: Based on a balanced panel of firms from Orbis, a large database on firms. See appendix D and box 3.1 for more details.
Note: Microfirms = 0–9 employees; small firms = 10–49 employees; medium and large firms = 50+ employees.

BOX 3.1 Definition of Sectors Dependent on Finance

Most of the empirical analysis in this section relies on comparing sectors of economic activity that depend on external finance with other sectors. Because the level of credit to GDP could be both a cause and a result of firms' economic performance, we cannot use this variable by itself to measure the effect of external financing conditions on firms. Instead, we combine it with an indicator of financial dependence that is not related to the actual level of finance received. Rajan and Zingales (1998) measure the degree of dependence on finance external to the firm as the difference between investments and cash generated from operations that is observed in publicly listed firms from the United States. Because capital

markets in the United States, especially for large listed firms, are relatively frictionless, this method can identify an industry's technological demand for finance external to the firm. Assuming that this technological requirement applies to other countries, throughout most of this chapter we use this measure to distinguish between financially dependent and other sectors. Table B3.1.1 displays examples of sectors by their levels of dependence on finance external to the firm. Holding everything else constant, a credit crunch is likely to affect an industry that requires a lot of external funding, such as pharmaceuticals, more than one that requires very little external funding, such as repair of computers.

TABLE B3.1.1 Examples of Sectors and Their Dependence on External Finance

Low dependence on finance	Medium dependence on finance	High dependence on finance
Financial services activities, except insurance and pension funding	Crop and animal production, hunting and related service activities	Remediation activities and other waste management services
Real estate activities	Forestry and logging	Motion picture, video, and television program production; sound recording and music publishing activities
Repair of computers and personal and household goods	Printing and reproduction of recorded media	
Fishing and aquaculture	Manufacture of electrical equipment	Programming and broadcasting activities
Other mining and quarrying	Manufacture of other transport equipment	Information service activities
Manufacture of food products		Publishing activities
Employment activities	Human health activities	Manufacture of coke and refined petroleum products
Services to buildings and landscape activities	Civil engineering	Manufacture of chemicals and chemical products
	Mining of coal and lignite	
		Manufacture of basic pharmaceutical products and pharmaceutical preparations

In summary, improving firms' external financing conditions has the potential to benefit households in ECA in terms of new and more productive jobs. Although the distributional effects of the efficiency gains from improved financing conditions are difficult to anticipate, the sharp differences between the bottom 40 and top 60 suggest that some of the labor market effects are likely to be different for these groups. In particular, firms' external financing conditions could be crucial to increasing the number of salaried jobs among the bottom 40 in ECA because the bottom 40 are more likely to work in firms that depend on external finance to grow.

What Impact Does Improving Firms' External Financing Conditions Have on Labor Market Volatility?

While improving firms' external financing conditions can bring about more and better job opportunities in ECA, it can also make firms' employment decisions—and hence labor demand—more sensitive to credit market volatility. Studies suggest that recessions resulting from financial crises are more severe and longer in duration compared with those originating in nonfinancial crises. The slower pace of recovery is due to the freezing of credit channels and the need for both firms and households to deleverage their debts (see Claessens et al. 2013 and Buera, Fattal Jaef, and Shin 2015).[3] Improved external financing conditions can promote the reallocation of resources, which is a key part of the recovery process from an economic crisis; but this channel of recovery does not work well when the source of the crisis itself is in the financial sector. Recessions that involved a financial crisis in their early stages also typically involve a stronger employment and unemployment response than nonfinancial recessions (Reinhart and Rogoff 2008; OECD 2010; Boeri 2012).[4] A study finds that, during the 10 years following a financial crisis, unemployment rates remain on average 5 percentage points above the average rate of the 10 years prior to the crisis (Reinhart and Rogoff 2014). Similarly, for the "big five" banking crises of the past (Spain 1977, Norway 1987, Finland 1991, Sweden 1991, and Japan 1992), unemployment rates were higher and more persistent than in recessions not associated with banking crises (Knotek and Terry 2009).

Thus, although better external financing conditions improve investment, productivity, and employment, they can also increase vulnerability to financial crises. Indeed, studies have found that highly leveraged firms and sectors are characterized by higher job destruction rates during financial recessions (Boeri 2012; Bernanke and Gertler 1989; Sharpe 1994). Firms more leveraged before a financial recession face a greater need to deleverage, and hence reduce employment to a greater extent. Leveraged firms may find their liquidity suddenly called back by the lender, which reduces their ability to maintain and manage existing jobs. A larger decline in the net worth of more leveraged firms, typically observed under financial recessions, could be another reason for the higher level of layoffs in such firms. The decline in net worth may cause firms to shut down part of their operations, and may destroy the associated existing jobs. Further, the impact of a financial recession seems to be higher in places with more well-developed capital markets (Boeri 2012), where firms will have an incentive to be more leveraged in normal times. In normal times, deep capital markets also lead to tight labor markets. An adverse

FIGURE 3.5 Better external financing conditions before the crisis were associated with larger GDP losses and unemployment increases

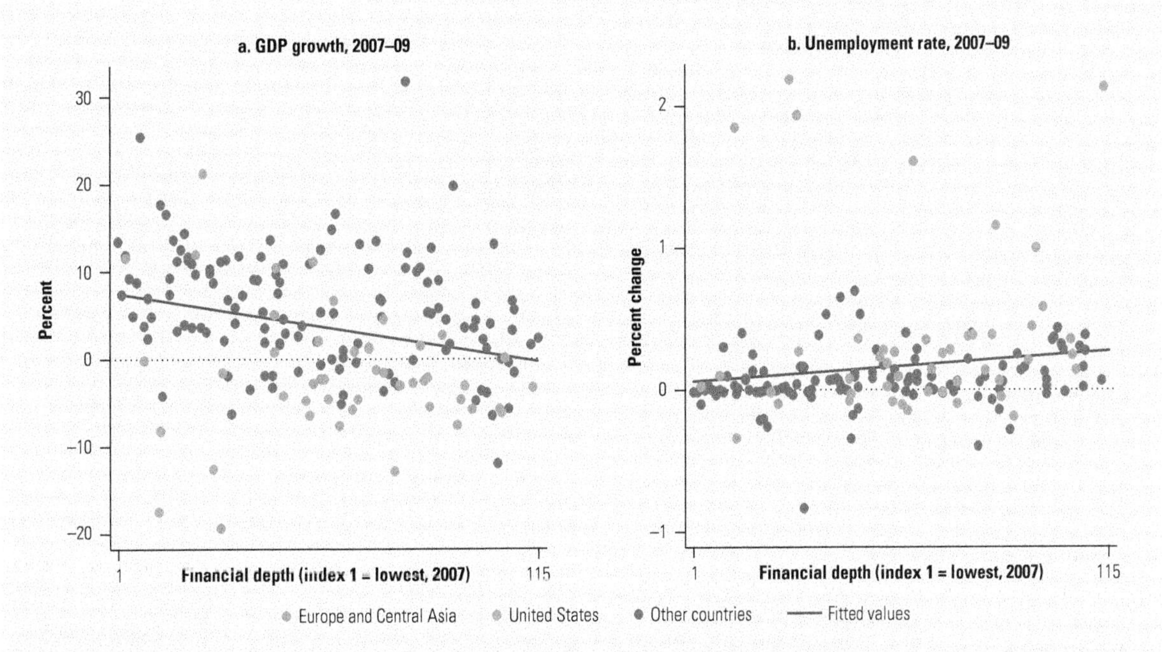

a. GDP growth, 2007–09

b. Unemployment rate, 2007–09

● Europe and Central Asia   ● United States   ● Other countries   —— Fitted values

Source: World Development Indicators.
Note: We approximate external financing conditions with an index of financial depth. To estimate the index of financial depth, countries are ranked according to two indicators: stock market capitalization to gross domestic product (GDP) and private sector credit to GDP. The index is the average of both rankings.

liquidity shock thus hits harder. This may explain why the unemployment rate in the United States at the beginning of the 2008 financial crisis increased much more than in European countries experiencing larger output losses (figure 3.5).

Indeed, credit tightening with the recent global financial crisis—through its effects on employment in firms—likely had a deep and persistent impact on the labor market in ECA. The increase in unemployment following the onset of the crisis is well known, but whether this was due to a reduction in finance or a fall in demand following the slowdown in the global economy requires analysis. To better isolate the impact of the financial tightening, our analysis adopts an approach similar to that pioneered by Rajan and Zingales (1998) in their seminal study of the impact of finance on growth. This approach isolates the impact of finance by comparing sectors that are "inherently" more dependent on external financing to those less dependent on finance, where a sector's inherent dependence on external financing is measured using U.S. data as a benchmark.[5] Assuming that during the 2008 crisis the impact of factors other than the credit crunch was similar across less and more financially dependent sectors, the observed gap in the performance of these sectors must reflect the impact of the credit tightening associated with the crisis.[6]

In most of the ECA region, the decline in firm-level employment during the 2008 crisis was indeed steeper in more financially dependent sectors, suggesting that the credit crunch had a significant negative effect on

In most of the ECA region, the decline in firm-level employment during the 2008 crisis was indeed steeper in more financially dependent sectors, suggesting that the credit crunch had a significant negative effect on employment.

FIGURE 3.6 **Financially dependent sectors experienced more employment reduction during the 2008 financial crisis in ECA**

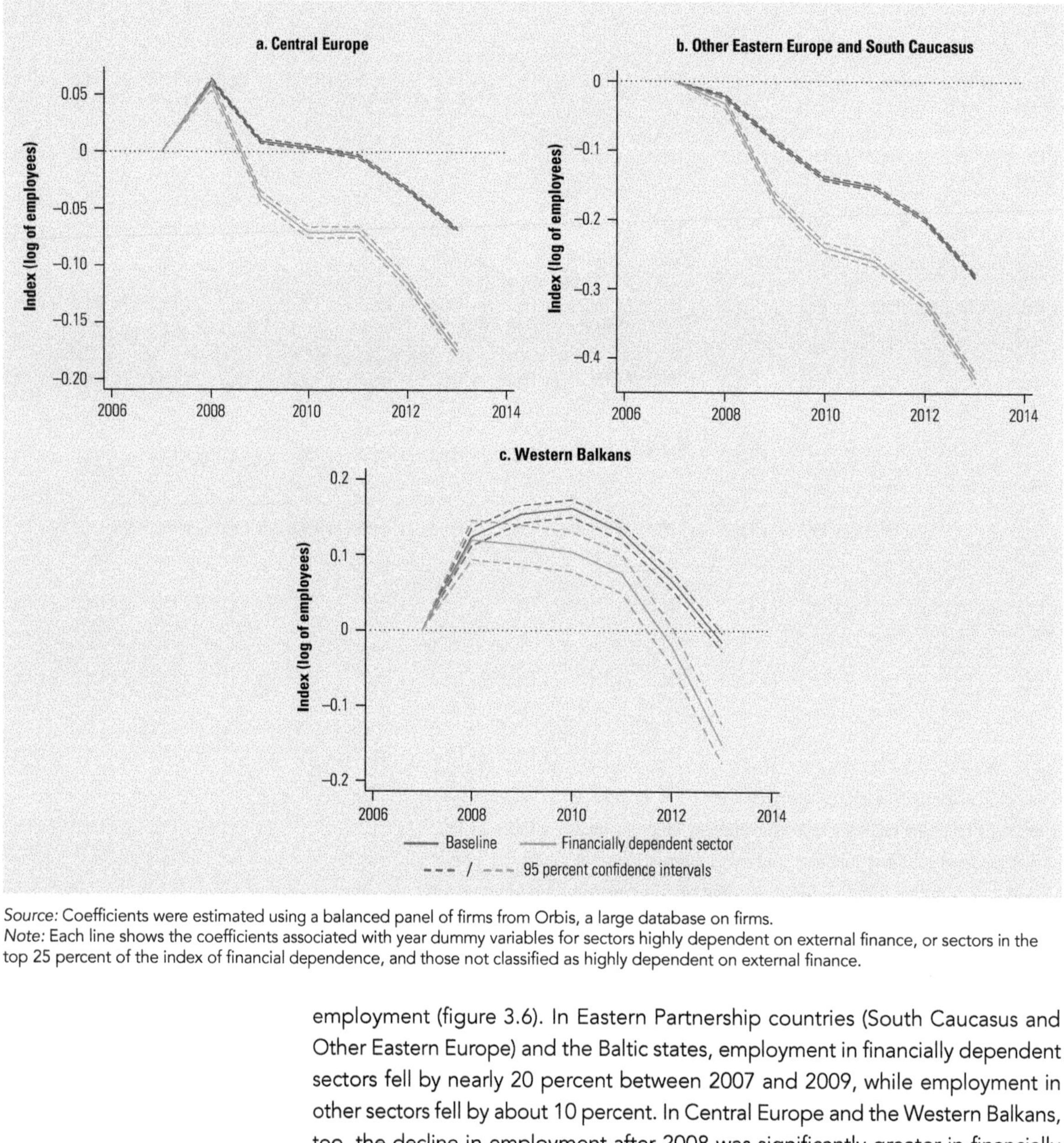

Source: Coefficients were estimated using a balanced panel of firms from Orbis, a large database on firms.
Note: Each line shows the coefficients associated with year dummy variables for sectors highly dependent on external finance, or sectors in the top 25 percent of the index of financial dependence, and those not classified as highly dependent on external finance.

employment (figure 3.6). In Eastern Partnership countries (South Caucasus and Other Eastern Europe) and the Baltic states, employment in financially dependent sectors fell by nearly 20 percent between 2007 and 2009, while employment in other sectors fell by about 10 percent. In Central Europe and the Western Balkans, too, the decline in employment after 2008 was significantly greater in financially dependent sectors. In each case, the widening gap in employment between financially dependent and other sectors is statistically significant, as shown by the 95 percent confidence interval lines. The Russian Federation is the only exception to this pattern.

By 2013, the final year in our data set, financially dependent sectors in ECA had experienced a substantial decline in employment, compared both to their own precrisis levels and to other sectors. And this gap showed no signs of narrowing. Consistent with previous studies on the impact of financial recessions, these patterns suggest that the 2008 financial crisis had a lasting impact on employment.

FIGURE 3.7 **Financially dependent sectors experienced more employment reduction during the 2008 financial crisis in high-income Europe**

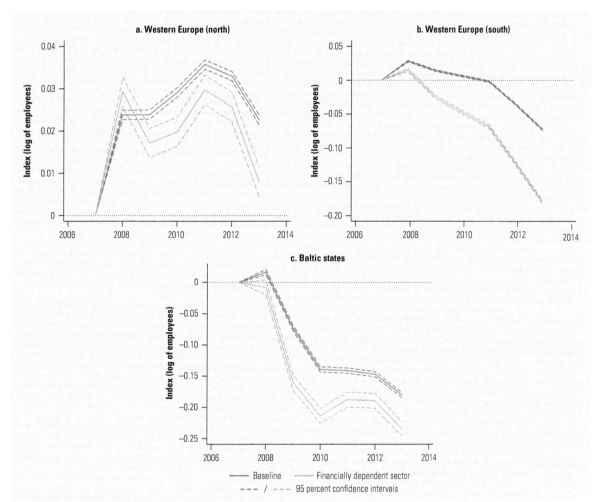

Source: Coefficients were estimated using a balanced panel of firms from Orbis. See appendix D for more details.
Note: Each line shows the coefficients associated with year dummy variables for sectors highly dependent on external finance and the rest.

Note that the data include not just manufacturing but also service sectors, the major source of employment in most of the region.

The financial crisis also adversely affected employment in high-income Europe (figure 3.7). In the northern part of Western Europe, although employment levels in general did not fall below precrisis levels, our indicator of the impact of the crisis—the gap between financially dependent and other sectors—did turn negative after 2008 and subsequently widened. In the southern parts of Western Europe, just like in most of ECA, employment levels declined below precrisis levels in both types of sectors, but more so in financially dependent sectors.

Regression analysis confirms that changes in the level of credit in ECA countries have a significantly greater impact on financially dependent sectors (as defined in the Rajan/Zingales methodology described in box 3.1) than on other sectors. The regressions, which are discussed in detail in appendix D, show that financially dependent sectors in Central European and Baltic economies performed better than other sectors when total credit in the economy expanded, and worse when it contracted.[7] To isolate the impact of the credit channel from other macroeconomic shocks, the regressions account for other country-specific shocks that were common to different sectors. A 1 percentage point decline in the ratio of credit to GDP from 2005–13 is associated with a 1.5 percent greater decline in employment in financially dependent sectors compared to other sectors. Consistent with other empirical studies, regression analysis also indicates that the impact of a decline in bank credit is greater for small firms than for large firms (box 3.2).

A decline in the credit-to-GDP ratio also was associated with a greater decline in the rate of firm entry and exit and the total number of firms in financially dependent

---

BOX 3.2 Small Firms More Vulnerable than Large Firms to a Decline in Credit

For the sector-level data from Eurostat, a 1.0 percentage point fall in the credit-to-GDP ratio is associated with a 2.2 percentage point fall in employment in firms with 1–9 employees and a 1.5 percentage point fall in self-employment, in financially dependent sectors relative to other sectors. In contrast, the corresponding estimate for firms with 10 or more employees is not significantly different from zero. Similarly, a decline in the credit-to-GDP ratio has a significantly negative impact on the entry and exit rate of firms with 1–9 employees in financially dependent sectors, relative to other sectors. Corresponding estimates for firms with 10 or more employees are not statistically significant. The greater impact of the credit crunch on small firms in financially dependent sectors may reflect their more limited access to capital markets (as in Gertler and Gilchrist 1994),[a] or that the decline in commercial bank lending is especially severe for small business loans because of differences in lender health and asymmetric information.[b]

Firm-level data from Orbis on 32 countries were used to confirm the finding that declines in the credit-to-GDP ratio have a disproportionate impact on small firms in financially dependent sectors.[c] These data allow us to control for unobserved firm characteristics that could affect a firm's response to a recession and that could vary systematically across financially dependent and other sectors.

Also, this analysis considers only firms that were operating during the full period being analyzed (firms that entered or shut down during the study period are ignored). Thus, it identifies changes within the same set of firms, unlike the analysis based on sector-level Eurostat data, which could not separate the effects of entry and exit in a sector from changes within existing firms in that sector. Moreover, in addition to countries in Central Europe and the Baltic states, this database includes the Russian Federation, Ukraine, and some Western Balkan economies as well as some non-Europe and Central Asia (ECA) countries (China, the Republic of Korea, and Japan).[d] This broader sample helps to verify, albeit in a limited sense, if the patterns observed in the Eurostat data set generalize beyond Central Europe and the Baltic states.

The results from firm-level data are consistent with the findings from sector-level data. A decline in the credit-to-GDP ratio is associated with a significant employment decline in firms in financially dependent sectors, relative to other sectors. The magnitude is lower than that observed in Eurostat sector-level data, perhaps because the latter also include the net employment effects of firm entry and exit. More important, these results control for firm-level fixed effects, which may absorb a large part of the omitted variable bias present in sector-level regressions.

(Continued)

BOX 3.2 *(continued)*

The effects are larger for small firms. A 10 percent decline in private sector credit to GDP reduced employment in firms with 10–49 employees by 3 percentage points more in financially dependent sectors than in other sectors. Regarding age, the impact is larger for small firms aged 7–11 years because a 10 percent decline in credit is associated with an additional 4 percent decline in employment in financially dependent sectors. Data availability makes it difficult to determine why this age group of small firms is more affected by the decline in credit. Perhaps very young small firms are more immune because, even in good times, they rely largely on internal financing. A robustness check using an alternative measure of financial depth—stock market capitalization as a share of GDP—shows the same pattern: firms in the 7–11 age range were the most affected by the financial crisis.

a. Fort et al. (2013) find that, during a credit crunch, the employment growth rate of small and young firms declines by more than that of large and old firms. Greenstone, Mas, and Nguyen (2014) find that small firms were more reliant on bank lending, and suffered larger employment losses during the 2008 financial crisis, than large firms.
b. According to Chodorow-Reich (2014), the predicted change in employment varies by as much as 5 percentage points depending on the health of its lenders. In the aggregate, these frictions can account for as much as one-third to one-half of the decline in employment at small and medium firms in the year following the collapse of Lehman Brothers. Firms that had precrisis relationships with less healthy lenders had a lower likelihood of obtaining a loan following the Lehman bankruptcy, paid a higher interest rate if they did borrow, and reduced employment by more compared to precrisis clients of healthier lenders. Consistent with frictions deriving from asymmetric information, the effects vary by firm type. In particular, lender health has an economically and statistically significant effect on employment at small and medium firms.
c. Orbis is a database collected by Bureau van Dijk of private and listed company information from around the world—all standardized for easy cross-border comparisons (https://orbis.bvdinfo.com/).
d. A list of countries in the sample is included in appendix D.

FIGURE 3.8

The credit crunch particularly reduced the churning of firms, especially small firms, in financially dependent sectors

Firm entry and exit rates

■ Entry rate
▨ Exit rate

Source: World Bank calculations based on Orbis database.
Note: Each bar represents the differential change in entry and exit rates of sectors highly dependent on finance versus the rest, when the private credit-to-GDP ratio declines by 10 percentage points. See appendix D for more details.

sectors, relative to other sectors (figure 3.8).[8] This may imply that the crisis reduced the productivity gains from the entry of productive firms and exit of unproductive firms (see, for instance, Larrain and Stumpner 2015). Better external financing conditions allow more entrepreneurs with ideas to enter the market, grow, and challenge inefficient incumbents. A credit crunch might reduce such productivity-enhancing churning among firms.

How Does Labor Market Volatility as a Result of Fluctuations in Credit Affect the Bottom 40?

Studies often find that unskilled workers (who are more likely to be poorer than their skilled counterparts) are often the first to lose their jobs during a recession because firms hoard their trained labor force (Halac et al. 2004; Habib et al. 2010). However, recent evidence suggests that the 2008 financial crisis affected the emerging middle class in developing countries more than the poor because the former were more likely to be employed in export-oriented sectors and salaried jobs in services, which appear to have suffered the largest declines in labor demand (Habib et al. 2010). The more limited impact on the poor may be due to their isolation from the global markets (and from the formal sector that gains the most from such links) that has prevented them from exiting poverty in the past. Habib et al. (2010) also pointed out that it is important to distinguish "crisis-vulnerable" or "newly poor" households during a financial crisis from those who are chronically poor. On average, the newly poor are more skilled and urban than the chronically poor, indicating that financial crises have a sizable effect on the number of "working poor."

Regression analysis based on data from Labor Force Surveys for 17 European countries indicates that declines in credit led to a greater reduction in salaried employment in regions (as defined in box 3.3) with labor markets that are more dependent on finance (figure 3.9).

Moreover, this effect was long lasting. Even by 2012, these regions displayed lower rates of salaried employment than less financially dependent regions. Further analysis using individual panel data for 18 European countries from 2008 to 2012 shows that a 10 percentage point decline in the share of credit to GDP was associated with a fall in the salaried employment rate by 1.45 percentage point more in regions whose labor markets were more dependent on finance external to the firm (in the sense that the share of employment in financially dependent sectors was 10 percentage points higher than in less financially dependent regions; see appendix D for details of this analysis).

The decline in finance seems to have affected only the total employment rate of individuals in the top 60, whereas the direct effect on the bottom 40 was statistically not different from zero. When focusing on the probability of having a salaried job, the effects are also stronger for the top 60 in both Western and Central Europe. It is striking that individuals in the bottom 40 in financially dependent regions of Central Europe were more likely to have a salaried job during the financial crisis than their equivalents in less financially dependent regions. Although more research is needed to understand this effect, a potential explanation is that some of the firms more affected by the credit crunch in Central Europe reacted by hiring lower-wage workers (who are more likely to be in the bottom 40) to substitute for

> Individuals in the bottom 40 in financially dependent regions of Central Europe were more likely to have a salaried job during the financial crisis than their equivalents in less financially dependent regions.

BOX 3.3 **A Regional Index Measuring the Degree of Dependence on Finance External to the Firm**

The index measures the share of employment in sectors highly dependent on finance, by region. We define the region at the Nomenclature of Territorial Units for Statistics of Europe (NUTS) 1 or 2 level, depending on the level of disaggregation for each country. NUTS (from the French *Nomenclature des Unités territoriales statistiques*) is a "geographical nomenclature subdividing the economic territory of the European Union (EU) into regions at three different levels (NUTS 1, 2, and 3 respec-

tively, moving from larger to smaller territorial units)."[a]

We also divide each region into three categories according to their population density. This leaves us with 278 regional units exhibiting a significant degree of variation in the degree of dependence on finance external to the firm in 2008. Most European regions had about 25 percent of their workers employed in financially dependent sectors (figure B3.3.1).

FIGURE B3.3.1 **There was significant variation in the degree of financial dependence of each region at the onset of the financial crisis in Europe**

Regional share of employment in sectors highly dependent on finance, 2008

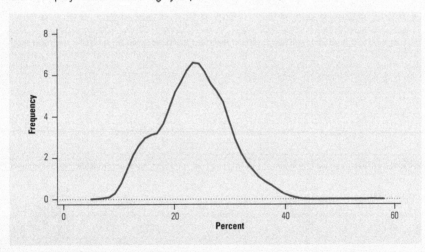

Source: Labour Force Surveys from Eurostat 2008.
Note: Sample includes Austria, Belgium, Bulgaria, Cyprus, the Czech Republic, Denmark, Estonia, Finland, France, Italy, Latvia, Lithuania, Luxembourg, Poland, the Slovak Republic, Spain, and the United Kingdom. There are 278 regions, each one defined at the Nomenclature of Territorial Units for Statistics of Europe (NUTS) 1 or 2 level depending on data availability, and at the same time split into three categories according to the level of urbanization.
a. For more information on NUTS, see the Glossary on the Eurostat website, http://ec.europa.eu/eurostat/statistics-explained/index.php/Glossary:Nomenclature_of_territorial_units_for_statistics_(NUTS).

higher-wage workers. Figure 3.10 shows evidence consistent with this hypothesis: firms in sectors more dependent on finance reacted to the credit crunch by decreasing their share of nonproduction workers (who are more likely to be in the top 60) relatively more than their counterparts in less financially dependent sectors. Moreover, even though on average firms increased their share of skilled production workers (who are more likely to be in the top 60 when compared to

FIGURE 3.9 Wage employment in regions with more financially dependent labor markets was more severely affected by the credit crunch

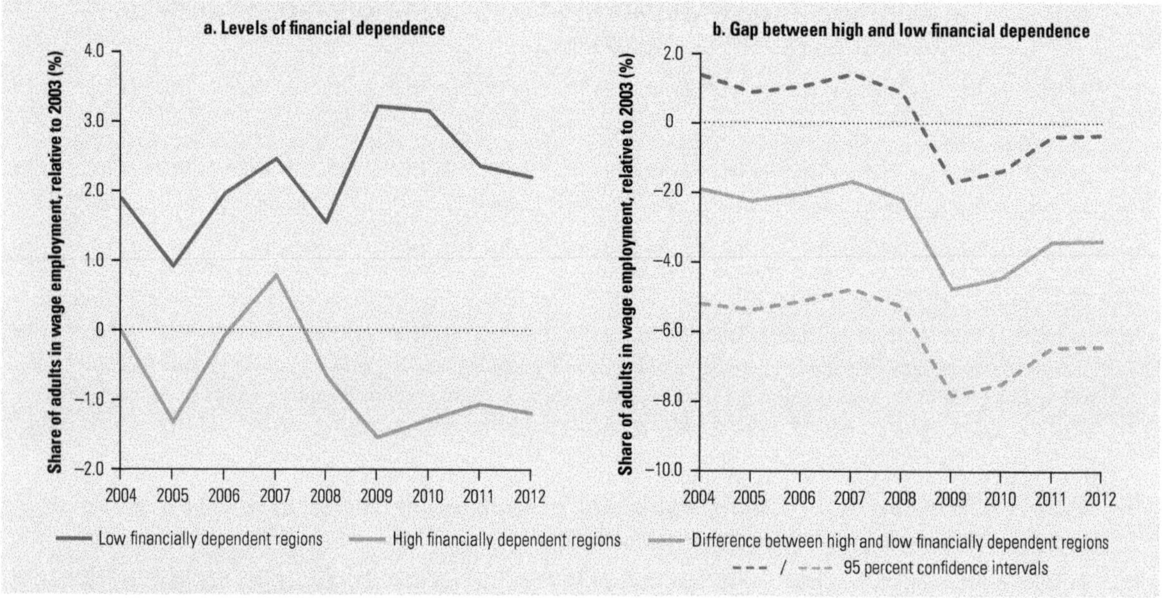

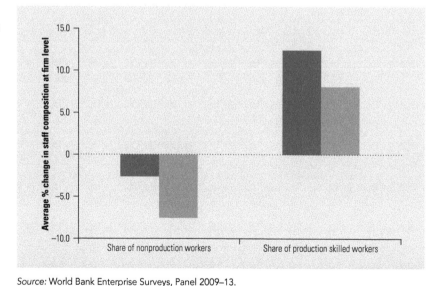

a. Levels of financial dependence

b. Gap between high and low financial dependence

—— Low financially dependent regions   —— High financially dependent regions   —— Difference between high and low financially dependent regions

--- / --- 95 percent confidence intervals

Source: Labour Force Surveys from Eurostat, 2004–13.
Note: Sample includes Austria, Belgium, Bulgaria, Cyprus, the Czech Republic, Denmark, Estonia, Finland, France, Italy, Latvia, Lithuania, Luxembourg, Poland, the Slovak Republic, Spain, and the United Kingdom. There are 278 regions, each one defined at the Nomenclature of Territorial Units for Statistics of Europe (NUTS) 1 or 2 level depending on data availability and at the same time split into three categories according to the level of urbanization. Regions are split between high and low financial dependence using the fraction of employment in financially dependent (FD) sectors in 2007 for each region. Those above the median value are classified as high FD.

FIGURE 3.10

Financially dependent firms became more intensive in production and skilled workers

Central Europe, 2008–12

■ Baseline
■ Financially dependent sectors

Source: World Bank Enterprise Surveys, Panel 2009–13.
Note: Each bar represents the change in the share of nonproduction (managers, professional and technical employees) and production skilled workers (those who have a special knowledge or ability in their work).

unskilled production workers), those in financially dependent sectors did so to a lesser extent than the rest.

Similar to the results for employment, the hourly wages of individuals who kept their jobs over 2008–12 declined more in financially dependent regions than in others. This evidence is consistent with previous studies showing that firms reduced the hours worked by their employees as an adjustment mechanism (see World Bank 2011). These aggregate effects, however, mask important differences across regions. Whereas in Central Europe the credit crunch seemed to affect labor markets mostly by reducing hours worked—especially by the self-employed—firms in Western Europe responded mostly by laying off employees (see table D.4 in appendix D). The fall in hours worked was in part driven by government-sponsored schemes to supplement wages of employees working reduced hours (Directorate-General for Economic and Financial Affairs of the European Commission 2009). Although the impact of the credit crunch on hours worked by salaried workers was larger among the top 60, the impact on the hours worked by the self-employed affected the bottom 40 and the top 60 to the same extent. In Western Europe, individuals living in regions highly dependent on finance did not experience larger cuts in hours of work than their counterparts living in less financially dependent regions, and this is true for those in both the top 60 and the bottom 40 of the income distribution.

We also estimated the effects of the credit crunch on the hourly earnings of individuals who remained employed from 2008 through 2012. As before, those in the top 60 suffered a larger reduction in their hourly earnings compared to the bottom 40. Also, in the top 60 of both Central and Western Europe, the effects are larger in magnitude for the earnings of the self-employed than for those of salaried workers. This result is expected because self-employment earnings are in general more volatile during the business cycle than are those of salaried workers (Jensen and Shore 2015).

The finding that individuals in the bottom 40 were less affected by the financial crisis than their counterparts in the top 60 may seem contradictory with the finding that small firms were hit the hardest during the credit crunch and that employed individuals in the bottom 40 are more likely to work in small firms than their peers in the top 60. However, two explanations may help reconcile these findings. First, small firms account for only about 15 percent of total employment in ECA, hence their performance does not have a significant influence in the overall evolution of the labor market (EBRD 2010). Second, individuals in the bottom 40 are less likely than their richer counterparts to have a job, and thereby are less likely to suffer the consequences of a labor market downturn.

Considering workers' individual characteristics can help us better understand the channels by which the top 60 were affected more severely than the bottom 40. In both Central and Western Europe, the effects of the credit crunch seem to have been larger for older individuals in terms of losing a job, cutting down hours of work, or reducing hourly wages (see figure D.1 in appendix D). Workers with a college degree also bore part of the negative effects in terms of the reduction of salaried jobs, especially in Western Europe. Because prime age and skilled individuals are likely to be richer, the fact that they were more likely to suffer the direct effects of the financial crisis through the labor market could help explain why the effects were larger for the top 60.[9]

To summarize the empirical evidence, the credit crunch had a larger negative direct effect (through the labor market channel) on individuals in the top 60 percent of the income distribution in Western and Central Europe than on their peers in the bottom 40 percent. Whereas in Western Europe the effects were mostly driven by a decrease in the number of salaried jobs, in Central Europe they were driven by a decline in the number of both self-employed and salaried jobs. Firms in Central Europe also responded to the credit crunch by reducing the number of work hours. The shortage in finance also had a greater negative effect on the hourly earnings of the top 60 compared to the bottom 40, especially for the self-employed in both Central and Western Europe.

It is important to mention two caveats to these findings. First, they do not account for general equilibrium effects—that is, for the fact that the financial shock experienced by some firms may eventually become a real shock for other firms in the region or in other regions through channels such as trade or migration. Second, they refer only to the labor market channel, whereas the crisis may have affected differently the bottom 40 and top 60 through other channels such as savings, real estate values, or insurance coverage.

These results highlight the trade-offs of improving external financing conditions for firms. Although the benefits in terms of job creation and wage growth could be large, increasing dependence on finance can also make labor markets more subject to the volatility of financial markets. Moreover, it is those already included—that is, those more likely to be in the top 60—who are more likely to suffer the fluctuations of the supply of credit for firms. Given the existing state of firms' external financing conditions in most of the ECA region, the trade-off between employment growth and volatility effects of finance has been less acute for households in the bottom 40. Not by choice, but because of a lack of good external financial conditions, households in the bottom 40 were less reliant on jobs in firms that were dependent on financing external to the firm than were households in the top 60. Hence, relative to top 60 households, there is scope to bring more opportunities to the bottom 40 by improving firms' *external financing conditions*. Relative to bottom 40 households, those in the top 60 are more vulnerable to the labor market effects of financial volatility, and have more to gain by *financial stability* (as long as stability does not come at the cost of substantially reduced financial depth).

What Policies Can Improve Income Growth among the Bottom 40 and Reduce Volatility for the Top 60?

The evidence reviewed in this chapter suggests that firms' external financing conditions matter for both the bottom 40 and the top 60 in ECA, but in a different way. Whereas improving firms' external financing conditions could benefit the bottom 40 disproportionately by contributing to job creation and creating incentives to be in the formal sector, the labor market outcomes of households in the top 60 are more sensitive to the volatility of financial flows. The higher stability of the incomes of households in the bottom 40 during a credit crunch is consistent with evidence from other chapters of this report, and it is largely driven by the bottom 40 percent's lower exposure to firms' access to finance, because they are more likely to depend on nonlabor income than their wealthier peers.

This section illustrates the importance both of improving external financing conditions faced by firms in the ECA region and of policies intended to reduce the volatility of financial flows. Although financial volatility may initially affect the top 60 directly, the effects eventually spread to the rest of the economy and can potentially affect the bottom 40 as well. This chapter shows that financial sector policies aimed at improving firms' external financing conditions in ECA—in particular in the Caucasus, Central Asia, Other Eastern Europe, the Baltic states, and Russia—could boost shared prosperity by creating jobs and raising productivity and wages. It also highlights the importance of financial sector policies aimed at reducing the volatility of capital flows, particularly among those economies with better external financing conditions. Our results also emphasize the importance of nonfinancial sector policies to reduce the vulnerability of households during a credit crunch through the development of well-targeted social programs to reach the most vulnerable households, or by increasing individuals' incentives to save and thereby raise their ability to cope with the negative income effects of financial volatility (see chapter 4).

Notes

1. A composite story.
2. Finance external to the firm refers to all finance, excluding internally generated resources (retained earnings) or contributions from owners. Examples include bank loans, bonds, and stock issuance.
3. Buera, Fattal Jaef, and Shin 2015 show that firms that become more financially constrained reduce their labor and capital demand and the surplus production factors get reallocated to unconstrained producers via the general equilibrium effect of lower factor prices. However, frictions in the labor market interfere with this labor reallocation. It takes time for the economy to absorb idled workers and, as a result, unemployment rates increase and remain high for a prolonged period.
4. Calvo, Coricelli, and Ottonello (2012) conduct an empirical analysis and conclude that the joblessness nature of recoveries is more severe during financial crises than in "normal" recessions.
5. See box 3.1 and appendix D for more details on the methodology.
6. The key assumption is that, on average, the impact of factors other than the credit crunch was similar across less and more financially dependent sectors. This analysis provides only suggestive evidence. A more precise measurement of the impact of the credit crunch would require more data and economic modeling because it would have to account for all the channels through which the 2008 crisis could have affected firms, including the general equilibrium effects of a credit crunch.
7. The unit of observation corresponds to a country-sector-year cell. The regressions measure how, during 2005–13, the relationship between the credit-to-GDP ratio of the economy and sector-level outcomes varied across baseline and financially dependent sectors by interacting the credit-to-GDP ratio variable with a binary indicator for whether a sector is at the top 25 percent of the indicator of financial dependence. The data are from Eurostat.
8. As discussed in box 3.2, the results on firm entry and exit are driven by firms with fewer than 10 employees, and are not statistically significant when firms of all sizes are

considered. A decline in credit can be associated with a fall in the number of firms exiting because regulatory restrictions limit firms' ability to fire workers and go bankrupt.

9. See the background paper for this report (Sharma and Winkler 2015) for more details on these results.

References

Beck, Thorsten, Asli Demirgüç-Kunt, and Ross Levine. 2007. "Finance, Inequality and the Poor." *Journal of Economic Growth* 12 (1): 27–49.

Beck, Thorsten, Asli Demirgüç-Kunt, and V. Maksimovic. 2005. "Financial and Legal Constraint to Growth: Does Firm Size Matter?" *Journal of Finance* 60 (1): 137–77.

Beck, Thorsten, Ross Levine, and Alexey Levkov. 2010. "Big Bad Banks? The Winners and Losers from Bank Deregulation in the United States." *Journal of Finance* 65: 1637–67.

Bernanke, B., and M. Gertler. 1989. "Agency Costs, Net Worth, and Business Fluctuations." *American Economic Review* 79 (1): 14–31.

Bloom, N., and J. Van Reenen. 2010. "Why Do Management Practices Differ across Firms and Countries?" *Journal of Economic Perspectives* 24 (1): 203–24.

Boeri, T. 2012. "Setting the Minimum Wage." *Labour Economics* 19 (3): 281–90.

Buera, Francisco J., Roberto N. Fattal Jaef, and Yongseok Shin. 2015. "Anatomy of a Credit Crunch: From Capital to Labor Markets." *Review of Economic Dynamics* 18 (1): 101–17.

Calomiris, C. W., M. Jaremski, H. Park, and G. Richardson. 2015. "Liquidity Risk, Bank Networks, and the Value of Joining the Federal Reserve System." NBER Working Paper 21684, National Bureau of Economic Research, Cambridge, MA.

Calvo, Guillermo A., Fabrizio Coricelli, and Pablo Ottonello. 2012. "The Labor Market Consequences of Financial Crises with or without Inflation: Jobless and Wageless Recoveries." NBER Working Paper 18480, National Bureau of Economic Research, Cambridge, MA.

Chodorow-Reich, Gabriel. 2014. "The Employment Effects of Credit Market Disruptions: Firm-Level Evidence from the 2008–9 Financial Crisis." *Quarterly Journal of Economics* 129 (1): 1–59.

Claessens, Stijn, Ayhan Kose, Luc Laeven, and Fabian Valencia. 2013. "Understanding Financial Crises: Causes, Consequences, and Policy Responses." Economic Research Forum Working Paper 1301, Koç University–TUSIAD, Istanbul.

Demirgüç-Kunt, A., L. F. Klapper, and G. A. Panos. 2011. "Entrepreneurship in Post-conflict Transition." *Economics of Transition* 19 (1): 27–78.

Demirgüç-Kunt, A., and R. Levine. 2009. "Finance and Inequality: Theory and Evidence." *Annual Review of Financial Economics* 1 (1): 287–318.

Directorate-General for Economic and Financial Affairs of the European Commission. 2009. *Economic Crisis in Europe: Causes, Consequences and Responses.* European Communities.

EBRD (European Bank for Reconstruction and Development). 2010. *Life in Transition: After the Crisis.* Life in Transition Survey (LITS) II. London: EBRD.

Fort, Teresa C., John Haltiwanger, Ron S. Jarmin, and Javier Miranda. 2013. "How Firms Respond to Business Cycles: The Role of Firm Age and Firm Size." *IMF Economic Review* 61 (3): 520–59.

Gertler, M., and S. Gilchrist. 1994. "Monetary Policy, Business Cycles, and the Behavior of Small Manufacturing Firms." *Quarterly Journal of Economics* 109 (2): 309–40.

Gine, X., and R. M. Townsend. 2004. "Evaluation of Financial Liberalization: A General Equilibrium Model with Constrained Occupation Choice." *Journal of Development Economics* 74 (2): 269–307.

Greenstone, Michael, Alexandre Mas, and Hoai-Luu Nguyen. 2014. "Do Credit Market Shocks Affect the Real Economy? Quasi-experimental Evidence from the Great Recession and 'Normal' Economic Times." NBER Working Paper 20704, National Bureau of Economic Research, Cambridge, MA.

Habib, Bilal, Ambar Narayan, Sergio Olivieri, and Carolina Sanchez-Paramo. 2010. "Assessing Ex Ante the Poverty and Distributional Impact of the Global Crisis in a Developing Country: A Micro-simulation Approach with Application to Bangladesh." Policy Research Working Paper 5238, World Bank, Washington, DC.

Halac, M., S. L. Schmukler, E. Fernández-Arias, and U. Panizza. 2004. "Distributional Effects of Crises: The Financial Channel [with comments]." *Economia* (Fall): 1–67.

Jensen, S. T., and S. H. Shore. 2015. "Changes in the Distribution of Earnings Volatility." *Journal of Human Resources* 50 (3): 811–36.

Klapper, L., R. Amit, and M. F. Guillén. 2010. "Entrepreneurship and Firm Formation across Countries." In *International Differences in Entrepreneurship*, edited by J. Lerner and A. Schoer, 129–58. University of Chicago Press, © National Bureau of Economic Research.

Klapper, L., L. Laeven, and R. Rajan. 2006. "Entry Regulation as a Barrier to Entrepreneurship." *Journal of Financial Economics* 82 (3): 591–629.

Knotek II, E. S., and S. Terry. 2009. "How Will Unemployment Fare Following the Recession?" *Federal Reserve Bank of Kansas City Economic Review* 94 (3): 5–33.

Krishnan, Karthik, Debarshi Nandy, and Manju Puri. 2014. "Does Financing Spur Small Business Productivity? Evidence from a Natural Experiment." *Review of Financial Studies* 28 (6): 1768–1809.

Larrain, Mauricio, and Sebastian Stumpner. 2015. "Capital Account Liberalization and Aggregate Productivity: The Role of Firm Capital Allocation." Available at SSRN: http://ssrn.com/abstract=2172349.

OECD (Organisation for Economic Co-operation and Development). 2010. *OECD Economic Outlook*. Paris: OECD Publishing. doi: http://dx.doi.org/10.1787/eco_outlook-v2010-1-en.

Rajan, Raghuram, and Zingales, Luigi. 1998. "Financial Dependence and Growth." *American Economic Review* 88 (3): 559–86.

Reinhart, Carmen M., and Kenneth S. Rogoff. 2008. "This Time Is Different: A Panoramic View of Eight Centuries of Financial Crises." *Annals of Economics and Finance, Society for AEF* 15 (2): 1065–1188.

———. 2014. "Recovery from Financial Crises: Evidence from 100 Episodes." NBER Working Paper 19823, National Bureau of Economic Research, Cambridge, MA.

Sharma, Siddharth, and Hernan Winkler. 2015. "The Distributional Impact of a Credit Crunch." Background paper for this report.

Sharpe, W. F. 1994. "The Sharpe Ratio." *Journal of Portfolio Management* 21 (1): 49–58.

World Bank. 2011. *The Jobs Crisis: Household and Government Responses to the Great Recession in Eastern Europe and Central Asia*. Directions in Development: Human Development. Washington, DC: World Bank.

SPOTLIGHT 3

Achieving Equilibrium Credit Provision in Europe and Central Asia with the Help of Cross-Border Supervision

Financial sector development is essential for growth. However, credit growth also can be excessive because rapid increases in lending can reflect a deterioration in credit evaluation that boosts nonperforming loans, and can lead to unsustainable levels of economic activity, inflation, and ultimately a crisis.

One approach to evaluating whether the level of credit is appropriate is to compare the extent of financial sector development with that in similar economies. Here we use a large, cross-country panel data set to establish financial sector benchmarks (see Barajas et al. 2013 and Beck et al. 2008 for other benchmark studies). These benchmarks represent levels of financial sector indicators predicted by a regression based on country characteristics (per capita income and population size, density, and age structure) that are not directly related to policies or the financial sector.[1] Countries with significantly greater (or smaller) levels of credit than in similar countries may have excessive (or insufficient) levels of credit to support sustainable growth.

This analysis illustrates the enormous changes in financial systems of Europe and Central Asia (ECA) over the past 25 years. The ratio of private credit to gross domestic product (GDP) in the median regional country increased nearly sevenfold from 1995 to 2013 (figure S3.1). The benchmark level of private credit to GDP also increased, driven by rising GDP per capita in regional countries and the global trend toward deeper financial systems.[2] In the early years of the period, the level of private credit to GDP was below the benchmark, but by 2005 this level exceeded the benchmark.

Credit expansion may have been excessive by the mid-2000s as the level of credit and deposits in the median ECA country moved beyond the bench-

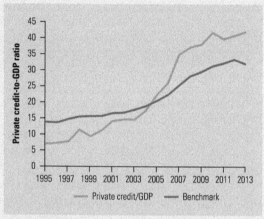

FIGURE S3.1 Private credit-to-GDP in transition ECA economies now exceeds the benchmark

Source: World Bank calculations based on Global Financial Development Indicators.

mark levels. Moreover, the credit increase was faster than the mobilization of domestic deposits, so that credit ultimately exceeded deposits and the ratio of credit to deposits moved beyond its predicted level after 2003 (figure S3.2). Much of this additional credit was allocated to households rather than enterprises, especially in the form of mortgage credit at longer maturities, and in some cases in foreign currency. The gap between the actual and benchmark credit-to-deposit ratio peaked in 2008, at the onset of the global financial crisis. The extensive funding of ECA's credit intermediation with external resources, and increasing aggregate liquidity risk, helps explain why the crisis has affected ECA more than Latin America—a region with similarly high dependence on cross-border banking (Cull and Martinez Peria 2013).

Financial sector reforms in ECA countries should reflect the dangers of excessive credit creation.

FIGURE S3.2 Credit-to-deposit ratios in ECA countries have moved above the benchmark level

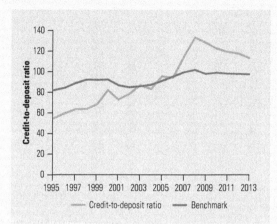

Source: World Bank calculations based on Global Financial Development Indicators.

Effective systems of credit information sharing, collateral creation and enforcement, and contract enforcement in general can increase the level of sustainable financial development, with positive repercussions for economic development (De la Torre, Feyen, and Ize 2013). Improved financial regulation could focus on capital and liquidity requirements and a greater focus on systemic risk, in addition to the soundness of individual banks. The latter implies introduction and strengthening of macroprudential regulatory frameworks that concentrate on interlinks and contagion between individual financial institutions and other sources of systemic risk. Financial safety nets that can effectively deal with bank failures and minimize their effects on other financial institutions and the real economy are critical. These institutional and supervisory reforms could help increase the sustainable level of credit provision (Buncic and Melecky 2014).

In addition, steps should be taken to diversify financial intermediation away from banking. Although in 2012 the median ECA country had a level of private credit to GDP above that of all regions (except for South Asia), its ratio of stock market capitalization to GDP was below that of any other region. Similarly, the median life insurance penetration is the lowest across the six regions.[3] This limited diversification of funding sources in the region can limit growth potential and lead to a more volatile funding landscape across the business cycle (Langfield and Pagano 2015).

Another important challenge for equilibrium credit provision is ensuring effective supervision of foreign banks, including through well-functioning cross-border supervision. Foreign banks have improved the efficiency, breadth, and stability of banking systems in transition economies (Cull and Martinez Peria 2013). However, foreign banks also can transmit instability in home country financial systems to host countries. Thus, the failure of a foreign bank in a home country in Europe may lead to contagion to important subsidiaries in ECA. For example, the ongoing uncertainty surrounding a potential Greek sovereign default and the risk of a currency redenomination had implications for the safety and soundness of the banking systems of jurisdictions hosting Greek banks.

Two issues exacerbate the risks that foreign banks present to financial stability in ECA banking systems. First, key operational functions of cross-border banks (for example, bank office operations, information technology [IT], infrastructure, compliance, internal audit, and treasury) have been increasingly centralized. Thus, an operational problem elsewhere in the banking group can have a significant impact on branches and subsidiaries in ECA, whereas ECA supervisors may have little information on, or ability to influence, these practices. For example, despite the host country being responsible for supervising liquidity risk in a foreign subsidiary or branch in its territory, the supervisor may be unable to do so because it has no insight on how the bank manages its liquidity.

SPOTLIGHT 3 *(continued)*

FIGURE S3.3 Foreign banks hold large asset shares in host ECA countries

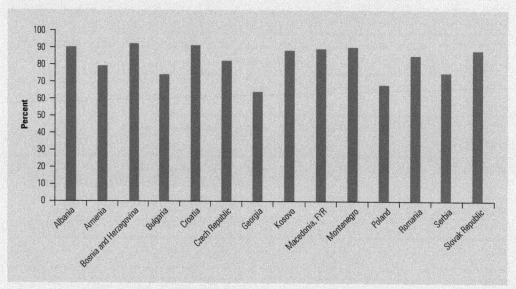

Sources: Figures compiled from central banks' websites.

Second, although a foreign bank may hold a significant share of banking assets in a small transition economy (figure S3.3 shows the share of foreign banks in ECA banking systems), that bank's assets in the host transition economy may account for only a small share of the bank's total assets. Thus, the ECA country's regulatory authorities may have little influence over the bank's risk management and business practices, and may have little role in, or even access to information on, cross-border cooperative efforts to resolve a crisis. Arrangements (for example, supervisory colleges, crisis management groups) exist for sharing information and coordinating actions by supervisors in resolving problems affecting cross-border banks. However, small host country supervisors may not participate in these forums, where for practical reasons participation is limited to the countries where the cross-border bank is

most exposed. Moreover, authorities responsible for the largest share of a bank's assets may have only a limited incentive to take into account the concerns of authorities with only a small share of these assets, even if this "small share" has systemic implications for the host country's financial system.

As the global financial crisis illustrated, the extent and nature of international banking integration led to unprecedented transmission of financial instability. Financial contagion can spread through the balance sheet of banks, but it can also be transmitted indirectly—through a common brand name, for example. Thus a bank crisis driven by a failure in the home country's investment bank activities could affect the reputation of the retail operations of a bank in ECA.

Therefore, host country supervisors cannot always rely exclusively on international cooperation to protect domestic financial stability. Where cooperation with home country supervisors is not practical or is unlikely to protect host country interests, host supervisors may require banks to hold liquidity and capital buffers locally. They may also require that domestic subsidiaries not depend on intragroup transfers and eliminate other operational group dependencies (IT, outsourcing, and back-office functions). Other measures, for example capital and liquidity requirements that are higher than the regulatory minimum, dividend restrictions, and restrictions on liquidity flows and subsidiarization may be necessary to ensure that the bank subsidiary can operate independently and protect its domestic assets from cross-border contagion.

These ring-fencing measures are generally described by adverse terms, such as fragmentation, home bias, balkanization, financial protection, and nationalism; and they do have costs in terms of forgoing some of the efficiency gains from financial integration. These costs will be higher if foreign operations are heavily integrated and will also rise for heavily interdependent markets. Imposing such requirements as a general rule, rather than abruptly during a financial crisis, would give the relevant banks time to adapt and embed the measures in their business practices.

Notes

1. First, the log of GDP per capita and its square (to account for possible nonlinearities) proxy for general demand and supply-side constraints related to low income. Second, the log of population proxies for market size and the possibilities of financial intermediaries and markets to benefit from scale economies. Third, the log of population density proxies for geographic barriers and thus the ease of financial service provision. Fourth, the log of the age dependency ratio

is included to capture demographic trends and corresponding saving behavior. Finally, dummy variables for off-shore centers, transition countries, and oil-exporting countries are included to control for specific country circumstances, as these countries face specific challenges and development experiences that impact their financial systems.

2. The decreasing value of the benchmark in 2013 might reflect a global retrenchment of financial systems in the wake of the global financial crisis.

3. The fact that the median life insurance penetration ratio is higher for Sub-Saharan Africa than for Eastern Europe and Central Asia is due to the fact that this statistic is available only for the most developed insurance markets in Africa.

References

Barajas, Adolfo, Thorsten Beck, Era Dabla-Norris, and Seyed Reza Yousefi. 2013. "Too Cold, Too Hot, or Just Right? Assessing Financial Sector Development Across the Globe." IMF Working Paper 13/81, International Monetary Fund, Washington, DC.

Beck, Thorsten, Erik H. B. Feyen, Alain Ize, and Florencia Moizeszowicz. 2008. "Benchmarking Financial Development." Policy Research Working Paper 4638, World Bank, Washington, DC.

Buncic, Daniel, and Martin Melecky. 2014. "Equilibrium Credit: The Reference Point for Macroprudential Supervisors." Journal of Banking and Finance 41 (April): 135–54.

Cull, Robert, and Maria Soledad Martinez Peria. 2013. "Foreign Bank Participation in Developing Countries: What Do We Know about the Drivers and Consequences of This Phenomenon?" In Encyclopedia of Financial Globalization, edited by Gerard Caprio. Oxford, U.K.: Elsevier.

De la Torre, Augusto, Erik Feyen, and Alain Ize. 2013. "Financial Development: Structure and Dynamics." World Bank Economic Review, February.

Langfield, Sam, and Marco Pagano. 2015. "Bank Bias in Europe: Effects on Systemic Risk and Growth." Economic Policy, April 13.

Weighing Different Strategies for Developing Capital Markets in Europe and Central Asia

Despite some progress, capital market development remains limited in most Europe and Central Asia (ECA) countries, for the most part below levels in Latin America and the Caribbean, Middle East and North Africa, and East Asia and Pacific (figure S4.1). Most regional equity markets list only a limited number of companies, and secondary markets are often illiquid. Government bond markets exhibit more development, at least in the largest countries, although even they require further progress to achieve a deep and liquid yield curve. Throughout the region corporate funding remains dominated by banks, although in a few countries corporate bond markets are starting to play a larger role in the funding of financial companies and also in short-term funding of corporations. On the demand side, the investor base across all countries is still very narrow. In general, direct retail investor participation is very limited; and the number of institutional investors (mutual funds, pension funds, and insurance companies), while growing, remains small in terms of assets under management and relative to the economy. Foreign participation in the local markets is almost nonexistent, except for participation in the government bond markets of just a few countries, usually the largest jurisdictions.

Two different approaches have been discussed to pursuing capital market development in ECA: regional integration of existing capital markets (countries harmonizing listing, regulatory, and supervisory standards) and individual countries becoming an international financial center (centralization of capital markets in one or a few country hubs).

Regional integration can be an attractive proposition, particularly for small countries whose

FIGURE S4.1 Market capitalization of stock markets in ECA is low compared to other regions

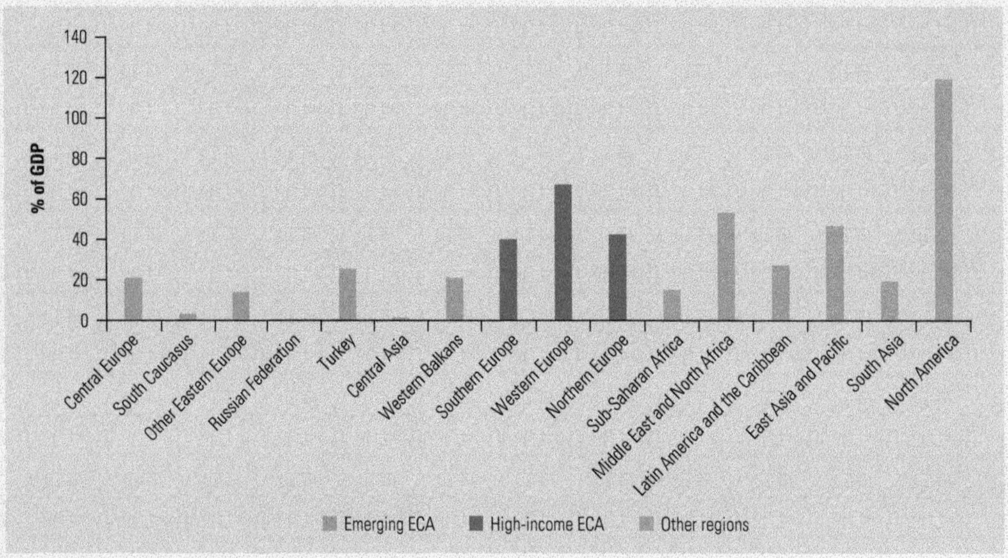

Source: World Bank Global Financial Development Database.

domestic markets do not offer the necessary diversification of investment opportunities to investors or of funding sources to companies. The free flow of capital that is at the core of regional integration should enable companies to reach a wider base of investors and enable investors to choose among a broader set of investment opportunities, which should in turn translate into better portfolio allocation.

In spite of its theoretical appeal, very few projects of regional integration have achieved much success. Only Europe has achieved a relative degree of capital markets integration. Regional integration is being pursued in the European Union through the initiative to create a capital markets union.[1] This would involve the creation of uniform rules for markets and for company reporting, so that investors would have sufficient confidence in their ability to evaluate the return and risk of companies and to trade on markets throughout the region. Yet the current proposal for a capital markets union highlights that more needs to be done to efficiently link investors and savers with growth and to unlock the potential of capital markets for long-term investment. In all other regions, including the MILA (*Mercado Integrado Latinoamericano*) and AMERCA (*Alianza de Mercados Centroamericanos*) initiatives in Latin America and the East Africa Community in Africa, projects of regional integration are at a much earlier stage.

Regional integration can raise significant concerns among stakeholders. Although companies and investors generally support regional integration to lower barriers to obtaining or allocating capital, securities intermediaries and the market infrastructure providers (the exchanges) may view integration as a competitive threat rather than as a potential vehicle to expand their customer or business base. Smaller exchanges are concerned that investors will gravitate toward the larger markets. These types of concerns are stronger in cases where there are material disparities in the state of development of the countries, and one or more countries are perceived to be dominant.

Authorities may be concerned that differences in the legal and regulatory framework for capital markets, and the intensity and quality of supervision and enforcement, could have several adverse consequences. Intermediaries may choose to relocate to countries with less stringent requirements, so authorities are faced with the choice of seeing a decline in the depth of capital markets or loosening their own standards. Investor protection could suffer if the legal framework or the supervisory program applicable to the distribution of products by intermediaries in one jurisdiction is considered to be deficient, thus increasing the risk of mis-selling or fraud to investors located in a host jurisdiction. The risk of financial instability could increase if it is considered that the prudential framework or the early warning program in place for securities intermediaries of one jurisdiction is too lax and not capable of dealing effectively with their failure. This could have spillover effects into the host jurisdictions given the increased interconnectedness brought by integration.

Regional integration of capital markets is a complex task. Integration is most successful where participating countries already have strong economic ties and are at similar levels of development. Ideally a single currency should be in place, but the experience of capital markets in Europe shows that the process of integration can start even with multiple currencies; however, in that case, the availability of hedging mechanisms is critical. A similar legal tradition facilitates integration but is not a necessary precondition.

Gradual implementation can provide stakeholders with the time to prepare and address potential risks. Such gradualism can apply to both markets and products as well as to the way in which services can be provided.

The regulatory framework that supports the offering and trading of securities and the provision of services in the region needs to provide comfort to the public authorities that the risk of regulatory arbitrage and harm to investor protection and

SPOTLIGHT 4 *(continued)*

financial stability are being minimized. Mutual recognition tends to work better when the legal and regulatory frameworks of the jurisdictions involved are perceived to provide a similar level of protection to investors (even if differences exist). If that perception does not exist, then regulatory harmonization might be needed. However, harmonization is complicated, because it is important to avoid a race to the bottom and adoption of the least stringent framework, but adoption of the most stringent framework could prevent entry by smaller participants and markets.

Strengthened coordination among supervisors is essential, including implementation of arrangements for the exchange of information, cooperation, and coordination. However, experience shows that as integration deepens, stronger supervisory arrangements are needed, including the creation of regional bodies, initially to better coordinate but over time to potentially assume direct supervisory and enforcement functions. The creation of regional supervisory and enforcement agencies gives rise to another host of concerns, including those related to the division of responsibilities between the domestic and the regional supervisory authorities.

Market infrastructure must be unified, in the sense that investors must be able to access all markets, although not necessarily through the creation of a single exchange. In the long run, full integration requires the harmonization of the enabling environment, including in sensitive areas such as the tax regime and the insolvency framework.

These requirements indicate that the integration of all capital markets in ECA is unrealistic. A few countries could deepen their integration with the European Union, while other clusters of countries with similar characteristics might develop a plan for integration. In any event, regional integration does not replace the need for ECA countries to think

about the role of capital markets at the domestic level. Where integration makes sense, domestic plans need to be fully integrated into this broader strategy.[2]

Becoming an international financial center (IFC)—that is, a location where a significant amount of financial services with no domestic connection takes place—is attractive for countries with large domestic markets. However, few countries have been successful in this goal.

There are different and somewhat contradictory theories about how and why IFCs develop. Some of them place particular importance on the role that the location of manufacturing and more basic services industries, mainly those for physical goods, have had in the development of IFCs. Others emphasize the economies of scale in concentrating financial business in one or a small number of places. The centralization brought by economies of scale would justify the existence of just a few large global IFCs (for example, New York, London, and Tokyo). However, smaller financial centers such as Singapore or Hong Kong SAR, China, also have emerged, perhaps because of other factors such as strategic location, the quality of the legal and regulatory framework, political stability, or functional specialization.

There is no single list of accepted attributes for IFCs. However, in general both research and surveys conducted on the topic point to the following attributes as determinant to the success of an IFC:[3]

• *Rule of law:* The existence of a legal framework that protects private property and has strong mechanisms for dispute resolution is key for an IFC to develop.

• *Appropriate regulation:* There is no unique model for the regulatory and supervisory framework that should govern the financial services provided in the IFC. The challenge lies in ensuring that regulations do not impede innovation but at the same time achieve their objectives of protecting investors, ensuring fair and liquid markets, and managing risks to financial stability. In tandem, a credible supervisory authority should be in place.

- *Availability of high-quality finance professionals and support services:* Attracting high-quality finance professionals—including not only investment bankers but also other specialized professionals, such as lawyers and accountants—depends on a variety of factors that include softer issues such as the quality of life that professionals can have in the place where the IFC is located.

- *Avoidance of excessive taxation:* Corporate and personal taxes play a role in determining the cost and profitability of financial firms. Excessive taxation can deter financial firms from placing their business in a particular location. However, what level of taxation should be considered "excessive" is difficult to determine.

- *High-quality infrastructure:* Having robust market infrastructure is key, including trading platforms that are appropriately linked to clearing, settlement, and custody services. All these services also depend on the availability of high-quality support infrastructure such as electricity and communications.

- *Reasonable operational costs:* Personnel costs are usually the largest expense component of investment banks, although there are other important costs such as real estate. The costs structure varies between different cities.

- *Openness to foreign entry:* Existing global IFCs have a strong foreign presence. Furthermore, such foreign presence can bring high-quality expertise to the IFC. Thus, it is important that the laws of the country do not impede the flow of talent.

- *Favorable time zone:* Although IFCs can compete across time zones, certain activities naturally must be done within a favorable time zone. This is particularly the case for trading.

- *Stable political and economic conditions:* Research has found that financial centers tend to prosper when their hinterlands are buoyant.

Meeting these requirements is not a realistic proposition for most ECA countries. Thus, a country that is committed to becoming an IFC needs to evaluate itself against the core attributes listed above and determine the type of measures that could help it to address weaknesses. Even with strong commitment, success is highly uncertain, because the advantages of scale are self-reinforcing: new business tends to go to the already established IFCs, so it is hard for new IFCs to gain traction. There has to be a clear advantage to attract companies and investors from the established IFCs. Efforts to become an IFC should be undertaken with caution because they can entail additional costs that might not be necessary for domestic market development. Nevertheless, most of the key attributes of an IFC are important also for the development of a domestic market. Thus, progress made in connection with the establishment of an IFC would likely benefit the development of the domestic market.

In conclusion, neither regional integration across ECA nor becoming an IFC is a likely path to capital market development for most ECA countries. Instead, it is essential to focus on establishing efficient capital markets that can serve primarily domestic investors.

SPOTLIGHT 4 *(continued)*

Notes

1. On September 30, 2015, the European Commission adopted an action plan setting out 20 key measures to achieve a true single market for capital in Europe. See http://ec.europa.eu/finance/capital-markets-union /index_en.htm.
2. For example, countries with strong expectations to join the European Union should be mindful of the regulatory framework for capital markets at the European Union level and try as much as possible to base their own regulatory approaches on such framework in order to facilitate future integration.

3. The following is taken from Elliott (2011) and Jarvis (2009).

References

Elliott, Douglas. 2011. "Building a Global Financial Center in Shanghai: Observations from Other Centers." Brookings, Washington, DC.

Jarvis, Darryl S. L. 2009. "Race for Money: International Financial Centres in Asia." Lee Kuan Yew School of Public Policy Research Paper LKYSPP09-012-CA, National University of Singapore, June 3.

Household Saving Behavior in Europe and Central Asia

We asked the keeper of a small shop in Tashkent, Uzbekistan, if he had enough savings to provide for him and his family if he got sick or was too old to work. He responded, "Why would I have to save? I have my family to support me!"[1] The propensity of people to save depends on many factors, including cultural traditions, perceived stability of the economy and the financial system, various saving options and their expected rate of return, size of publicly and privately provided pension systems, financial sector regulations, and financial literacy, among other factors. Across Europe and Central Asia (ECA) countries and periods of time, some factors are more important than others in influencing household saving behavior. However, there is one common outcome that could be observed across ECA. Despite ECA's relatively high level of income, the share of households there that save is among the lowest of all world regions.

This chapter analyzes the determinants of saving in ECA. The chapter is divided in two sections. The first uses the 2014 Global Financial Inclusion Database (Global Findex),[2] new worldwide data on financial literacy, and a range of secondary sources to provide an overview of saving behavior in ECA. The second section uses a unique data set (OeNB Euro Survey) to provide a more detailed view of saving behavior in a subset of ECA countries focusing on financial inclusion in savings and their allocation across a broader range of formal financial tools than considered by Global Findex.[3] The section conducts analysis of the main determinants of the saving behavior in Central Europe and the Western Balkans to inform policy initiatives to boost household savings in the region.

Main messages:

- The share of people in ECA who save is low compared with other world regions whereas saving informally in cash is widespread. This is particularly true among the bottom 40 percent of income earners but is also widespread among the top 60. Among those who do save, bank deposits are the main form of formal saving, and diversification across different instruments is very low, apart from saving in foreign currency.

- Mistrust in banks is widespread in Emerging ECA and discourages people from saving formally. Trust in deposit safety is higher than trust in banks. Although deposit insurance has improved, concerns about the stability of banks prevail.

- Policies could increase adoption and use of formal savings accounts. International experience shows that promoting increased competition to lower account fees, providing incentives for opening an account, and paying wages and social benefits through bank accounts could nudge more people to start saving formally. Financial education programs can have an uncertain impact and have a better chance of working if targeted and tailored to country context.

What Characterizes the Saving Behavior in ECA, and Which Policies Can Boost Savings?

Saving is low in ECA: only about 38 percent of adults hold savings compared with the developing world average of 54 percent (figure 4.1). And just 8 percent of adults hold their savings in formal financial institutions such as banks; in the developing world, only the Middle East and North Africa has a lower rate. Although the region's population is rapidly aging, just 12 percent of adults save for old age. The shares of adults with savings vary dramatically within the region, from a low of 13 percent in Georgia to above 50 percent in some countries of Central Asia with mandated savings.

Only about 38 percent of adults hold savings compared with the developing world average of 54 percent. And just 8 percent of adults hold their savings in formal financial institutions such as banks; in the developing world, only the Middle East and North Africa has a lower rate.

The share of adults who save money varies significantly by income. In ECA, 32 percent of adults living in the poorest two-fifths of households save money, compared to 43 percent of adults in richer households. ECA's 11 percentage point income gap is significant but slightly smaller than the developing world average of 16 percentage points, and about half the size of the gap in South Asia. Nevertheless, certain countries in the region suffer from severe inequalities. For example, in Bulgaria, Georgia, and Montenegro, wealthier adults are twice as likely to save money as poorer adults. Yet in other countries—notably Kosovo and Tajikistan—there is virtually no income gap in saving, with about one-third of both rich and poor adults saving money.

Men are more likely to save than women. About 41 percent of men in ECA save money, compared to 37 percent of women. This 4 percentage point gender gap is comparable to the developing world average of 5 percentage points. A few countries in the region, including Belarus, Kazakhstan, Moldova, and Montenegro, have achieved relative gender parity in savings. Other countries struggle with

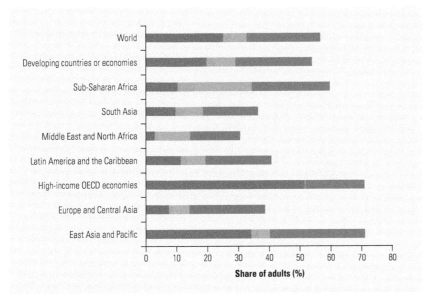

FIGURE 4.1

Worldwide, few adults save formally

Saving behavior by region

- ■ Saved formally
- ▥ Saved both formally and semiformally
- ▨ Saved semiformally
- ■ Saved using other methods only

Source: Global Findex database.
Note: OECD = Organisation for Economic Co-operation and Development.

sizable gender gaps, for example 11 percentage points in Kosovo and 9 percentage points in Tajikistan.

Formal saving, like total savings, differs by income and gender. About 4 percent of adults in the poorest two-fifths of households use formal saving methods, compared to 11 percent of richer households. Bulgaria struggles with the largest income gap, with 33 percent of adults in the richest households using formal saving methods, about eight times as many as at the bottom of the ladder. About 10 percent of men save formally, compared to 6 percent of women.

Some nonformal saving is carried out through semiformal organizations. About 8 percent of ECA adults use formal saving methods, and 6 percent use semiformal methods exclusively (figure 4.1). For example, in the Kyrgyz Republic, where about 10 percent of adults have semiformal savings (figure 4.2), many adults provide their savings to mutual aid groups, which take out microloans against their members' savings. However, the most popular saving method in ECA, reported by 24 percent of adults, is to simply store cash ("Saved using other methods only" in figures 4.1 and 4.2). This practice is especially common in Turkmenistan, where it is used by 54 percent of adults, and in Ukraine, where the figure is 30 percent.

Painful memories of bank failures and currency devaluations make cash, including foreign currency cash, a popular option. Adults in many former Soviet economies saw their savings vanish during a wave of inflation that accompanied the transition to a market economy (Caprio and Honohan 2010). Around the same time, bank failures in several countries—including Bulgaria, the Czech Republic, Romania, and the Baltic states—crippled growth and wiped out household investments (Steinherr 1997). Coupe (2011) examines survey data from Ukraine and reports that more than half of respondents use cash to save, while those who distrust banks are 10 to 15 percentage points more likely to keep all their savings in cash. The picture is similar in Central Asia. A recent study by the Kazakhstani

FIGURE 4.2

In ECA, few adults save through formal financial institutions

Saving behavior in select ECA economies

- ■ Saved formally
- ▨ Saved both formally and semiformally
- ▨ Saved semiformally
- ■ Saved using other methods only
- ■ Did not save

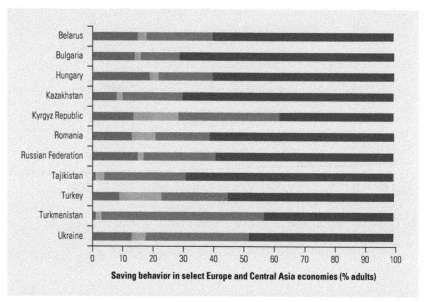

Saving behavior in select Europe and Central Asia economies (% adults)

Source: Global Findex database.

government found that 44 percent of the population prefers to keep their savings at home, because of weak confidence in banks and fear of currency devaluations (Interfax-Kazakhstan News Agency 2015). Stix (2013) and Brown and Stix (2015) show that memories of previous economic crises during transition have an impact on trust in the financial system and affect the demand for informal versus formal savings, as well as the currency denomination of savings.

On average, the saving behavior of most adults in the region does not appear to take into account their need for retirement income. The 2014 Global Findex Survey reports that only 12 percent save for old age, roughly half the rate in developing regions overall. Low-income adults are most likely to face savings shortfalls upon retirement, with just 8 percent of those in the poorest two-fifths of households saving for old age, roughly half the rate of those in richer households. However, countries with large, aging populations do seem to prioritize saving for old age. The share of adults who save for old age is 22 percent in Belarus, 18 percent in Hungary, and 15 percent in the Russian Federation. But in countries with relatively youthful populations, saving for retirement is relatively uncommon. Just 5 percent of adults in the Kyrgyz Republic, and only about 10 percent in Albania and Turkey, save for old age. Overall, there is a need to boost retirement savings in the ECA region.

The region's low formal saving may also increase vulnerability to shocks and complicate the recovery from the low-growth performance since the financial crisis. Low formal saving correlates to low national savings rates. For ECA as a whole, a 1.0 percentage point decrease in the share of adults who save at a financial institution is associated with about a 0.6 percentage point fall in the national savings rate. Aging populations, declining revenues, and depleted pensions have policy makers scrambling for ways to care for the elderly. During a period of strong growth spanning the late 1990s and early 2000s, a number of countries in the region abandoned or complemented

> Low-income adults are most likely to face savings shortfalls upon retirement, with just 8 percent of those in the poorest two-fifths of households saving for old age, roughly half the rate of those in richer households.

government-funded pay-as-you-go pensions by adopting mandatory, privately funded programs (Rudolph and Price 2013). These reforms were partially or totally reversed in some economies later on, but soaring debts, shriveled tax bases, and low returns on pension fund assets mean that pensioners will have to work longer and collect fewer benefits (see spotlight 5).

There Are Policies to Encourage Formal Saving

Globally, five key factors impede saving in poor households.[4] Transaction costs—including account fees, paperwork requirements, and distance to service providers—deter adoption of bank accounts. Second, lack of trust in financial institutions and regulatory barriers such as know-your-customer requirements also prevent poor households from saving through banks. A third factor is lack of information or low financial literacy. Finally, social constraints—such as pressure to lend money to relatives—and behavioral biases like impetuous spending habits are also found to weaken saving behavior.

There are interventions of financial firms and public policy that could help boost saving and savings rates, such as reducing account fees, shortening the distance—including the virtual one—to service providers, and linking savings accounts to specific purposes (investment, purchase of durable goods) that are relevant to potential savers. Commitment savings accounts—which limit users' access to funds until a specific date or goal has been reached—usually have adoption rates of about 20 to 30 percent (Karlan, Ratan, and Zinman 2014). In the Philippines, 28 percent of women who were offered such an account accepted, and users' average savings balances increased by 82 percent after one year (Ashraf, Karlan, and Yin 2006). Similar interventions can be used for pension savings. Automatically including workers in a direct deposit to an individual pension plan (unless they opt out) leads to much higher participation than if workers must affirmatively sign up for the plan. In the United States, setting automatic enrollment as the default option for 401(k) programs increased participation by 50 percent (Klapper and Singer 2014).

Moving wage payments and government social benefit payments into accounts can also encourage formal saving while reducing the number of unbanked individuals. About half of adults in ECA are unbanked, according to the 2014 Global Findex Survey. About 15 percent of these adults receive government wages or government social payments in cash, and an additional 15 percent receive private sector wages in cash. Digitizing agricultural payments provides another opportunity: about 16 percent of adults in the region receive cash payments for livestock or produce.

The link between financial literacy and saving is tenuous. The new S&P Global FinLit Survey[5] shows that adults who use financial services are more likely to be financially literate. According to the survey's definition, 30 percent of adults in ECA are financially literate—about the same as the average in developing economies (28 percent) and worldwide (33 percent). Financial literacy rates vary dramatically within the region, from 54 percent in Hungary to 14 percent in Albania. About half of ECA adults who use formal savings are financially literate, compared to 28 percent of adults who do not use formal savings. But there is no significant difference in financial literacy between adults who save for old age and those who do not.

Together, the 2014 Global Findex and S&P Global FinLit Survey present a sobering picture. In Bulgaria, for example, nearly 90 percent of adults don't save for old age, and about 70 percent of them are financially illiterate; in Romania, the numbers are 85 percent and 80 percent, respectively. Increasing the financial skills of these adults might lead to smarter investment decisions.

Financial literacy rates vary dramatically within the region, from 54 percent in Hungary to 14 percent in Albania.

Karlan et al. (2014) argue that the causal link between low knowledge and undersaving "looks increasingly weak," but they do suggest that targeted interventions focused on particular behaviors, such as savings account adoption, can have positive results. In a meta-analysis of 188 papers, Miller et al. (2014) conclude that financial literacy programs can increase savings, but they emphasize that the small size of the sample and lack of comparability between studies make this finding highly tentative. Lusardi and Mitchell (2014) observe that financially literate adults are more likely to plan for retirement and accumulate greater retirement wealth when exposed to targeted financial literacy programs. Considering that low financial literacy has been correlated with missing profitable investment opportunities (Lusardi and Mitchell 2014), policy makers could consider programs aimed at helping these adults get the most out of their savings.

Policy makers should be careful before investing too much even into targeted financial literacy programs. They should first carefully also consider other policy options and use focus groups to test the program design and impact before launching the programs at their full scale. Here, learning by doing could apply to both the content of financial literacy programs and the learning about which policy designs work best in the context of a country and targeted group.

To sum up, both formal and total saving are low in ECA compared to other developing regions. Expanding formal savings—especially among the elderly—is critical to the region's ability to recover from the low-growth performance after the financial crisis, increase investment, and improve retirement income, particularly given the lack of fiscal space in many countries. Although low formal savings is largely driven by lack of trust in financial institutions, studies suggest several policies that could increase adoption and use of savings accounts.

What Drives Saving Behavior in Emerging ECA?

This section provides a more detailed analysis of the determinants of saving and savings allocation, based on the OeNB Euro Survey conducted by the Austrian central bank since 2007 on a regular basis as a repeated cross-sectional survey in 10 Central European and Western Balkan countries (see appendixes E and F).[6] Elements of this analysis are applicable to the region as a whole because of the common experience of transition from planned to market economies.

Household Savings Are Low in Central Europe and the Western Balkans

Among the 10 sample ECA countries, the share of individuals who save varies from just below 80 percent in the former Yugoslav Republic of Macedonia to

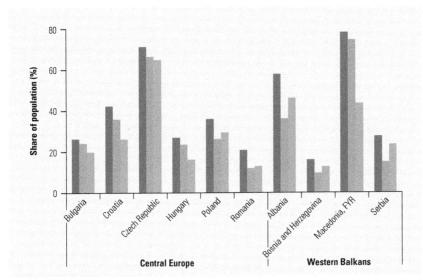

FIGURE 4.3
Participation in saving varies considerably among the sample of 10 Emerging ECA countries

■ Any savings
▩ Formal savings
▨ Informal savings

Source: OeNB Euro Survey 2012–13.
Note: All percentages are weighted by sampling weights.

below 20 percent in Bosnia and Herzegovina (figure 4.3). In Central Europe more individuals save through formal financial institutions than informally, whereas in the Western Balkans a higher percentage of individuals save through informal means.

The Drivers of Private Saving Are Diverse

A relatively small body of empirical research has investigated the main determinants of aggregate consumption and saving patterns across countries. The recent, most comprehensive study by Grigoli, Herman, and Schmidt-Hebbel (2014), which covers 165 countries from 1981 to 2012, shows that private saving rates are persistent and driven by income levels, past and expected income growth, inflation, foreign borrowing, the old-age dependency ratio, urbanization, and public saving. Similarly, among our 10 countries, private saving is positively correlated with gross domestic product (GDP) per capita, old-age dependency, and credit growth, and negatively correlated with inflation (table 4.1). In addition, private saving is negatively correlated with spending on social safety nets, which could be interpreted as evidence that better social safety nets reduce (precautionary) saving. However, these results are based on only 10 observations and should not be overinterpreted.

The Global Economic Crisis Reduced Household Savings

Households in Central Europe and the Western Balkans were hit much harder by the global economic crisis than those in Western Europe (EBRD 2011). As a consequence, households' ability to save declined between 2008 and 2013 (figure 4.4, panel a). Furthermore, 43 percent of households had to reduce the amount set aside for savings, and a quarter of households tapped into savings or sold

TABLE 4.1 Spearman Rank Correlation of Saving Determinants

	Household savings	GDP per capita	Inflation	Old-age dependency	Public pension spending	Social security contribution	Coverage social protection	Credit/ GDP	Credit growth
Household savings	1								
GDP per capita	0.20	1							
Inflation	−0.31	−0.20	1						
Old-age dependency	0.42	0.55	0.00	1					
Public pension spending	−0.43	0.56	0.32	0.03	1				
Social security contribution	−0.10	0.69	−0.37	0.26	0.52	1			
Coverage social protection	−0.36	0.55	0.18	0.96*	0.43	0.37	1		
Credit/GDP	−0.07	0.21	−0.63*	0.02	0.20	0.31	0.14	1	
Credit growth	0.25	−0.12	−0.25	−0.08	−0.23	−0.67	−0.43	0.35	1

Sources: OeNB Euro Survey 2012–13; World Bank Development Indicators (http://data.worldbank.org/data-catalog/world-development -indicators). Household savings denotes the percentage of individuals with any savings based on the Euro Survey question.
* Statistically significant at 10 percent confidence level or better.

FIGURE 4.4 Households' ability to save and stock of savings were reduced by the global economic crisis

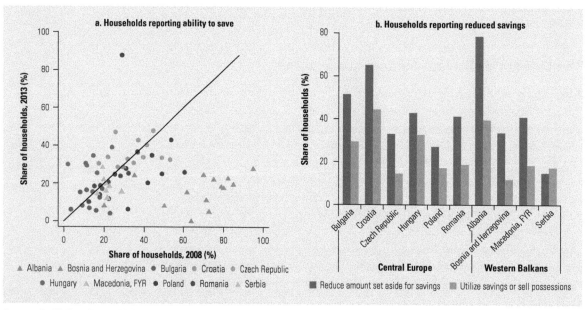

Sources: OeNB Euro Survey 2012–13.
Note: Panel a shows the within-country regional averages (there are multiple regions within each country) of the percentage of households who report "currently being able to save" in fall 2008 and fall 2013. Panel b reports the percentage of households who report they had to "reduce the amount set aside for savings" or "utilize savings or sell possessions" in response to the global financial crisis.

possessions because of the crisis (figure 4.4, panel b). These findings confirm the conclusion by the European Bank for Reconstruction and Development (EBRD) that the macroeconomic environment exerts a strong impact on households in Central Europe and the Western Balkans.

Cash and Bank Deposits Are the Main Saving Instruments

Theoretical models of household investment behavior predict that all households should participate in all financial markets and thus hold a diversified portfolio that includes risky financial assets (Panizza 2015). Empirical evidence on actual investment behavior, including investment in risky assets, is scarce and mainly limited to high-income countries. Guiso and Sodini (2013) gather evidence on direct and indirect stock holding for 12 countries; more recently the Household Finance and Consumption Survey in the euro area collected new data on the saving behavior of households in 15 euro area countries.[7]

In Central Europe and the Western Balkans, among those individuals who save (40 percent on average), an equal percentage of households have informal savings (74.6 percent) and bank savings (74.1 percent). The very high percentage of informal savings is mostly in the form of (foreign currency) cash, a feature of households' saving behavior in transition economies that has been documented and analyzed in depth by previous research (Stix 2013).

The high percentage of informal savings could imply that access to banks is low. Savings are positively correlated with account ownership, as expected (see also table F.1 in appendix F). However, with the exception of Albania (and FYR Macedonia) the percentage of account holders is (significantly) higher than the percentage of savers (figure 4.5).

Current accounts or savings deposits are the predominant form of formal savings (figure 4.6). Contractual retirement savings are held by 23 percent of savers or 9 percent of households, well below the 33 percent average in the euro area (Guiso and Sodini 2013). In line with the well-known puzzle of why individuals

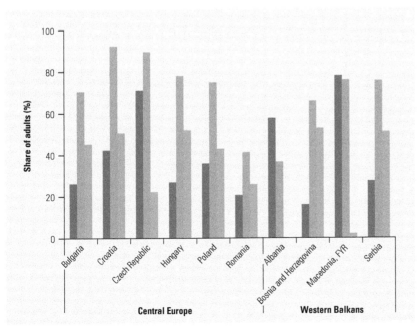

FIGURE 4.5
The share of adults who save is generally much lower than the share with an account

- ■ Any savings
- ▨ Account at financial institution
- ▨ Account but no savings

Source: OeNB Euro Survey 2012–13.
Note: All percentages are weighted by sampling weights.

FIGURE 4.6 Participation in saving instruments is diverse across the 10 countries

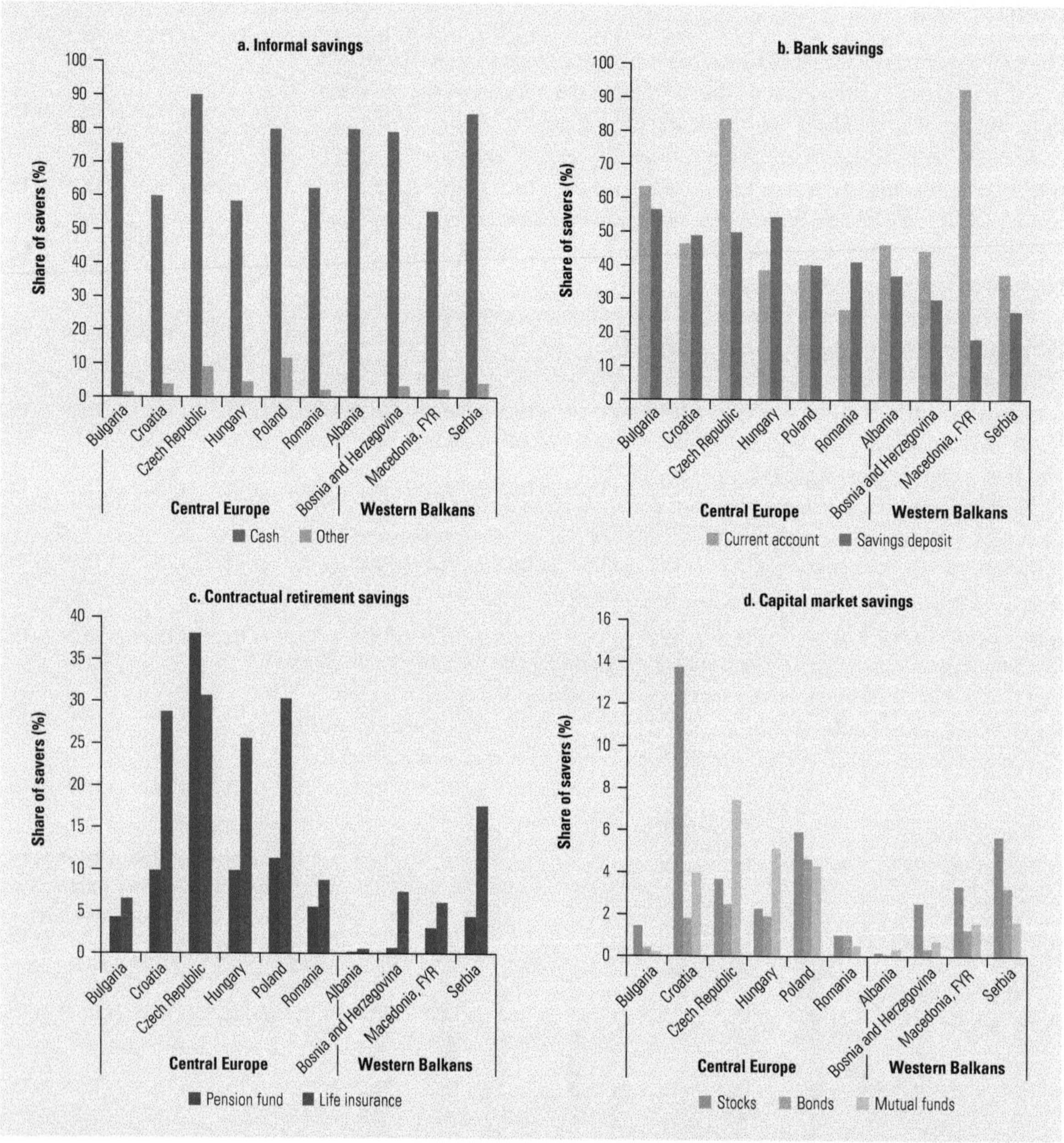

Source: OeNB Euro Survey 2012–13.
Note: Figures show the percentage of savers who save using the respective saving instrument. All percentages are weighted by sampling weights.

invest less in stock markets than anticipated by theoretical models, less than 3 percent of households and 7 percent of savers hold capital market savings. Capital markets remain underdeveloped in most ECA countries, and proposals for integration across the region or the investment in efforts to become an international financial center may face some headwinds (see spotlight 4).

The shares of different saving instruments vary considerably across countries. Less than 40 percent of savers in Serbia save with banks; but, in Bulgaria, the Czech Republic, and FYR Macedonia, the percentage is as much as 90 percent. The cross-country differences in pension funds or life insurance participation range from below 1 percent of savers in Albania to above 30 percent of savers in the Czech Republic. Finally, less than 1 percent of savers in Albania invest in stocks, bonds, or mutual funds compared to nearly 14 percent in Croatia.

Diversification of Saving Instruments Is Limited, but Foreign Currency Holdings Are High

On average, savers hold 1.36 formal saving instruments (figure 4.7, panel a). The Czech Republic has the highest level of diversification whereas Albania, Bosnia and Herzegovina, Romania, and Serbia are significantly below the average.

As in many transition economies, the share of foreign currency savings deposits is high. On average, 42 percent of savings deposits and 45 percent of cash are denominated in foreign currency. However, the range is high. In some countries, for instance Serbia, it is about 90 percent. As longer time series based on aggregate data show, the share of foreign currency denominated deposits increased strongly in Southeastern Europe and the Western Balkans during the financial crises of the 1990s and has since remained persistently high. In most of Central

FIGURE 4.7 Diversification of saving instruments is low, but foreign currency holdings are high

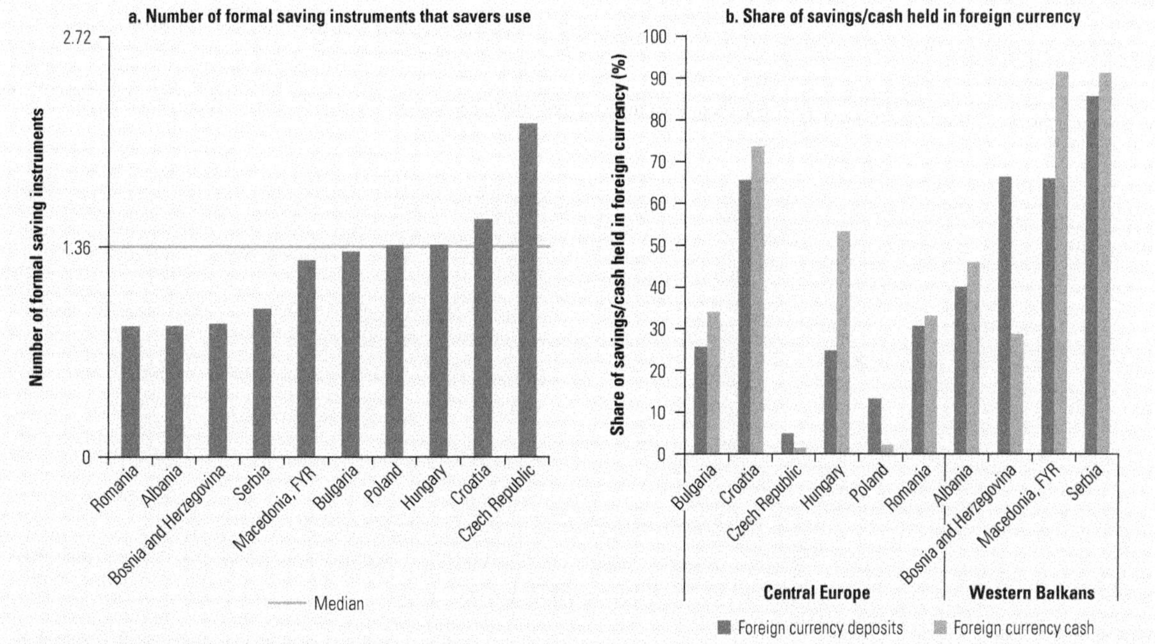

Source: OeNB Euro Survey 2012–13.

BOX 4.1   An Econometric Model of Saving

We relate the indicators of saving behavior $S_{i,c}$ of individual i in country c to household characteristics X, controlling for country-level determinants by including interacted country and survey wave fixed effects (α_{cw}):

$$S_{i,c} = \alpha_{cw} + \beta_1 X_i + \varepsilon_{i,cw}. \qquad \text{(B4.1.1)}$$

Given that a large fraction of households do not save, our regression might suffer from selection bias (Palia, Qi, and Wu 2014). Following Shum and Faig (2006), we exclude households that do not have sufficient funds to save. We estimate probit models and calculate average marginal effects for participation in saving and saving instruments for each of the following dependent variables: any savings (based on the entire sample), formal savings, savings in cash only, savings in bank accounts, contractual savings, capital market savings, and more

than one formal saving instrument, based on the sample of savers. Standard errors account for clustering at the primary sampling unit and time level.

We check for the robustness of our results by estimating a Heckman selection model where we jointly estimate the probability of having savings and the probability of holding specific asset categories, following Allen et al. (2014). We further conduct robustness checks by including control variables step by step instead of jointly. To check that our results are not driven by a particular country, we repeat estimations dropping one country at a time. Finally, we ensure that our dependent variables do not capture insignificant savings by using the information from the survey question on the ranking of saving instruments in terms of amounts, and repeat estimations only including up to three saving instruments.

Europe, the share of foreign currency denominated deposits is much lower and has been declining (Brown and Stix 2015).

What Further Insights Can Be Gained by Analyzing Saving Determinants through an Econometric Model?

In order to analyze the saving determinants, we use an econometric model to explain what household characteristics are related to the probability of saving and the choice of saving instruments (box 4.1). The issues addressed through the econometric model include the main differences in the saving decisions between households in the bottom 40 percent and top 60 percent of the income distribution, and whether the limited use of formal bank and capital market saving products is due to the lack of access to or trust in the financial system. The main regression results, where all control variables enter jointly, are provided in appendix G.

In Contrast to the Early Transition Period, the Wealth-Age Saving Profile Is Now Similar to That of the Advanced Economies

The life-cycle hypothesis implies a hump-shaped wealth-age profile (savings rise in the early adult years, reach a maximum at some point, and then decline during retirement).

Early analyses did not confirm, or found only limited evidence, that savings in transition economies followed the hump-shaped relationship with age that is often found in advanced economies and assumed by the life-cycle hypothesis. The failure to confirm the life-cycle hypothesis was attributed to the high level of macroeconomic instability during transition (Denizer, Wolf, and Ying 2002; Leszkiewicz-Kedzior and Welfe 2012). Our results, however, do indicate a hump-shaped relationship between age and savings, suggesting that the differences in household savings between ECA and nontransition regions may be declining.

Income and Wealth Are More Associated with Saving than with Account Ownership

Individuals in the bottom 40 percent of the income distribution are on average 12 percentage points less likely to have any savings and 10 percentage points less likely to have a financial account than are richer households (figure 4.8). The effect of income is particularly strong in Albania and Croatia (almost 20 percentage points) whereas it is the weakest in Serbia, where the impact of income on the probability of having savings is not significant. Croatia and the Czech Republic stand out as examples where income strongly increases the probability of saving but not the probability of account ownership. By contrast, for Albania and Romania income exerts a stronger impact on account ownership than on saving.

Home ownership is positively associated with the probability of household saving in only some countries. However, households that own real estate in addition to their home are more likely to have savings. If ownership of other real estate is interpreted as an indicator of wealth, then these results are in line with results from the euro area (Arrondel et al. 2014).

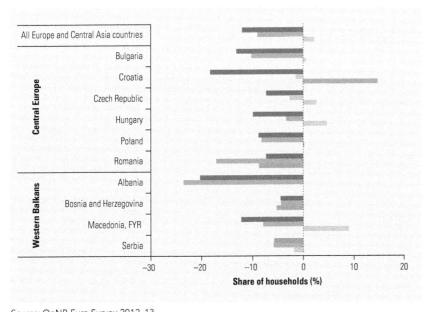

FIGURE 4.8

Households in the bottom 40 percent are less likely than richer households to save or have accounts

■ Any savings
■ Account
▨ Account but no savings

Source: OeNB Euro Survey 2012–13.
Note: Average marginal impact on saving of being in the bottom 40 percent, from country probit models. The models also control for additional socioeconomic characteristics and region/time fixed effects. Lighter bars indicate that coefficients are insignificant.

Income, Remittances, Receipt of Income in Euros, and Real Estate Ownership Affect Saving

Conditional on having any savings, households in the bottom 40 percent are 5 percentage points less likely to have any formal savings (6 percent of the sample mean), 4 percentage points more likely to save in cash (25 percent of the sample mean), and 7 percentage points less likely to save at banks (9 percent of the sample mean). For contractual retirement savings (such as private pensions and annuities) and capital market savings, income does not have a significant effect; very few households in the bottom 40 percent have any of these saving instruments. Some of these results, however, are driven by individual countries that have very different relationships between the income and the dependent variables.[8] Income is a significant determinant of the share of contractual retirement savings in all countries except the Czech Republic. Also, income has an insignificant impact on cash savings if Albania is excluded, perhaps indicating that the lack of formal savings in Albania is significantly driven by transaction costs whereas the results in other countries may reflect lack of trust (Stix 2013).

Remittances appear to be an important determinant of savings; recipients of remittances are 13 percentage points more likely to have savings than households that do not receive remittances—a result that is particularly important for the Western Balkans, where some countries have a significant inflow of remittances.

Households that receive income denominated in euros are 11 percentage points more likely to save; about 5 percent of households receive some income in euros, and 3 percent receive a regular income in euros. Conditional on having savings, those with regular income in euros are more likely to save in cash, which is probably related to the high percentage of foreign currency cash savings (see figure 4.7). Finally, ownership of the primary residence does not influence the choice of saving instruments. However, ownership of other real estate increases the probability of investments in capital markets and diversification of formal saving instruments, probably because this variable is an indicator of wealth.

Considerable Differences in Saving Behavior Exist among Households in the Bottom 40 Percent

Savings among the bottom 40 percent differ by education, labor market status, and real estate ownership (see appendix G for estimation results). In general, individuals with tertiary education are more likely to save, with a substantial variation of the impact of tertiary education on savings between countries ranging from 11 percentage points in Croatia up to 27 percentage points in Albania. Savers in the bottom 40 percent with tertiary education are more likely to have bank savings than less-educated savers in the bottom 40 percent.

Self-employed and retired savers in the bottom 40 percent are more likely to save informally; the former result likely is due to the nature of self-employment. By contrast, employed savers in the bottom 40 percent are more likely to save formally, but less likely to hold contractual savings.

Ownership of the primary residence does not affect the choice of saving instruments by individuals in the bottom 40 percent. However, there appears to be a substitution effect between investment in real and financial assets: individuals in the bottom 40 percent who own real estate other than the primary residence are 8 percentage points less likely to save (equal to 17 percent of the sample mean) compared to those who do not own other real estate. This substitution effect between real and financial assets also holds for the choice of saving instrument: households in the bottom 40 percent who own other real estate are less likely to have formal savings, and more likely to save informally, than households in the bottom 40 percent who do not own other real estate.

Trust Is an Important Determinant of Saving

Trust has been found to have an important influence on the financial decisions of households (see, for example, Guiso, Sapienza, and Zingales 2008; Balloch, Nicolae, and Philip 2015; Delis and Mylonidis 2015; and Stix 2013). To ensure that trust is not a proxy for other determinants of saving instrument participation, we control for risk aversion and individual expectations (following Guiso, Sapienza, and Zingales 2008). Risk-averse individuals are 4 percentage points more likely to save. Those who think that the economic situation of their country will improve are 5 percentage points more likely to save and 3 percentage points more likely to hold formal savings—at banks or in pension funds or life insurance. The Euro Survey finds that trust in both foreign and domestic banks is low compared to that in nontransition economies.[9] However, trust in the safety of deposits, and in the stability of the financial system, is higher than trust in banks (figure 4.9).

Further regression analysis shows that trust in deposit safety and financial stability are correlated with trust in government. However, the correlation between trust in government and financial stability is relatively weak, whereas the correlation between financial stability and trust in the European Union (EU) is stronger. This may indicate that respondents are aware on the one hand of possible spillover effects from instability in the euro area and on the other hand believe that the EU institutions have a stabilizing cross-border effect.

Respondents in Central Europe and the Western Balkans who trust their government or the EU are 3 percentage points more likely to save (see table G.2 in appendix G). Trust in government does not affect the choice of saving instruments. However, those who trust the EU are 2 percentage points more likely to invest in capital markets, a sizeable effect compared to the sample average of 8 percent. Households in the bottom 40 percent who trust the government have a lower propensity to save than those who do not trust the government. Unfortunately, we do not have information on which households receive government benefits, which would improve our understanding of this effect.

Trust in financial institutions has a strong effect on savings and the choice of saving instruments (see appendix G, table G.2). Individuals who trust deposit safety and those who trust the stability of the financial system are 5 percentage points more likely to have savings, compared to a sample mean of 43 percent. Conditional on having savings, trust in deposit safety increases the probability of holding formal savings by 4 percentage points and the probability of saving at banks by 5 percentage points—an effect similar in magnitude to having secondary education. In line with Stix (2013), we find that trust in the safety of deposits decreases the probability of saving in cash by 3 percentage

Individuals who trust deposit safety and those who trust the stability of the financial system are 5 percentage points more likely to have savings, compared to a sample mean of 43 percent.

FIGURE 4.9

Trust in financial institutions is low in transition economies and does not vary significantly between the top 60 and bottom 40 percent of income earners

- ■ Trust domestic banks, top 60
- ▨ Trust domestic banks, bottom 40
- ▨ Trust foreign banks, top 60
- ▨ Trust foreign banks, bottom 40
- ■ Trust in safety of deposits, top 60
- ▨ Trust in safety of deposits, bottom 40
- ■ Financial system is stable, top 60
- ▨ Financial system is stable, bottom 40

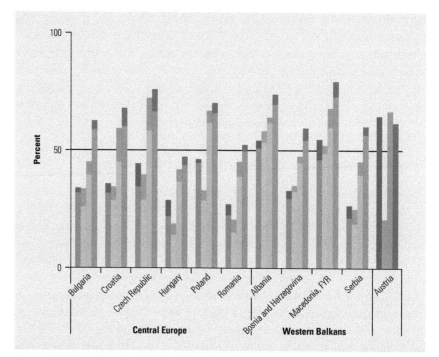

Source: OeNB Euro Survey 2012–13.
Note: Austria is used as a comparator country with no distinction between the top 60 and bottom 40 percent of income earners.

points. Interestingly, those who trust financial stability are more likely to invest in life insurance or pension funds (4 percentage points) and stocks, bonds, or mutual funds (2 percentage points). Compared to the sample means of 24 percent and 8 percent, the effect is sizeable, although not as large as that reported for the United States. Trust in the stability of the financial system has the largest effect on diversification of saving instruments: 6 percentage points, or a third of the sample mean.

A more detailed analysis including the indicators of trust separately in the regression equation shows that trust in banks (whether foreign or domestic) has the strongest impact on whether respondents hold any savings. The decision to save formally is influenced by trust in domestic banks and trust in deposit safety. By contrast, lack of trust in deposit safety increases the probability of saving in cash only. Trust in the stability of the financial system has the strongest impact on the decision to hold nonbank formal savings and to diversify savings.

Finally, there is no significant difference between the impact of trust in financial institutions on the choice of saving instruments for the bottom 40 percent and top 60 percent of households (appendix G, table G.2).

The Experience of Banking Crises during Transition and Lack of Trust in Financial Institutions Affect the Choice of Saving Instruments

Many countries in ECA went through economic and banking crises during transition from planned to market economies—the experience of which had an important impact on saving decisions (see also Beckmann, Scheiber, and Stix 2011;

FIGURE 4.10 **Trust in domestic banks and in the stability of the banking system are important influences on saving decisions**

Average marginal effect of trust in financial institutions on probability of having savings and saving instruments

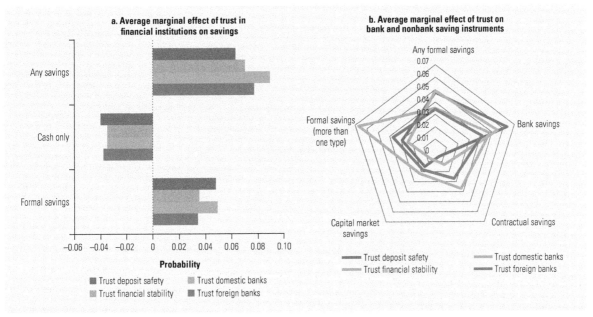

Source: OeNB Euro Survey 2012–13.
Note: Panel a shows the average marginal effect for each trust indicator on the respective saving instrument. Panel b shows the marginal effect on bank and nonbank saving instruments.

Stix 2013; and Brown and Stix 2015). Those who experienced a financial loss during transition are more likely to save, and conditional on having savings are more likely to save formally, in particular using contractual savings (3 percentage points compared to a sample mean of 24 percent) and capital market savings (4 percentage points compared to a sample mean of 8 percent). The effect on bank savings is only 4 percentage points, or 5 percent of the sample mean. This "preference" for nonbank formal savings is likely related to the experience of banking crises during the transition. Furthermore, individuals who experienced a banking crisis are 6 percentage points more likely than others to hold a diversified savings portfolio.

However, even after accounting for the experience of banking crises, trust in financial institutions has a strong and significant impact on participation in formal saving instruments and the choice between bank and nonbank formal savings. Lack of trust in the banking system—not only because of the experience of economic crisis during the transition—is an important reason for holding savings in the form of cash (figure 4.10, panel a). Trust in the stability of the financial system has the strongest impact on the decision to hold nonbank formal savings and to diversify savings (figure 4.10, panel b).

Unemployment Significantly Reduces the Probability of Having Savings or Owning an Account

In the euro area unemployment does not have a significant impact on saving, which, as Arrondel et al. (2014) argue, could be explained by the transitory and

FIGURE 4.11
The unemployed are less likely to save or own accounts

■ Any savings
■ Account
■ Account but no savings

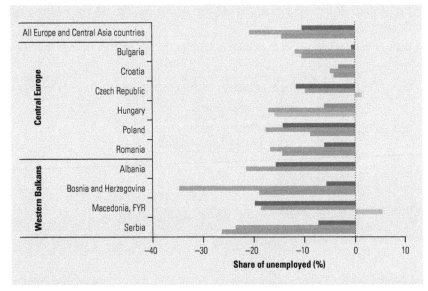

Source: OeNB Euro Survey 2012–13.
Note: Average marginal effect of unemployment on participation in savings, accounts, and accounts without savings from probit models by country. The models also control for additional socioeconomic characteristics and region-time fixed effects. Lighter bars indicate that coefficients are insignificant.

unexpected nature of unemployment. By contrast, the unemployed in Central European and Western Balkan countries are 10 percentage points less likely than employed workers to have savings, although there is considerable variation among countries (figure 4.11). In Bulgaria, Croatia, Hungary, and Romania, unemployment is not significantly correlated with the probability of having savings. By contrast, the unemployed are 21 percentage points less likely to have savings in FYR Macedonia (where the 28 percent unemployment rate is the highest in our sample). In FYR Macedonia and Poland, unemployment has a stronger negative effect on saving than does income. As our sample comprises only 10 countries, the variation is too small to analyze the effect of unemployment insurance in depth. Better social safety nets appear to be negatively associated with saving (table 4.1), although this may reflect both the receipt of social benefits and reduced saving (or asset liquidation) by the unemployed.

Unemployment exerts a stronger impact on account ownership than on saving (the unemployed are 21 percentage points less likely to have an account). The effect of unemployment is stronger for account ownership than for savings in all countries except the Czech Republic and FYR Macedonia. The strongest effect of unemployment on account ownership is observed in Bosnia and Herzegovina (35 percentage points). For Central Europe the impact of unemployment on account ownership is lower on average, and ranges between 5 percentage points in Croatia and 17 percentage points in Poland.

Unemployment Reduces the Share of Savings in Formal Instruments

Conditional on having savings, employed individuals are more likely to save formally. The effect is sizeable, at 5.3 percentage points or 24 percent of the sample mean. Employment also marginally increases the probability of capital market investment except in Albania, Bulgaria, and Romania.

Self-employed individuals are more likely to save and, if saving, more likely to save using life insurance or pension funds, or invest in stocks, bonds, or mutual funds. Albania is an exception: self-employed individuals in that country are more likely to be working in low-skilled jobs in comparison to the other nine countries and more likely to save in cash.

Physical Access Does Not Have a Strong Influence on Formal Savings

Globally, lack of physical access to banks impedes the adoption of formal savings (Karlan et al. 2014). However, bank branch density in Central Europe and the Western Balkans is high on average; less than 2 percent of households live more than 15 kilometers from the nearest bank, even though the distribution of bank branches varies greatly within countries (Beckmann, Reiter, and Stix, forthcoming). This would suggest that physical access to banks is not a significant constraint on formal savings. Indeed, after controlling for local economic activity (appendix G, table G.2), distance to a bank does not have an effect on participation in bank savings or on informal savings. There is some indication that households that are farther from a bank are more likely to use alternative formal savings, but the size of the effect is small.

Internet Access Is Related to the Composition of Savings, but Only for the Financially Literate

Poor households often face high costs from information barriers. Bogan (2008) argues that improvements in Internet access lowered transaction and information costs for stock market participation—estimating that the increased probability of participation due to overall improvements in Internet access was equivalent to U.S.$27,000 in additional household income. Glaser and Klos (2013) obtain similar results over a longer time horizon, employing instrumental variable techniques to address the endogeneity of Internet access. They argue that Internet diffusion lowers information costs and helps households to make better financial decisions. However, because early Internet adopters tend to have higher financial literacy, providing universal Internet access would not necessarily promote stock market participation.

In our sample of 10 countries, Internet access is significantly related to formal savings, in particular contractual and capital market savings, as well as diversification of formal savings. However, this does not imply that increasing Internet access would significantly promote formal savings. Even though we control for a long list of characteristics, including trust, risk aversion, and education, it is difficult to measure the independent impact of Internet access on savings. To investigate this, we follow Glaser and Klos (2013) and Liang and Guo (2015) in examining the impact of financial literacy and social interaction on the correlation between Internet access and savings. Although the impact of Internet access on savings is almost unchanged once indicators of financial literacy are included as independent variables (panel a of table G.5, appendix G), Internet access only increases the probability of holding contractual savings, capital market savings, and a diversified savings portfolio for financially literate individuals (panel b of table G.5).[10] Internet access does not have an effect on participation in bank savings or on the saving behavior of those who are financially illiterate.

Conclusion

There is ample scope for advancing household saving in Emerging ECA. The percentage of savers is low, particularly among households in the bottom 40 percent of the income distribution. Moreover, informal saving is widespread even among households in the top 60 percent. Formal savings mainly include bank deposits; participation in nonbank formal savings is very low. Diversification in terms of the number of saving instruments held by households is very low, and foreign currency savings are widespread.

Building on the policies to encourage formal savings outlined above, the more detailed analysis in the second section of this chapter bears some additional policy implications.

Improving physical access to banks is unlikely to increase bank savings, as the density of banks is already high. Although information on formal savings could be improved by increasing Internet access, this will affect the saving behavior of financially literate individuals only.

Mistrust in banks is widespread and has a significant negative impact on formal saving. However, trust in deposit safety is higher than trust in banks, suggesting that, although policies to improve deposit insurance have been successful, trust in the stability of individual banks remains weak. Improving trust in banks may take time as memories of prior crises remain fresh in people's minds and transparency remains a challenge. Furthermore, given that the overall trust in the stability of the financial system is higher than trust in banks, there is some indication of a substitution effect between bank savings and nonbank formal savings.

Notes

1. Based on World Bank informal interviews of businesses and individuals on the state of financial sector development in Central Asia, June 2015.
2. For more information, see Global Financial Inclusion (database), World Bank, Washington, DC, http://datatopics.worldbank.org/financialinclusion/.
3. For more information, see the Oesterreichische National Bank website, https://www.oenb.at/en/Monetary-Policy/Surveys/OeNB-Euro-Survey.html.
4. This typology is based on an exhaustive literature review by Karlan, Lakshimi Ratan, and Zinman (2014).
5. The new S&P Global FinLit Survey, based on survey data collected in 143 economies, provides unprecedented insight into financial numeracy and literacy skills of adults around the world. And, by identifying gaps in the financial knowledge of adults who save and do not save, this data could help policy makers design responses to the region's savings problem. The survey asked adults about four basic topics: risk diversification, inflation, interest, and compound interest. Adults who correctly answered at least 3 out of 4 topics were deemed financially literate for the purposes of the survey.

For more information, see https://www.spglobal.com/corporate-responsibility/global-financial-literacy-survey.

6. This includes six European Union member states that are not part of the euro area—Bulgaria, Croatia, the Czech Republic, Hungary, Poland, and Romania—and four (potential) candidate countries—Albania, Bosnia and Herzegovina, FYR Macedonia, and Serbia.

7. Information on the survey is available from the European Central Bank website. Although there is no direct link to download data, the data can be requested through the website: https://www.ecb.europa.eu/pub/economic-research/research-networks/html/researcher_hfcn.en.html.

8. We test for this by repeating the estimations, dropping one country at a time from the sample.

9. In seven out of ten countries, trust in domestic banks is higher than trust in foreign banks. See Knell and Stix (2015) for comparable indicators of trust in domestic banks, foreign banks, deposit safety, and financial stability.

10. Households may acquire information on saving products from neighbors. Including the percentage of respondents in the primary sampling unit who hold formal savings also does not affect the significance or magnitude of the "Internet effect."

References

Allen, F., E. Carletti, R. Cull, J. Qian, I. Senbet, and P. Valenzuela. 2014. "Improving Access to Banking—Evidence from Kenya." CEPR Discussion Paper 9840, Centre for Economic Policy Research, London.

Arrondel, L., L. Bartiloro, P. Fessler, P. Linder, T. Y. Mathä, C. Rampazzi, and P. Vermeulen. 2014. "How Do Households Allocate Their Assets? Stylised Facts from the Eurosystem Household Finance and Consumption Survey." European Central Bank Working Paper Series 1722, European Central Bank, Frankfurt, Germany.

Ashraf, N., D. Karlan, and W. Yin. 2006. "Tying Odysseus to the Mast: Evidence from a Commitment Savings Product in the Philippines." *Quarterly Journal of Economics* 121 (2): 635–72.

Balloch, A., A. Nicolae, and D. Philip. 2015. "Stock Market Literacy, Trust, and Participation." *Review of Finance* 19: 1925–63.

Beckmann, E., S. Reiter, and H. Stix. Forthcoming. "The Banking Landscape of Households in Central, Eastern and Southeastern Europe." *Focus on European Economic Integration.*

Beckmann, E., T. Scheiber, and H. Stix. 2011. "How the Crisis Affected Foreign Currency Borrowing in CESEE: Microeconomic Evidence and Policy Implications." *Focus on European Economic Integration* Q1/11: 25–43.

Bogan, V. 2008. "Stock Market Participation and the Internet." *Journal of Financial and Quantitative Analysis* 43: 191–212.

Brown, M., and H. Stix. 2015. "Euroization of Bank Deposits." *Economic Policy* 81: 95–139.

Caprio, G., Jr., and P. Honohan. 2010. "Banking Crises." In *The Oxford Handbook of Banking*, edited by A. N. Berger, P. Molyneux, and John O. S. Wilson. Oxford, U.K.: Oxford University Press.

Coupe, T. 2011. "Mattresses versus Banks—The Effect of Trust on Portfolio Composition." Kyiv School of Economics Discussion Paper No. 40, Kyiv, Ukraine.

Delis, M. D., and N. Mylonidis. 2015. "Trust, Happiness, and Households' Financial Decisions." *Journal of Financial Stability* 20: 82–92.

Denizer, C., H. Wolf, and Y. Ying. 2002. "Household Savings in Transition." *Journal of Comparative Economics* 30: 463–75.

EBRD (European Bank for Reconstruction and Development). 2011. *Transition Report 2011: Crisis and Transition—The People's Perspective*. London: EBRD.

Glaser, M., and A. Klos. 2013. "Causal Evidence on Internet Use and Stock Market Participation." University of Munich Working Paper.

Grigoli, F., A. Herman, and K. Schmidt-Hebbel. 2014. "World Saving." IMF Working Paper 14/204, International Monetary Fund, Washington, DC.

Guiso, L., P. Sapienza, and L. Zingales. 2008. "Trusting the Stock Market." *Journal of Finance* 63 (6): 2557–600.

Guiso, L., and P. Sodini. 2013. "Household Finance: An Emerging Field." Chapter 21 in *Handbook of the Economics of Finance*, Volume 2B, edited by G. M. Constantinides, M. Harris, and R. M. Stulz, 1397–532. Oxford, U.K. and Amsterdam: Elsevier.

Interfax-Kazakhstan News Agency. 2015. "Nearly Half of Kazakhs Prefer to Keep Savings at Home." July 22.

Karlan, D., A. Lakshimi Ratan, and J. Zinman. 2014. "Savings by and for the Poor: A Research Review and Agenda." *Review of Income and Wealth* 60 (1): 36–78.

Klapper, L., and D. Singer. 2014. *The Opportunities of Digitizing Payments*. Washington, DC: World Bank.

Knell, M., and H. Stix. 2015. "Trust in Banks during Normal and Crises Times—Evidence from Survey Data." *Economica* 82 (S1): 995–1020.

Leszkiewicz-Kedzior, K., and W. Welfe. 2012. "Consumption Function for Poland: Is the Life-Cycle Hypothesis Legitimate?" *Kredit I Bank* 48 (6): 6–15.

Liang, P., and S. Guo. 2015. "Social Interaction, Internet Access and Stock Market Participation—An Empirical Study in China." *Journal of Comparative Economics* 43 (4): 883–901.

Lusardi, A., and O. S. Mitchell. 2014. "The Economic Importance of Financial Literacy: Theory and Evidence." *Journal of Economic Literature* 52 (1): 5–44.

Miller, M., J. Reichelstein, C. Salas, and B. Zia. 2014. "Can You Help Someone Become Financially Capable? A Meta-Analysis of the Literature." Policy Research Working Paper 6745, World Bank, Washington, DC.

Palia, D., Y. Qi, and Y. Wu. 2014. "Heterogeneous Background Risks and Portfolio Choice: Evidence from Micro-level Data." *Journal of Money, Credit and Banking* 46 (8): 1687–720.

Panizza, Ugo. 2015 "Billions on the Sidewalk: Improving Savings by Reducing Investment Mistakes." Working Paper HEIDWP18-2015, Graduate Institute of International and Development Studies, International Economics Department, Geneva.

Rudolph, Heinz P., and William Joseph Price. 2013. *Reversal and Reduction, Resolution and Reform: Lessons from the Financial Crisis in Europe and Central Asia to Improve Outcomes from Mandatory Private Pensions*. Washington, DC: World Bank.

Shum, P., and M. Faig. 2006. "What Explains Household Stock Holdings?" *Journal of Banking and Finance* 30 (9): 2579–97.

Steinherr, Alfred. 1997. "Banking Reforms in Eastern European Countries." *Oxford Review of Economic Policy* 13 (2): 106–25.

Stix, H. 2013. "Why Do People Save in Cash? Distrust, Memories of Banking Crises, Weak Institutions and Dollarization." *Journal of Banking and Finance* 37 (11): 4087–106.

SPOTLIGHT 5
Developing Private Pension Schemes in Europe and Central Asia

Mandatory, funded private pension systems (pillar 2) can help ensure that workers have adequate income during retirement and can support a reduction in future obligations under public pension programs.[1] However, regulatory requirements and misguided strategies for creating private pension schemes have impeded these objectives.

Regulatory requirements limiting investment in "risky" assets have resulted in low returns and made it difficult for private pensions to provide adequate levels of retirement income. On average, 65 percent of investments by pension systems in Europe and Central Asia (ECA) are in low- or zero-return government securities or bank deposits (figure S5.1). Requirements that funds achieve a minimum rate of return or protect the principal value also have steered funds toward safer yet lower-growth investments. Instead of regulating minimum rates of return during the investment period, financial

authorities should ensure that *at the time of retirement* a worker's pension has obtained a minimum asset level to generate an acceptable pension. Such a guarantee at retirement, rather than setting a minimum rate of return on an annual basis, would allow pension funds to invest in higher-growth assets prior to a worker's retirement. The government could cover a portion of this guarantee, financed through an annual fee charged to pension funds.

Excessive reliance on domestic or regional investments, as opposed to investments in advanced countries, also has lowered pension fund returns. These policies may reflect concerns over currency risk if foreign investments must ultimately fund expenditures in domestic currency, or the desire to use pension funds to promote domestic growth. However, domestic corporate and government investments also can be high risk, and returns on domestic investments often have been lower than

FIGURE S5.1 Share of pension fund investments in safe assets is high in ECA

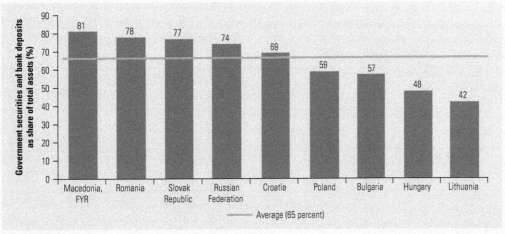

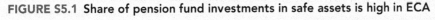

Source: FinStats.
Note: Includes all Europe and Central Asia countries with mandatory pension schemes and with adequate data.

SPOTLIGHT 5 *(continued)*

FIGURE S5.2 Pension fund management fees as a percent of total net assets are high in ECA

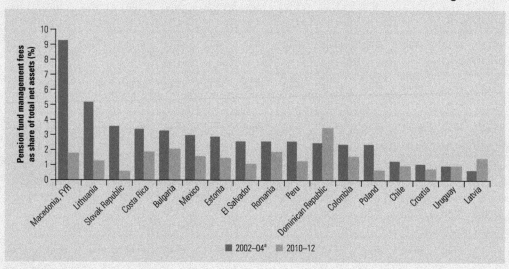

Source: FinStats.
a. Or implementation.

returns on foreign investments. For example, from 2003 to 2012, the U.S. Standard and Poor's (S&P) index earned 9.15 percent compared to an average of 4.3 percent by pension plans in 11 selected ECA countries with available data.[2] An index combining S&P equities and fixed income assets also outperformed ECA pension funds over this period. In short, regulatory efforts to minimize pension fund losses and pursue other objectives have reduced the ability of pension funds to provide targeted replacement income levels.

High management fees also have reduced pension returns. Management fees have fallen from the very high levels at the beginning of ECA's pension reforms (see figure S5.2), reflecting the expansion of the asset base available to cover the fixed costs of pension fund managers. Nevertheless, the current average of just over 1 percent, although comparable to (and sometimes lower than) fees in Latin American funds, could still be reduced. For example, Croatia reduced its fees by centralizing the back-office operations of pension funds, allowing the pension fund managers to focus on their core work of investing. Other steps to lower fees include the more strategic use of benchmark index funds to lower the costs of securities trading.

Fiscal problems have led to the dismantling of Hungary's private pension system and the redirection of a share of payroll contributions to the public pension system in several countries. In some countries, these fiscal problems were exacerbated when the private pensions were created: a portion of the salary contributions to public pensions was redirected to the new private pensions while the government issued debt to cover the increased expenditures now required to maintain public pension payments. An important lesson is that it is critical to consider the fiscal implications of creating a private pension system. Establishing a mandatory private pension scheme can reduce future government obligations under public pension programs. However, creation of a large fiscal gap to cover immediate public pension obligations during the transition to a new system can threaten the sustainability of the private pension system.

If it is impossible to create a private pension system without exacerbating a difficult fiscal position, then pension reform can begin by establishing a voluntary (pillar 3) system. Encouraging aging workers to save more could facilitate a gradual reduction in public pension obligations, until there is adequate fiscal room to move toward a funded system.

Experience shows that voluntary systems are difficult to build up, but some lessons should be kept in mind. Contrary to intuition, the use of matching government funds (Australia, Czech Republic) or tax incentives (Denmark, United States, and others) has been less successful in increasing participation than automatic enrollment with the option to opt out (Canada, New Zealand, United Kingdom). Also, the use of blind accounts (as in Sweden), where the investment manager does not know the identity of the worker contributing funds, helps to avoid aggressive customer poaching that raises costs (and thus lowers returns) to the overall pension fund industry.

In conclusion, private pension systems in the ECA region suffered financial convulsions during the 2008 crisis and subsequent reversals in fiscally fragile countries. Nevertheless, given an appropriate regulatory framework, funded systems can provide adequate retirement income while reducing government's future liabilities. This requires focusing on achieving adequate returns over the long term, rather than excessive concern with asset volatility and short-term returns, or using the pension system to achieve domestic investment objectives. It also requires that private pensions be established in the context of a strong fiscal program.

Notes

1. Pension systems are typically classified as one of the following: pillar 1—state-run pension with basic coverage, often covering all workers (for example, social security in the United States); pillar 2—funded pension based on contributions from employers and workers (for example, 401(k) plans offered by employers); and pillar 3—voluntary, private funded accounts (for example, personal savings).
2. The countries include Bulgaria, Croatia, Estonia, Kazakhstan, Latvia, Lithuania, the former Yugoslav Republic of Macedonia, Poland, Romania, the Russian Federation, and the Slovak Republic. Data for some countries reflect a shorter period, depending on the start dates of the private pension systems.

5

The Nexus of Financial Inclusion and Financial Stability: Identifying Trade-Offs and Synergies for Europe and Central Asia

In 1984, Carlos Díaz-Alejandro wrote "Good-Bye Financial Repression, Hello Financial Crash," discussing how Latin American countries dismantled many of the financial sector controls that had been roundly criticized for holding back (financial) development, only to be beset by severe financial crises and deep recessions. In Europe and Central Asia (ECA), the liberalization of financial markets and an opening to external financial flows were also associated with financial instability, although the origins of the instability could have been more external than internal. These are dramatic examples of how efforts to increase the ability of firms and individuals to use financial services such as credit (referred to as financial inclusion in credit) could increase volatility and lower growth, at least in the short term.

This chapter considers how ECA's policies on financial inclusion should be designed to avoid an adverse impact on stability. To that end, the chapter examines the relationship between measures of financial inclusion and financial stability and provides lessons for Emerging ECA countries. It discusses the existing measures of financial inclusion and stability and how ECA performs on these measures. The chapter explains why studying the relationship between the two policy objectives is important and proposes an analytical approach for studying this relationship. It discusses policy recommendations based on the estimated relationship between financial inclusion and stability, taking into account different country contexts.

Main messages:

- Global and ECA experience implies a trade-off between financial inclusion and financial stability, so that advancing financial inclusion may be associated with greater instability on average. However, closer inspection of this result reveals that synergies could arise with almost equal probability as trade-offs.

- Policies to increase the financial inclusion of firms are less likely to be associated with instability, whereas policies to increase the financial inclusion of individuals, particularly in using credit, are much more likely to be associated with instability and unintended consequences.

- ECA experience is consistent with the finding that financial openness and inflows of capital may increase the trade-off between advancing financial inclusion and maintaining financial stability. However, this potential increase can be mitigated by improving macroprudential supervision of capital flows and their prudent allocation to creditworthy firms and individuals.

- Low marginal tax rates and tax burdens are associated with a lower trade-off and potential synergies between inclusion and stability by encouraging precautionary savings due to smaller safety nets and a greater potential for discretionary tax increases. Improving education can increase financial literacy and boost financial inclusion and stability. Moreover, deeper credit information systems can improve the screening of creditworthy customers and facilitate more precise estimation of expected losses, allowing for greater financial inclusion with stability.

Both financial inclusion and financial stability are high on the agendas of ECA and international policy makers. In Emerging ECA, many policy makers are still grappling with high levels of firm and household debt and mechanisms to boost savings and sustained growth. In the international arena, the G20 has called for global commitments to both advancing financial inclusion (the Maya Declaration and the Global Partnership for Financial Inclusion) and enhancing financial stability (the Financial Stability Board, Basel III Implementation, and other regulatory reforms). One challenge is that there may be important policy trade-offs between the two objectives. For instance, a rapid increase in credit can impair financial stability, because not everyone is creditworthy or can manage credit responsibly—as illustrated in the last decade by the subprime mortgage crisis in the United States; foreign currency–denominated mortgages in Hungary, Poland, and other ECA countries; and the Andhra Pradesh microfinance crisis in India. In addition, trade-offs between inclusion and stability could arise as an unintended consequence of bad, or badly implemented, policies. In contrast, advancing financial inclusion by increasing the use of electronic payments, deposits, or insurance may not impair financial stability, but rather may enhance it. There may be important synergies between some forms of inclusion and stability. For example, a broader use of financial services could help financial institutions diversify risks and aid stability. Similarly, financial stability can encourage trust in financial systems and the use of financial services. Understanding the synergies and trade-offs is thus important for policy makers who strive to advance financial inclusion and stability in sync.

Box 5.1 discusses the recent economic literature on the relationship between financial inclusion and stability.

Understanding the potential trade-offs and synergies in advancing financial inclusion and stability is especially important for central bankers and other policy

---

BOX 5.1 **The Economic Literature on the Relationship between Financial Inclusion and Stability**

The literature on the relationship between financial inclusion and financial stability is relatively thin, and provides contradictory views on how these outcomes are related. One view sees financial inclusion as having limited importance for systemic risk, because greater inclusion entails numerous exposures of limited amounts that are fairly manageable with existing prudential tools (Hannig and Jansen 2010). Nevertheless, financial inclusion may generate issues for central banks, as it affects the transmission of monetary policy and has an impact on financial stability (Mehrotra and Yetman 2015). Another view is that greater financial inclusion through irresponsibly rapid credit growth poses risks for financial stability (Mehrotra and Yetman 2015). The quick expansion of unregulated parts of the financial system might also impair the stability of regulated financial intermediaries. The benefits of participation in good times can turn into negative spillover effects in bad times (De la Torre, Feyen, and Ize 2013).

There is also a view that financial inclusion can enhance stability directly (Hawkins 2006; Han and Melecky 2013) and indirectly (Claessens 2006). Hawkins (2006) argues that promoting access to finance enhances financial stability both in the short and in the long run. For instance, to improve access and stability at the same time, the author suggests a tiered banking system where different types of banks provide a restricted number of services (for example, deposit banks). Prasad (2010) suggests that increased savings deposited in the financial system enhances the financing of domestic investments by decreasing reliance on foreign financing, thus leading to greater stability. Han and Melecky (2013) find that a 10 percent increase in the use of

deposits can reduce the withdrawal rate for deposits in stress times on average from 20 percent to about 15 percent. For credit, Adasme, Majnoni, and Uribe (2006) and Morgan and Pontines (2014) argue that lending to small and medium-size enterprises lowers nonperforming loans (NPLs) and the probability of default by credit institutions because diversified loans to small and medium-size enterprises pose less systemic risk than concentrated, large loans. By the same token, Mehrotra and Yetman (2014) suggest that increasing financial inclusion provides firms and households with better risk management tools, which indirectly boosts the resilience of financial institutions (that is, more resilient borrowers imply more resilient banks).

Another line of argument is that excessive or increased emphasis on financial stability may limit financial inclusion. An inappropriate calibration of the regulatory framework for basic financial services according to their contribution to risks for the entire financial system can become a cause for exclusion. Financial institutions may limit access to financial services by low-income groups, especially in times of regulatory tightening, in an attempt to boost profits and cut off risky customer segments. This response can reduce households' welfare because financial services ease consumption smoothing, expand investment opportunities, reduce poverty, and reduce income inequality (Claessens 2006). Nevertheless, Dittus and Klein (2011) point to the need to design regulation of financial innovations in terms of the nature and risks of each different financial service or innovation. Excessive emphasis on financial stability can prolong involuntary financial exclusion by preventing innovation (Basel Committee on Banking Supervision 2015). Conversely,

(Continued)

BOX 5.1 **The Economic Literature on the Relationship between Financial Inclusion and Stability** (continued)

financial stability can enhance trust in the financial system, improving financial inclusion (Mehrotra and Yetman 2014) and the likelihood that households save formally (Beckmann and Mare 2016). Small denomination instruments enable households to hold diversified portfolios. The pooling of these resources allows for financing projects on a bigger scale. Moreover, financial inclusion enables more effective adjustment in saving and investment decisions, thereby insulating households' consumption from output volatility (Mehrotra and Yetman 2014). Dabla-Norris et al. (2015) use a calibrated theoretical model to illustrate the importance of country-specific characteristics for assessing the implications of financial policies on access to credit, depth of credit markets, and intermediation efficiency for gross domestic product (GDP) and inequality in developing countries.

In a recent contribution to this debate, Sahay et al. (2015) use selected cross-country data, relying mostly on the International Monetary Fund's Financial Access Survey, to illustrate that financial stability risks increase when access to credit is expanded without proper supervision. Financial buffers tend to decline when access to credit expands; they decline faster in countries with weaker banking supervision. In contrast, countries with strong supervision could see some financial stability gains from higher inclusion. The paper points to large differences in the effectiveness of supervision across countries, signaling the potential risks to financial stability from an unchecked broadening of access to credit. Sahay et al. (2015) also suggest that increasing access to financial services other than credit does not impact financial stability adversely.

makers in ECA, the developing region that underwent rapid financial liberalization but was also hardest hit by the 2008 global financial crisis. Policy makers have increasingly taken on mandates, tasks, and public commitments on financial stability (BIS 2011; Čihák, Muñoz, et al. 2012). At the same time, countries increasingly prepare and implement financial inclusion strategies (Pearce and Ortega 2012; World Bank 2014), and central bankers are often asked to lead these efforts. For these reasons, new evidence is needed on the relationship between financial inclusion and stability, and the trade-offs and synergies that could characterize it. Ignoring interlinks in advancing financial inclusion and stability could result in costly financial crises or continued financial exclusion.

How Do We Measure Financial Inclusion and Stability?

Although there are alternative ways to measure financial inclusion, for the purposes of this analysis we define financial inclusion as the *use of* rather than *access to* a range of financial services by individuals and firms. We focus on the use of financial services (account ownership, payments, savings, credit, and insurance), rather than access to them, because access by itself does not mean that individuals and firms will actually use these financial services (consistent with definitions in Beck, Demirgüç-Kunt, and Martinez Peria 2007; Demirgüç-Kunt and Klapper 2012; Allen et al. 2012; World Bank 2014; Basel Committee on Banking Supervision 2015; and Sahay et al. 2015). For example, individuals may not use financial services because they lack understanding of finance (Cole, Sampson, and Zia 2011), or because they wish to avoid official notice because of complicated regulations, taxes, low quality of public services, or poor governance. With poor overall governance, financial authorities may not be able to greatly affect the incentives for financial inclusion.

Financial stability is defined in a broad sense to capture (a) resilience of the financial system; (b) volatility in key segments of financial intermediation; and (c) negative, low-probability events associated with financial crises. Our measures focus primarily on banks because, given the dominant role of banks in ECA and most of the world's financial systems, the data available on financial sectors other than banking are limited. Conceptually, however, we aim to measure stability of the broader financial system. The first element of stability, resilience, is important because it indicates the degree to which the system can withstand future shocks. The second element, volatility, is important because instability implies greater uncertainty and risk. Even seemingly resilient financial systems can underdeliver because of contagion and high volatility from other markets. Third, to properly account for low-probability risks in our analysis, we explicitly cover financial crises, which are extreme events when the financial sector fails to perform its core functions. Figure 5.1 exemplifies these concepts of financial inclusion and financial stability, along with the measures used in this study.

The complete list of variables used in the analysis, along with the description and data sources, appears in appendix I, table I.1. The data are primarily from the World Bank's Global Findex database,[1] the Financial Access Survey of the International

FIGURE 5.1 Financial stability and inclusion can be measured in many ways

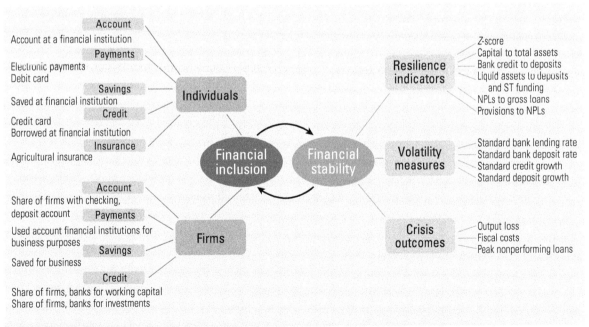

Sources: The use of financial services is measured primarily with data from the World Bank's Global Findex and Enterprise Surveys.
Note: We distinguish between individuals and firms and classify our variables according to the type of financial services. The distinction between firms and individuals can become blurry at the microenterprise level, but for practical purposes, we refer to firms when financial services are used for business purpose. We choose a parsimonious set of indicators that consistently measure our definition of financial inclusion. The variables are selected on the basis of past research (see for instance Beck et al. 2008; Čihák, Demirgüç-Kunt, et al. 2012; and World Bank 2013), and available country coverage. NPLs = nonperforming loans; ST = short-term.

Monetary Fund (IMF),[2] the IMF's Financial Soundness Indicators database,[3] World Bank's Global Financial Development Database,[4] and the Systemic Banking Crises Database of Laeven and Valencia (2013). The set of empirical indicators is described in appendix H.

ECA Has Similar Levels of Financial Inclusion as Other Developing Regions

Among the World Bank regions, ECA shows average overall financial inclusion. Although the region performs well in the use of bank financing by firms, the use of savings deposits—both by firms and individuals—is low. Across ECA, 54 percent of adults report having an account at a formal financial institution, with the share ranging from about 1 percent in Turkmenistan to more than 80 percent in Croatia, the Czech Republic, and Slovenia. The use of debit cards and electronic payments in ECA is average among the developing regions and much lower than in high-income countries. Improvements in policies in ECA are necessary to expand the use of electronic payments (box 5.2). The large differences between the maximum and minimum values of these financial indicators for ECA countries suggest that

---

BOX 5.2　Increasing the Use of Electronic Payments

Electronic payments offer tremendous potential to increase financial sector efficiency and integrate low-income households and communities, small-scale agriculture producers and vendors, and informal or marginalized economic segments into the financial system. Transitioning from a heavy reliance on cash to the broad use of electronic payments will require improvements in financial and communications infrastructure, the legal and regulatory framework governing financial transactions, the attractiveness of electronic services (product design and proximity and reliability of points of service), and the financial know-how of the target customer base.

Efforts are underway in several Europe and Central Asia (ECA) countries to improve the legal and regulatory framework. All but two ECA countries now have laws governing payment systems, compared to only about half in 2010. These laws, or their implementing regulations, typically include provisions to add consumer protections, recalibrate anti-money laundering and combatting the

financing of terrorism (AML/CFT) requirements, and enable the launch of innovative approaches that would support electronic payments.

Transforming the payments infrastructure to support electronic finance is a greater challenge. The financial infrastructure in most ECA countries is designed to process traditional bank-based electronic payments. Few ECA countries have the capacity to efficiently process the magnitude and diversity of small-value electronic transactions that would accompany a large-scale shift to electronic payments.

The broad adoption of electronic transactions also requires services that are easy to use and offer attractive terms and conditions, convenient and reliable points of service, and a consumer base with sufficient financial knowledge. The most basic of these is the availability of points of service (or access) to conduct transactions, but all ECA countries except Turkey have only a small number of traditional payment acceptance points relative to population (figure B5.2.1). At the same time, apart from

(Continued)

BOX 5.2 *(continued)*

FIGURE B5.2.1 **The number of points of service for retail payments is relatively modest in ECA**

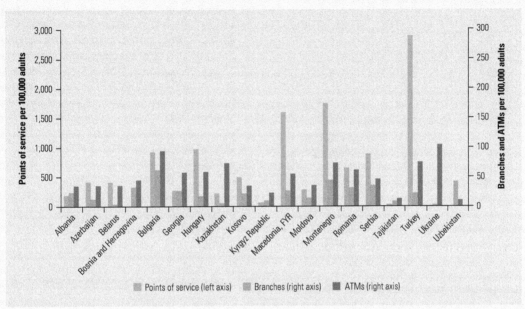

Sources: World Bank 2012 Global Payment Systems Survey and International Monetary Fund 2014 Financial Access Survey.

bill payment kiosks, newer types of access channels have yet to achieve a significant presence.

A particular challenge in achieving the large-scale adoption of electronic payments is ensuring that products are appropriate for low-income households, which tend to conduct very frequent, low-value transactions in cash and require ready access to their funds (see Collins et al. 2009 and related studies). Thus, the poor may particularly value payment services with dependable access points and low costs per transaction. On the other hand, marginalized economic entities, such as vendors or farmers, may conduct person-to-person transactions with a wide range of counterparties (using payment services offered by a variety of payment service providers), and may need to have immediate access to business proceeds. Such entities may value transaction speed and interoperability across payment services the most.

The transition to greater use of electronic payments can be encouraged by focusing on existing

transactions that are used by many households, including the delivery of government benefits, wage payments, utility bill payments, and remittances:

- Government benefit payments can be particularly valuable in introducing low-income households to electronic payments. Government transfers, which encompass more than just social benefit payments, reach significant numbers of those in the bottom 40 percent of the income distribution (B40).[a] In ECA, 10 to 20 percent of the B40 among lower-middle-income countries (LMICs), and 20 to 30 percent among upper-middle-income countries (UMICs), receive a government transfer. Governments in two-thirds of ECA's UMICs (with available data) pay the benefits of over 50 percent of their recipients in electronic form through direct deposit.[b]

- There is considerable potential in ECA to promote financial inclusion through the electronic

(Continued)

BOX 5.2   **Increasing the Use of Electronic Payments** (continued)

payment of utility bills. Apart from Kosovo, over 65 percent of adults in ECA's low-income countries and LMICs pay utility bills; and, according to the Global Findex Survey, low-income residents across ECA are just as likely to pay utility bills as higher-income individuals. However, little progress has been made. For example, in Belarus, Turkey, and Uzbekistan, 95 to 100 percent of adults who pay utilities—including those with transaction accounts—report that they pay their utility bills in cash. The widespread network of cash kiosks, used in ECA to pay utility bills, to accept noncash forms of payment (for example, prepaid cards, mobile and Internet payments) could be modified to encourage electronic payment.

• Remittances, both domestic and cross-border, could be used to advance the adoption of electronic payments and boost financial inclusion. ECA residents received an estimated US$48 billion in cross-border remittances in 2015, and the top three ECA remittance recipient countries received flows equivalent to 49, 32, and 25 percent of GDP in 2014 (World Bank 2015). Although comparable estimates on the value of domestic remittance flows are not available, the 2014 Findex survey reports that 10 to 20 percent of adults in ECA countries send or receive domestic remittances, most commonly "in cash by hand." Increasing the use of electronic payments for remittances in ECA is likely to require significant changes in the remittance market, particularly the greater availability of services that are connected to the broader retail market.

a. Findex provides figures on government transfers, not just government benefit payments. According to Findex figures, the B40 are only somewhat more likely than the T60 (top 60 percent) to receive government transfers.
b. Findex data on the means by which government payments are received are available only for countries where 10 percent or more of the adult population receive government transfers.

levels of these indicators differ significantly across the region (figure 5.2). For instance, the use of debit cards and electronic payments varies greatly across ECA, with the countries in Central Asia showing the smallest use and the countries in Central and Eastern Europe showing the greatest use. Interestingly, across all indicators, ECA shows higher inclusion of firms than of individuals.

About 12 percent of adults in ECA borrowed money from a formal financial institution (such as a commercial bank), which is below the median level for the most advanced countries but higher than the value observed in other developing regions. The same pattern holds for credit cards. These figures may reflect depressed borrowing following the global financial crisis, which hit the region particularly hard. By contrast, only about 7 percent of adults in ECA saved money at a formal financial institution, the lowest median level among all World Bank regions. Nonetheless, the best-performing country in ECA (the Slovak Republic) shows a rate of saving in a formal financial institution that is closer to the median for industrial countries.

Saving for business purposes is relatively rare among firms in ECA. The median value for the region is about 5 percent of all firms; in the best-performing country (Turkmenistan) just 12 percent of firms report saving for business purposes in the last 12 months. One possible explanation is that businesses in Central and Eastern Europe are more likely to operate in the formal sector than are businesses in Central Asia. The ECA median value is significantly smaller than the value in several developing regions (that is, East Asia and Pacific [EAP], Latin America and the

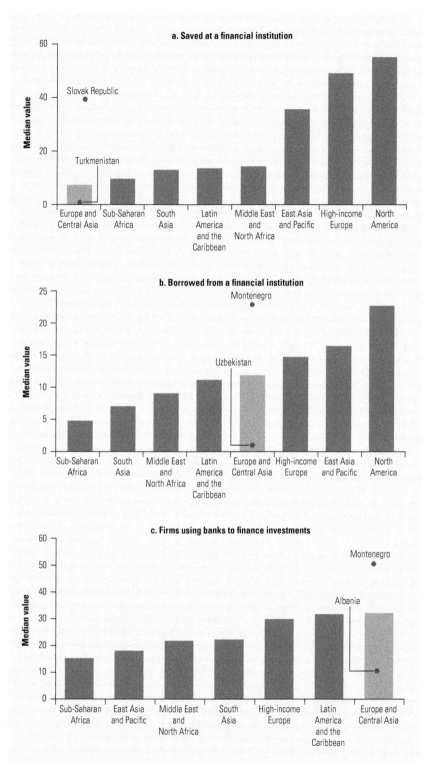

FIGURE 5.2
ECA's ranking differs across indicators of financial inclusion

Source: Global Findex.
Note: Data represent the median regional average. For Europe and Central Asia only, we report the data for the countries with the lowest and highest values of the specific indicator.

Caribbean [LAC], the Middle East and North Africa [MENA], and Sub-Saharan Africa [SSA]). In contrast, the median level for the use of individual accounts for business purposes in ECA is comparable to the median level in LAC but is well below that of EAP. In Slovenia, which has the highest level in ECA, the use of individual accounts for business is as frequent as in other high-income countries.

Account ownership in ECA firms is high—at the median, about 92 percent of firms report having a checking or savings account. ECA firms are most likely among all the regions to borrow, which could reflect excessive levels of debt among ECA firms, especially in countries that experienced big boom-and-bust cycles (such as Montenegro). About 32 percent of ECA firms report using banks to finance investments, and almost 35 percent of firms use banks to finance working capital.

The use of insurance among the population is important for increasing economic resilience of people and firms. Moreover, this greater use indirectly supports the stability of financial systems that serve individuals and households. Despite the increased availability of high-quality flood and earthquake insurance packages that cost between €14 and €40 annually, the demand for catastrophe insurance products continues to be low. Moral hazard due to expectations of government support and lack of accurate assessment of risks by individuals and the public sector need to be addressed (see spotlight 7).

The complete individual distributions of the financial inclusion indicators included in the analysis appear in appendix I, figures I.1 and I.2.

Financial Instability Is High in ECA

ECA appears to underperform on financial stability compared to other World Bank regions (figure 5.3). Nonetheless, as observed for the financial inclusion indicators, the levels of financial stability differ widely across the region (see chapter 1). For resilience, the ECA region has the second-lowest median value for the z-score (10.7), a measure of the probability of insolvency of a banking system, though the best-performing country in the region (the Czech Republic) has a value above 50.[5] However, the ratio of banks' capital to total assets is high, with the median value above 10 percent. On liquidity, the loan-to-deposit ratios for about half of the ECA countries exceed 100 percent, meaning that there is an imbalance between local savings and credit provision. The median value for the share of liquid assets in total assets is about 30 percent, lower than the median level of developing regions. ECA has the highest ratio of nonperforming loans (NPLs) to total loans (almost 9 percent) across all regions, with two countries (Serbia and Kazakhstan) above 15 percent at end-2014. The median provisioning of NPLs is the third highest among all the regions (62 percent), but the number varies from 1 percent for Azerbaijan to about 130 percent for Serbia.

The volatility of financial intermediation shows a mixed picture. The median volatility of lending rates across ECA countries is the second lowest (0.08) whereas the volatility of deposit rates is the third highest (0.26) among the regions. However, the high standard deviations of the annual growth in loans (0.13) and in deposits (0.07) could point to an intrinsic systematic vulnerability. On crisis outcomes, ECA has been the developing region most affected by the global financial

> The ECA region has the second-lowest median value for the z-score (10.7), a measure of the probability of insolvency of a banking system, though the best-performing country in the region (the Czech Republic) has a value above 50.

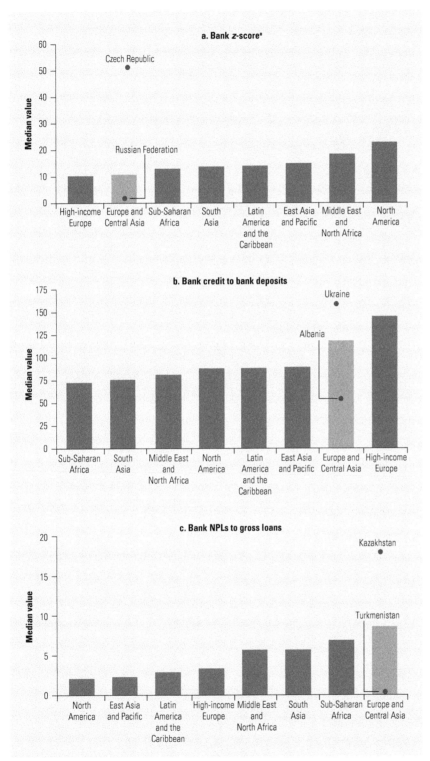

FIGURE 5.3
Financial instability is high in ECA

Source: World Bank Global Financial Development Database.
Note: Data represents the median regional average. For Europe and Central Asia only, we report the data for the countries with the lowest and highest value of the specific indicator. NPLs = nonperforming loans.
a. The z-score is a measure of the likelihood of insolvency in the banking system.

crisis. Moreover, the emerging market crisis of the 1990s hit ECA hard. Overall, ECA has gone through big boom-and-bust cycles in the last 25 years.

The complete individual distributions of the financial stability indicators included in the analysis appear in appendix I, figures I.3 and I.4.

How Do We Assess the Relationship between Inclusion and Stability?

This section presents the framework for evaluating the interactions between financial inclusion and financial stability. The framework aims to (a) demonstrate that the *interactions* between inclusion and stability are important for policy, and (b) motivate our empirical analysis of these interactions using cross-country data.

In the framework, we assume that financial stability and financial inclusion are both important outcomes for financial policy makers.[6] When evaluating financial sector outcomes, and when prioritizing design and implementation of alternative financial policies, policy makers could miss important aspects by ignoring the interactions between financial stability and inclusion. To illustrate this point, it is useful to consider the following intuitive framework:[7]

Achieving joint financial stability and inclusion	=	Achieving financial stability	+	Achieving financial inclusion	+	Exploiting synergies and mitigating trade-offs between financial inclusion and stability

That is, policies to achieve financial stability and inclusion may not deliver the intended results if there are large trade-offs between achieving inclusion and stability. But, if there are important synergies between inclusion and stability, then policies to achieve one can reinforce the other. While most empirical work has typically focused on achieving the outcomes of stable or inclusive financial systems independently, limited attention has been paid to the interdependence between the two outcomes.

This chapter focuses on the interdependence between financial stability and inclusion, highlighted by the last interdependence term in the above equation, and its practical relevance for a country. Note that, if financial inclusion and stability were completely independent outcomes, the interdependence term would be zero. However, if the two outcomes are interrelated, the interdependence term will be significantly different from zero, either positive or negative. This term can be significantly negative when the two outcomes (stability and inclusion) involve a trade-off for policy makers—for instance, increasing the use of credit among people involves more systemic risk. Conversely, the interdependence term can be significantly positive when achieving the two outcomes leads to synergies—for instance, greater financial stability improves trust in the financial sector and increases the likelihood of using bank deposit accounts.

We study the interdependence between stability and inclusion in terms of different economic agents (firms and individuals), financial services (account, payments, savings, credit, and insurance), and dimension of financial stability (resilience, volatility, and crises) to gain deeper insights into this relationship. The analysis is done using average correlations between indicators of stability and inclusion, emphasizing that our estimates indicate an *association*, but do not necessarily imply causality between inclusion and stability. A formal presentation of the analytic approach is given in appendix J.

How Are Stability and Inclusion Related?

This section analyzes how the measures of financial stability and inclusion are related (correlated) to gain an understanding of the overall association between the two concepts. The discussion is grouped into four subsections. The first subsection analyzes the overall correlation between indicators of stability and inclusion, as well as separately for individuals and firms. The second subsection estimates the average correlations by individuals and firms, financial service, and element of financial stability (resilience, volatility, and crises). The third subsection computes the aggregate correlations between inclusion and stability using constructed aggregate indexes from measures of inclusion and, separately, stability for each country. The final subsection presents the results of the regression analyses to identify country characteristics that explain the variation of the aggregate correlations across countries.

There Is Some Evidence that Higher Inclusion Can Increase Instability

Our results suggest that there is a negative association (trade-off) between some indicators of resilience and financial inclusion variables. Higher bank capitalization is negatively correlated with the use of financial services, particularly for individuals (table 5.1). Moreover, there is a trade-off between several indicators of financial inclusion and the costs of banking crises. Greater financial inclusion (increase in account ownership or use of debit cards) is associated with more costly financial crises (measured by losses in output, higher government expenditures required to resolve the crisis, and the peak NPL ratio). The median ratios of private credit and deposits to GDP in ECA had reached significantly higher levels than in similar economies by the mid-2000s, indicating that excessive inclusion may have contributed to the depth of the 2008 crisis (see spotlight 3). Nonetheless, financial systems with higher inclusion of individuals are generally associated with lower average NPLs. Looking at all of the correlations between financial stability and inclusion, a negative association between the two is more common, including between banking crises and the various uses of credit.[8] However, statistical tests indicate that both negative and positive associations between stability and inclusion are likely, although negative relationships occur with the greatest frequency (this is illustrated in figure 5.4, which shows the distribution of correlation coefficients by frequency, called a *histogram*).[9]

The importance of trade-offs and synergies between inclusion and stability differs for firms compared to individuals (panels a and b of figure I.5 in appendix I). Trade-offs between inclusion and stability for firms are likely in extreme

TABLE 5.1 Correlations between Measures of Inclusion and Stability

			Stability			
			Resiliency			
			Bank z-score[a]	Bank capital to total assets	Low bank credit to bank deposits	Liquid assets to deposits and short-term funding
Inclusion	Individuals	Borrowed from a financial institution	0.062	−0.172	−0.449	−0.256
		Used a credit card	0.025	−0.439	−0.449	−0.258
		Saved at a financial institution	0.154	−0.527	−0.269	−0.316
		Used an account at a financial institution	0.068	−0.507	−0.474	−0.351
		Purchased agriculture insurance	0.131	0.064	0.289	0.261
		Used a debit card	0.085	−0.404	−0.505	−0.332
		Used either Internet payments or electronic	0.100	−0.426	−0.519	−0.295
	Firms	Used a checking or savings account	−0.058	−0.017	−0.349	−0.271
		Used banks to finance investments	0.049	−0.042	−0.408	−0.404
		Used banks to finance working capital	0.203	0.027	−0.334	−0.330
		Saved to start, operate, or expand a farm or business	0.016	0.104	0.334	−0.016
		Used an account at a financial institution for business purposes	0.056	−0.395	−0.258	−0.228

Note: The variables are transformed so that an increase in a variable measures improvement in financial inclusion (or financial stability). A positive correlation coefficient thus denotes the presence of potential synergy between inclusion and stability, and a negative correlation the presence of a trade-off. The Spearman correlation coefficients between financial stability and financial inclusion are computed using equation (J.2) in appendix J. The table includes the values for the linear dependence of each financial inclusion indicator (rows) and each individual financial stability indicator (columns). Red and green highlight coefficients that are included in the left tail and right tail of the distribution of the Spearman coefficients: lighter green in the highest 5 percent; darker green in the highest 10 percent; darker red in the lowest 10 percent; and lighter red in the lowest 5 percent. NPLs = nonperforming loans; — not available.
a. The z-score is a measure of the likelihood of insolvency in the banking system.

FIGURE 5.4 Both trade-offs and synergies between inclusion and stability are likely (pairwise correlations between measures of inclusion and stability)

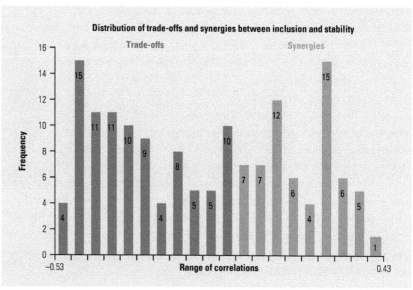

Source: World Bank elaboration.
Note: This figure represents the distribution of the frequency of pairwise correlation coefficients between financial stability and financial inclusion included in table 5.1.

Stability								
Resiliency		Volatility				Crisis		
Low bank NPLs to gross loans	High provisions to NPLs	Low variability lending rate growth	Low variability credit growth	Low variability bank deposit rate growth	Low variability deposit growth	Low output loss	Low fiscal cost	Low peak NPLs
0.282	−0.354	−0.173	−0.202	0.147	0.193	−0.243	−0.229	−0.182
0.432	−0.244	−0.323	−0.374	0.260	0.281	−0.427	−0.376	−0.402
0.382	−0.334	−0.162	−0.349	0.357	0.375	−0.409	−0.382	−0.357
0.291	−0.366	−0.272	−0.379	0.313	0.331	−0.467	−0.461	−0.448
−0.113	0.029	0.110	−0.002	−0.147	−0.065	—	0.132	0.132
0.299	−0.296	−0.330	−0.424	0.265	0.265	−0.471	−0.469	−0.459
0.338	−0.317	−0.370	−0.398	0.248	0.265	−0.473	−0.452	−0.447
0.123	−0.006	−0.178	−0.166	0.249	0.122	−0.113	−0.033	−0.073
0.048	−0.131	−0.088	−0.236	0.265	0.228	−0.077	−0.009	−0.008
0.100	0.047	0.021	−0.126	0.359	0.249	0.055	0.130	0.172
0.182	0.172	0.131	0.111	−0.020	−0.026	0.229	0.263	0.284
0.156	−0.259	−0.139	−0.190	0.262	0.261	−0.453	−0.437	−0.417

circumstances, such as banking crises. However, extreme events are not very likely.[10] Overall, financial inclusion of firms appears to be less interlinked with stability than for individuals, so that policies to improve the financial inclusion of firms may not have a significant impact on stability in most circumstances. By contrast, for individuals, the distribution of correlation coefficients indicates that policy makers will be confronted with significant trade-offs and possible synergies when implementing policies for inclusion of individuals.[11]

Implementing policies for individual and firm inclusion independently and ignoring their interlinks could result in poor financial sector outcomes (future crises or continued financial exclusion) and unintended consequences. Note that financial inclusion for individuals may also reinforce stability, particularly by increasing resilience and lowering volatility by reducing the level of NPLs compared to loans, and reducing the volatility of deposits and deposit interest rates. Increasing the use of saving instruments (Han and Melecky 2013) could improve both inclusion and stability; this information could be fundamental for setting priorities for policy, particularly for developing countries in ECA.

A More Detailed Look Reveals a Complex Relationship between Inclusion and Stability

Investigating the relationship between inclusion and stability for different types of financial stability (resilience, volatility, and crises) provides further information (table 5.2). High *resilience* and low *volatility*—the first two elements of financial stability—are not consistently associated with financial inclusion of firms for any

TABLE 5.2 Average Pairwise Spearman Correlation Coefficients by Agent, Type of Financial Service, and Stability Measures

	Inclusion										
	Account ownership		Payments		Savings		Credit		Insurance		
	Individuals	Firms	Individuals	Firms	Individuals	Firms	Individuals	Firms	Individuals		
Stability measure									Agri.	Life	Nonlife
High resilience	−0.223	−0.096	−0.189	−0.155	−0.152	0.132	−0.152	−0.098	0.101	−0.095	−0.081
Capital	−0.220	−0.037	−0.161	−0.170	−0.187	0.060	−0.131	0.059	0.098	−0.240	−0.251
Liquidity	−0.413	−0.310	−0.413	−0.243	−0.293	0.159	−0.353	−0.369	0.275	0.022	0.171
NPLs	−0.038	0.058	0.006	−0.052	0.024	0.177	0.029	0.016	−0.071	−0.065	−0.162
Low volatility	−0.002	0.007	−0.060	0.049	0.055	0.049	−0.024	0.084	−0.026	−0.272	0.046
Low volatility lending rate	−0.272	−0.178	−0.350	−0.139	−0.162	0.131	−0.248	−0.033	0.110	−0.053	0.282
Low volatility credit growth	−0.379	−0.166	−0.411	−0.190	−0.349	0.111	−0.288	−0.181	−0.002	−0.684	−0.017
Low volatility bank deposit rate	0.313	0.249	0.257	0.262	0.357	−0.020	0.204	0.312	−0.147	0.069	−0.035
Low volatility deposit growth	0.331	0.122	0.265	0.261	0.375	−0.026	0.237	0.239	−0.065	−0.418	−0.044
Milder/no crisis	−0.459	−0.073	−0.462	−0.436	−0.383	0.259	−0.310	0.044	0.132	0.117	0.153

Note: The average value of the correlation coefficients for each category reported in table 5.1. Rows are organized according to the stability measure; columns refer to the types of financial services, split by agent. Red denotes negative average correlations statistically different from 0; green marks positive average correlations statistically different from 0. Statistical significance (5 percent level) is determined using Fisher's z-transformation. Agri. = agricultural; NPLs = nonperforming loans.

financial service. For individual inclusion, however, there does appear to be a trade-off between resilience and account ownership, and between resilience and the use of the Internet or electronic systems to make payments. A greater probability and higher cost of *crisis*—the third element of financial stability—are associated with the use of the Internet or electronic systems to make payments by individuals and firms, as well as increasing account ownership, increased savings at financial institutions, and the greater use of consumer credit by individuals.[12] However, as shown in table 5.2, more stability (lower cost of crises) is positively associated with the share of firms that save. Also, when crises hit or become more severe, people use deposit savings less often—including because of decreasing trust in banks (see chapter 4 for more details). Understanding these relationships is important so that governments can emphasize financial policies focused on creating synergies (greater use of savings by firms is associated with lower financial volatility) and give lower priority to financial policies that generate significant trade-offs and unintended consequences (greater use of consumer credit is associated with more costly financial crises).

When crises hit or become more severe, more firms save in formal financial institutions. This behavior is partly to hoard liquidity to finance firms' costs as access to credit becomes more uncertain, and partly to have resources to purchase assets should prices fall. This association between crises and savings by firms could explain the positive relationships between firms' financial inclusion and stability discussed earlier. However, the correlations between types of financial inclusion and crises are still too few to explain the overall association of inclusion with resilience and volatility. The association of inclusion with resilience and volatility appears to be complex, so that analysis of the correlations by different types of resilience and volatility is needed to gain further insights.

The relationship between financial inclusion and indicators of the resilience element of financial stability—including bank capitalization, liquidity, and NPLs—differs sharply by indicator, which explains our failure to detect a significant relationship between inclusion and resilience as a whole. Whereas high levels of bank capital and liquidity (implying a high level of resilience) are associated with low levels of financial inclusion, a low level of NPLs (also implying a high level of resilience) is associated with greater inclusion as measured by account ownership, electronic payments, and credit (the relationship is stronger for individuals than for firms). This finding may reflect the different purposes of bank capital, liquidity, and NPLs in dealing with expected versus unexpected losses. Holding high levels of capital and liquidity enables banks to accommodate unexpected losses, so that capital-to-assets ratios tend to fall with the onset of a crisis (and the size of the fall is related to the cost of the crisis). By contrast, a higher average level of NPLs over the macroeconomic cycle reflects an increase in expected loss for the banking business in a given country, so that the correlation between NPLs and crises is mildly positive (appendix K, table K.2). These correlations provide only limited information on the direction of causality. Thus, higher financial inclusion may be associated with higher unexpected losses because rapidly expanding credit can lead to a crisis. Alternatively, a tightening of regulatory requirements to ensure greater resilience against a crisis could reduce financial inclusion.

Similar to the analysis of resilience indicators, the relationship between financial inclusion and different indicators of the volatility element of financial stability—including the low variability of the lending rate, credit growth, the deposit interest rate, and deposit growth—differs across indicators. There are significant trade-offs between financial inclusion (particularly as measured by account ownership, electronic payments, savings, and credit) and the low volatility of the lending rate and credit growth. We also find a negative relationship between life insurance and credit, perhaps because borrowers with limited capacity to repay are more likely to be required to take out mortgage insurance in higher-income countries.[13] Thus, the estimated relationships between inclusion and volatility, as measured by the variability of the lending rate and credit growth, are consistent with the relationships found between inclusion and crises, bank capital, and liquidity (discussed above).

By contrast, there is a significant, positive association between inclusion in the form of accounts, payments, savings, and credit and the low volatility of the deposit rate and deposit growth. These relationships are stronger for individuals than for firms, which could reflect differences in the quality of the measures of inclusion for individuals (Findex) and firms (Enterprise Surveys).[14] For instance, our finding of a significant correlation (of about 0.4) between the low volatility of deposit growth and the use of deposits by individuals is consistent with the finding of Han and Melecky (2013) that a 10 percent increase in the use of deposits can reduce deposit withdrawal rates in stress times by about 5 percentage points.

We do not detect any significantly positive relationship between insurance and volatility, or between insurance and financial stability at large. Although nonlife insurance appears to be associated with lower volatility of credit, the large variability and limited country coverage of the data prevent us from drawing a clear inference.

Overall, the results suggest that, in normal times, financial inclusion aids financial stability, especially by decreasing banks' average expected losses over the financial cycle and their business costs (recall the results for NPLs) and by lowering the volatility of deposit growth and deposit interest rates. However, financial inclusion is associated with lower financial stability as measured by the volatility of credit, capital, and liquidity buffers, as well as crises, because higher inclusion may increase unexpected losses.

On Average across Indicators, Higher Inclusion Is Related to Greater Instability

The overall correlation between the summary indexes of inclusion and stability, including both firms and individuals, is −0.455 (which is significantly different from zero), suggesting that the relationship between inclusion and stability could create trade-offs for policy making (table 5.3).[15] Interestingly, the correlation between the financial inclusion of individuals and financial stability (−0.501) is more negative than the overall correlation between inclusion (firms and individuals together) and stability. The correlation between the inclusion of firms and stability is not significantly different from zero. These results do not appear to differ significantly at different levels of financial stability (see appendix I, figure I.6). Overall, this analysis suggests that it may be safe to overlook the impact of inclusion on stability when considering policies on the inclusion of firms. But policy makers should be concerned with potential trade-offs between inclusion and stability when considering policies for the inclusion of individuals.

A note of caution is warranted here because the quality of data on the inclusion of firms may not be as good as the quality of data on the inclusion of individuals. Therefore, the trade-offs between the financial inclusion of firms and stability may be as important as for the financial inclusion of individuals, but measurement errors in the data for firms could have obscured these relationships.

TABLE 5.3 Correlation between Stability and Inclusion

	Overall inclusion	Individuals	Firms
Matrix using unweighted average indexes (range)[a]			
Overall stability	−0.455***	−0.501***	−0.072
Matrix using unweighted average indexes (standardized)[b]			
Overall stability	−0.395***	−0.460***	−0.116

a. The indexes are built using equation (J.4) in appendix J.
b. Each variable is normalized by subtracting the cross-sectional mean and dividing by the cross-sectional standard deviation. We then take the average of the indicators included in a specific financial outcome to compute the separate indexes.
*** = 1 percent.

The Relationship between Inclusion and Stability Is Affected by Country Characteristics

To explore this, we calculate the correlation between inclusion and stability taking into consideration one country characteristic (for example, growth in GDP per capita, school enrollment, age dependency ratio—see the list in table K.3 in appendix K) at a time, to maximize the number of available observations. We divide the sample into two groups according to the median value of a given country characteristic, and then compare the difference between the correlations for the country groups above and below the median, using an appropriate statistical test. Second, we use regression analysis to take account of all relevant country characteristics at the same time.

To study country characteristics that affect the relationship between stability and inclusion we employ a wide range of country characteristics (appendix I, table I.2, reports the results taking into consideration one country characteristic at a time). We discuss the statistically significant results only. Countries with higher informality, as measured by the number of years firms operated without formal registration (other indicators of informality are not significant), experience a lower trade-off between financial inclusion and stability. A plausible explanation is that previously informal firms that enter the formal sector are relatively greater risk-takers because informal credit is more expensive and thus is taken by firms with a greater appetite for risk.[16] Because risk appetites are unlikely to change quickly, rapid increases in credit to previously informal firms that enter the formal sector should be monitored for potential threats to financial stability. Greater openness to external capital could impose a higher trade-off between inclusion and stability. To manage this trade-off, financial account liberalization may need to be accompanied by adequate prudential supervision to ensure prudent levels of borrowing.

Limited restrictions on investment appear to increase the trade-off between inclusion and stability, perhaps because such policies allow for greater risk-taking. In contrast, low marginal tax rates and tax burden[17] may reduce the trade-off between inclusion and stability. Low taxes and smaller social safety nets may encourage greater precautionary savings by individuals and firms that could decrease financial volatility. Also, stronger governance could significantly reduce the overall negative correlation between inclusion and stability and thus mitigate the trade-off facing policy makers.

The regression results including all of the country characteristics at once (reported in appendix I, table I.3) are broadly consistent with the conclusions reached by considering each country characteristic separately. However, the sample of countries is more representative of developing countries (column "Included" of appendix K, table K.4) because several indicators are not available for high-income countries.[18] Countries with more open financial systems may face a higher trade-off between increasing financial inclusion and fostering financial stability. In contrast, low tax rates are estimated to have a significant, positive effect on the interdependence between inclusion and stability—that is, to generate or increase synergies between the two. Greater formalization of the economy—increase in the percentage of firms that formally registered when they started operations in the country—is estimated to introduce or significantly increase the trade-off between inclusion and stability (this variable is more significant than when considered separately from other country characteristics). Education—enrollment rates in secondary education—is found to generate synergies between financial inclusion and stability (although this effect was insignificant when considered separately). Perhaps the impact of education reflects improved financial literacy that ensures responsible financial inclusion and thus improves financial stability, especially in developing countries (Klapper, Lusardi, and Panos 2013).

The results are somewhat different when the maximum number of countries are included (column 2 of table I.3, appendix I), including many high-income countries that were excluded in the first exercise immediately above. Here the impact of financial openness on the trade-off between inclusion and stability is not significant, probably because higher-income countries with greater capacity to manage capital flows are included. Low tax rates retain their positive effect on the trade-off between inclusion and stability, at the 5 percent significance level (a stronger result than the 10 percent level in the sample that is more representative of developing countries). Population density is estimated to have a significant (at the 10 percent level), positive effect on this relationship and can thus introduce or increase synergies between inclusion and stability—even though population density was not significant when considered separately. More densely populated countries may benefit from more intensive social networks that improve the efficiency of screening and monitoring of financial customers as well as facilitate the emergence of self-monitoring groups—for instance, credit cooperatives and private guarantee schemes. Other things equal, finance could thus be more responsible in densely populated countries and generate synergies with financial stability by increasing the size of the market and diversifying bank lending. Finally, the depth of the credit information index (the coverage and richness of credit reporting systems) is significant in generating or enhancing synergies between inclusion and stability at the 5 percent level.

The relationship between inclusion and stability among developing countries in ECA is not significantly different from that of other regions. This finding suggests that the region, and the geographic location of countries in ECA, does not play a role in explaining systematic variations in the relationship between inclusion and stability across countries. It could also suggest that we have not omitted any country characteristics of ECA that would be important for distinguishing the relationship between inclusion and stability in ECA from that of other regions.

Conclusion

This chapter confirms that there is indeed much to gain from coordinated policies that take into account synergies and trade-offs between financial inclusion and financial stability. On average, there appears to be a trade-off between financial inclusion and stability that should be considered by policy makers. However, both trade-offs and synergies are found in cross-country experience depending on the indicator of stability and inclusion one is examining. This implies that, although trade-offs can dominate the relationship between inclusion and stability, synergies can occur with almost equally high probability. Excluding periods of crisis, we find that greater financial inclusion is associated with greater stability and may mitigate expected losses of the financial sector. But greater financial inclusion, particularly associated with extensive borrowing by individuals, may also increase the risk of extreme events, unexpected losses of the financial system, and ultimately more frequent banking crises.

The relationship between inclusion and stability is systematically influenced by country characteristics, such as financial openness, tax rates, education, and the depth of credit information systems. While financial openness increases trade-offs between inclusion and stability, low tax rates, education, and credit information depth help generate synergies between the two goals. Greater financial openness and movement of capital are particularly challenging in middle- and low-income countries that tend to have a limited capacity to manage capital flows and ensure prudent and efficient allocation of the funding to creditworthy firms and individuals. Low tax rates may generate synergies by stimulating precautionary savings because of smaller social safety nets and greater probability of unexpected increases in taxes. Education can generate a positive relationship between inclusion and stability by improving financial literacy and responsible financial inclusion that help the financial system reap the benefits of economic scale and risk diversification. The depth of credit information systems generates synergies by improving screening of creditworthy customers, including new users of credit, and aids stability by, for example, improving the accuracy of estimations of expected losses. Finally, greater information depth also promotes competition in oligopolistic markets, decreases the cost of finance, and encourages more firms and people to start using a financial service or use more than one financial service.

Our findings have important policy implications. Because trade-offs and synergies between financial inclusion and financial stability are significant, they need to be addressed in policy making. Because policy on both financial inclusion and financial stability involves multiple government agencies (in many countries the central bank and other financial supervisors) and ministries (in many countries the ministry of finance, economic development, or strategic planning), the trade-offs and synergies must be addressed at a high enough policy-making level. One important tool to formulate high-level policy for the financial sector is the financial sector strategy (Maimbo and Melecky 2016; Melecky and Podpiera, forthcoming). So far, financial sector strategies around the world have tended to pay little attention to trade-offs, but some good examples exist, such as Malaysia and Switzerland (Melecky and Podpiera, forthcoming). The findings in our chapter can thus be interpreted as a call for greater use of financial sector strategies to explicitly mitigate trade-offs and promote synergies between financial inclusion and financial stability. These financial sector development strategies are addressed in the following chapter.

Notes

1. For more information, see the World Bank website at http://www.worldbank.org/en/programs/globalfindex. The World Bank partners with the Bill & Melinda Gates Foundation and the Gallup World Poll to produce the data set.

2. For more information, see the IMF website at http://data.imf.org/?sk=E5DCAB7E
-A5CA-4892-A6EA-598B5463A34C.

3. For more information, see the IMF website at http://data.imf.org/?sk
=9F855EAE-C765-405E-9C9A-A9DC2C1FEE47.

4. For more information, see the World Bank website at http://data.worldbank.org/data
-catalog/global-financial-development.

5. The z-score is a measure of the likelihood of insolvency in the banking system, combining information on leverage (equity to assets) with performance (return on assets) and risk (standard deviation of return on assets).

6. Note that the other important outcome for financial policy makers could be financial efficiency. The proposed framework can be readily extended to three outcomes. Here, we focus on inclusion and stability.

7. Formally:

$$E[stable \cdot inclusive] = E[stable] + E[inclusive] + Cov[inclusive, stable],$$

where $E[\cdot]$ is the expectation operator and $Cov[\cdot]$ captures the (linear) dependency between the two outcomes: financial inclusion and financial stability. While empirical work typically focuses on the expected outcomes of stable or inclusive financial systems separately, limited attention has been paid to the covariance term. For an in-depth discussion of the conceptual framework, see Čihák, Mare, and Melecky (2016).

8. This calculation assumes that all the estimated pairwise correlations are drawn from the same distribution characterizing the association between financial inclusion and stability. The distribution ranges from −0.53 to 0.43, and the distribution is not normal as suggested by a formal test (D'Agostino, Belanger, and D'Agostino, Jr. 1990; Royston 1991). Moreover, it is left skewed and leptokurtic, meaning that we observe longer and fatter lower tails.

9. This conclusion is based on the shape of the estimated kernel density for the distribution and the formal test of unimodality.

10. The support of the distribution is narrower than the one for the overall financial inclusion. The distribution is significantly left skewed, but we do not find a significant evidence of kurtosis, meaning that we observe a long lower tail that is not significantly different from the tail of the normal distribution. Statistical tests also indicate that the distribution of correlations for firms' inclusion is characterized by only one mode. This finding is also reflected in the shape of the estimated kernel density for the distribution.

11. The support of the distribution is about as wide as one of the correlations for the overall financial inclusion. The distribution is not significantly skewed but it is leptokurtic, meaning that we observe fatter tails (positive and negative) than in the normal distribution. The formal test for unimodality and the shape of the estimated kernel density for the distribution suggest multimodality. The kernel density indicates two visible modes of which the left one (the peaking negative values) has higher probability.

12. Note that account ownership and credit are related because getting credit from an institution often requires the prospective borrower to open an account with the prospective lender. Use of electronic payments with the account then follows. Indeed, account ownership, the use of debit cards, and the use of Internet or electronic payments are highly positively correlated (appendix K, table K.1).

13. Note that the insurance sample is much smaller than for other services, and mainly includes higher-income countries reporting to the International Monetary Fund's Financial Access Survey.

14. For more information, see http://www.enterprisesurveys.org/data. The World Bank partners with other institutions, such as the European Bank for Reconstruction and Development, the Inter-American Development Bank, Compete Caribbean, the European Investment Bank, and the U.K. Department for International Development, to conduct the survey in different parts of the world.

15. Each index is an equally weighted average of all indicators (rescaled to lie between 0 and 1) included in a specific subcategory—for instance, the average of all the stability indicators for the overall stability index. Using these aggregate indexes, we also

calculate the average correlation between inclusion and stability for different levels of financial stability (by deciles). To determine if these relationships are stable, we also examine two alternative approaches: (a) standardizing each indicator before computing the indexes; and (b) using the principal components and the factor weights associated with each individual variable included in a specific index. For the sake of space, we do not present the findings using the first principal component and the normalization using the standard deviation of each variable. The results are available upon request.

16. To support our conjecture, appendix K, figure K.1, provides estimates of the difference between the risk-taking appetite between self-employed in the formal and informal sectors using the Life in Transition Survey II for countries with available data, http://www.ebrd.com/news/publications/special-reports/life-in-transition-survey-ii.html. We thank Hernan Winkler for helping us with the estimates.

17. This is the "fiscal freedom" indicator in the Heritage Foundation's Index of Economic Freedom, http://www.heritage.org/index/.

18. This exercise uses a much smaller sample than was available for the analysis of individual country characteristics. Thus, the results are complementary to, but not necessarily more reliable than, the latter exercise. To partially address the influence of the different sample sizes, we run two regressions constraining the sample size to 99 observations (appendix I, table I.3, column 1) and 144 observations (appendix I, table I.3, column 2, which drops indicators for which coverage is not almost complete). It was mostly high-income countries that dropped out in the smaller sample (appendix K, table K.4).

References

Adasme, O., G. Majnoni, and M. Uribe. 2006. "Access and Risk: Friends or Foes? Lessons from Chile." Policy Research Working Paper 4003, World Bank, Washington, DC.

Allen, F., A. Demirgüç-Kunt, L. F. Klapper, and M. S. Martinez Peria. 2012. "The Foundations of Financial Inclusion: Understanding Ownership and Use of Formal Accounts." Policy Research Working Paper 6290, World Bank, Washington, DC.

Basel Committee on Banking Supervision. 2015. "Range of Practice in the Regulation and Supervision of Institutions Relevant to Financial Inclusion." Bank for International Settlements, Basel, Switzerland.

Beck, T., A. Demirgüç-Kunt, and M. S. Martinez Peria. 2007. "Reaching Out: Access to and Use of Banking Services across Countries." Journal of Financial Economics 85 (1): 234–66.

Beck, T., E. Feyen, A. Ize, and F. Moizeszowicz. 2008. "Benchmarking Financial Development." Policy Research Working Paper 4638, World Bank, Washington, DC.

Beckmann, Elisabeth, and Davide Salvatore Mare. 2016. "Household Savings and Trust in the Financial System." Unpublished manuscript.

BIS (Bank for International Settlements). 2011. "Central Bank Governance and Financial Stability." Report by a study group chaired by Stefan Ingves, Governor, Sveriges Riksbank, Bank for International Settlements, Basel, Switzerland.

Čihák, M., A. Demirgüç-Kunt, E. Feyen, and R. Levine. 2012. "Benchmarking Financial Systems around the World." Policy Research Working Paper 6175, World Bank, Washington, DC.

Čihák, M., D. S. Mare, and M. Melecky. 2016. "The Nexus of Financial Inclusion and Financial Stability: A Study of Trade-Offs and Synergies." Policy Research Working Paper 7722, World Bank, Washington, DC.

Čihák, M., S. Muñoz, S. Sharifuddin, and K. Tintchev. 2012. "Financial Stability Reports: What Are They Good For?" IMF Working Paper 12/1, International Monetary Fund, Washington, DC.

Claessens, S. 2006. "Access to Financial Services: A Review of the Issues and Public Policy Objectives." *World Bank Research Observer* 21 (2): 207–40.

Cole, S., T. Sampson, and B. Zia. 2011. "Prices or Knowledge? What Drives Demand for Financial Services in Emerging Markets?" *Journal of Finance* 66 (6): 1933–67.

Collins, Daryl, Jonathan Morduch, Stuart Rutherford, and Orlanda Ruthven. 2009. *Portfolios of the Poor*. Princeton, NJ: Princeton University Press.

Dabla-Norris, E., Y. Ji, R. M. Townsend, and D. F. Unsal. 2015. "Distinguishing Constraints on Financial Inclusion and Their Impact on GDP, TFP, and Inequality." NBER Working Paper 20821, National Bureau of Economic Research, Cambridge, MA.

D'Agostino, R. B., A. J. Belanger, and R. B. D'Agostino, Jr. 1990. "A Suggestion for Using Powerful and Informative Tests of Normality." *American Statistician* 44: 316–21.

De la Torre, A., E. Feyen, and A. Ize. 2013. "Financial Development: Structure and Dynamics." *World Bank Economic Review* 27 (3): 514–41.

Demirgüç-Kunt, A., and L. Klapper. 2012. "Measuring Financial Inclusion: The Global Findex Database." Policy Research Working Paper 6025, World Bank, Washington, DC.

Díaz-Alejandro, Carlos F. 1984. "Good-Bye Financial Repression, Hello Financial Crash." Working Paper 24, Helen Kellogg Institute for International Studies, University of Notre Dame, Notre Dame, IN.

Dittus, P., and M. Klein. 2011. "On Harnessing the Potential of Financial Inclusion: The Case of 'Mobile Payments.'" BIS Working Papers 347, Bank for International Settlements, Basel, Switzerland.

Han, R., and M. Melecky. 2013. "Financial Inclusion for Stability: Access to Bank Deposits and the Deposit Growth during the Global Financial Crisis." Policy Research Working Paper 6577, World Bank, Washington, DC.

Hannig, A., and S. Jansen. 2010. "Financial Inclusion and Financial Stability: Current Policy Issues." ADBI Working Paper 259, Asian Development Bank Institute, Tokyo.

Hawkins, P. 2006. "Financial Access and Financial Stability." In *Central Banks and the Challenge of Development*, 65–79. Basel, Switzerland: Bank for International Settlements.

Klapper, L., A. Lusardi, and G. A. Panos. 2013. "Financial Literacy and Its Consequences: Evidence from Russia during the Financial Crisis." *Journal of Banking and Finance* 37 (10): 3904–23.

Laeven, L., and F. Valencia. 2013. "Systemic Banking Crises Database." *IMF Economic Review* 61 (2): 225–70.

Maimbo, Samuel Munzele, and Martin Melecky. 2016. "Financial Policy in Practice: Benchmarking Financial Sector Strategies around the World." *Emerging Markets Finance and Trade* 52 (1): 204–22, January.

Mehrotra, A. N., and J. Yetman. 2014. "Financial Inclusion and Optimal Monetary Policy." BIS Working Papers 476, Bank for International Settlements, Basel, Switzerland.

———. 2015. "Financial Inclusion: Issues for Central Banks." *BIS Quarterly Review* March: 83–96.

Melecky, M., and A. Podpiera. Forthcoming. "Financial Sector Strategies and Financial Sector Outcomes: Do the Strategies Perform?" Unpublished manuscript.

Morgan, P. J., and V. Pontines. 2014. "Financial Stability and Financial Inclusion." ADBI Working Paper 488, Asian Development Bank Institute, Tokyo.

Pearce, D., and C. R. Ortega. 2012. "Financial Inclusion Strategies: Reference Framework." Policy Research Working Paper 78761, World Bank, Washington, DC.

Prasad, E. S. 2010. "Financial Sector Regulation and Reforms in Emerging Markets: An Overview." IZA Discussion Paper 5233, Institute for the Study of Labor, Bonn, Germany.

Royston, P. 1991. "Comment on sg3.4 and an Improved D'Agostino Test." *Stata Technical Bulletin* 3: 23–24. Reprinted in *Stata Technical Bulletin Reprints*, vol. 1, 110–12. College Station, TX: Stata Press.

Sahay, R., M. Čihák, P. N'Diaye, A. Barajas, S. Mitra, A. Kyobe, Y. Mooi, and S. R. Yousefi. 2015. "Financial Inclusion: Can It Meet Multiple Macroeconomic Goals?" IMF Staff Discussion Note 15/17, International Monetary Fund, Washington, DC.

World Bank. 2013. *World Development Report 2014: Risk and Opportunity. Managing Risk for Development*. Washington, DC: World Bank.

———. 2014. *Global Financial Development Report 2014: Financial Inclusion*. Washington, DC: World Bank.

———. 2015. "Migration and Remittances: Recent Developments and Outlook." Migration and Development Brief 24, April 13.

Setting Up the Framework for Macroprudential Policy in Europe and Central Asia

Most Europe and Central Asia (ECA) countries have established the basic institutional framework for macroprudential policy making, which often involves using financial regulations (for example, reserve requirements, loan-to-value limits, payment-to-income limits, and sectoral credit limits) to ensure financial stability. In the vast majority of ECA countries, the central bank has the legal mandate to ensure financial stability. And 20 of the 23 ECA central banks have direct responsibility for banking supervision. Thus, most central banks have direct access to supervisory information and to the full range of microprudential tools required for macroprudential policies. Following the global financial crisis, central banks in ECA took steps to increase their focus on systemic risk. Almost all ECA central banks have set up financial stability units (most recently in Ukraine) and have started to publish financial stability reports.

Nevertheless, within ECA central banks, the delineation of micro- and macroprudential policy and the systematic integration of the new macroprudential function into central bank policy making are progressing at a slow pace and with varying degrees of success. In some cases, coordination and data sharing between the newly established financial stability units (generally staffed from economics/research divisions) and the traditional bank supervisors have been problematic. Staff working in the financial stability units often come from the economics/research areas of the central bank and sometimes struggle to speak the same language as their supervisor colleagues. Such problems are more limited where former bank supervisors are mixed with the research/economics types in the unit's staff (for example, the former Yugoslav Republic of Macedonia) and where supervision and

financial stability are under the same deputy governor (for example, Armenia).

Most central banks in ECA have not adopted the clear institutional division between macroprudential policies, banking supervision, and monetary policy that is viewed as best practice in some advanced countries (for example, the United Kingdom's Monetary Policy Committee and Financial Stability Committee). In ECA, the central bank's board generally retains the responsibility for policy making in all three areas. The internal advisory bodies established to channel policy advice from the staff to the board typically address all three issues as well, although in a few ECA countries separate internal committees exist for micro- and macroprudential discussions.

Many ECA countries have established financial stability councils (FSCs) designed to facilitate macroprudential coordination, among other tasks. The FSCs typically consist of the central bank, the ministry of finance, and sometimes various other stakeholders (deposit insurance, securities market regulator, parliamentary committee, and the like). However, these organizations mix crisis management (for example, bank resolution), where the likely use of public funds means that the ministry of finance plays a crucial role, with crisis prevention (micro- and macroprudential policies), where it is desirable to limit political influence to maintain central bank independence. As a result, the ministry tends to have a limited role at FSC meetings when there is no crisis, and the ministry's representation tends to be delegated to staff level, or meetings cease altogether.

Most central banks in ECA already have had some experience with using macroprudential policy tools. In the aftermath of the global financial crisis and with sluggish or negative credit growth, the macroprudential stance in ECA countries has typically tilted toward easing. However, some market segments (for example, consumer loans) recently started to show signs of excess in some countries, which triggered some macroprudential tightening (typically payment-to-income caps).

The use of "pure" macroprudential tools, such as the countercyclical capital buffer (CCB) or the systemic capital surcharge, is at the moment limited in ECA.[1] The identification of banks that are systemically important for the domestic economy (D-SIBs) is widespread in ECA, but more for the purpose of crisis preparation than for determining capital requirements. ECA countries that are European Union (EU) members (Bulgaria, Croatia, Poland, Romania) have to introduce these tools under the EU's Capital Requirements Directive (CRD IV); the CCB started to phase in in 2016. Countries wishing to join the EU will have to endorse CRD IV to meet EU standards. ECA countries that are not EU members or candidates, but have endorsed Basel III (for example, the Russian Federation and Turkey), are set to introduce these tools in the near future.

For the rest of the ECA countries, there are no known timetables or clearly identifiable motivating mechanisms for implementation. That said, ECA countries with substantial presence of Western European banks in their financial systems should be interested in the domestic implementation of macroprudential tools such as the CCB; otherwise the home country supervisor will set the buffer for the subsidiary at its discretion.

Recent financial stability reports show that ECA central banks are gradually improving their capacity for macroprudential analysis, in both the time-series and cross-sectional dimensions. Stress tests, especially to evaluate credit risk, are now widespread in the region. However, the quality of this analysis varies, with some central banks relying on simple scenario analysis and others estimating credit risk models with feedback loops. Regular stress tests of banks' liquidity positions, typically following the principles of the Basel III liquidity coverage ratio, are less universal in ECA countries (see table S6.1 for the stress-testing practices of the new EU member states). There has been less progress on analytical tools aimed at (a) measuring the current degree

TABLE S6.1 Stress-Testing Practices in the New EU Member States

| | Stress-testing methodology | | | | | |
| | Target variables | | Type of risk assessment in stress tests | | | |
	Solvency	Liquidity	Credit risk	Market risk	Concentration risk	Liquidity risk
Bulgaria						
Croatia	■		■			
Czech Republic	■		■		■	
Estonia	■		■			
Hungary	■	■	■	■		■
Latvia	■		■			
Lithuania	■		■			
Poland	■		■		■	
Romania	■		■			■
Slovak Republic	■		■			
Slovenia	■		■			

Source: World Bank 2013.
Note: Blue cells indicate which types of risk are covered by the individual country stress tests.

SPOTLIGHT 6 *(continued)*

FIGURE S6.1 Macroprudential analysis = systemic risk monitoring + policy simulation

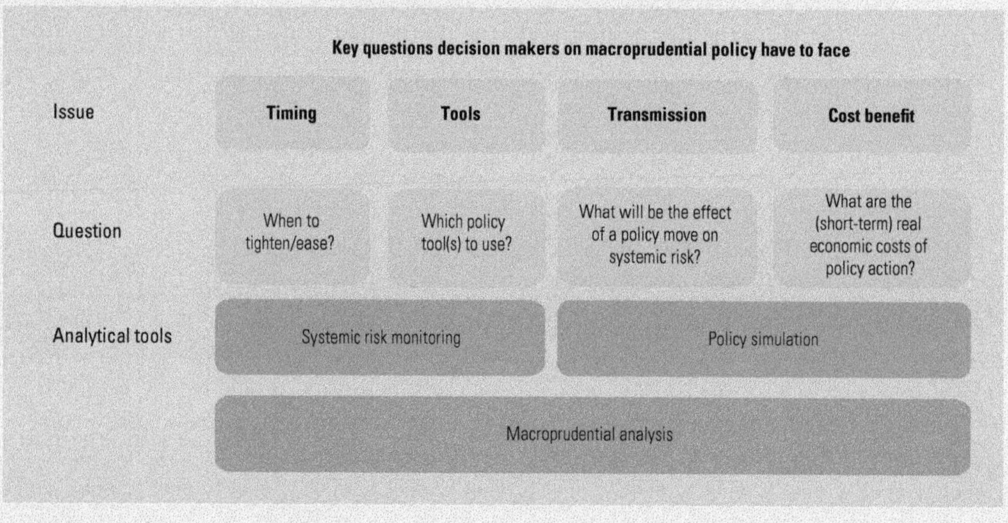

of stress (financial stress indexes); (b) forecasting future stress (early warning systems); and (c) measuring the policy stance and its impact (financial conditions indexes). Nevertheless, regular surveys to capture lending conditions are already in place in a number of countries (such as Albania, Armenia, Kazakhstan, Kosovo, FYR Macedonia, Romania, Serbia, and Ukraine).

Macroprudential analysis in ECA has predominantly focused on systemic risk monitoring rather than policy simulations. However, more activist macroprudential policy making, especially in the tightening phase when it meets political resistance and needs to be publicly defended, will require strong arguments substantiated with robust impact assessments of various policy alternatives (see figure S6.1). Such policy simulations should be based on a macro model with a representation of the financial system, which is a work in progress even in advanced country central banks. Until such models become available, analysis has to rely on shortcuts,

such as rules-of-thumb for bank behavior in reaction to macroprudential tightening or loosening (expressed in credit supply) and some quantifiable views on the impact of credit supply shocks on the real economy. Very few central banks in ECA have started to address these analytical challenges.

Note

1. The countercyclical capital buffer requires banks to set aside capital during periods of strong credit growth that they can then use during periods of financial stress. The systemic capital surcharge refers to higher capital requirements for large banks whose failure would pose a risk to the financial system.

Reference

World Bank. 2013. "Establishing Effective Macroprudential Frameworks in the New EU Member States." Unpublished internal document, World Bank, Washington, DC.

SPOTLIGHT 7
Promoting the Use of Insurance for Increased Risks from Climate Change

The countries of Southeastern Europe (SEE) face a difficult challenge from natural disasters. For example, the 2014 floods in Serbia and Bosnia and Herzegovina triggered massive landslides, destroying homes and damaging agriculture, with estimated losses totaling $4.5 billion. Although this was a one-in-a-hundred-year event, all countries in SEE have to cope with floods of varying severity, as well as earthquakes, forest fires, and drought, almost annually. Moreover, climate change is expected to increase the likelihood of hydrometeorological disasters. Rainfall is projected to increase by 5 percent in the northwest tip of the SEE region and to decline by 10 to 20 percent in the rest of the region. Lower rainfall and rising temperatures will increase the frequency and severity of drought, thus raising the potential for forest fires. And rainfall, when it comes, will be of greater intensity, leading to flash floods and landslides.

Households in the bottom 40 percent of the income distribution are hardest hit by natural disasters. Low-income households tend to depend on agriculture, which is particularly vulnerable to disasters. Low saving rates and the lack of a public safety net make it difficult to maintain consumption in the face of a sudden decline in income. In Serbia, an estimated 125,000 people fell below the poverty line after the 2014 floods, with vulnerable groups and the rural population particularly affected.[1]

The government cannot afford to provide adequate financial assistance to all those affected by natural disasters. The Serbian government's 2014 budget for dealing with natural disasters was about $57 million, whereas the estimated economic loss from the flooding was more than $2.1 billion. Thus, private sector insurance will be necessary to cover the risks presented by natural disasters. However, in the SEE region only 1–3 percent of homeowners and small and medium enterprises (SMEs) are insured against natural disasters. This lack of insurance was clearly felt in Bosnia and Herzegovina and in Serbia after the 2014 floods, when only $125 million of the $4.5 billion in losses were insured (Aon Benfield 2013).

The lack of indemnity-based catastrophe and parametric weather-risk insurance products such as Area Yield Index Insurance reflects limited supply and demand. The supply of disaster insurance is low because individual SEE countries have relatively small markets with little premium volume. Moreover, local companies are faced with undiversified risks and often cannot acquire reinsurance at affordable prices, and a lack of historical data and prohibitively expensive risk models of natural disasters make the development of disaster insurance products uneconomical for local companies. The few catastrophe insurance products that are offered are often too expensive for the average consumer, or are simply unreliable given the low capital base and often-insufficient reinsurance coverage of local companies that sell them.

Nevertheless, the supply of disaster insurance products in the region is increasing. The World Bank, jointly with the Global Environmental Fund (GEF) and the Swiss State Secretariat for Economic Affairs (SECO), are supporting the Southeastern Europe Catastrophe Risk Insurance Facility (SEE CRIF), a program to develop affordable, high-quality catastrophe and weather-risk insurance products for local homeowners, SMEs, and farmers. Countries become members of SEE CRIF by providing equity contributions financed by the World Bank. Albania became the first country to join the SEE CRIF in 2008, followed by Serbia and the

SPOTLIGHT 7 *(continued)*

former Yugoslav Republic of Macedonia in 2012. These countries established the Europa Reinsurance Facility Ltd. (Europa Re) as a specialized regional Swiss licensed reinsurer. Europa Re has launched numerous catastrophe insurance products, as well as weather-risk products such as the Agriculture Yield Index Insurance to protect farmers from a reduction in crop yields. To support these disaster insurance products, Europa Re has developed unique probabilistic risk models for earthquakes and floods and completed the underlying pricing and actuarial work. To get these products to market, Europa Re has also entered into partnership agreements with eight local private insurers, which already provided insurance coverage of more than $10 million to the public and local municipalities.

The demand for catastrophe insurance products continues to be low, despite the increased availability of high-quality flood and earthquake insurance packages that cost between $17.5 and $50 annually. When a disaster has not occurred recently, individuals tend to underestimate the probability of a catastrophe (Dumm, Johnson, and Watson 2015), and may not fully understand their risk exposure and potential losses or the benefits of catastrophe insurance. Low demand also reflects expectations that the government will provide assistance in response to natural disasters.[2] For example, less than 1 percent of Serbian households affected by flood had flood insurance during the 2014 floods. A survey by the Government of the Republic of Serbia (2014) noted that Serbians tend not to purchase disaster insurance because they expect that "losses due to natural disasters will be compensated by the government." Such expectations may be reinforced by government commitments: the Serbian government promised to rebuild homes after the 2014 floods, despite the lack of sufficient budgetary resources to help most affected households (see figure S7.1).

FIGURE S7.1 May 2014 floods in Serbia: government aid dominates insurance

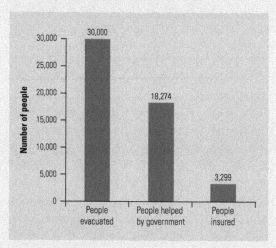

Source: NBS 2014.

Although it is difficult (and likely socially undesirable) for the government to ignore the plight of individuals devastated by a natural disaster, such government assistance may mean that individuals are likely to forgo insurance. This moral hazard issue should be addressed by requiring the purchase of insurance against catastrophes. Compulsory catastrophe insurance has been introduced elsewhere in ECA. The Romanian Catastrophic Insurance Pool has faced difficulties in enforcement but nevertheless insures more than 2 million homes, or about 30 percent of housing stock. The Turkish Catastrophe Insurance Pool, which was established with extensive technical and capital support from the World Bank, insures close to 7 million homes or about 40 percent of insurable housing. Compulsory disaster insurance is also slowly gaining traction in SEE. Advanced technical work is being undertaken in Albania, with World Bank support, to draft a compulsory catastrophe insurance law. Europa Re also continues to encourage member states to require catastrophe insurance for all homes and SMEs.

A similar moral hazard issue can be seen in the public sector. Because the government is responsible for compensating municipalities for disaster losses, municipalities have no incentive to purchase catastrophe insurance (Michel-Kerjan 2013). Transferring at least a part of the fiscal responsibility for natural disasters to the local level would increase municipalities' incentive to purchase insurance. For example, some Serbian municipalities sought disaster insurance after the central government indicated uncertainty over its ability to cover the losses from the 2014 floods. Sremska Mitrovica, a city that was devastated by the floods, purchased an Area Yield Index Insurance contract that insures the municipality's corn output against all perils, including flood. Specifically, if the city's average yield of maize drops below 20 percent, the municipality receives several million dollars in compensation. Increasing these contracts from only a few municipalities led by visionary mayors to *hundreds* of cities across SEE would require changing the intergovernmental fiscal system to increase the responsibility of local municipalities for covering the costs of recovery from disaster, hopefully before another major disaster occurs.

Increasing public education and risk awareness is an important complement to compulsory insurance. To this end, Europa Re has developed CATMonitor, an interactive consumer website for the SEE public to better understand and measure risk. The website includes several features for effectively visualizing hazard, property risk exposure, and loss information before and after natural disaster events. Europa Re also has implemented a regional public relations strategy and intends to develop country-specific communication strategies in order to increase public understanding of disaster risk.

In conclusion, although SEE now has a facility— SEE CRIF—that can provide a supply of accessible, good-quality, inexpensive catastrophe and weather-risk insurance products, low demand continues to hinder the development of local catastrophe insurance markets. Making disaster insurance compulsory for individuals, as well as requiring cities to take on more fiscal responsibility for disaster-related damages, will increase demand for catastrophe and weather-risk insurance, and ensure that more risk is transferred to the private sector. This would not only protect governments from unforeseen budgetary outlays but also enable them to channel scarce public resources to help the most vulnerable.

Notes

1. For more information, see the Serbian government's Public Investment Management Office website, http://www.obnova.gov.rs/english.
2. In the United States, a recent study showed that a $1,000 increase in the average individual disaster assistance grant decreased the average insurance coverage by $4,300 (Michel-Kerjan 2013).

References

Aon Benfield. 2013. *Global Climate and Catastrophe Report: Impact Forecasting—2013.* London: Aon Benfield.

Dumm, Randy E., Mark Johnson, and Charles Watson. 2015. "An Examination of the Geographic Aggregation of Catastrophic Risk." *Geneva Papers on Risk and Insurance: Issues and Practice* 40 (1): 159–77.

Government of the Republic of Serbia. 2014. *Serbia Floods 2014.* Belgrade: European Union, United Nations, and World Bank.

Michel-Kerjan, Erwann. 2013. "How We Entered an Ever-Growing Cycle on Government Disaster Relief." Roundtable presentation, U.S. Senate Committee on Small Business and Entrepreneurship, Washington, DC, March 14.

NBS (National Bank of Serbia). 2014. "Insurance Sector in Serbia: Report for 2014." Insurance Supervision Department, NBS, Belgrade.

Financial Sector Strategies and Financial Sector Outcomes: Do the Strategies Perform?

When a group of people heads out for a hike, it is useful for them to have a travel map with marked directions and planned time for completing the trip. This does not guarantee that the group won't run into unexpected obstacles and have to solve problems on the go, but it anchors the group's expectations, avoids misunderstandings about which path to take at each cross-section, and gives everyone a sense of how fast the group needs to hike. Sectoral policy strategies, including for the financial sector, are similar to travel maps. A particular challenge faced by a financial sector strategy is to weigh the systemic risk that advancing financial depth, efficiency, or inclusion entails. In other words, while aiming to better satisfy the demand of people, firms, and governments for financial services (payments, saving instruments, credit, equity, and insurance), the strategy needs to find ways for public policy to ensure prudent management of systemic risk in the financial sector (banks, nonbank financial institutions, and capital markets). Evaluating the scope and quality of financial sector strategies in Europe and Central Asia (ECA) and their impact on financial sector development can provide key insights into improving financial sector outcomes in the region.

This chapter considers whether the existence of a national financial sector strategy over 1985–2014, and its scope and quality, had a significant impact on financial sector outcomes, such as financial depth, stability, efficiency, and inclusion. We do not focus on whether all financial sector strategies fulfilled their goals because many of them do not set their goals using quantitative measures. Instead, we assess whether the existence of a comprehensive strategy can improve the development of the financial sector. In addition, we aim to understand how the

strategies support sustained financial development. For the latter, we try to identify whether the strategies had a direct role in shaping the regulatory framework or an indirect effect by bringing together the main institutions involved in the financial sector in an inclusive and consultative manner, ensuring a greater ownership of the agreed reform program, improving coordination within the public sector, and providing the private sector a clear view of policy intentions.

Main messages:

- The articulation of financial sector strategies has had a positive impact on financial deepening, stability, and inclusion, and this impact is greater for high-quality strategies. However, financial sector strategies do not appear to be significantly related to improved efficiency or profitability of banks.

- Financial sector strategies can affect financial outcomes not only by strengthening the regulatory framework but also by improving the coordination of policy within the government and across private sector firms and individuals, including by reducing uncertainty and providing a clear view of authorities' intentions.

- The quality of financial sector strategies in ECA, and around the world, could be improved greatly. One particular defect in ECA strategies is the failure to account for possible trade-offs between financial development and increases in systemic risk.

ECA is in particular need of effective financial sector strategies, given its recent experience of the rapid liberalization of financial markets, integration into global capital markets, and large capital inflows that helped feed credit booms. ECA has gone through two boom-and-bust cycles over the past 25 years. In the late 1990s, Central and Eastern Europe liberalized financial markets and then was hit by the emerging markets financial crisis in 1997–99. In the early 2000s, Southeastern Europe and Central Asia liberalized financial markets and were hit by the 2008 global financial crisis. It is unclear whether ECA authorities intentionally took on the systemic risk associated with financial liberalization and rapid financial deepening, or whether the extent of systemic risk, as well as the trade-off between financial development and systemic risk management, was poorly understood. The World Bank is assisting ECA countries in improving their ability to manage systemic risk through crisis simulation exercises (see spotlight 8).

Our work contributes to the literature by constructing a new database (not yet publicly available) of financial sector strategies, based on published documents across 150 low-, middle-, and high-income countries from all regions of the world. Using the assessment criteria proposed in Maimbo and Melecky (2014), we evaluate the quality and scope of the strategies in our database. That is, we assess whether the strategy adequately covers the objectives of financial development and systemic risk management, whether the stated objectives are accompanied by an implementation plan, and to what extent the strategy addresses the potential trade-off between financial development and systemic risk management. Although determining how strategies were formulated is not a major goal of this chapter, we provide some insight into the role of different actors in the origination and formulation of strategies. The origins of strategies are diverse, but good strategies often reflect the participation of major institutions involved in financial sector policy in one coordinated, consultative process.

To estimate the effect of financial sector strategies on financial sector outcomes, we control for several macroeconomic, social, and institutional factors commonly found in the literature (see Barajas et al. 2013; De la Torre, Feyen, and Ize 2013; De la Torre, Gozzi, and Schmukler 2007; Feyen, Lester, and Rocha 2011; and Yartey 2008). The set of macroeconomic indicators considered includes gross domestic product (GDP) per capita, GDP growth, the money market rate, inflation, and the change in exchange rate. To measure institutional development, we include the governance indicator developed by Kaufmann, Kraay, and Mastruzzi (2010) and the financial openness index of Chinn and Ito (2006). Socioeconomic indicators considered are the age dependency ratio and population density. A financial sector strategy is the highest-level policy document for the financial sector. Therefore, we do not include financial indicators as independent variables in the estimation of the relationship between strategies and financial outcomes because the development of financial sector indicators could have been directly influenced by the financial sector strategy.[1] Because reforms can be implemented also in countries with no explicit financial sector strategies, we further analyze whether there is a direct connection between financial strategies and the evolution of financial policy reforms. To this end, we use several indicators compiled in the World Bank's Doing Business database, including the distance to frontier[2] for getting credit, enforcing contracts, and resolving insolvency.

The overall scope and quality of financial sector strategies could be improved significantly. The strategies could pay greater attention to systemic risk associated with achieving the targeted development outcomes (financial depth, efficiency, and inclusion) as well as acknowledge and try to manage trade-offs in financial policy—particularly between the speed of financial development and systemic risk management. Financial sector strategies are more recent phenomena in ECA compared with East Asia and Pacific (EAP) or Latin America and the Caribbean (LAC). Although fewer countries in ECA have adopted financial sector strategies than in EAP, ECA strategies tend to be of higher quality and greater scope. Nevertheless, ECA strategies do not address trade-offs between financial development and systemic risk management, and they fall behind EAP, LAC, and in particular Organisation for Economic Co-operation and Development (OECD) economies in that respect.

Regression analysis suggests that the presence and quality of a strategy had a significant, positive impact on financial sector development in our sample of 150 countries over 1985–2014. The quality of the financial sector strategy was associated with increased financial deepening, as measured by the ratio of deposits to GDP, and reduced financial volatility, as measured by the standard deviation of deposits to GDP. The strategies increased financial inclusion as measured by the number of deposit accounts per 1,000 adults, but had no effect on the number of credit accounts per 1,000 adults. One explanation could be that the consideration of inclusion in financial sector strategies is only a recent phenomenon. We do not find strong evidence that the quality and scope of strategies have a greater impact on financial outcomes than does the simple presence of a strategy. This could be because the average quality of strategies was historically low, so that our criteria for measuring quality and scope do not reveal substantial differences in the strategies.

Overall, our evidence suggests that formulating financial sector strategies would help ECA countries to cope with future financial cycles. To strike the right balance in financial policy, ECA's financial sector strategies must pay attention to trade-offs between financial development and systemic risk management. In this respect, ECA can learn from some best practice examples from OECD and EAP economies such as Switzerland and Malaysia.

The remainder of this chapter is organized as follows: the first section provides an overview of the financial sector strategies, how they were formulated, and an assessment of their quality. The second section presents the data and the model for the analysis of the effect of financial strategies on financial development. The third section discusses the estimation results, and the last section concludes.

What Has Driven Financial Sector Strategies, and How Can They Be Evaluated?

A New Database Has Been Developed to Assess Financial Sector Strategies

The database of financial strategies includes all published financial sector strategies for which implementation began by 2012.[3] Our primary sources were the websites of ministries of finance, central banks, or financial sector supervisors. We contacted the country authorities if a strategy was not available on the Internet but was known to exist. We also included national development plans that contained comprehensive sections on financial sector development. Among the strategy documents, 39 are "financial sector development strategy" documents and 26 are "national development strategy" documents that include dedicated strategies for financial sector development.

Overall, we examined a sample of 150 countries around the world, with 45 of them having at least one financial sector strategy or a written plan for financial sector development. Of these 45 countries, 12 had two strategies (for example, Ghana had a four-year financial sector strategy starting in 2003 and a new six-year strategy starting in 2010) and four had three, so that a total of 65 documents were used in the analysis. The average implementation period of a strategy was about 5 years, with the minimum period 2 years and the maximum period 16 years.

The total number of strategies in place peaked around 2006–07 (figure 6.1) and decreased substantially during the global crisis, when authorities likely focused more on crisis preparedness and resolution than on development strategies. At the same time, the lessons from the global crisis were only slowly emerging, as beliefs about finance were changing and new global regulation standards were being formulated. A smaller number of strategies were in place in 2012 because

FIGURE 6.1 The number of strategies in place increased in the 150 countries analyzed

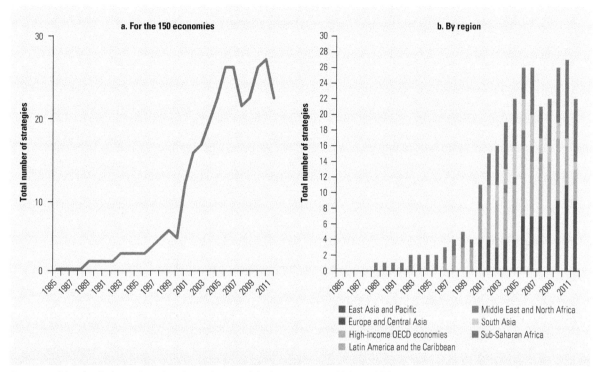

Source: World Bank calculations based on the newly created database (not yet publicly available).
Note: OECD = Organisation for Economic Co-operation and Development.

the implementation period for several finished in 2011, including strategies initiated during the crisis.

Financial sector strategies are a more recent phenomenon for ECA than for EAP and LAC. According to our database, the first strategies in ECA appeared only in the early 2000s (for instance, Turkey in 2001), perhaps prompted by the recovery from the emerging markets crisis of 1997–98 and the need for a strategic approach to managing the upcoming financial cycle. However, no financial sector strategy was initiated in ECA in 2003–05, when a number of strategies were being prepared in EAP and LAC. In 2006, ECA's interest in financial sector strategies restarted (Georgia and the Kyrgyz Republic initiated strategies in 2006) and, by 2011–12 the number of strategies in ECA was on par with LAC, but still behind EAP. Whether financial sector strategies were originated independently by governments, or reflected the initiatives of international development organizations, has some bearing on our analysis. For example, if a strategy was formulated in the context of an International Monetary Fund (IMF) program, then subsequent changes in financial sector development may in part reflect program requirements rather than strategy developed by the national authorities. Although it is difficult to account for this in our analysis, it appears that international organizations have played a role in the development of several strategies, although not necessarily in the context of an explicit program. Other strategies, however, reflect the initiative of national actors (box 6.1).

BOX 6.1 The Origination of Financial Sector Strategies

Some early strategy documents resulted from the collaboration between national governments or central banks with international development organizations. For instance, Botswana's 1989 *Financial Policies for Diversified Growth* resulted from a collaborative effort between Botswana's Ministry of Finance and Development Planning and the Bank of Botswana on one side, and the World Bank on the other side (World Bank 1989). Similarly, Madagascar's 1993 financial strategy resulted from close collaboration between the government of Madagascar and the World Bank (World Bank 1993). Cambodia's "Financial Sector Blueprint for 2001–2010" was based on consultations between the national Financial Sector Steering Committee and the Asian Development Bank (ADB), which followed a preliminary financial sector "roadmap" drafted in 1999 by ADB at the request of the Cambodian government (Chun et al. 2001). The following 10-year financial sector strategy for Cambodia, which started in 2006, reflected the national effort to encourage a broader participatory approach involving stakeholders from the financial sector and consultations among line ministries, private sectors, and nongovernmental organizations. ADB, the International Monetary Fund (IMF), and the World Bank helped coordinate the consultations (Kingdom of Cambodia 2006).

Some recent strategies also benefitted from the support of international development organizations. Ghana's 2003 Financial Sector Strategic Plan was supported by the U.S. Agency for International Development and benefitted from contributions of participants from the financial sector, the private sector, and academia (Republic of Ghana 2003). However, the ensuing 2011 "Financial Sector Strategic Plan II," outlined by the Ministry of Finance and Economic Planning, originated from the effort of more developed and capacitated national institutions and it was finalized after "extensive consultation with the regulatory agencies, financial institutions, and other public and private sector stakeholders" (Republic of Ghana 2011). Other examples include the African Development Bank's support for the Arab Republic of Egypt's 2006–10

Financial Sector Reform Programme (African Development Bank 2012), the World Bank's support for the Lao People's Democratic Republic's Financial Institution Development Strategy 2009–20 (Governor of the Bank of Lao PDR 2006), and financial support provided by the multi-donor-funded Financial Sector Reform and Strengthening (FIRST) Initiative, and technical assistance from the German Development Cooperation for Sierra Leone's 2009 Financial Sector Development Plan (Bank of Sierra Leone 2009). The FIRST initiative also supported the development of Rwanda's 2007 and 2012 strategies (Murgatroyd et al. 2007; Andrews et al. 2012).

Other developing countries prepared financial sector strategies after their participation in a Financial Sector Assessment Program (FSAP).[a] Burundi prepared its 2011–17 Financial Sector Strategy after the 2009 FSAP (Republic du Burundi 2010). Rwanda's 2007 strategy is also based on the 2005 FSAP recommendations. Other strategies, for example by the National Bank of Georgia (2006) for the development of the banking sector over 2006–09, include among the featured tasks and goals the fulfillment of the recommendations of the FSAP. In other cases, for instance Ethiopia's 2002 *Sustainable Development and Poverty Reduction Strategy*, the countries incorporated the recommendations from technical assistance by IMF and the World Bank (FDRE MOFED 2002).

On the other hand, many governments and central banks took the initiative to conduct consultations and prepare strategies for developing their financial sectors. Trinidad and Tobago's Ministry of Finance (2001, 2004) prepared both the 2002 *Medium-Term Policy Framework* and the 2004 "Reform of the Financial System." In 2004, Zambia's Ministry of Finance and National Planning laid out the 2004–09 "Financial Sector Development Plan for Zambia" (Republic of Zambia 2004). In the Kyrgyz Republic, the 2006 and 2009 strategies were prepared by the central bank (National Bank of the Kyrgyz Republic 2011). Thailand's Ministry of Finance and the Bank of Thailand designed the 2004 and 2010 "Financial

(Continued)

BOX 6.1 *(continued)*

Sector Master Plans I and II." Turkey's 2001 and 2010 Strategic Plans were formulated by the Banking Regulation and Supervision Agency (Banking Regulation and Supervision Agency 2001).

For some developed countries, the establishment of a particular institution was the trigger for laying down a strategic plan for future development of the financial sector. In Canada, the government established in 1996 the Task Force on the Future of the Canadian Financial Services Sector to provide advice on the future of the sector. After two years of study and consultations, the newly created institution proposed a number of measures to be implemented in a strategic document (Department of Finance Canada 1999). The global financial crisis prompted some countries to rethink the path for financial sector development. For instance, in Switzerland, the Federal Department of Finance in collaboration with the Swiss Financial Market Supervisory Authority and the Swiss National Bank formulated a set of objectives and strategic directions to strengthen the financial sector in the aftermath of the crisis (Federal Council of Switzerland 2009). In Ukraine, a program of reforms was developed by the working groups of the Economic Reform Committee (Committee on Economic Reforms under the President of Ukraine 2010).

Among the financial strategies in our database, 26 were part of national development strategies—comprehensive plans considering a wide area of development objectives. In Jordan, the financial strategy was included in the government's "National Social and Economic Development Plan" for the years 2004–06. Similarly, the governments of Uganda and Lesotho included objectives for financial sector development in Uganda's National Development Plan for 2010–14 and Lesotho's

National Strategic Development Plan for 2002–16. In Vietnam, the party congress laid out the strategy for socioeconomic development for 2001–10, while the State Bank of Vietnam formulated the 2011 "Banking Development Strategy." In 2002, the Danish government adopted the "Danish Growth Reform Program" that also refers to financial sector areas that need strategic development. One important side benefit of developing the strategy was that the process brought together stakeholders involved in the financial sector for extensive consultations before and after the strategies were formulated.

Cambodia is a good example of how developing a strategy can trigger the needed policy dialogue. Although ADB played an important role in the formulation of the first financial sector strategy for Cambodia, the next strategy involved active contributions from key stakeholders in the financial sector. Ethiopia's 2002 *Sustainable Development and Poverty Reduction Strategy* emphasizes that the document was prepared after conducting "extensive, transparent and inclusive consultations" (FDRE MOFED 2002). South Africa's 2011 plan, *A Safer Financial Sector to Serve South Africa Better*, also highlights that the strategy is meant to be the ". . . beginning of an important conversation with the society including all other stakeholders" (Republic of South Africa, National Treasury 2011). After China's State Council approved *The 12th Five-Year Plan for the Development and Reform of the Financial Industry*, the People's Bank of China conducted a series of surveys, organized expert seminars, solicited comments from the public, and carried out research on major issues regarding the development and reform of the financial industry under the plan (People's Bank of China et al. 2012).

a. The joint World Bank-IMF program provides countries with a comprehensive and in-depth analysis of their financial sector.

Financial Strategies Should Be Assessed by Measuring Their Relationship to Financial Outcomes

The quality and scope of financial sector strategies can be assessed on the basis of four categories of strategic objectives: financial development, systemic risk management, implementation arrangements, and policy trade-offs (table 6.1 provides the rating criteria used, based on Maimbo and Melecky 2014).

TABLE 6.1 Financial Sector Strategy Rating Criteria Developed by Maimbo and Melecky (2014)

Development objectives	Clear	Is the objective of the document clearly identified somewhere in the strategy?
	Quantified	Is the objective of the document quantified?
	Tools to implement them	Are there tools identified in the document to support the development goals?
Systemic risk	Identified	Does the document refer to systemic risk and macroprudential regulation?
	Quantified	Are these issues, or issues related to capital adequacy, liquidity risk, and increase in reserve charges, quantified?
	Tools	Does the document make reference to tools to affect capital adequacy, risk-based capital regulation, and other reserves allocation in financial institutions?
Implementation	Development	Does the document make reference to how it will implement the growth in the banking sector part of the strategy?
	General risk (looking for a financial sector board)	Does the government have a financial sector board, or at least a body that will implement macroprudential regulation? Or does the government at least refer to using macroprudential tools to control systemic risk beyond individual bank risk?
Trade-off	Trade-off is communicated (change in regulatory approach)	Does it acknowledge that imposing more stringent banking capital adequacy requirements and additional capital charges will reduce potential growth in the banking sector?

Source: Maimbo and Melecky 2014.

Key evaluation criteria for the financial development objective are whether a strategy has clear and well-quantified objectives and whether it identifies tools to support its development goals. For instance, the financial strategy for Rwanda in 2007[4] states that "Rwanda seeks to develop a financial sector that is effective, in particular, by: (1) Expanding access to credit and financial services; (2) Enhancing savings mobilization, especially long-term savings; and (3) Mobilizing long-term capital for investment" (Murgatroyd et al. 2007). This description is clear, but it does not provide quantitative objectives or tools to achieve them. By contrast, to strengthen banks' role in providing better access to financial services, Rwanda's strategy quantifies the development objectives for the market shares and the pricing of bank products and supports them with one main action, namely the transformation of Union des Banques Populaires du Rwanda into a commercial bank, Banque Populaire du Rwanda.

Elements of an effective strategy to address systemic risk include: (a) the identification of potential risks, such as a significant increase in private sector indebtedness or imprudent behavior of financial institutions that could lay the foundations for instability; and (b) specification of an adequate set of measures or tools for mitigating and managing such risks. For instance, the 10-year financial sector strategy for Cambodia acknowledges that unsafe banking can lead to a systemic financial crisis, emphasizes the need for financial regulation and supervision to avoid future crises, and recognizes that rapid financial liberalization in the absence of appropriate sequencing and development of the legal and regulatory framework can increase the likelihood of crises. The strategy, initiated in 2011 by the Royal Government of Cambodia, states that "a crisis management framework will need to be established and will require periodic testing to ensure it fits the local economic and financial situation as well as be designed to address increasing interconnections and new risks within the financial sector" (Kingdom of Cambodia 2011).

The quality and scope of a strategy is also assessed on the basis of its plan for implementation of the strategy and the coordination mechanism that will be used, and whether the strategy assigns responsibilities and has a clear time frame for implementing both the development goals and systemic risk management. For instance, the 2006–09 strategy to develop the Georgian banking system sets 58 development actions with corresponding time frames for implementation (National Bank of Georgia 2006). In addition, the strategy declares that the National Bank of Georgia considers close cooperation with international financial institutions as one priority for successful implementation of the adopted strategy.

Finally, an effective strategy should acknowledge, and have plans to address, the trade-off between development goals and systemic risks. In particular, strategies should recognize that overambitious development involves excessive risk-taking by the financial system. And conversely, that imposing more stringent requirements on bank capital adequacy and additional capital charges to reduce macroprudential and systemic risk could hinder banking sector development. Although ECA authorities have improved the institutional framework for macroprudential policy and have some experience in using macroprudential policy tools, further efforts are required to strengthen the analysis of macroprudential risks and implementation of policies (see spotlight 6).

The strategy index assigns equal weights to each of the nine criteria that are assessed as fully or largely met (scored 1) or not met (scored 0). The resulting total score is the overall index of the strategy. The median of the strategy index for our sample is 4.0, with a standard deviation of 2. On average, strategies focus more on development than on systemic risk—the median development index (including implementation of the development objective) is 3.05 whereas the median systemic risk index (including implementation of the systemic risk objective) is 1.15. Figure 6.2 shows the evolution of the subindexes for financial development and for systemic risk management separately across all strategies in our sample. Only 10 strategies focus on the trade-off between development and systemic risk.[5] Figure 6.3 illustrates the country distributions of the overall index, development subindex, systemic risk subindex, and the trade-off subindex.

After 2006, ECA financial sector strategies focused more on systemic risk management than strategies prepared in LAC, but ECA still lags behind EAP on the systemic risk considerations. Both ECA and LAC experienced a dip in the development of financial sector strategies toward the end of our sample.

Most often the strategies were rated 3 on our 0–9 scale (figure 6.3), so that the strategies of many countries are considered of a low quality and narrow scope. However, 13 strategies were rated around 6, which is above the midpoint of our scale. There is only one strategy (for Switzerland) in the database rated with the maximum index of 9. The ratings of the subindexes help to explain the poor results for the overall rating. Whereas more than 55 strategies focus on financial development outcomes and receive a rating of 3 or 4 on the development index, only 17 strategies focus on systemic risk management. Moreover, fewer than 10 strategies focus historically on the trade-offs between financial development and systemic

FIGURE 6.2 More strategies focus on development than on systemic risk

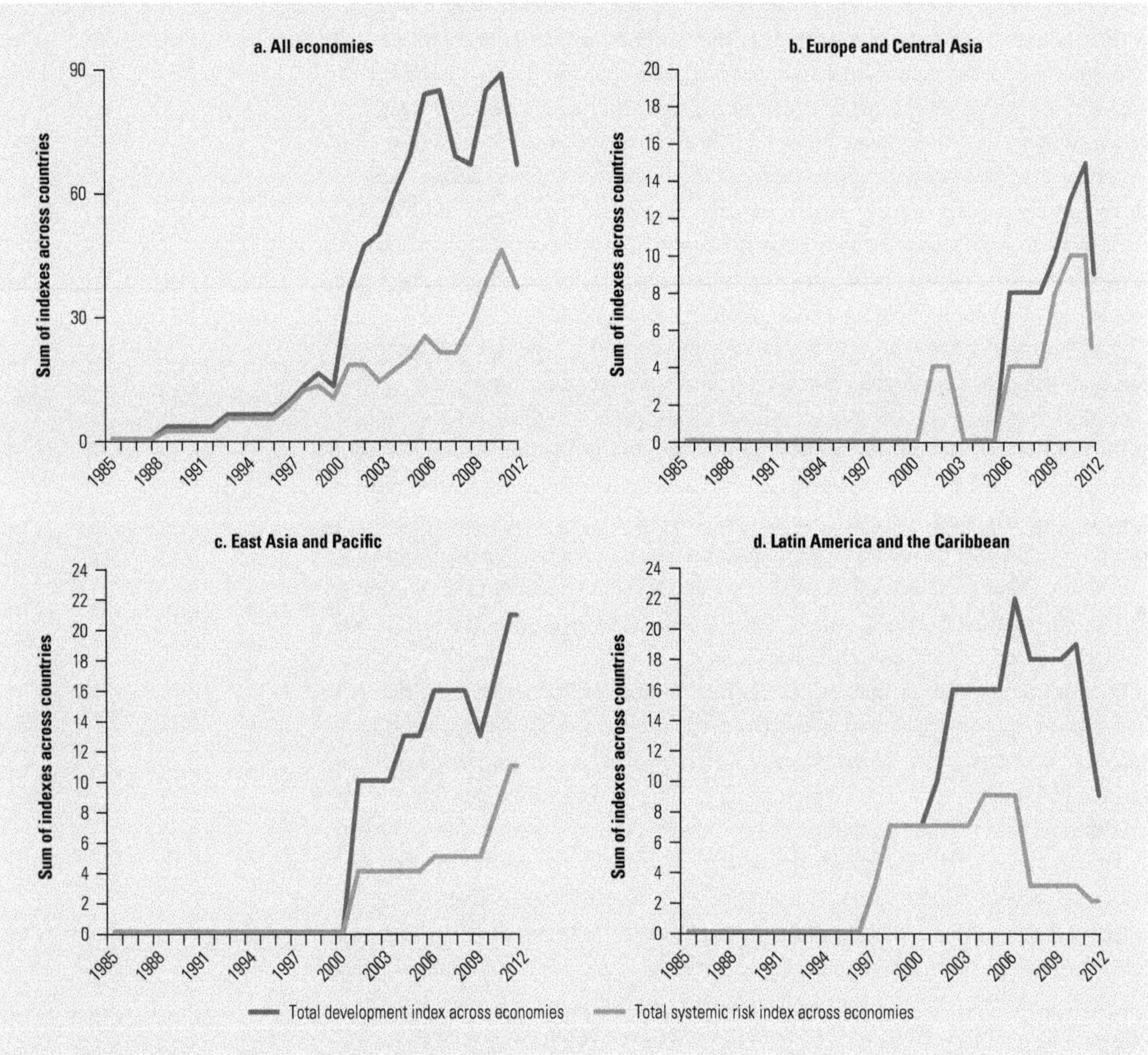

Source: World Bank calculations based on the newly created database.

risk management. Finally, although this cannot be seen in the distributions given in figure 6.3, most strategies lack measurable goals that would strengthen the ability to monitor their implementation and help increase accountability for results.

Figure 6.4 shows that ECA countries, followed by EAP and OECD economies, have the highest scores on the overall index for financial sector strategies—that is, ECA leads on the quality and scope of its strategies. This result is mainly due to the high scores that ECA achieves on the development index, including using measurable goals for development targets, and on the systemic risk index because of its much greater focus on financial stability. However, ECA scores very badly when it comes to considering trade-offs, for the most part disregarding trade-offs between the returns from fast financial development and the risk of occasional financial crises.

FIGURE 6.3 Most strategies receive low ratings

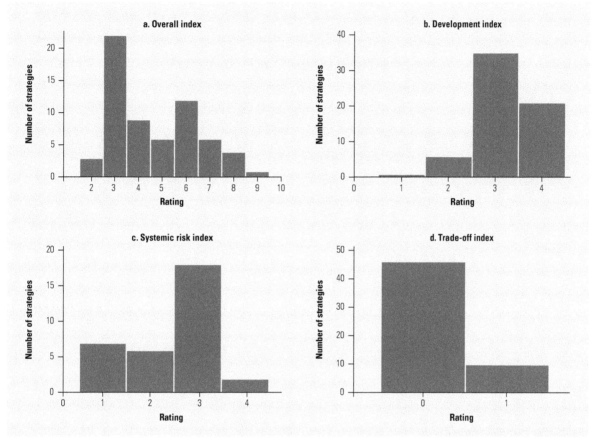

Source: World Bank calculations based on the newly created database.

How Do We Estimate the Relationship between Strategies and Financial Outcomes?

Several Indicators of Financial Development Are Used

This section provides an estimate of the effect of the strategies on financial sector outcomes, as measured by indicators of financial depth, inclusion, efficiency, and stability. We focus on the measures that have been used in the literature and have good data coverage, so the maximum number of countries can be included:

- To measure financial *depth*, we use the change in the logarithm (the percentage change) of the deposit-to-GDP ratio and the ratio of private credit to GDP. These ratios are often used as measures of financial depth (Panizza 2014). The change in logarithm is used to control for possible trends and the impact of the initial level of an indicator in order to better isolate the effect on financial deepening due to the strategies.

- To measure financial *inclusion*, we use the logarithm of total number of deposit accounts per 1,000 adults and the logarithm of the total number of borrowers per

FIGURE 6.4 ECA strategies have the highest ratings, except when considering the trade-off between stability and inclusion

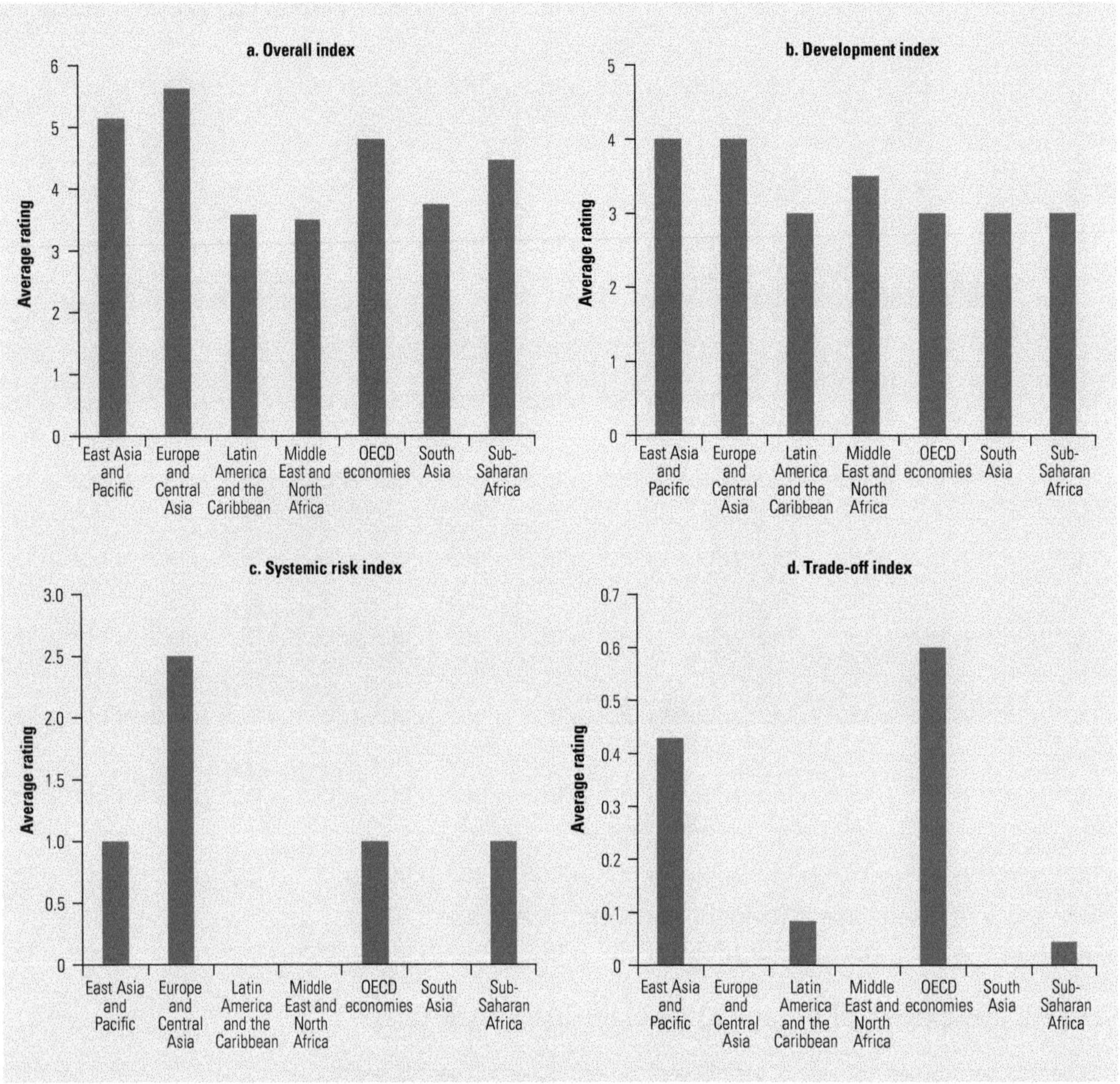

Source: World Bank calculations based on the newly created database.

1,000 adults. The two indicators have annual data available since 2004, and thus offer a better coverage compared with other measures of financial inclusion such as those from the Global Findex.

- To measure financial *efficiency*, we use the logarithm of the ratio of overhead costs to income (Bikker 2010), and a profitability indicator—the return on assets (ROA) ratio.[6]

- To measure financial stability, we use the volatility of the change in the logarithm of the deposits-to-GDP ratio and the credit-to-GDP ratio (volatility is measured by a moving five-year standard deviation for each of the two variables).[7] In addition, we use an alternative measure of financial stability, the output loss during banking crises computed by Laeven and Valencia (2013), to determine if our results are greatly affected by the particular measure used to represent stability.[8] Figure 6.5 illustrates the evolution of financial sector development indicators.

FIGURE 6.5 Financial indicators for the median country have been roughly stable in ECA, except financial inclusion has risen

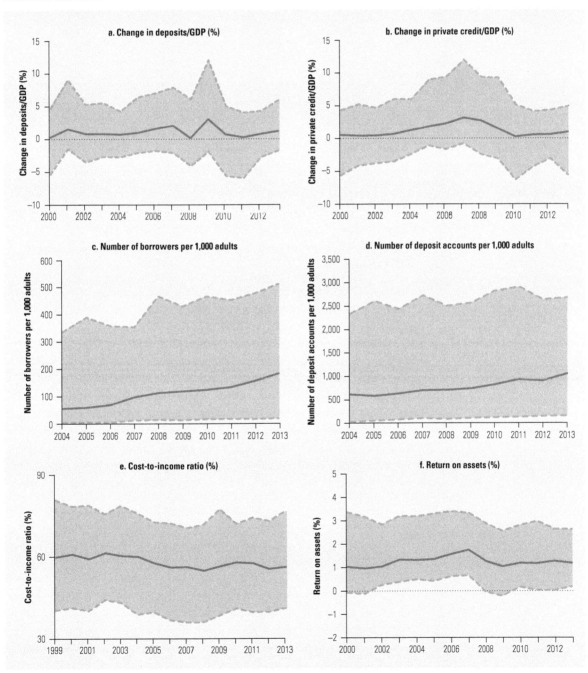

(Continued)

FIGURE 6.5 Financial indicators for the median country have been roughly stable in ECA, except financial inclusion has risen *(continued)*

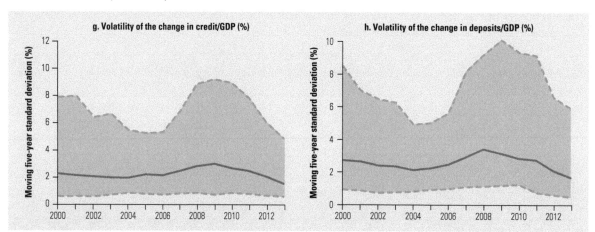

Sources: World Bank calculations based on data from the World Bank's FinStats database and the International Monetary Fund's Financial Access Survey.
Note: The dark, solid line in the middle of each graph is the median level of the indicated variable. The dashed line on top indicates the level of the variable below which 90 percent of observations fall. The dashed line at the bottom indicates the level of the variable below which 10 percent of the observations fall.

Regression Analysis Is Used to Estimate the Relationship between Strategies and Financial Sector Outcomes

Financial sector strategies have had a meaningful effect on financial development. These estimations are based on annual data for 150 countries over 1985–2014. Figures 6.6 (ratio of deposits to GDP), 6.7 (overhead costs to income), and 6.8 (volatility of the change in the private credit to GDP) show that initiation of a strategy was associated with an improvement in financial development variables in several countries.

To determine whether the apparent improvement in financial development is significantly related to initiation of a strategy, we use regression analysis to estimate the relationship between financial sector development and indicators of the existence and quality of a strategy, macroeconomic indicators, socioeconomic indicators (the variables are defined below), and particular country characteristics not otherwise captured:[9]

We use four transformations of the strategy indicators to measure the impact of the strategies over time. Two of these are referred to as *dummy* variables, meaning that they are set equal to 1 in the period affected by a strategy and zero otherwise. The other two are *index strategy* variables, meaning that they are set equal to the index value measuring the quality and scope of the strategy during the period affected, and zero otherwise. Each of these two types of variables is structured both as an *impulse* variable and as a *shift* variable, as follows:

FIGURE 6.6 Ratio of deposits to GDP often rose during implementation of a strategy (selected countries)

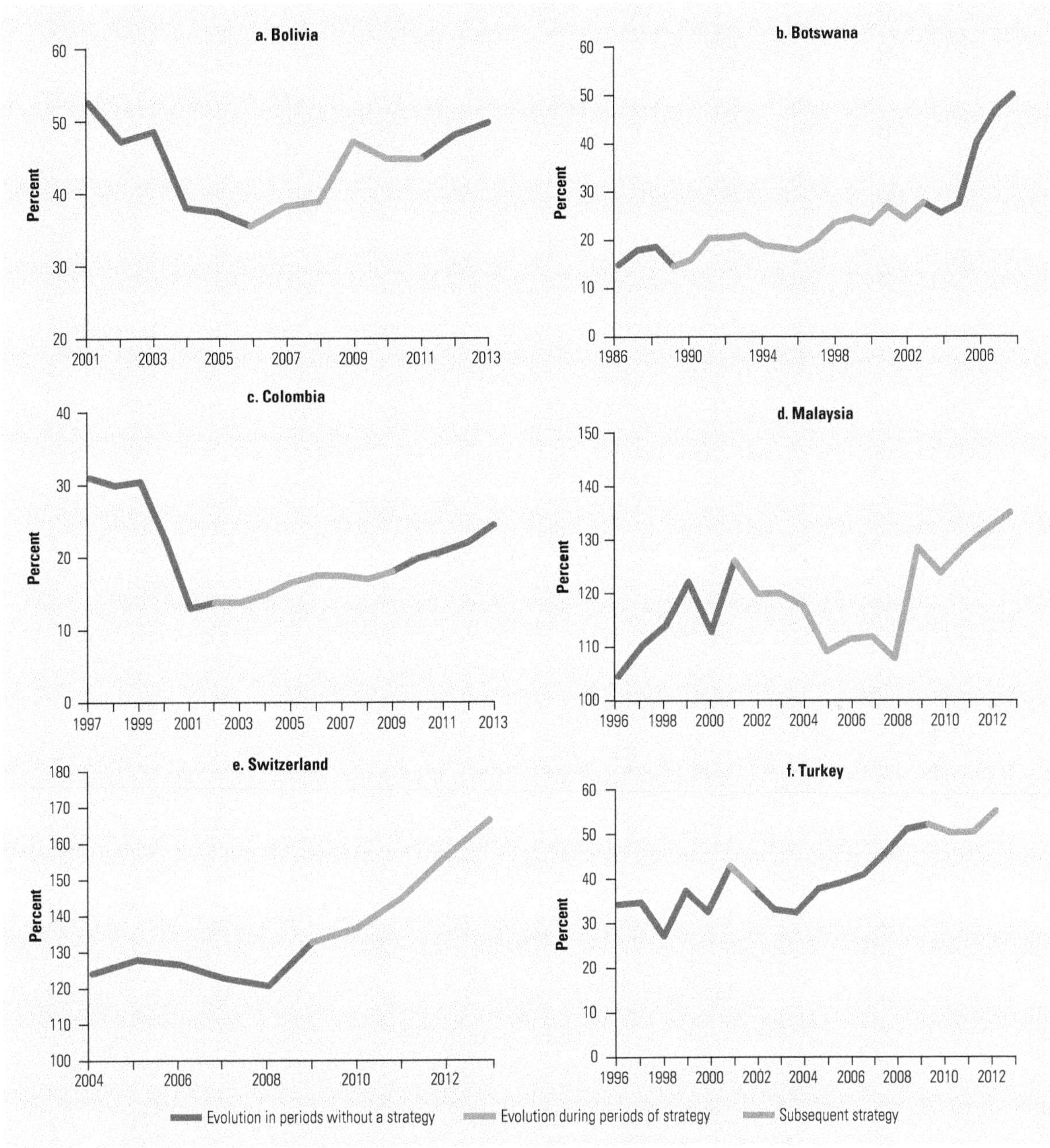

Evolution in periods without a strategy — Evolution during periods of strategy — Subsequent strategy

Sources: World Bank's FinStats for the deposits-GDP ratio and World Bank data set of financial strategies.

- The *impulse variables* measure the impact of the strategy during its period of effectiveness. Thus the *dummy strategy* indicator for the *impulse* variable equals 1 during the strategy's implementation period and 0 otherwise. For instance, Mozambique had two financial sector strategies during 2001–05 and 2010–20. In our database, the *dummy strategy* for Mozambique has the value of 1 during 2001–05 and 2010–13, and 0 otherwise. By contrast, the *index strategy* indicator for the *impulse* variable equals the value of the index

FIGURE 6.7 Ratio of overhead costs to income often fell during implementation of a strategy (selected countries)

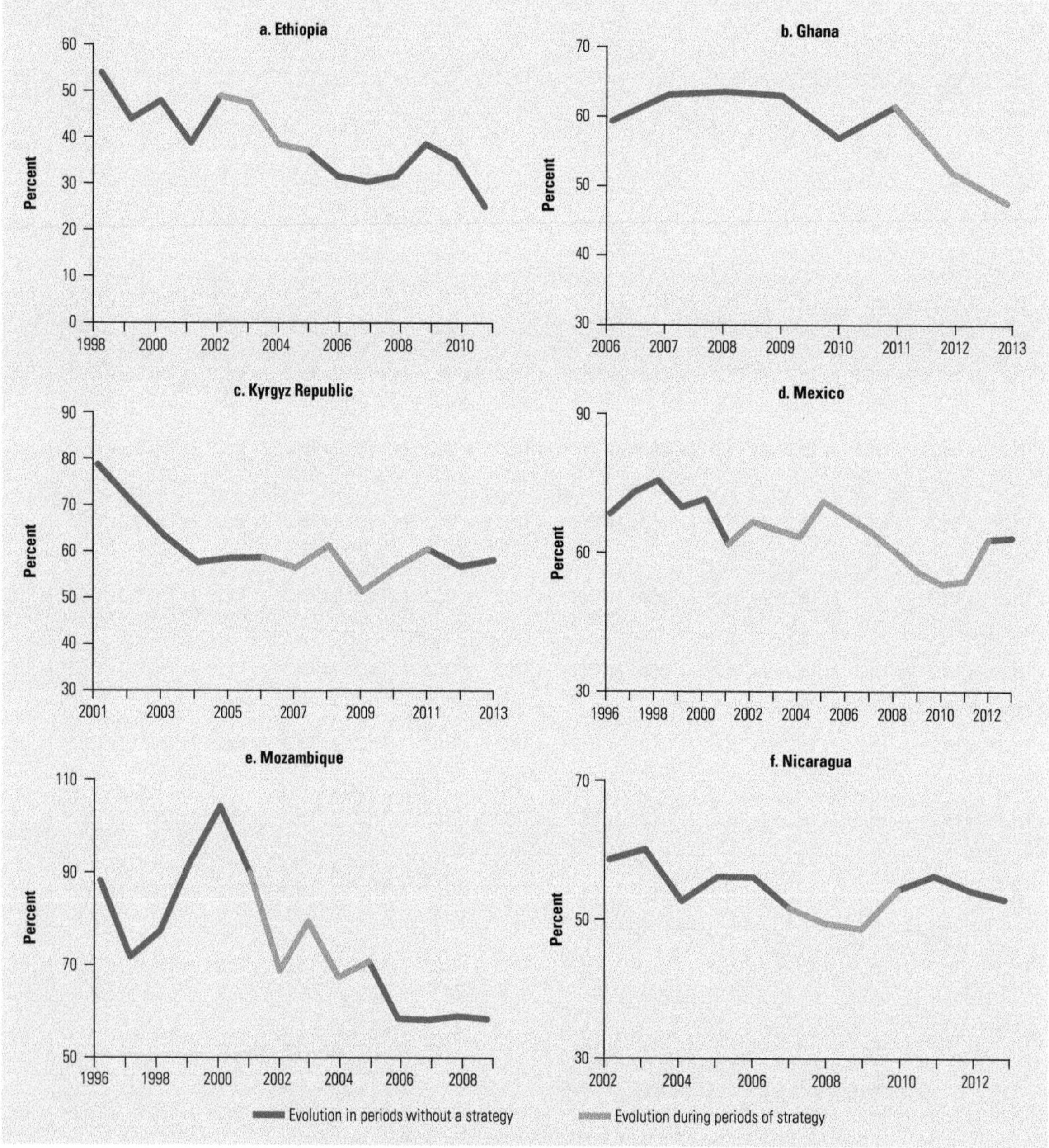

Sources: World Bank FinStats for the ratio of overhead costs to income and World Bank data set of financial strategies.

(assessed scope and quality previously discussed) during the strategy's implementation period and 0 otherwise. The *index strategy* for Mozambique has the value of 3 during 2001–05, 7 during 2010–13, and 0 otherwise.

- `The *shift* variables measure the effects of strategies on financial development that may extend beyond the implementation period for the strategy. We do this

FIGURE 6.8 **Instability often fell during implementation of a strategy (ratio of the volatility of the change in private credit to GDP, selected countries)**

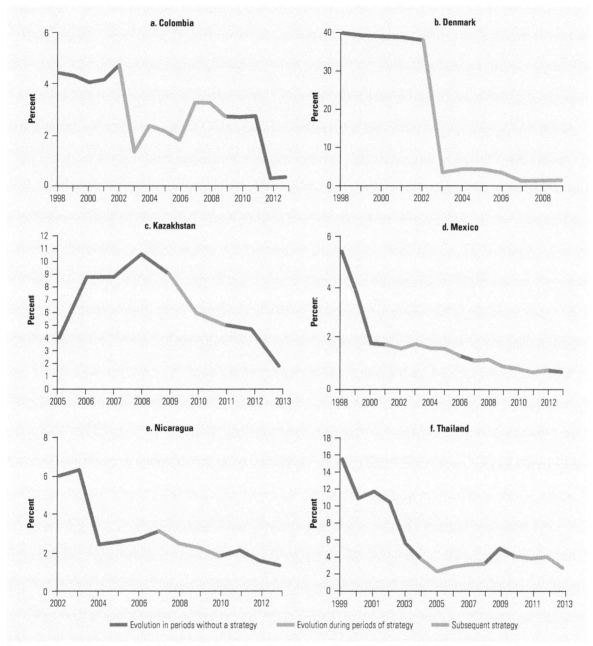

Sources: Computations based on World Bank's FinStats for the ratio of private credit to GDP and World Bank data set of financial strategies.

by extending the nonzero values of the *impulse* variables (both the *dummy strategy* and the *index strategy*) over time until the implementation period of the next strategy, or until 2013 if no strategy follows in our sample. For instance, Denmark had a strategy during 2002–10, and the *dummy strategy* indicator for the *shift* variable takes the value of 1 from 2002 until 2013. We run separate regressions for all *impulse* and *shift* strategy variables.

We control for the impact on financial outcomes of several macroeconomic, institutional, demographic, and social factors commonly found in the literature. The macroeconomic factors include GDP per capita, GDP growth, the interest rate, inflation, and the change in the exchange rate (De la Torre, Gozzi, and Schmukler 2007; Barajas et al. 2013; Feyen, Lester, and Rocha 2011). The set of institutional variables includes indicators of governance and financial openness. The governance indicator is the updated indicator of governance by Kaufmann, Kraay, and Mastruzzi (2010)[10] that measures the quality of the institutions and the legal and regulatory environment—all of which affect financial sector outcomes (Barajas et al. 2013; Feyen, Lester, and Rocha 2011; Yartey 2008). The financial openness indicator is the updated indicator by Chinn and Ito (2006) that measures the extent of regulatory controls over current or capital account transactions, the existence of multiple exchange rates (where governments require that certain transactions be valued at a more favorable exchange rate than others), and the requirements of surrendering export proceeds. The socioeconomic indicators considered are the age dependency ratio and population density.[11] The last two indicators are used as control variables when relevant, namely, in regressions for financial depth, inclusion, and efficiency. The population density should have a positive effect, and the age dependency a negative effect, on financial depth and inclusion (De la Torre, Feyen, and Ize 2013).[12]

The possibility that the strategy indicator is endogenous, that is, in part affected by the dependent variable of financial development, is a concern for the estimation of the regression model.[13] Financial development could influence the emergence of a strategy, and its scope and quality, although it is unclear whether lower or higher financial sector development would trigger the preparation of a financial sector strategy. As discussed in box 6.1, the reason for initiating a strategy differed greatly across countries. Strategies have arisen from a close collaboration of countries with international development organizations, for example following recommendations from the Financial Sector Assessment Program (FSAP), or may have been a reaction to measures taken after the global financial crisis, or may have primarily reflected the initiatives of governments and central banks to signal their commitment to give a financial sector a greater push and direction for development. The very diverse origins of the financial sector strategies, together with our several unsuccessful attempts to find a relevant instrument (FSAPs, development assistance including FIRST [Financial Sector Reform and Strengthening], governance, and economic freedom) explain why we consider the strategies as a weakly exogenous variable in our regression model.[14] The other approach employed to address this problem is to use the value of the strategy variable in the previous period, rather than the concurrent value.

We also briefly examine the mechanisms through which the strategies worked. Namely, we examine whether they led to implementation of broad-based regulatory reforms. Ideally, we would like to determine whether the implementation plan for each strategy, including deployment of tools and measures, was followed. But we are unable to perform this analysis because of data limitations, especially on earlier strategies. Instead, we analyze whether the strategies in our sample have an impact on the development of regulatory policy, while including as many strategies as possible in the analysis. The quantitative analysis of the impact of strategies on regulatory reforms focuses on three indicators from the World Bank's Doing Business database that are relevant for financial sector development: getting credit, enforcing contracts, and resolving insolvency. The coverage of the Doing Business database starts in 2004, so this part of the analysis considers a more limited period than in our extensive historical database on strategies. Nevertheless, this exercise can provide some insight into whether the more recent strategies have affected the implementation of regulatory policies in the financial sector.

ECA-specific dummy variables (where each ECA country has a value of 1 and other countries a value of zero) are included in all our estimations to determine whether location in ECA affects the relationship between the independent variables and the financial development indicators. However, these dummies do not capture any additional effects beyond that of the other variables included in the equation. Therefore, the specific results for ECA dummies are not discussed in the next section.

What Are the Estimation Results?

Strategies Help Increase the Financial Depth

Financial deepening, particularly an increase in the ratio of deposits to GDP, is positively affected by the presence and the quality of a strategy. The coefficients of all four strategy variables (the *index* and *dummy* strategy indicators for both the *impulse* and *shift* variables—see above) are significant and positively related to the change in the deposits-to-GDP ratio (table 6.2), showing that the presence and quality of a strategy have an important impact on financial deepening. The estimated relationships between our four strategy indicators and the change in the credit-to-GDP ratio are positive, but the coefficients are not significantly different from zero. One possible explanation is that the ratio of credit to GDP is an ambiguous measure of sustainable financial deepening because it also can be a predictor of crises, and in particular a rise in credit to GDP from an already high level can increase instability. Also, increases in credit-to-GDP ratios can have opposite effects on growth in the short run and the long run (Loayza and Ranciere 2006; Arcand, Berkes, and Panizza 2012; and Ranciere, Tornell, and Westermann 2008).

Most of the control variables also have important effects on financial development. Governance has a positive effect on financial depth, highlighting the importance of strong institutions for supporting the provision of, and demand for, financial services. Furthermore, a depreciation of the local currency can slow the rise in credit compared to GDP, possibly because of the uncertainty caused by local currency depreciation. The change in credit to GDP is also positively associated with population density and negatively associated with the age dependency ratio. Both GDP growth and inflation have a negative effect on the growth in deposits to GDP. This result suggests that deposits grew, in general, at a slower pace than GDP. One possible explanation of these estimated effects is that higher GDP growth is associated with higher returns on investment, which means that individuals and

TABLE 6.2 Estimation Results for Depth

| | | Dependent variable | | | | | | | |
| | | 100*Δ log (deposits/GDP) | | | | 100*Δ log (credit/GDP) | | | |
	Explanatory variables	1	2	3	4	5	6	7	8
Strategy variables	Index strategy impulse variable	0.435* (0.245)				ns			
	Index strategy shift variable		0.631** (0.256)				ns		
	Dummy strategy impulse variable			2.171* (1.281)				ns	
	Dummy strategy shift variable				3.794** (1.627)				ns
Institutional and macroeconomic variables	Log (GDP per capita)	−12.5*** (3.800)	−13.1*** (3.858)	−12.2*** (3.756)	−12.84*** (3.835)	−15.25*** (4.533)	−15.32*** (4.609)	−15.03*** (4.493)	−15.01*** (4.575)
	Financial openness	ns	ns	ns	ns	ns	ns	ns	ns
	Governance	5.066* (2.943)	5.409* (2.949)	4.979* (2.939)	5.051* (2.935)	6.212* (3.362)	6.257* (3.397)	6.117* (3.370)	6.090* (3.375)
	GDP growth	−0.63*** (0.102)	−0.63*** (0.101)	−0.63*** (0.102)	−0.63*** (0.102)	−0.275* (0.152)	−0.276* (0.151)	−0.276* (0.152)	−0.276* (0.152)
	Interest rate	ns	ns	ns	ns	ns	ns	ns	ns
	Δ log (exchange rate)	ns	ns	ns	ns	−14.90** (6.531)	−14.94** (6.525)	−14.94** (6.503)	−14.99** (6.483)
	Inflation	−0.15*** (0.0473)	−0.15*** (0.0475)	−0.15*** (0.0473)	−0.15*** (0.0476)	ns	ns	ns	ns
Social variables	Age dependency ratio	ns	ns	ns	ns	−0.384** (0.154)	−0.382** (0.154)	−0.384** (0.154)	−0.385** (0.155)
	Log (population density)	ns	ns	ns	ns	17.02** (7.480)	16.87** (7.485)	17.09** (7.480)	17.09** (7.500)
	Constant	95.07** (39.33)	102.5** (39.91)	91.47** (38.99)	101.3** (39.90)	97.49* (50.78)	98.56* (51.53)	95.29* (50.34)	95.23* (51.15)
	Observations	1,498	1,498	1,498	1,498	1,487	1,487	1,487	1,487
	R-squared	0.154	0.155	0.154	0.155	0.158	0.158	0.158	0.158

Note: ns = not statistically significant at 10 percent. Robust standard errors in parentheses.
* $p < 0.1$, ** $p < 0.05$, *** $p < 0.01$.

firms are more likely to invest than to place their assets in low-return bank deposits. Similarly, high inflation and price uncertainty increase the risk that the value of bank deposits will decline in real terms, which encourages individuals and firms to hold real assets (for example, durable goods). Finally, the level of development is negatively correlated with financial deepening, with less-developed countries experiencing more rapid increases in financial depth.

Strategies Can Improve Some Aspects of Financial Inclusion

The existence and quality of financial sector strategies tend to increase financial inclusion, as measured by the total number of deposit accounts; and this effect persists beyond the implementation period for the strategy. However, strategies do not appear to have a significant effect on the number of borrowers. Table 6.3

TABLE 6.3 Estimation Results for Inclusion

	Explanatory variables	Dependent variable							
		Log (total deposit accounts per 1,000 adults)				Log (total number of borrowers per 1,000 adults)			
		1	2	3	4	5	6	7	8
Strategy variables	Index strategy impulse variable	0.0177* (0.00961)				ns			
	Index strategy shift variable		0.0256* (0.0135)				ns		
	Dummy strategy impulse variable			0.102** (0.0510)				ns	
	Dummy strategy shift variable				0.253** (0.105)				ns
Institutional and macroeconomic variables	log (GDP per capita)	1.172*** (0.351)	1.145*** (0.354)	1.204*** (0.344)	1.167*** (0.352)	1.727*** (0.307)	1.732*** (0.308)	1.765*** (0.307)	1.745*** (0.307)
	Financial openness	ns	ns	ns	ns	−0.0807** (0.0353)	−0.0702** (0.0342)	−0.0807** (0.0348)	−0.0551 (0.0342)
	Governance	0.566*** (0.201)	0.575*** (0.202)	0.555*** (0.199)	0.520*** (0.188)	1.024*** (0.256)	1.016*** (0.256)	1.017*** (0.259)	0.960*** (0.236)
	GDP growth	−0.009** (0.004)	−0.009** (0.004)	−0.009** (0.004)	−0.008** (0.004)	−0.016*** (0.0053)	−0.016*** (0.0053)	−0.016*** (0.0054)	−0.016*** (0.0052)
	Interest rate	ns	ns	ns	ns	ns	ns	ns	ns
	Δ log (exchange rate)	ns	ns	ns	ns	0.485** (0.247)	0.458* (0.251)	0.478* (0.248)	0.475* (0.250)
	Inflation	ns	ns	ns	ns	0.00951* (0.00573)	0.00963* (0.00573)	0.00958* (0.00574)	0.0101* (0.00574)
Social variables	Age dependency ratio	0.0344** (0.0143)	0.0364** (0.0141)	0.0346** (0.0141)	0.0389*** (0.0142)	ns	ns	ns	ns
	Log (population density)	6.203*** (0.930)	6.197*** (0.924)	6.192*** (0.930)	6.146*** (0.920)	3.525*** (0.653)	3.475*** (0.638)	3.532*** (0.664)	3.505*** (0.647)
	Constant	−32.0*** (5.030)	−31.9*** (4.978)	−32.3*** (4.968)	−32.08*** (4.961)	−25.80*** (3.347)	−25.65*** (3.290)	−26.21*** (3.490)	−26.09*** (3.399)
	Observations	630	630	630	630	510	510	510	510
	R-squared	0.943	0.943	0.943	0.944	0.951	0.951	0.950	0.951

Note: ns = not statistically significant at 10 percent. Robust standard errors in parentheses.
* $p < 0.1$, ** $p < 0.05$, *** $p < 0.01$.

displays the results of the regressions in which the dependent variables are the number of deposit accounts per 1,000 adults and of borrowers per 1,000 adults (both variables in logarithms). The data coverage for the two variables is different; hence the results are not fully comparable. Nevertheless, the levels of development, governance, and population density have positive effects on both financial inclusion indicators. Inflation and changes in the exchange rate tend to increase the number of borrowers but not the number of deposit accounts. GDP growth is negatively correlated with financial inclusion. One explanation could be that richer countries with greater levels of financial inclusion may have experienced lower growth on average. Finally, a higher age dependency ratio significantly increases the number of deposit accounts among the adult population.

Because our measures of financial inclusion could include a time trend, we also estimate the regressions for financial inclusion using the percentage growth in the deposit and credit accounts per 1,000 adults (see table L.2 in appendix L). This approach reduces the sample size because the number of time periods is reduced by one. The results show general positive effects of strategies on inclusion as measured by deposits, particularly of the strategies that are highly rated on quality and scope. Based on an even smaller sample, the presence or quality of a financial sector strategy does not have a significant impact on the use of credit.

Strategies Do Not Appear to Have an Important Impact on the Efficiency of Financial Systems

Neither the presence of a strategy nor its quality has a significant impact on bank efficiency, as measured by the ratio of overhead costs to income and the return on assets (table 6.4). One possible explanation is that strategies lack specific measures focused on reducing banks' operational costs or raising profitability.

The control variables have various effects on efficiency. As anticipated, GDP growth helps decrease cost inefficiencies and increase bank profitability. The size

TABLE 6.4 Estimation Results for Efficiency

| | | Dependent variable | | | | | | | |
| | | Log (cost/income) | | | | Return on assets | | | |
	Explanatory variables	1	2	3	4	5	6	7	8
Strategy variables	Index strategy impulse variable	ns				ns			
	Index strategy shift variable		ns				ns		
	Dummy strategy impulse variable			ns				ns	
	Dummy strategy shift variable				ns				ns
Institutional and macroeconomic variables	log (GDP per capita)	−0.163*** (0.0411)	−0.157*** (0.0421)	−0.162*** (0.0408)	−0.154*** (0.0415)	ns	ns	ns	ns
	Financial openness	ns	ns	ns	ns	ns	ns	ns	ns
	Governance	ns	ns	ns	ns	ns	ns	ns	ns
	GDP growth	−0.0022** (0.0011)	−0.0022** (0.0011)	−0.0022** (0.0011)	−0.0022** (0.0011)	0.0479** (0.0191)	0.0479** (0.0191)	0.0479** (0.0192)	0.0481** (0.0191)
	Interest rate	ns	ns	ns	ns	−0.0660* (0.0378)	−0.0660* (0.0379)	−0.0661* (0.0378)	−0.0647* (0.0382)
	Δ log (exchange rate)	0.101* (0.0645)	0.0991* (0.0647)	0.101* (0.0645)	0.0967* (0.0649)	−4.782** (2.091)	−4.766** (2.079)	−4.790** (2.098)	−4.744** (2.075)
	Inflation	ns	ns	ns	ns	0.0218* (0.0118)	0.0215* (0.0116)	0.0218* (0.0118)	0.0210* (0.0116)
Social variables	Age dependency ratio	0.0032* (0.0019)	0.0032* (0.0019)	0.0032* (0.0019)	0.003 (0.0018)	ns	ns	ns	ns
	Log (population density)	−0.126 (0.08)	−0.120 (0.081)	−0.126 (0.081)	−0.110 (0.081)	ns	ns	ns	ns
	Constant	5.810*** (0.502)	5.741*** (0.516)	5.798*** (0.499)	5.687*** (0.511)	ns	ns	ns	ns
	Observations	1,507	1,507	1,507	1,507	1,498	1,498	1,498	1,498
	R-squared	0.598	0.598	0.598	0.598	0.188	0.188	0.188	0.188

Note: ns = not statistically significant at 10 percent. Robust standard errors in parentheses.
* $p < 0.1$, ** $p < 0.05$, *** $p < 0.01$.

of overhead costs in relation to income is positively associated with the change in the exchange rate. Depreciation of the local currency directly affects the cost of banks' foreign currency financing. Overhead costs are also positively associated with the age dependency ratio, and negatively associated with population density. Greater population density could enable more efficient outreach, screening, and monitoring by banks, including through more intensive social networks.[15] Finally, bank profitability is negatively associated with the interest rate, indicating that banks may not be able to pass the increased cost of financing on to borrowers, in particular in a more competitive banking sector. Local currency depreciation can erode profitability by increasing the cost of credit and of debt financing.

Strategies Can Improve Financial Stability

Financial sector strategies can foster financial stability by helping to reduce the volatility of financial cycles (see table 6.5 for the results of the regressions with the volatility of the changes in the credit-to-GDP ratio and in the deposits-to-GDP ratio as dependent variables).[16] The presence of a strategy (the dummy strategy

TABLE 6.5 Estimation Results for Stability

| | | Dependent variable | | | | | | | |
| | | Volatility of Δ log (deposits/GDP) | | | | Volatility of Δ log (private credit/GDP) | | | |
	Explanatory variables	1	2	3	4	5	6	7	8
Strategy variables	Index strategy impulse variable	−0.155* (0.0865)				ns			
	Index strategy shift variable		ns				ns		
	Dummy strategy impulse variable			−0.725* (0.434)				ns	
	Dummy strategy shift variable				ns				ns
Institutional and macroeconomic variables	GDP per capita	ns	ns	ns	ns	−3.86** (1.65)	−3.91** (1.68)	−3.93** (1.63)	−3.79** (1.68)
	Financial openness	−0.566* (0.301)	−0.537* (0.300)	−0.556* (0.300)	−0.570* (0.304)	ns	ns	ns	ns
	Governance	−2.99* (1.76)	−2.86 (1.77)	−2.95* (1.76)	−2.93* (1.76)	ns	ns	ns	ns
	GDP growth	ns	ns	ns	ns	ns	ns	ns	ns
	Interest rate	7.45* (4.48)	7.43* (4.44)	7.35* (4.45)	ns	0.227*** (0.049)	0.227*** (0.0496)	0.226*** (0.0493)	0.223*** (0.0499)
	Exchange rate	ns	ns	ns	ns	ns	ns	ns	ns
	Inflation	ns	ns	ns	ns	0.0771*** (0.0244)	0.0770*** (0.0245)	0.0774*** (0.0244)	0.0783*** (0.0246)
Social variables	Age dependency ratio	ns	ns	ns	ns	ns	ns	ns	ns
	Constant	0.255 (0.167)	0.274 (0.169)	0.268 (0.165)	0.263 (0.168)	0.379** (0.171)	0.383** (0.173)	0.388** (0.170)	0.379** (0.171)
	Observations R-squared	1,592 0.602	1,592 0.601	1,592 0.602	1,592 0.602	1,585 0.482	1,585 0.482	1,585 0.482	1,585 0.483

Note: ns = not statistically significant at 10 percent. Robust standard errors in parentheses.
* $p < 0.1$, ** $p < 0.05$, *** $p < 0.01$.

indicator) and the quality and scope of the strategy (the index strategy indicator) significantly reduce the volatility of deposits to GDP, but only during the implementation period of the strategy (the impulse variables previously defined). Simply the presence of a strategy may help reduce volatility by improving financial sector participants' ability to understand and anticipate, and thus act upon, authorities' financial sector policies. By contrast, the estimated relationships between the strategy variables and the volatility of changes in credit to GDP are not significantly different from zero.

The coefficients on the control variables provide interesting insights into the effect of macroeconomic and institutional variables on stability. Good governance can help reduce the volatility of deposits to GDP, whereas high interest rates can increase the volatility of both deposits and credit to GDP. Furthermore, financial openness is associated with greater volatility of deposits to GDP and thus potentially greater financial instability.

> **Countries with financial sector strategies are less vulnerable to banking crises or experience lower economic losses from banking crises. More comprehensive strategies can reduce the cost of financial crises even further.**

Countries with financial sector strategies are less vulnerable to banking crises or experience lower economic losses from banking crises (table L.1 in appendix L). More comprehensive strategies can reduce the cost of financial crises even further. Finally, GDP per capita and the interest rate are positively associated with the cost of crises.[17] One explanation is that banking crises, in particular the 2008 crisis, mostly affected upper-middle- and high-income countries. Also, countries might suffer a higher output loss if the interest rate is kept high to limit capital outflows.

Strategies Can Help Strengthen the Regulatory Framework

If we take into account the potential for strategies to affect financial outcomes beyond the implementation period, the strategies appear to have a significant and positive impact on the regulatory framework for getting credit, resolving insolvency, and enforcing contracts. Table 6.6 presents the results of regressions

TABLE 6.6 Estimation Results for Regulatory Policy

		Dependent variable											
	Explanatory variables	Getting credit DTF				Enforcing contracts DTF				Resolving insolvency DTF			
Strategy variables	Index strategy impulse variable	ns				ns				ns			
	Index strategy shift variable		0.93** (0.37)				ns				ns		
	Dummy strategy impulse variable			ns				ns				ns	
	Dummy strategy shift variable				10.88*** (1.83)				0.86** (0.38)				2.41*** (0.4)
	Constant	50.6*** (0.39)	49.3*** (0.523)	50.7*** (0.38)	47.4*** (0.56)	58.04*** (0.07)	57.9*** (0.0972)	58.11*** (0.08)	57.81*** (0.124)	37.74*** (0.15)	37.6*** (0.22)	37.8*** (0.15)	37.1*** (0.17)
	Observations	1,131	1,131	1,131	1,131	1,241	1,241	1,241	1,241	1,241	1,241	1,241	1,241
	R-squared	0.859	0.860	0.859	0.863	0.979	0.979	0.979	0.979	0.975	0.975	0.975	0.975

Note: DTF = distance to frontier; ns = not statistically significant at 10 percent. Robust standard errors in parentheses.
** $p < 0.05$, *** $p < 0.01$.

that measure the effect of strategies on the quality of regulatory policies governing finance (each regression relates one strategy indicator to one regulatory indicator). We use the distance to frontier (DTF—see note 2 at the end of this chapter) measure for the three regulatory frameworks. The *shift* variables for both the existence, and quality and scope, of a strategy have a significant and positive impact on the quality of the regulatory framework for getting credit. Moreover, the *shift* variable for the existence of a strategy also is positively associated with the regulatory framework for resolving insolvency and enforcing contracts.

As discussed previously, one issue is whether financial strategies affect financial development only by improving the regulatory framework. To examine this, we include indicators of regulatory reform (instead of the strategy variables) as independent variables in our main regression model explaining financial outcomes. In a few cases regulatory reform variables have a significant impact on financial outcomes, in the expected direction: the DTF for enforcing contracts has a significant impact on financial depth, and the DTF for resolving insolvency is significant in the regressions for efficiency and stability. In the remaining regressions, however, the regulatory variables lack significance. These results suggest that, although the strategies have a positive impact on regulations, there might be additional ways in which the positive impact of strategies on financial development works. One possibility is through the positive effect of the strategies on overall coordination of financial policy, for instance, across the central bank, ministry of finance, and other financial sector regulators. Another way that strategies could have a direct positive impact on financial development is by reducing uncertainty: private sector financial institutions, firms, and individuals can improve their planning because they gain a better understanding of policy intentions.

Summary and Policy Recommendations

Our review of the origination of strategies reveals that, although the preparations of early strategies were often supported by international development organizations, in many cases government institutions, including the central bank, took the initiative to consult public and private entities involved in the financial sector and formulate the national financial sector strategy. The number of adopted strategies around the world peaked around 2006–07 and then decreased substantially during the global financial crisis. One possible explanation is that during the crisis period countries focused more on crisis preparedness and resolution and other short-term issues, rather than on medium-term strategies. Our assessment suggests that overall the scope and quality of strategies could be improved substantially. The strategies could pay greater attention to the systemic risk associated with advancing financial depth, efficiency, or inclusion, as well as acknowledge and try to manage various policy trade-offs, in particular those that can arise between the efforts to speed up financial development and foster financial stability.

The estimation results show that financial sector strategies support financial sector deepening, inclusion, and stability, in particular if the strategies are of a good quality. This effect is more evident if it is assumed that the impact of the strategy on financial outcomes continues beyond the implementation period for the strategies. We do not find any significant effect of the strategies on cost efficiency and profitability of banks. Further, we find that the strategies have a significant and positive impact on the regulatory framework for getting credit, resolving insolvency, and enforcing contracts. The analysis also indicates that the strategies' positive impact on financial development is not limited to their role in improving the regulatory framework. Other ways in which strategies may improve financial development are through improving coordination of financial policy and reducing policy uncertainty for the private financial and real sectors.

Our preliminary results should encourage a greater number of countries to use financial sector strategies to plan, communicate, and coordinate their financial sector policies. However, the quality and scope of strategies need to improve across all countries, as the average rating of the quality and scope of strategies is low. Only a few high-quality strategies, such as those for Malaysia and Switzerland, can serve as role models for other countries in their efforts to deploy financial strategies effectively.

Country Pointers to Focus Policy Efforts with the Help of Financial Sector Strategies

To provide some country guidance on the focus of financial sector strategies, we summarize the overall findings of this report by bringing together in a quantitative way the three aspects to consider in decision making on financial policy: (a) the existing financial development gaps—that is, the distance to the financial development frontier the country should aim to close; (b) how much the closing of a particular gap—for financial stability, efficiency, inclusion, or depth—could advance growth and shared prosperity; and (c) whether the closing of one gap, such as the one for financial inclusion, can actually increase other gap(s), such as the one for financial stability, and pose a policy trade-off or whether the closing of one gap can help close another gap and create synergies. This parametric summary can point individual ECA subregions and countries to important country-specific areas that may need to be addressed by financial policy, and alert the policy makers about the importance of trade-offs.

> Across ECA, focusing financial policy on advancing financial efficiency and inclusion is the most important area for supporting equal upturn in aggregate growth and shared prosperity.

We bring aspects (a)–(c) together assuming, as an example, that ECA policy makers wish to promote financial sector reforms aimed at boosting aggregate and bottom 40 incomes in parallel. Because bottom 40 growth primarily depends on financial inclusion, policy makers may need to emphasize inclusion over other financial development areas. As figure 6.9 suggests, across ECA, focusing financial policy on advancing financial efficiency and inclusion is the most important area for supporting equal upturn in aggregate growth and shared prosperity. Although financial efficiency is more important than inclusion for aggregate growth in ECA as a whole, the picture changes at the level of ECA subregions and countries. While the Russian Federation is the subregion in greatest need of improvement in financial efficiency, focusing on improving financial inclusion is even more important for the country's inclusive growth. Central Asia and to a smaller extent Eastern Europe are in a similar situation. In contrast, Turkey needs to improve financial efficiency in tandem with financial stability, which is a lower

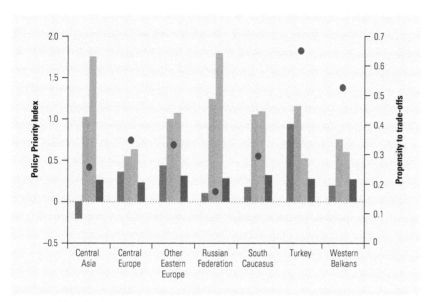

FIGURE 6.9 **Financial sector strategies can help ECA countries focus their financial policy in priority areas for inclusive income growth, while considering important policy trade-offs**

■ Stability
■ Efficiency
■ Inclusion
■ Depth
● Propensity to trade-offs (right axis)

Source: World Bank calculations.
Note: The calculation of utility assumes linear, additive objective function with equal weights on aggregate and bottom 40 income growths. The calculation uses the regression estimates from chapter 2 and the identified distance to financial development frontier from chapter 2. The propensity to trade-offs is computed using the regression estimations from appendix I (table I.3, column 2). We use column 2 estimates because of their greater country coverage and thus robustness.

policy priority for inclusive growth in other countries. Central Europe appears to be the closest to the financial development frontier, but further improvements in financial inclusion and efficiency could pay off.

Focusing on advancing financial efficiency, inclusion, or stability is not a clear-cut task because country policy makers could confront important trade-offs in achieving these objectives. The predictive score from the estimated cross-country regression in appendix I (table I.3, column 2) could be used to calculate a propensity to trade-offs based on individual country characteristics (figure 6.9, propensity to trade-offs). Policy makers in Turkey and the Western Balkans could be confronted with the highest trade-offs in achieving their policy objectives compared with other ECA subregions. In contrast, policy makers in Russia and Central Asia could face the smallest trade-offs when trying to boost inclusive growth through financial sector reforms. It is important to keep both the priority policy objectives and trade-offs in mind when deliberating reforms and formulating financial sector strategies that could help rebalance financial policy in ECA for sustained financial development and inclusive growth.

Notes

1. One assumption of a regression model is that the explanatory variables are independent—that is, not highly correlated with each other.
2. An economy's distance to frontier is the difference between a financial sector outcome for that economy and the outcome of the most successful economies. The distance to frontier is measured on a scale from 0 to 100, where 0 represents the lowest performance and 100 represents the frontier.

3. That is, we consider the strategies that have been in place for at least two years.

4. A FIRST initiative–funded team was recruited and prepared the Rwanda financial sector development strategy under the guidance of the central bank (BNR) and worked closely with a national steering committee composed of key stakeholders in each of the areas addressed by the Financial Sector Development Program.

5. Possibly, policy makers could intentionally disregard trade-offs in favor of synergies that they aim to achieve, for example, by advancing financial inclusion in deposits and diversifying the funding base of banks to make them more resilient (Han and Melecky, 2013). However, neglecting trade-offs, especially in developing credit markets, and hoping only for synergies may result in unbalanced strategies with unintended consequences for systemic risk.

6. We prefer these two measures over the net interest margin and lending-deposit rate spread because they are less controversial. An increase or decrease in the net interest margin can signal a rise or a fall in efficiency, depending on country circumstances. The same applies for the lending-deposit rate spread because its evolution can be heavily influenced by changes in monetary policy.

7. The volatility at time t is measured as the standard deviation of the variable for the [t-2, t+2] time period.

8. This is computed as the cumulative sum of the differences between actual and trend real GDP, expressed as a percentage of trend real GDP, over the period [T, t+3] where T is the start of the crisis.

9. As is typical in many regression estimations using data from many countries, each country (except one) is assigned a variable equal to 1 for that country and zero otherwise (referred to as fixed effects). The purpose is to control for the impact of country characteristics on the relationship being studied that are not captured by the other independent variables. For the output loss during banking crises—which is a truncated variable that takes the cumulative value of output loss during the crisis and zero otherwise—we use a Tobit model to estimate the regression.

10. We consider the average of the six indexes estimated by Kaufmann, Kraay, and Mastruzzi (2010) regarding the control of corruption, government effectiveness, political stability, regulatory stability, rule of law, and voice and accountability.

11. Initially, we considered life expectancy and education level as well, but realized that these are highly correlated with the level of development measured by GDP per capita. For that reason, we dropped them.

12. GDP per capita and population density are expressed in logarithms.

13. This is a common problem in the use of regression analysis in economic research. The regression model assumes that the explanatory variables are not affected by the dependent variable. If this is not the case, then the relationship between the explanatory variables and the dependent variable may not be estimated correctly.

14. In regression analysis, there is often a concern that the dependent variable may affect the independent variables (that is, the independent variables may be endogenous). Often a variable that is clearly unaffected by the dependent variable, but is closely correlated with the independent variable, is substituted for the latter in the regression. This variable is referred to as an *instrument*. In this example, an indicator of governance may be correlated with the strategy formulation, but may not be driven by financial sector development (the dependent variable).

15. Additional regressions using a smaller data set for which data for the presence of foreign banks were available shows that this variable also has the effect of improving the cost efficiency of banks.

16. Both variables are expressed as the change in the logarithmic value.

17. We do not include the GDP growth because its impact on the output loss is tautological: the higher the growth, the smaller the difference between the potential output and actual output.

References

African Development Bank. 2012. *Financial Sector Reform Programme. Egypt: Program Completion Report*. Department OSGE, African Development Bank.

Andrews, A. Michael, Keith Jefferis, Robert Hannah, and Paul Murgatroyd. 2012. *Rwanda: Financial Sector Development Program II*. Washington, DC: World Bank.

Arcand, Jean-Louis, Enrico Berkes, and Ugo Panizza. 2012. "Too Much Finance?" IMF Working Paper WP/12/161, International Monetary Fund, Washington, DC.

Bank of Sierra Leone. 2009. *Financial Sector Development Plan 2009*. Republic of Sierra Leone.

Barajas, Adolfo, Thorsten Beck, Era Dabla-Norris, and Seyed Reza Yousefi. 2013. "Too Cold, Too Hot, or Just Right? Assessing Financial Sector Development across the Globe." IMF Working Paper WP/13/81, International Monetary Fund, Washington, DC.

BDDK (Banking Regulation and Supervision Agency). 2001. *Towards a Sound Turkish Banking Sector*. Istanbul: BDDK, May.

Bikker, Jakob. 2010. "Measuring Performance of Banks: An Assessment." *Journal of Applied Business and Economics* 11 (4): 141–59.

Chinn, Menzie D., and Hiro Ito. 2006. "What Matters for Financial Development? Capital Controls, Institutions, and Interactions." *Journal of Development Economics* 81 (1): 163–92.

Chun, Byoung-Jo, Xuechun Zhang, Ashok Sharma, and Arun Hsu. 2001. *Financial Sector Blueprint for 2001–2010*. Kingdom of Cambodia and Asian Development Bank.

Committee on Economic Reforms under the President of Ukraine. 2010. *Prosperous Society, Competitive Economy, Effective State: Program of Economic Reforms 2010–2014*.

De la Torre, Augusto, Erik Feyen, and Alain Ize. 2013. "Financial Development: Structure and Dynamics." *World Bank Economic Review* 27 (3): 514–41.

De la Torre, Augusto, Juan Carlos Gozzi, and Sergio L. Schmukler. 2007. "Capital Market Development: Whither Latin America?" Policy Research Working Paper 4156, World Bank, Washington, DC.

Department of Finance Canada. 1999. *Reforming Canada's Financial Services Sector. A Framework for the Future*. Ottawa: Department of Finance.

FDRE MOFED (Federal Democratic Republic of Ethiopia, Ministry of Finance and Economic Development). 2002. *Ethiopia: Sustainable Development and Poverty Reduction Program*. Addis Ababa: FDRE MOFED.

Federal Council of Switzerland. 2009. *Strategic Directions for Switzerland's Financial Market Policy: Report in Response to the Graber Postulate*. Bern: Federal Council.

Feyen, Erik, Rodney Lester, and Roberto Rocha. 2011. "What Drives Development of the Insurance Sector? An Empirical Analysis Based on a Panel of Developed and Developing Countries." Policy Research Working Paper 5572, World Bank, Washington, DC.

Governor of the Bank of the Lao PDR. 2006. *Financial Institution Development Strategy of Lao PDR from 2009 to 2020*. Vientiane: Governor of the Bank of the Lao PDR.

Han, Rui, and Martin Melecky. 2013. "Financial Inclusion for Financial Stability: Access to Bank Deposits and the Growth of Deposits in the Global Financial Crisis." Policy Research Working Paper 6577, World Bank, Washington, DC.

Kaufmann, Daniel, Aart Kraay, and Massimo Mastruzzi. 2010. "The Worldwide Governance Indicators: A Summary of Methodology, Data, and Analytical Issues." Policy Research Working Paper 5430, World Bank, Washington, DC.

Kingdom of Cambodia. 2006. *Financial Sector Development Strategy 2006–2015*. Royal Government of Cambodia.

———. 2011. *Financial Sector Development Strategy 2011–2020*. Mandaluyong City: Asian Development Bank.

Laeven, Luc, and Fabian Valencia. 2013. "Systemic Banking Crises Database." *IMF Economic Review* 61 (2): 225-70.

Loayza, Norman, and Romain Ranciere. 2006. "Financial Development, Financial Fragility, and Growth." *Journal of Money, Credit and Banking* 38 (4): 1051-76, June.

Maimbo, Samuel, and Martin Melecky. 2014. "Financial Sector Policy in Practice: Benchmarking Financial Sector Strategies around the World." Policy Research Working Paper 6746, World Bank, Washington, DC.

Murgatroyd, Paul, James Dry, Tom Power, and William Postgate. 2007. *Rwanda Financial Sector Development Program Report*. Washington, DC: World Bank.

National Bank of Georgia. 2006. *Georgian Banking System Development Strategy for 2006–2009*. Tbilisi: National Bank of Georgia.

National Bank of the Kyrgyz Republic. 2011. *Main Areas of Development of the Banking Sector of the Kyrgyz Republic by the End of 2014*. Bishkek: National Bank of the Kyrgyz Republic.

Panizza, Ugo. 2014. "Financial Development and Economic Growth: Known Knowns, Known Unknowns, and Unknown Unknowns." *Revue d'économie du développement* 22 (HS02): 35–65.

People's Bank of China, China Banking Regulatory Commission, China Securities Regulatory Commission, China Insurance Regulatory Commission, and State Administration of Foreign Exchange. 2012. *The 12th Five-Year Plan for the Development and Reform of the Financial Industry*. Beijing.

Ranciere, Ramain, Aaron Tornell, and Frank Westermann. 2008. "Systemic Crises and Growth." *Quarterly Journal of Economics* 123 (1): 359–406.

Republic du Burundi. 2010. *Strategie et Plan d'Actions pour le Developpement du Secteur Financier Elabores sous la Coordination du Ministere des Finances du Burundi 2011–2017*. Ministere des Finances du Burundi.

Republic of Ghana, Ministry of Finance. 2003. *Financial Sector Strategic Plan*. Ministry of Finance.

Republic of Ghana, Ministry of Finance and Economic Planning. 2011. *Financial Sector Strategic Plan II*. Ministry of Finance and Economic Planning.

Republic of South Africa, National Treasury. 2011. *A Safer Financial Sector to Serve South Africa Better*. Pretoria: National Treasury.

Republic of Trinidad and Tobago, Ministry of Finance. 2001. *Medium-Term Policy Framework 2002–2004*. Port of Spain: Ministry of Finance.

———. 2004. "Reform of the Financial System of Trinidad and Tobago." White paper, Ministry of Finance, Port of Spain, June.

Republic of Zambia, Ministry of Finance and National Planning. 2004. *Financial Sector Development Plan for Zambia 2004–2009*. Ministry of Finance and National Planning.

World Bank. 1989. *Botswana: Financial Policies for Diversified Growth*. Washington, DC: World Bank.

———. 1993. *Madagascar: Financial Policies for Diversified Growth*. Washington, DC: World Bank.

Yartey, Charles A. 2008. "The Determinants of Stock Market Development in Emerging Economies: Is South Africa Different?" IMF Working Paper WP/08/32, International Monetary Fund, Washington, DC.

Learning from Crisis Simulation Exercises in Europe and Central Asia

Financial crisis simulation exercises (CSEs) are role-playing games designed to improve authorities' ability to act in a crisis. CSEs enable financial authorities to practice information sharing and decision making under existing or proposed legal and operational arrangements, for example legal powers to compel corrective actions or resolve failed institutions, or limits and operational rules and procedures to grant emergency liquidity assistance. These games often can help identify potential improvements in legal and operational arrangements, or create consensus behind reforms under consideration. Since its inception in 2012, the World Bank's Vienna Financial Sector Advisory Centre has conducted eight CSEs in its client countries.[1]

Nature and purpose of CSEs. CSEs are games of interaction among financial sector decision makers, including policy makers and operational departments in the finance ministry, the central bank, or agencies responsible for bank and nonbank supervision and deposit insurance. Financial sector authorities from other jurisdictions dealing with common issues (such as host supervisors of subsidiaries of a regional/global financial group and the group's home supervisor) may also participate.

World Bank CSEs are designed as games of asymmetric information: participating teams representing different decision makers receive both "public information" (simultaneously available to all participants and the public) in the form of national and international press articles, and "private information" in the form of e-mail messages from a large number of sources (staffs of participating teams, bankers, foreign authorities, politicians, journalists, and the like). Participating teams can take appropriate decisions only after sharing the information they have privately received and their respective

understanding of it. The outputs of the exercise are the decisions made and a series of dialogues reflecting this exchange of information. Because the interaction normally takes place exclusively in writing, it allows for a detailed analysis of the decision-making process.

Although the scope of the scenario is specific to each client, CSEs generally focus on systemic vulnerabilities (quality and structure of assets and liabilities, cyberincidents, and other operational risks), shortcomings in the legal and regulatory frameworks or operational arrangements, the extent of information sharing and coordination among relevant agencies or departments, and their strategies of communication with the public.

The main purpose of these games is "learning by doing." CSEs may or may not lead to major reforms in the existing framework for crisis preparedness and management, but they can improve coordination among financial sector authorities during financial crises.

What makes a CSE successful? The ideal game is one in which all participating teams truly want to "play," and in which the problems sound plausible to all of them. When some of the participating teams would rather not play but must do so because more influential participants want it, or when executing the simulation derives from conditionality in an international financial institution (IFI) program without strong client ownership, or when the game does not reflect scenarios the participants truly worry about, the resulting interactions are unlikely to be particularly revealing.

Stylized facts observed in Europe and Central Asia CSEs. With important variations from exercise to exercise, we have observed the following facts in Europe and Central Asia (ECA) simulations:

SPOTLIGHT 8 *(continued)*

Limited progress with recovery and resolution planning. Although some of our CSE countries, notably the European Union (EU) candidates, were in the process of establishing a resolution framework and aligning it with the EU's Bank Recovery and Resolution Directive, this process was at best in its infancy.

Provision of public funds. Resolving a systemic bank usually involves the use of public money. Because ex ante resolution funds are very rare in ECA countries, requests for an extraordinary use of public funds typically require parliamentary approval. This may take too much time or be impossible to obtain in some periods of the year (for example during the parliament's summer recess).

Lack of preparedness to assess resolution costs. Assessing the cost of bank resolution options (liquidation, purchase and assumption, bridge bank, nationalization, and so on) is a key step in managing a banking crisis and typically has to be done under a strict time constraint. In several countries the authorities may be underestimating the importance, complexity, and resources necessary to do this quickly and properly.

Solvency as a hard constraint for liquidity assistance. In many countries, legislation or central bank bylaws prevent the central bank from providing liquidity support to insolvent banks. This constraint could risk escalating a crisis if a systemic bank becomes illiquid and insolvent. However, this constraint may also encourage politicians to provide public funding in a timely manner.

Financial stability councils (FSCs). An FSC, consisting of the central bank, the ministry of finance, and sometimes other stakeholders (deposit insurance, securities market regulator, parliamentary committee, and the like) was set up in many ECA countries following the global financial crisis. Most of these FSCs are designed to be a coordination forum rather than a decision-making body. FSCs often have both crisis management and crisis prevention functions, which can lead to the wrong composition of participants. That is, during a crisis that is likely to require extra public funds, high-level officials from the ministry of finance typically play a crucial role. In contrast, the ministry has little role to play in regular FSC meetings focused on crisis prevention, so that participation may be delegated to staff level, become less frequent, or cease altogether. The wrong membership does not help in crisis times either, when FSC members may resist taking responsibility for crisis prevention, which is mainly the responsibility of the independent supervisor or regulator.

Financial stability departments. The extent to which the central bank's financial stability department, with responsibility for monitoring the stability of the financial system as a whole (as opposed to that of individual banks, the task of banking supervision) is integrated into the decision-making process varies. Some only produce regular reports on stress tests and financial stability, whereas others play a pivotal role in handling interdepartmental information flows and proposing critical decisions to the Board.

Declaring a crisis as systemic. In a number of CSEs, declaring that a crisis has reached systemic proportions was either a precondition to, or improved the chance of, parliamentary approval of public funds. Yet, even if the importance of the declaration was clear in many cases, the practical response to the crisis was often problematic.

Liquidity provision in a twin (currency and banking) crisis. Widespread currency substitution and foreign exchange (FX) lending in ECA financial systems meant that the CSE scenarios often involved significant pressure on the domestic currency to depreciate. In general, authorities were fully aware that it is not enough to minimize (through regulation) the open FX position of the banking system if there is a maturity mismatch between FX assets and liabilities. They recognized that FX liquidity may become scarce and the central bank is expected to find ways of providing it. Not all countries have, however, a properly designed mechanism to do so.

Integrating monetary policy in crisis response. In twin (currency and banking) crises, some central banks did not hesitate to increase interest rates substantially, while others tried to separate monetary policy from managing the banking crisis. In one case, the central bank refused to change interest rates during the simulated crisis, claiming that financial stability and monetary policy goals should not be mixed. However, following an external shock shortly after the CSE, the country found itself in a real-life twin crisis, in which the central bank did resort to substantial interest rate hikes.

Deposit guarantee funds (DGFs). Most DGFs in ECA were limited to paying out depositors in a bank resolution process, although some DGFs did top up a failed bank's assets in order to facilitate a private selector solution. Another issue was that DGF funds were often invested in public debt, and there was no clear way to make these funds liquid when they are needed to pay out deposits. Although a straightforward solution would be to enter into a sale and repurchase agreement with the central bank, a recurring technical problem is that central banks typically have a predefined list of clients (mostly commercial banks), which does not include the DGF. Some countries have more cumbersome arrangements, such as a central bank loan to the DGF against a government guarantee.

Home-host and host-host supervisory coordination. Given the high penetration of foreign (mostly euro area) banks in ECA client countries, our CSE scenarios almost always featured coordination with foreign authorities. However, in some countries memoranda of understanding on information sharing with the relevant home supervisors were not in place. Moreover, errors were common in contacting potential sources of information, such as demanding information from the parent bank instead of the parent supervisor. The launch of the EU's Single Supervisory Mechanism also has made some host

supervisors uncertain whether they should contact the home supervisor or the European Central Bank in case of a crisis. Also, the opportunities for host-host information sharing (keeping in touch with supervisors of subsidiaries of the same parent group in other countries) were not effectively used.

Overconfidence in parent banks' support. Local authorities often believed that euro area parent banks would provide full capital and liquidity support for their local subsidiaries (although authorities in countries with exposure to Greek parents were much more cautious).

Lack of focus on cybersecurity issues. Our CSE scenarios have started to feature cyberincidents, typically as triggers for a loss in public confidence. It appears that authorities viewed cyberissues as technical questions to be handled by information technology departments, rather than a matter of concern for the highest decision-making levels. One consequence was a lack of a public communication strategy regarding cyberincidents. Dealing with cyberattacks was also typically considered the sole responsibility of affected banks, disregarding any potential systemic implications.

Analyzing the action: statistics, metadata, and slicing the scenario. Understanding the output of a simulation, made up of between 250 and 600 not necessarily well-written e-mails reflecting multiple dialogues (on different matters, among different counterparts), is not easy. Sequentially reading all these e-mails is quite difficult, and it may easily lead to overlooking important patterns. To detect these patterns we have increasingly analyzed e-mail metadata (such as the history of senders and addressees in conversations), and segmented the full record according to the various stories that we typically include in our scenarios, even to the level of the multiple extended conversations that took place.

The public and private messages that we use to describe the scenario are primarily intended to motivate exchanges among the participants (the

SPOTLIGHT 8 *(continued)*

FIGURE S8.1 Share of interactions occurring among participants in total interactions is important for managing crises

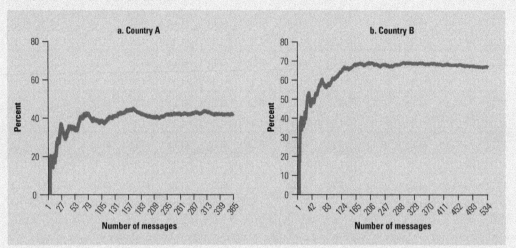

a. Country A

b. Country B

Number of messages

Number of messages

"players") rather than between them and us (the "control team"). One measure of the success of a simulation is the evolution over time of the number of messages among playing teams as a fraction of total messages (which also includes conversations between them and the control team). For example, in figure S8.1, Country B's exercise was clearly more successful in eliciting interaction among the players than Country A's exercise, and consequently much more informative regarding the way players process information and reach decisions on each of the problems posed by the scenario.

Network graphs derived from the volume and direction of the interaction between teams of decision makers, and between each one of them and the control team, reveal important patterns. The network graph in figure S8.2 shows that the flow of information between supervision and operations in a particular country was quite small relative to the total volume of information (revealed by the width of the links between pairs of nodes), and highly asymmetric (revealed by the relative size of the arrows pointing in the respective directions). These central bank departments don't talk much to each other, choosing to communicate their views and

information directly to the governor; and the limited communication that takes place between them is more likely to be from operations to supervision than the reverse.

Finally, when the time comes actually to read the content of the e-mails, their metadata allow us to disentangle the multiple conversations, frequently among different sets of counterparts, which are triggered by a single message. Figure S8.3 (which identifies the sender with the colored nodes) shows the e-mails in the different branches of the leafy tree of conversations triggered by one of the most fruitful messages in the exercise, making it possible to easily understand the matter being discussed, and who was included in or excluded from each branch.

Note

1. CSEs were carried out in Albania, Armenia, Croatia, Kosovo, the former Yugoslav Republic of Macedonia, Moldova, Montenegro, and Romania. Additionally, two multijurisdictional exercises were conducted in 2011 in Frankfurt, at the European Central Bank, with the participation of, respectively, Albania, Kosovo, FYR Macedonia, and Turkey; and Bosnia and Herzegovina, Croatia, Montenegro, and Serbia.

FIGURE S8.2 Network volume and direction of communication are important for policy makers

Network volume and direction of communication between decision makers

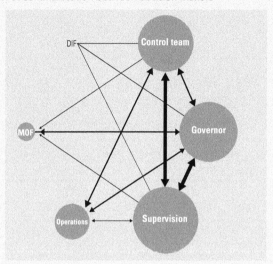

Source: World Bank staff, based on e-mail metadata of selected crisis simulation exercises.
Note: Larger width of arrows indicates greater volumes of communication flows. DIF = deposit insurance fund; MOF = ministry of finance.

FIGURE S8.3 E-mails sent, content, and how they were distributed between actors help demonstrate information flows

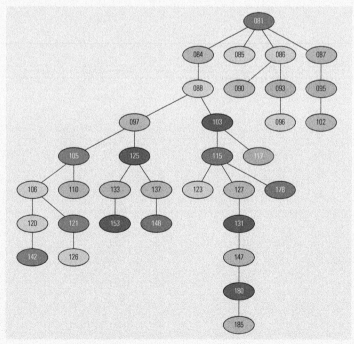

Note: The six colors represent the typical participants in a crisis simulation exercise (CSE): the central bank governor, minister of finance, bank supervisor, head of open market operations, director of financial stability, and head of the deposit insurance fund. Nonbank supervisors also could be present in some CSEs.

Appendixes

Appendix A
Econometrics

The econometric model outlined in chapter 2 was used to address the missing observations with many financial indicators. Some of the most interesting variables from the point of view of policy makers (for example, the various inclusion indicators) lack the long data series typically required to study their effects on long-term growth. In fact, including these indicators in a traditional growth regression will cause such a significant loss of degrees of freedom that the estimates and confident intervals for the traditional growth determinants are meaningless. This is why we propose the following two-stage estimation:

We assume that the underlying model is

$$y = X\beta + f\gamma + \varepsilon, \tag{A.1}$$

where y is economic growth, X is an N-by-K matrix of growth determinants (initial GDP, schooling, and so on), and f is an indicator for financial development. We only have M nonmissing observations for the financial variables where $M < N$. Estimating the full growth model above will yield consistent estimates, but their precision will be low. The variance of the ordinary least squares (OLS) estimator for β is

$$VAR(\hat{\beta}) = \frac{\sigma_\varepsilon^2}{M - K - 1}(X_f'X_f)^{-1}, \tag{A.2}$$

where X_f is the matrix of growth determinants and the financial development indicator (K+1 columns). Depending on the size of M, the loss of degrees of freedom can cause a substantial increase in the precision of the OLS estimator. In fact, this is often the problem that economists face when working with macrodata on financial development and growth. We have relatively good series and cross-sectional coverage for many of the traditional growth indicators—such as initial GDP, schooling, inflation, and so on—but very sparse data for some of the financial indicators. This probably is one of the reasons that researchers focus on the size of the private credit as a measurement of financial development in the finance and growth literature.

To address this problem we propose the following two-stage estimation procedure. We first estimate the following model:

$$y = Xb + e \qquad\qquad (A.3)$$

and then use the residuals from this estimation in the second stage:

$$e = fg + u. \qquad\qquad (A.4)$$

If finance is correlated with the other growth determinants X, then b and g are biased estimators for β and γ. In fact, if we expect a positive correlation between finance and the other growth determinants, then b will be biased upward and g downward. It is not hard to derive that bias in each stage is

$$bias(b) = (X'X)^{-1}(X'f)\gamma \qquad\qquad (A.5)$$
$$bias(g) = -(f'f)^{-1}(f'X)bias(b). \qquad\qquad (A.6)$$

As can be seen, in the case of a positive covariance between X and f, the bias in the first stage is positive and negative in the second. Also, the bias is larger the greater the covariance between finance and the other growth determinants and the greater the importance of finance in the growth equation γ. However, introducing this estimation bias also gave us increased precision in the estimation of b (and β): the variance of our estimator b will be

$$VAR(b) = \frac{\sigma_e^2}{N-K}(X'X)^{-1}, \qquad\qquad (A.7)$$

where σ_e^2 depends positively on γ. Therefore the bias-precision trade-off between the two econometric procedures (full model versus two-stage estimation) depends mostly on the

- loss of degrees of freedom $(N - M)$,
- overall weight of finance in the underlying growth model γ, and
- variance covariance structure of the data.

This breakdown allows us to quantify the trade-off between the two approaches. The particular choice between either of these will depend on the cost function of the researcher where she adequately weighs how "costly" bias is and how beneficial precision is. However, it is not difficult to come up with a simple rule of thumb: if our prior belief for the size of γ is low, and the loss of degrees of freedom incurred by the inclusion of the f in the estimation is significant, then the researcher should consider the two-stage estimation.

Given the financial data used in this report, the choice was simple. Although the repeated cross-section data on growth and the basic growth determinants have more than 460 observations, the inclusion of some of the financial indicators on the right-hand side would cause a loss of degrees of freedom of the magnitude of 80 percent (some of the financial indicators only have about 100 nonmissing observations). This problem is exacerbated when dealing with the bottom 40 data where the missing data problem is twice as acute.

In addition to the benefits of additional degrees of freedom, we assume that most of long-term growth is determined by economic factors such as capital accumulation and education, with finance having smaller marginal effects. If this is indeed the case, then the estimation bias will be small and the gain in precision significant. Furthermore, it is very likely that the second-stage estimation will have not only a downward bias for the value of the coefficient but also a wider confidence interval. This is expected to produce more conservative results and reduce the likelihood of false positives.

Appendix B
Controlling for the Effect of Growth on Finance

In order to investigate the causal relationship between growth and financial development we reestimated the model, substituting in the initial values for all control variables and financial development indicators for each respective period. If the initial value is missing, we used the first nonmissing observation for that period (the dependent variable remains the average growth for the period).

Initial values for financial development are significantly correlated with the realized long-term overall growth for each period and continue to have the expected signs. The association between overall growth and financial efficiency and household inclusion increases in comparison with the base results. The correlation coefficients for financial development and the growth of the bottom 40 do not pass the commonly used significance thresholds. The results are summarized in table B.1.

TABLE B.1 Financial Development and Growth—Correlation versus Causality

	Overall growth	Bottom 40 growth
Depth	0.65***	−0.12
Efficiency	0.87***	0.44
Stability	0.42***	−0.10
Firm inclusion	0.71***	0.29
Household inclusion	0.73**	0.56

Note: Each row represents a bivariate regression with a dependent variable either the overall growth residual or the bottom 40 growth residual. The independent variables are composite indexes composed of mean and standard deviation–centered variables. The choice of variables in each index was made on the basis of the significance level of the overall growth regression. Each index represents a simple average of the values of its elements with the weights properly adjusted for missing observations.
** $p < 0.05$, *** $p < 0.01$.

Although substituting initial values addresses some issues about contemporaneous codetermination between growth and financial development, it does not address all aspects of endogeneity. There have been many attempts in the economic literature to address this problem. However, an in-depth treatment of the potentially endogenous relationships between the numerous financial indicators and growth is beyond the scope of this study. For a more detailed coverage of the econometric issues relating to endogeneity, we refer the reader to Beck (2008).

Reference

Beck, Thorsten. 2008. "The Econometrics of Finance and Growth." Policy Research Working Paper 4608, World Bank, Washington, DC.

Appendix C
Financial Development Data

Financial Depth Indicators

TABLE C.1 Financial Depth Indicators

Indicator	Description	Coverage
Total financial assets to GDP	Total assets held by bank and nonbank financial institutions as a share of gross domestic product (GDP).	1960–2011
Loans from nonresident banks	Ratio of net offshore bank loans to GDP. An offshore bank is a bank located outside the country of residence of the depositor, typically in a low tax jurisdiction (or tax haven) that provides financial and legal advantages.	1993–2011
External loans and deposits in relation to all sectors (%)	The share of loans and deposits of reporting international banks in external financing of the domestic banks and the real sector (all sectors of the economy).	1995–2011
Private credit by deposit money banks to GDP (%)	The financial resources provided to the private sector by domestic money banks as a share of GDP. Domestic money banks comprise commercial banks and other financial institutions that accept transferable deposits, such as demand deposits.	1960–2011
Nonlife insurance premium volume to GDP (%)	Ratio of nonlife insurance premium volume to GDP. Premium volume is the insurer's direct premiums earned (if property/casualty) or received (if life/health) during the previous calendar year.	1961–2011
Life insurance premium volume to GDP (%)	Ratio of life insurance premium volume to GDP. Premium volume is the insurer's direct premiums earned (if property/casualty) or received (if life/health) during the previous calendar year.	1990–2011
Liquid liabilities to GDP (%)	Ratio of liquid liabilities to GDP. Liquid liabilities are also known as broad money, or M3. They are the sum of currency and deposits in the central bank (M0); plus transferable deposits and electronic currency (M1); plus time and savings deposits, foreign currency transferable deposits, certificates of deposit, and securities repurchase agreements (M2); plus travelers' checks, foreign currency time deposits, commercial paper, and shares of mutual funds or market funds held by residents.	1961–2011
NBFI assets to GDP (%)	Ratio of assets of nonbank financial institutions (NBFI) to GDP. NBFIs include assets of mutual funds, insurance companies, and pension funds. The composite indicator represents an average of each of the indicators that were centered on their mean.	1980–2011
Stock market capitalization to GDP (%)	Total value of all listed shares in a stock market as a percentage of GDP.	1989–2011
Bank deposits to GDP (%)	The total value of demand, time, and savings deposits at domestic deposit money banks as a share of GDP. Deposit money banks comprise commercial banks and other financial institutions that accept transferable deposits, such as demand deposits.	1961–2011
Loans from nonresident banks (net) to GDP (%)	Ratio of net offshore bank loans to GDP. An offshore bank is a bank located outside the country of residence of the depositor, typically in a low tax jurisdiction (or tax haven) that provides financial and legal advantages.	1993–2011
Consolidated foreign claims of BIS reporting banks to GDP (%)	The ratio of consolidated foreign claims to GDP of the banks that are reporting to the Bank for International Settlements (BIS). Foreign claims are defined as the sum of cross-border claims plus foreign offices' local claims in all currencies. In the consolidated banking statistics, claims that are granted or extended to nonresidents are referred to as cross-border claims. In the context of the consolidated banking statistics, local claims refer to claims of domestic banks' foreign affiliates (branches/subsidiaries) on the residents of the host country (that is, country of residence of affiliates).	1983–2011

Source: World Bank Global Financial Development Database (GFDD) and Bank for International Settlements.

Financial Efficiency Indicators

TABLE C.2 Financial Efficiency Indicators

Indicator	Description	Coverage
Lending deposit spread (%)	Difference between lending rate and deposit rate. Lending rate is the rate charged by banks on loans to the private sector, and deposit interest rate is the rate offered by commercial banks on three-month deposits.	1980–2012
Bank overhead costs to total assets (%)	Operating expenses of a bank as a share of the value of all assets held. Total assets include total earning assets, cash and due from banks, foreclosed real estate, fixed assets, goodwill, other intangibles, current tax assets, deferred tax assets, discontinued operations, and other assets.	1998–2011
Bank cost-to-income ratio (%)	Operating expenses of a bank as a share of sum of net-interest revenue and other operating income.	1997–2011
Stock market turnover ratio (%)	Total value of shares traded during the period divided by the average market capitalization for the period.	1989–2011
Bank concentration (%)	Assets of three largest commercial banks as a share of total commercial banking assets. Total assets include total earning assets, cash and due from banks, foreclosed real estate, fixed assets, goodwill, other intangibles, current tax assets, deferred tax assets, discontinued operations, and other assets.	1997–2011
Boone indicator	A measure of degree of competition based on profit-efficiency in the banking market. It is calculated as the elasticity of profits to marginal costs. An increase in the Boone indicator implies a deterioration of the competitive conduct of financial intermediaries.	1997–2010
Bank net interest margin (%)	Accounting value of bank's net interest revenue as a share of its average interest-bearing (total earning) assets.	1998–2011
Bank return on assets (%, before and after tax)	Commercial banks' after-tax net income to yearly averaged total assets.	1998–2011
Bank return on equity (%, before and after tax)	Commercial banks' pretax income to yearly averaged equity.	1999–2011
H-statistic	A measure of the degree of competition in the banking market. It measures the elasticity of banks' revenues relative to input prices. Under perfect competition, an increase in input prices raises both marginal costs and total revenues by the same amount, and hence the H-statistic equals 1. Under a monopoly, an increase in input prices results in a rise in marginal costs, a fall in output, and a decline in revenues, leading to an H-statistic less than or equal to 0. When H-statistic is between 0 and 1, the system operates under monopolistic competition. However, it is possible for H-stat to be greater than 1 in some oligopolistic markets.	2010
Lerner index	A measure of market power in the banking market. It compares output pricing and marginal costs (that is, markup). An increase in the Lerner index indicates a deterioration of the competitive conduct of financial intermediaries.	1996–2010

Source: World Bank Global Financial Development Database (GFDD).

Financial Stability Indicators

TABLE C.3 Financial Stability Indicators

Indicator	Description	Coverage
Volatility of private credit	Private credit by deposit money banks and other financial institutions to gross domestic product (GDP).	1980–2012
Number of years spent in banking crisis	Average number of years spent in a systemic banking crisis.	1960–2013
Fiscal cost of crisis	Estimation of the fiscal cost of a banking or financial crisis.	1960–2013
Output loss due to banking crisis as a share of GDP	Average number of years spent in a systemic banking crisis.	1960–2013
Bank z-score	It captures the probability of default of a country's commercial banking system. Z-score compares the buffer of a country's commercial banking system (capitalization and returns) with the volatility of those returns.	1998–2011
Change in bank nonperforming loans (NPLs) to gross loans (%)	Change in the ratio of defaulting loans (payments of interest and principal past due by 90 days or more) to total gross loans (total value of loan portfolio). The loan amount recorded as nonperforming includes the gross value of the loan as recorded on the balance sheet, not just the amount that is overdue.	1998–2011
Bank capital to total assets (%)	Ratio of bank capital and reserves to total assets. Capital and reserves include funds contributed by owners, retained earnings, general and special reserves, provisions, and valuation adjustments.	1998–2011
Provisions to NPLs (%)	Provisions to NPLs. NPLs are loans for which the contractual payments are delinquent, usually defined as an NPL ratio being overdue for more than a certain number of days (for example, usually more than 90 days).	1998–2011
Stock price volatility	Stock price volatility is the average of the 360-day volatility of the national stock market index.	1960–2011
Bank credit to bank deposits (%)	The financial resources provided to the private sector by domestic money banks as a share of total deposits.	1960–2011

Source: World Bank Global Financial Development Database (GFDD).

Financial Inclusion Indicators

Firms

TABLE C.4 Financial Inclusion Indicators for Firms

Indicator	Description	Coverage
Investments financed by equity or stock sales (%)	Estimated proportion of purchases of fixed assets that was financed by owners' contribution or issue of new equity shares.	2002–2011
Working capital financed by banks (%)	Proportion of the working capital that was financed by bank loans.	2002–2011
Investments financed by banks (%)	Estimated proportion of purchases of fixed assets that was financed from bank loans.	2002–2011
Small firms with line of credit (%)	Percentage of small firms (5–19 workers) in the formal sector with a line of credit or a loan from a financial institution.	2006–2011
Firms using banks to finance investment (%)	Percentage of firms using banks to finance purchases of fixed assets.	2002–2011
Firms with line of credit (%)	Percentage of firms with a line of credit from a financial institution.	2002–2011
Firms using banks to finance working capital (%)	Percentage of firms using bank loans to finance working capital.	2002–2011
Firms not needing a loan (%)	Percentage of firms that did not apply for a loan in the last fiscal year because they did not need a loan. The denominator is the sum of all firms who applied and did not apply for a loan. The numerator is the number of firms who did not apply for a loan and also stated that they did not need a loan.	2006–2011
Firms with a checking or savings account (%)	Percentage of firms with a checking or savings account.	2006–2011
Firms identifying access to finance as a major constraint (%)	Percentage of firms identifying access/cost of finance as a "major" or "very severe" obstacle.	2002–2011
Firms with a bank loan or line of credit (%)	Percentage of firms in the formal sector with a line of credit or a loan from a financial institution.	2006–2011

Source: World Bank Enterprise Survey data.

Households

TABLE C.5 Financial Inclusion Indicators for Households

Indicator	Description	Coverage
Mobile phones used to pay bills (% age 15+)	The percentage of respondents who used a mobile phone to pay bills in the past 12 months (% age 15+).	2011
Borrowed from a financial institution in the past year (% age 15+) (and % of poorest 40%)	The percentage of respondents who borrowed any money from a bank, credit union, microfinance institution, or another financial institution such as a cooperative in the past 12 months (% age 15+).	2011 and 2014
Purchased agricultural insurance (% age 15+)	The percentage of respondents who purchased agricultural insurance.	2011
Loan in the past year (% age 15+) (and % of poorest 40%)	The percentage of respondents who borrowed any money in the past 12 months from any of the following sources: a formal financial institution, a store by using installment credit, family or friends, employer, or another private lender (% age 15+). (Note that getting a loan does not necessarily require having an account.)	2011
Saved at a financial institution in the past year (% age 15+) (and % of poorest 40%)	The percentage of respondents who saved at a financial institution in the past year.	2011 and 2014
Loan from a private lender in the past year (% age 15+)	The percentage of respondents who had a loan from a private lender in the past year.	2011
Bank accounts per 1,000 adults	Number of depositors with commercial banks per 1,000 adults.	2001–2011
Bank branches per 100,000 adults	Number of commercial bank branches per 100,000 adults.	2001–2011
Depositors with commercial banks per 1,000 adults	Depositors with commercial banks per 1,000 adults.	2001–2011
Accounts used to receive government payments	The percentage of respondents who had an account in which they received government payments.	2011
ATMs per 100,000 adults	Number of ATMs per 100,000 adults.	2001–2011
Credit card (% age 15+)	The percentage of respondents with a credit card (% age 15+).	2011 and 2014
Debit card (% age 15+)	The percentage of respondents with a debit card (% age 15+).	2011 and 2014
Electronic payments used to make payments (% age 15+)	The percentage of respondents who used electronic payments (payments that one makes or that are made automatically including wire transfers or payments made online) in the past 12 months to make payments on bills or to buy things using money from their accounts (% age 15+).	2011

Source: Global Findex.

Appendix D
Regression Analysis of the Impact of Credit on Firm-Level Outcomes

Table D.1 presents the results of regression analysis using sector-level data from Eurostat. The regressions estimate how changes in credit conditions in the economy correlate with outcome gaps between financially dependent sectors and other sectors, measuring the level of finance in the economy by the total credit-to-GDP ratio. The specification is

$$y_{s,c,t} = \alpha_0 + \alpha_1 FD_{s,2008} \times Credit_{c,t} + yc_{c,t} + \mu_s + \varepsilon_{s,c,t} \qquad \text{(D.1)}$$

where y is an outcome of sector s in country c and year t. $FD_{s,2008}$ is the measure of financial dependence of sector s in 2008, measured as the difference between investments and cash generated from operations that is observed in U.S. firms in that sector, as in Rajan and Zingales (1998). $Credit_{c,t}$ is the private sector credit flow as a share of GDP in country c and year t. We include country-year fixed effects $yc_{c,t}$, which absorb the effects of the aggregate level of credit supply as well as other omitted macro factors that are common across sectors. We also include sector fixed effects μ_s to account for unobserved, fixed heterogeneity at the sector level. The coefficient of interest is α_1, which we expect to be greater than zero—that is, a tightening in credit conditions at the country level would lead to worse outcomes for more financially dependent sectors, relative to other sectors.

Column 1 in table D.1 presents the results when all firms are included in the sector outcomes. Columns 2, 3, 4, and 5 consider only the self-employed (no employees), firms with 1–4 employees, firms with 5–9 employees, and firms with 10 or more employees, respectively.

TABLE D.1 Credit to GDP and Total Employment, Entry, Exit, and Number of Firms in Sectors—Regression Results Based on Eurostat Sector-Level Data for Central Europe and the Baltics

	1	2	3	4	5
	All firms	Self-employed	1–4 employees	5–9 employees	10+ employees
Outcome			Total employment (log)		
FD × Credit	0.0143*	0.0148**	0.0229***	0.0220***	0.0158
	(0.0087)	(0.0068)	(0.0065)	(0.0065)	(0.0097)
Observations	1,904	1,904	1,904	1,904	1,904
Adjusted R-squared	0.6801	0.8053	0.8212	0.8023	0.6408
Outcome			Firm entry (as proportion of existing firms)		
FD × Credit	0.0007	0.0012*	0.0015**	0.0013***	0.0007
	(0.0005)	(0.0007)	(0.0006)	(0.0005)	(0.0005)
Observations	1,720	1,720	1,720	1,720	1,720
Adjusted R-squared	0.7997	0.7348	0.7914	0.7914	0.7489
Outcome			Firm exit (as proportion of existing firms)		
FD × Credit	0.0003	0.0007	0.0007*	0.0008**	0.0005
	(0.0004)	(0.0005)	(0.0004)	(0.0004)	(0.0004)
Observations	1,720	1,720	1,720	1,720	1,720
Adjusted R-squared	0.8603	0.8150	0.8580	0.8061	0.7627
Outcome			Total number of firms		
FD × Credit	0.0142***	0.0154**	0.0171***	0.0175***	0.0142***
	(0.0055)	(0.0063)	(0.0054)	(0.0045)	(0.0041)
Observations	1,904	1,904	1,904	1,904	1,904
Adjusted R-squared	0.8438	0.8376	0.8562	0.8724	0.8519

Note: Robust standard errors in parentheses. Regressions include country-year fixed effects. FD = financial development.
* $p < 0.1$, ** $p < 0.05$, *** $p < 0.01$.

Tables D.2 and D.3 present the results of regression analysis using firm level data from Orbis, pooled across 31 countries (listed in table D.4). The regressions estimate how changes in credit conditions in the economy correlate with employment in firms, comparing financially dependent sectors and other sectors. The specification is

$$y_{i,s,c,t} = \alpha_0 + \alpha_1 FD_{s,2008} \times Credit_{c,t} + yc_{c,t} + \mu_i + \varepsilon_{i,s,c,t,} \qquad (D.2)$$

where y is an outcome of firm i belonging to sector s, country c, and year t. As before, $FJ_{s,20008}$ is the measure of financial dependence of sector s in 2008, and $Credit_{c,t}$ is the private sector credit flow as a share of GDP in country c and year t. Country-year fixed effects $yc_{c,t}$ absorb the effects of the aggregate level of credit supply as well as other omitted macro factors that are common across sectors. We also include firm fixed effects μ_i to account for unobserved, fixed heterogeneity at the firm level. The coefficient of interest is α_1, which we expect to be greater than zero—that is, a tightening in credit conditions at the country level would lead to worse outcomes for firms in more financially dependent sectors, relative to other sectors. The regression is estimated on a balanced sample of firms.

TABLE D.2 Credit to GDP and Firm-Level Employment—Regression Results Based on Orbis Firm-Level Data

	1 All firms	2 Age 0–2 years	3 Age 3–6 years	4 Age 7–11 years	5 Age 12–21 years	6 Age >21 years	7 0–9 employees	8 10–49 employees	9 50–249 employees	10 >249 employees
				All Countries						
FD × Private sector credit flows by banks (% GDP)	0.00292***	0.00168***	0.00254***	0.00384***	0.00304***	0.00204***f	0.000722***	0.00275***	0.00176***	0.00206***
	(0.000116)	(0.000536)	(0.000289)	(0.000223)	(0.000203)	(0.000215)	(0.000171)	(0.000193)	(0.000281)	(0.000644)
Observations	921,305	77,021	189,252	215,467	271,292	168,273	528,591	266,077	100,191	26,446
R-squared	0.059	0.205	0.064	0.070	0.070	0.041	0.120	0.114	0.094	0.084
Number of firms	131,615	11,003	27,036	30,781	38,756	24,039	75,513	38,011	14,313	3,778
			Excluding China, the Republic of Korea, and Japan							
FD × Private sector credit flows by banks (% GDP)	0.00299***	0.00170***	0.00259***	0.00394***	0.00311***	0.00212***	0.000737***	0.00283***	0.00191***	0.00217***
	(0.000118)	(0.000537)	(0.000290)	(0.000225)	(0.000205)	(0.000228)	(0.000173)	(0.000200)	(0.000296)	(0.000670)
Observations	846,566	75,152	180,866	199,724	252,854	137,970	511,931	233,051	81,214	20,370
R-squared	0.061	0.207	0.064	0.074	0.074	0.045	0.118	0.117	0.101	0.102
Number of firms	120,938	10,736	25,838	28,532	36,122	19,710	73,133	33,293	11,602	2,910

Note: Robust standard errors in parentheses. Regressions include firm fixed effects and country-year fixed effects. Balanced panel of firms. FD = financial development.
* $p < 0.1$, ** $p < 0.05$, *** $p < 0.01$.

TABLE D.3 Stock Market Capitalization and Firm-Level Employment—Regression Results Based on Orbis Firm-Level Data

	1 All firms	2 Age 0–2 years	3 Age 3–6 years	4 Age 7–11 years	5 Age 12–21 years	6 Age >21 years	7 0–9 employees	8 10–49 employees	9 50–249 employees	10 >249 employees
				All Countries						
FD × Stock market capitalization (% GDP)	0.00147***	0.00158***	0.00102***	0.00214***	0.00130***	0.00101***	0.000274***	0.00150***	0.000818***	0.000401
	(7.08e-05)	(0.000342)	(0.000185)	(0.000147)	(0.000121)	(0.000114)	(9.70e-05)	(0.000119)	(0.000196)	(0.000411)
Observations	781,104	65,646	161,094	180,636	230,388	143,340	450,000	224,478	84,348	22,278
R-squared	0.061	0.227	0.070	0.070	0.067	0.033	0.130	0.113	0.082	0.077
Number of firms	130,184	10,941	26,849	30,106	38,398	23,890	75,000	37,413	14,058	3,713
				Excluding China, the Republic of Korea, and Japan						
FD × Stock market capitalization (% GDP)	0.00153***	0.00152***	0.000953***	0.00226***	0.00133***	0.00111***	0.000280***	0.00150***	0.000810***	1.00e-05
	(7.53e-05)	(0.000347)	(0.000193)	(0.000154)	(0.000127)	(0.000129)	(9.96e-05)	(0.000128)	(0.000225)	(0.000520)
Observations	717,042	64,044	153,906	167,142	214,584	117,366	435,720	196,170	68,082	17,070
R-squared	0.064	0.230	0.070	0.074	0.071	0.036	0.129	0.115	0.087	0.096
Number of firms	119,507	10,674	25,651	27,857	35,764	19,561	72,620	32,695	11,347	2,845

Note: Robust standard errors in parentheses. Regressions include firm fixed effects and country-year fixed effects. Balanced panel of firms. FD = financial development.
* $p < 0.1$, ** $p < 0.05$, *** $p < 0.01$.

TABLE D.4 List of Countries in Orbis Sample

Country code	Country name	Country code	Country name
AT	Austria	IS	Iceland
BA	Bosnia and Herzegovina	IT	Italy
		JP	Japan
BE	Belgium	KR	Republic of Korea
BG	Bulgaria	LT	Lithuania
CN	China	LV	Latvia
CZ	Czech Republic	NL	Netherlands
DE	Germany	PL	Poland
EE	Estonia	PT	Portugal
ES	Spain	RO	Romania
FI	Finland	RS	Serbia
GB	Great Britain (United Kingdom)	RU	Russian Federation
GR	Greece	SE	Sweden
HR	Croatia	SI	Slovenia
HU	Hungary	SK	Slovak Republic
IE	Ireland	UA	Ukraine

Source: Orbis database.

Estimates Using Household Surveys

We estimate the following equation using individual panel data from the European Union Statistics on Income and Living Conditions (EU-SILC) for the period from 2008 to 2012 to investigate whether the effect of the crisis was larger in regions whose labor markets were more dependent on external finance:

$$y_{i,r,c,t} = \alpha_0 + \alpha_1 FD_{r,2008} \times Credit_{c,t} + yc_{c,t} + \mu_i + \varepsilon_{i,r,t,} \qquad (D.3)$$

where y is a labor market outcome of individual i, $FD_{r,2008}$ is the measure of financial dependence of the region r in 2008 obtained from the Labor Force Surveys, and $Credit_{c,t}$ is the private sector credit flow as a share of GDP. We include country-year fixed effects $yc_{c,t}$, which absorb the effects of the aggregate level of credit supply as well as other omitted factors that may be correlated with labor market conditions. We also include individual fixed effects μ_i to account for unobserved heterogeneity at the individual level. The coefficient of interest is α_1, which we expect to be greater than zero—that is, a tightening in credit conditions at the country level would lead to worse labor market outcomes for individuals living in more financially dependent regions. As can be seen in table D.5, the credit crunch had a larger effect on labor markets more dependent on finance external to firms. Moreover, in Western Europe, salaried workers were much more affected by the tighter credit conditions than other workers. In Central Europe, much of the impact of credit tightening was felt in hours worked by the self-employed, not necessarily in overall employment levels (table D.6).

TABLE D.5 The Credit Crunch Had a Larger Effect on Labor Markets More Dependent on External Finance

	Binary outcomes, all			Hourly earnings, employed individuals		
	Employed	Salaried job	Self-employed	Employed	Salaried job	Self-employed
FD × Credit	0.00284	0.0145***	0.00163	0.0123	0.0167**	0.000843
	(0.00551)	(0.00534)	(0.00231)	(0.0145)	(0.00810)	(0.0724)
Observations	185,068	185,068	185,068	96,110	84,746	10,840
R-squared	0.002	0.065	0.003	0.021	0.047	0.025
Number of individuals	46,267	46,267	46,267	24,212	22,282	2,852

Note: This table shows the estimates of α_1 from equation (D.3). Errors are clustered at the regional level. Robust standard errors in parentheses. FD = financial development.
* $p < 0.1$, ** $p < 0.05$, *** $p < 0.01$.

TABLE D.6 Labor Markets in Central and Western Europe Adjusted in a Different Way

	Binary outcomes, all			Hours worked, employed individuals		
	Employed	Salaried job	Self-employed	Employed	Salaried job	Self-employed
Central Europe						
FD × Credit	−0.00252	−0.00520	0.00307	0.0120*	0.00231	0.0351**
	(0.00526)	(0.00593)	(0.00361)	(0.00626)	(0.00261)	(0.0153)
Observations	68,976	68,976	68,976	34,668	29,010	4,007
R-squared	0.002	0.036	0.001	0.004	0.004	0.020
Number of individuals	17,244	17,244	17,244	8,678	7,287	1,006
Western Europe						
FD × Credit	0.00373	0.0178***	0.00140	0.00630	0.00299	−0.0234
	(0.00641)	(0.00601)	(0.00264)	(0.00664)	(0.00592)	(0.0167)
Observations	116,092	116,092	116,092	61,442	56,222	7,015
R-squared	0.003	0.075	0.003	0.004	0.003	0.018
Number of individuals	29,023	29,023	29,023	15,534	15,044	1,853

Note: This table shows the estimates of α_1 from equation (D.3). Errors are clustered at the regional level. Robust standard errors in parentheses. FD = financial development.
* $p < 0.1$, ** $p < 0.05$, *** $p < 0.01$.

To investigate the distributional impact of the financial crisis through the labor market, we estimate the following specification of equation (D.1):

$$y_{i,r,c,t} = \alpha_0 + \alpha_1 FD_{r,2008} \times Credit_{c,t} + \alpha_2 FD_{r,2008} \times Credit_{c,t} \times Top60_{i,2008} + yc_{c,t} + \mu_i + \varepsilon_{i,r,t,} \tag{D.4}$$

where $Top60_{i,2008}$ is a dummy variable equal to 1 if the individual was at the top 60 of the income distribution in 2008. In other words, although α_1 would capture the overall effect of the credit crunch, α_2 would be informative of the distributional impact. A value of α_2 greater than zero would imply that the credit crunch had a larger negative effect on individuals in the top 60 than among those in the bottom 40. As indicated in table D.7 and figure D.1, workers in the top 60 percent of the income distribution and older workers were the most adversely impacted by the financial crisis.

TABLE D.7 Financial Volatility Has Important Distributional Consequences

	Employment outcomes			Hours of work, employed individuals			Hourly earnings, employed individuals		
	Employed	Salaried job	Self-employed	Employed	Salaried job	Self-employed	Employed	Salaried job	Self-employed
Central Europe									
FD × Credit	-0.00765	-0.0111**	0.00238	0.0110*	0.000755	0.0353**	-0.0223*	-0.00325	-0.0477
	(0.00630)	(0.00516)	(0.00352)	(0.00604)	(0.00252)	(0.0154)	(0.0119)	(0.0147)	(0.0347)
FD × Credit × Top 60	0.0104***	0.0119***	0.00145**	0.00162	0.00248*	-0.000531	0.0296***	0.0234***	0.0365***
	(0.00262)	(0.00192)	(0.000587)	(0.00119)	(0.00143)	(0.00324)	(0.00420)	(0.00306)	(0.00815)
Observations	68,876	68,876	68,876	34,656	28,998	4,007	34,656	28,884	4,005
R-squared	0.004	0.038	0.001	0.005	0.005	0.020	0.038	0.073	0.023
Number of individuals	17,219	17,219	17,219	8,675	7,284	1,006	8,675	7,284	1,006
Western Europe									
FD × Credit	-0.00632	0.00761	0.000824	0.00252	-0.000948	-0.0265	-0.0238	0.00431	-0.0489
	(0.00743)	(0.00595)	(0.00299)	(0.00668)	(0.00650)	(0.0170)	(0.0176)	(0.0101)	(0.0792)
FD × Credit × Top 60	0.0115***	0.0114***	0.000506	0.00454	0.00413	0.00782	0.0472***	0.0143***	0.151***
	(0.00235)	(0.00280)	(0.00144)	(0.00289)	(0.00317)	(0.00813)	(0.00809)	(0.00361)	(0.0309)
Observations	115,768	115,768	115,768	61,311	56,185	6,927	61,311	55,815	6,781
R-squared	0.003	0.076	0.003	0.004	0.003	0.018	0.025	0.046	0.041
Number of individuals	28,942	28,942	28,942	15,499	15,034	1,829	15,499	14,985	1,824

Note: This table shows the estimates of α_1 and α_2 from equation (D.4). Errors are clustered at the regional level. Robust standard errors in parentheses. FD = financial development.
* p < 0.1, ** p < 0.05, *** p < 0.01.

FIGURE D.1 Older workers were hurt the most by the credit crunch

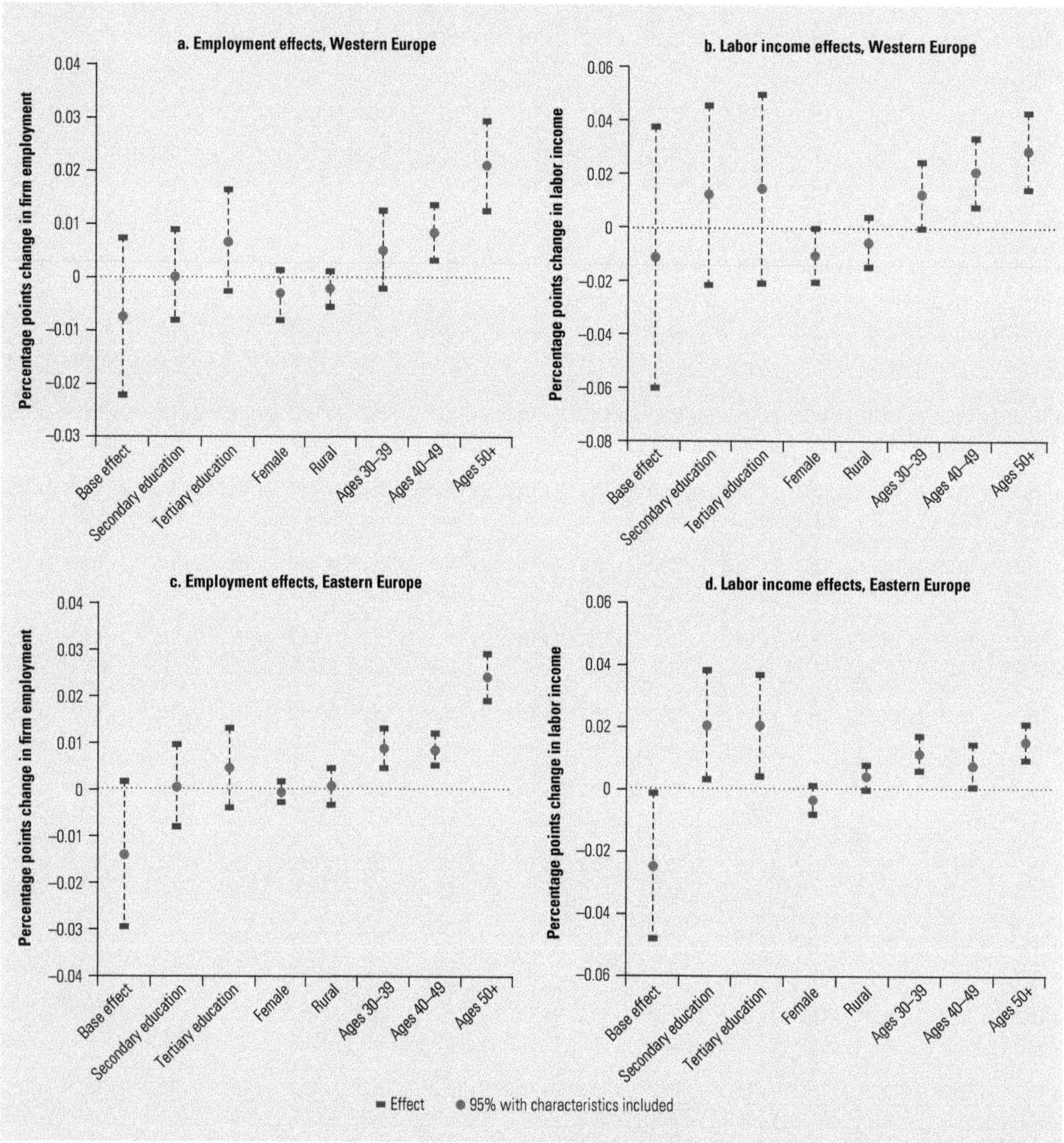

Note: This figure shows the estimates of α_1 from equation (D.3) and its interactions with individuals' age and employment characteristics included. Errors are clustered at the regional level. The omitted categories are individuals with primary education, males, urban, and younger than 30 years.

Reference

Rajan, Raghuram G., and Luigi Zingales. 1998. "Which Capitalism? Lessons from the East Asian Crisis." *Journal of Applied Corporate Finance* 11 (3): 40–48.

Appendix E
Data Source for the Analysis

The main data source for the analysis is the OeNB Euro Survey conducted by the Austrian central bank since 2007 on a regular basis as a repeated cross-sectional survey in 10 Central European and Western Balkan countries: six European Union member states that are not part of the euro area (Bulgaria, Croatia, the Czech Republic, Hungary, Poland, and Romania) and four (potential) candidate countries (Albania, Bosnia and Herzegovina, the former Yugoslav Republic of Macedonia, and Serbia).[1] The surveys are conducted in the major languages of each country—for example, in FYR Macedonia the survey is conducted in both Macedonian and Albanian. The surveys are centrally organized by the Austrian Gallup Institute and carried out by national contractors. The surveys may be conducted as part of an omnibus survey or as a stand-alone survey. Respondents do not receive incentives for participating.

In each country and wave, a nationally representative sample of 1,000 individuals aged 15 years or older is polled using multistage random sampling procedures. Data weighting ensures a nationally representative sample for each country using population statistics on gender, age, and region and (where available) education, socioeconomic status, and ethnicity.

The questionnaire consists of a core set of questions that focus on the role of the euro in households' portfolios and additional questions on varying special topics. We employ data from two surveys conducted in fall 2012 and 2013. Thus, our analysis focuses on 10 countries and around 20,000 individuals. In these surveys, the questionnaire elicits respondents' evaluations and expectations of current and future economic conditions, enquires about saving and borrowing activities of the household and personal experience of previous economic crises during transition, covers socioeconomic information of respondents, and includes four basic questions on financial literacy. In addition, the 2012 and 2013 surveys include the address of each primary sampling unit (PSU) for which we obtain geographical coordinates. This allows us to combine our data with data on all bank branches serving households (see Beckmann, Reiter, and Stix, forthcoming, for a detailed description of the bank branches). We further combine our data with information on light intensity at night, which Henderson, Storeygard, and Weil (2011) show is a useful proxy for local economic activity.

In general, the surveys contain information on the existence of savings and assets but not on amounts. Thus, percentages reflect participation rates only and not amounts invested in the respective assets. A further difference with household wealth surveys is that the questionnaire focuses on individuals rather than households. However, the questionnaire partly accounts for this issue by asking whether individuals hold financial assets alone or together with their partner. Finally, we do not impute missing values, but assume that nonresponse is random. For household income, we include a dummy variable for those respondents who refuse to answer the question on income.

The central variable of our analysis is based on the following questions:

1. *[ASK ALL] There are several ways in which one can hold savings. For example, one can hold cash, use bank accounts, have life insurances, hold mutual funds or pension funds, etc. Do you currently have any savings? Please refer to savings you hold personally or together with your partner.*

   Yes / No / Don't Know / No Answer

2. *[If 1 = Yes] Please take a look at this card that lists various saving instruments— could you please select the ones you are currently using and rank them according to the amounts you have saved on the respective instrument.*

   Cash
   Current account / transaction account / wage card
   Savings deposits / savings accounts (in foreign or in [LOCAL CURRENCY])
   Life insurance
   Mutual funds
   Stocks
   Pension funds (voluntary contributions)
   Bonds
   Other (for example, gold)
   Do not know
   No answer

Based on the above question, we employ seven main indicators of households' saving, each defined as a dummy variable and shown in table E.1.

TABLE E.1 Main Indicators of Household Saving

Dummy variable	Takes on value 1 for the following saving instruments
1. Any savings	Cash, current account, savings deposit, life insurance, mutual funds, stocks, pension funds, bonds
2. Formal savings	Current account, savings deposit, life insurance, mutual funds, stocks, pension funds, bonds
3. Bank savings	Current account, savings deposit
4. Contractual savings	Life insurance, pension funds
5. Capital market savings	Stocks, bonds, mutual funds
6. Cash only	Cash savings, no other savings
7. More than one formal savings	More than one of the following: current account, savings deposit, life insurance, mutual funds, stocks, pension funds, bonds

Source: Survey conducted by the Oesterreichische National Bank: https://www.oenb.at/en/Monetary-Policy/Surveys/OeNB -Euro-Survey.html.

Note

1. Further details on the survey can be found on the Oesterreichische National Bank website, https://www.oenb.at/en/Monetary-Policy/Surveys/OeNB-Euro-Survey.html.

References

Beckmann, E., S. Reiter, and H. Stix. Forthcoming. "The Banking Landscape of Households in Central, Eastern and Southeastern Europe." *Focus on European Economic Integration.*

Henderson, V., A. Storeygard, and D. Weil. 2011. "A Bright Idea for Measuring Economic Growth." *American Economic Review: Papers and Proceedings* 101: 194–99.

Appendix F
Comparability of Global Findex and OeNB Euro Surveys

As the survey data provide no information on the amounts of savings, it is difficult to compare these findings with aggregate indicators of savings. However, rank correlations reported in table F.1 suggest that our survey-based indicators are positively (and highly) correlated with aggregate stock (deposits to GDP) and flow (household saving rate) indicators of household savings. This is in line with previous analyses based on the Euro Survey data, which have shown that survey-based indicators provide a surprisingly accurate match with aggregate data (see, for example, Brown and Stix 2015 and Beckmann, Scheiber, and Stix 2011). Furthermore, table F.1 shows Euro Survey results are positively correlated with indicators of household savings from the Global Findex Survey. The survey questions are not directly comparable, as the Euro Survey question on savings is an indicator of the stock of savings whereas the Findex question enquires about flows. Table F.2 provides a comparison of the questions from Global Findex and table F.3 compares results on informal and formal savings as well as on the use of bank accounts both from Global Findex and the OeNB Euro Survey.[1] In summary, we conclude that despite limited comparability, our survey results match fairly well with evidence from aggregate data and from other surveys.

TABLE F.1 Spearman Rank Correlations of Savings Measurements from Aggregate and Survey Data

	ES savings	Hh saving rate	Gross savings	Deposits	GF saving rate	GF account	ES account	ES saving rate
ES savings	1.00							
Hh saving rate	0.90*	1.00						
Gross savings	0.35	0.30	1.00					
Deposits	0.47	-0.10	0.20	1.00				
GF saving rate	0.65*	0.60	0.40	0.09	1.00			
GF account	0.52	0.90*	0.43	0.07	0.49	1.00		
ES account	0.46	0.82	0.47	0.27	0.57	0.88*	1.00	
ES saving rate	0.35	0.60	0.16	0.05	0.88*	0.33	0.46	1.00

Source: Survey conducted by the Oesterreichische National Bank: https://www.oenb.at/en/Monetary-Policy/Surveys/OeNB-Euro-Survey.html.
Note: The table reports Spearman rank correlations between the country averages for each variable. Variables are defined as follows: *ES savings* denotes the percentage of individuals with any savings based on the Euro Survey question. *Hh saving rate* is taken from Eurostat and denotes the gross saving rate of households (including nonprofit institutions serving households) and is defined as gross savings divided by gross disposable income, with the latter being adjusted for the change in the net equity of households in pension fund reserves. *Gross savings* is taken from World Bank national accounts data and defined as gross national income less total consumption, plus net transfers. *Deposits / GDP* are taken from the World Bank Global Financial Development database and denote financial system deposits to GDP (%). *GF saving rate* and *GF account* are taken from the Global Findex Survey and denote the percentage of individuals who (a) saved over the last 12 months and (b) have an account at a financial institution. *ES account* and *ES saving rate* are taken from the Euro Survey and denote the percentage of individuals who (a) have an account at a financial institution and (b) are currently able to save.
* $p < 0.05$.

TABLE F.2 Comparison of Questions—Global Findex and OeNB Euro Survey

Global Findex	OeNB Euro Survey
Savings In the past 12 months, have you saved or set aside any savings?	There are several ways in which one can hold savings. For example, one can hold cash, use bank accounts, have life insurance, hold mutual funds, pension funds, etc. Do you currently have any savings? Please refer to savings you hold personally or together with your partner.
	Please tell me whether you agree or disagree with the following statement:
	Currently, I am able to save money.
Formal savings If saved: In the past 12 months, have you saved or set aside money by using an account at a bank, a credit union (or another financial institution, where applicable—for example cooperatives in Latin America), or microfinance institution?	If has savings: Please take a look at this card that lists various saving instruments. Could you please select the ones you are currently using and rank them according to the amounts you have saved on the respective instrument.
	Cash
	Current account
	Savings deposit / savings account
	Life insurance
	Mutual funds
	Stocks
	Pension funds
	Bonds
	Other (e.g., gold)
Account Do you, either by yourself or together with someone else, currently have an account at any of the following places? An account can be used to save money, to make and receive payments, or to receive wages and remittances. Do you currently have an account at a bank or credit union (or another financial institution, where applicable—for example, cooperatives in Latin America).	Do you have a current account or savings deposit? Please refer only to those accounts you hold personally or together with your partner.
	Answers coded separately for current account and savings deposit.
Do you currently have an account at the post office?	If respondent has current account / debit card / wage card or savings deposit: At which bank do you have this account / debit card / wage card / savings deposit?
	List of banks includes microfinance banks and postal savings bank. Answers are coded separately for (1) current account, debit and wage card, and (2) savings deposit.

Source: Global Findex and survey conducted by the Oesterreichische National Bank: https://www.oenb.at/en/Monetary-Policy/Surveys/OeNB-Euro-Survey.html.

TABLE F.3 Comparison of Descriptive Statistics—Global Findex and OeNB Euro Survey

Global Findex, 2011				
	Saved over the last 12 months (%)	Has any savings (%)	Saved at financial institution (% of those who saved over the last 12 months)	Account at financial institution (%)
Bulgaria	11	—	47	53
Croatia	22	—	57	89
Czech Republic	50	—	74	81
Hungary	27	—	65	73
Poland	32	—	62	70
Romania	18	—	48	45
Albania	23	—	38	28
Bosnia and Herzegovina	14	—	45	56
Macedonia, FYR	23	—	38	74
Serbia	15	—	22	63

OeNB Euro Survey, spring and fall 2011[a]				
	Currently able to save (%)	Has any savings (%)	Saves at formal financial institution if currently able to save[b] (%)	Account at financial institution (%)
Bulgaria	15	46	57	31
Croatia	15	60	73	88
Czech Republic	34	91	95	89
Hungary	13	48	62	71
Poland	35	68	77	86
Romania	19	45	46	15
Albania	27	86	43	27
Bosnia and Herzegovina	20	47	45	68
Macedonia, FYR	27	85	81	79
Serbia	14	51	59	68

Source: Global Findex and survey conducted by the Oesterreichische National Bank: https://www.oenb.at/en/Monetary-Policy/Surveys/OeNB-Euro-Survey.html.
Note: — = not available.
a. Data on credit cards are for fall 2014.
b. Includes current account, savings deposit, life insurance, and pension funds, excluding stocks, bonds, and mutual funds.

Note

1. For more information, see Global Financial Inclusion (database), World Bank, Washington, DC, http://datatopics.worldbank.org/financialinclusion/ and the Oesterreichische National Bank website, https://www.oenb.at/en/Monetary-Policy/Surveys/OeNB-Euro-Survey.html.

References

Beckmann, E., T. Scheiber, and H. Stix. 2011. "How the Crisis Affected Foreign Currency Borrowing in CESEE: Microeconomic Evidence and Policy Implications." *Focus on European Economic Integration* Q1/11: 25–43.

Brown, M., and H. Stix. 2015. "Euroization of Bank Deposits." *Economic Policy* 81: 95–139.

Appendix G
Detailed Tables of Results

TABLE G.1 Average Marginal Effects from Probit Model of Savings

	All	BG	HR	CZ	HU	PL	RO	AL	BA	MK	RS
Age	−0.004**	0.003	−0.005	−0.011**	−0.003	0.004	−0.011***	−0.006	0.002	0.001	−0.005
	0.002)	(0.005)	(0.005)	(0.005)	(0.006)	(0.004)	(0.004)	(0.005)	(0.004)	(0.002)	(0.005)
Age-squared	0.005**	−0.003	0.006	0.015***	0.006	−0.003	0.013***	0.006	−0.002	−0.003	0.007
	(0.003)	(0.005)	(0.005)	(0.006)	(0.006)	(0.004)	(0.003)	(0.007)	(0.004)	(0.002)	(0.005)
Female	−0.012	−0.001	−0.014	0.026	−0.064***	0.050*	−0.027	−0.008	0.020	−0.025	0.012
	(0.008)	(0.024)	(0.021)	(0.021)	(0.022)	(0.029)	(0.025)	(0.023)	(0.016)	(0.025)	(0.024)
1-person household	−0.033*	−0.062	−0.069**	−0.041	−0.053	−0.139***	−0.041	0.028	0.036	0.011	−0.034
	(0.018)	(0.060)	(0.034)	(0.050)	(0.047)	(0.053)	(0.041)	(0.089)	(0.052)	(0.037)	(0.060)
2-person household	−0.021*	−0.074*	0.009	−0.091***	−0.061	−0.064*	−0.026	0.020	−0.000	0.022	0.011
	(0.012)	(0.040)	(0.027)	(0.030)	(0.047)	(0.035)	(0.033)	(0.018)	(0.023)	(0.027)	(0.031)
Children in household	0.008	−0.009	0.029	−0.005	−0.010	−0.062**	−0.044	0.021	0.024	0.024	0.025
	(0.009)	(0.027)	(0.028)	(0.033)	(0.037)	(0.030)	(0.030)	(0.026)	(0.021)	(0.020)	(0.029)
Married	0.031**	0.052*	−0.017	0.125***	0.020	0.024	0.002	0.024	0.041	0.027	0.069
	(0.013)	(0.029)	(0.024)	(0.032)	(0.020)	(0.030)	(0.031)	(0.042)	(0.028)	(0.032)	(0.044)
Head of household	−0.001	−0.018	0.048*	0.027	−0.037	0.067***	−0.044*	0.011	0.006	0.036*	0.001
	(0.008)	(0.032)	(0.025)	(0.032)	(0.026)	(0.024)	(0.027)	(0.011)	(0.025)	(0.022)	(0.035)
Bottom 40 percent	−0.118***	−0.105***	−0.180***	−0.065*	−0.094***	−0.100**	−0.088***	−0.198***	−0.044*	−0.124***	−0.044
	(0.018)	(0.037)	(0.033)	(0.036)	(0.025)	(0.045)	(0.028)	(0.057)	(0.023)	(0.031)	(0.038)
Income answer refused	−0.080***	−0.128***	−0.091***	−0.227***	−0.078***	−0.070*	−0.039*	−0.087	−0.018	−0.034	−0.089**
	(0.012)	(0.030)	(0.033)	(0.060)	(0.025)	(0.039)	(0.022)	(0.070)	(0.034)	(0.036)	(0.040)
Own house	0.049***	−0.031	0.097***	0.067	0.054	0.104*	0.030	0.020	0.050*	0.011	−0.000
	(0.017)	(0.073)	(0.033)	(0.043)	(0.049)	(0.061)	(0.032)	(0.035)	(0.028)	(0.038)	(0.036)
Own other real estate	0.091***	0.110***	0.110***	0.092***	0.090*	0.127***	0.118**	0.043	0.172***	0.061**	0.118***
	(0.013)	(0.025)	(0.021)	(0.034)	(0.050)	(0.044)	(0.047)	(0.055)	(0.048)	(0.031)	(0.022)
Loan	0.039**	−0.098***	0.014	−0.006	0.018	0.032	0.022	0.144***	0.034	0.124***	0.104***
	(0.017)	(0.030)	(0.027)	(0.054)	(0.018)	(0.052)	(0.020)	(0.048)	(0.022)	(0.024)	(0.019)
Unemployed	−0.104***	−0.026	−0.036	−0.141***	−0.064	−0.139**	−0.051	−0.143***	−0.054**	−0.207***	−0.079**
	(0.020)	(0.033)	(0.037)	(0.037)	(0.052)	(0.054)	(0.033)	(0.042)	(0.024)	(0.021)	(0.035)
Self-employed	0.068***	0.118***	0.072	0.130***	0.048	0.068*	0.087**	−0.014	0.042	0.037	0.106**
	(0.018)	(0.027)	(0.054)	(0.031)	(0.046)	(0.035)	(0.034)	(0.043)	(0.067)	(0.049)	(0.048)
Retired	−0.032	0.081	−0.071	−0.124***	−0.034	−0.036	−0.024	−0.151**	−0.005	−0.107***	−0.058
	(0.020)	(0.057)	(0.049)	(0.039)	(0.036)	(0.040)	(0.042)	(0.066)	(0.031)	(0.029)	(0.060)
Secondary education	0.087***	0.111**	0.036**	0.126***	0.111***	0.017	0.043	0.117**	0.048	0.094***	0.112***
	(0.016)	(0.046)	(0.018)	(0.013)	(0.020)	(0.028)	(0.040)	(0.047)	(0.029)	(0.015)	(0.039)
Tertiary education	0.185***	0.185***	0.109**	0.229***	0.218***	0.114**	0.125***	0.268***	0.093***	0.114***	0.244***
	(0.019)	(0.049)	(0.045)	(0.033)	(0.027)	(0.046)	(0.040)	(0.032)	(0.031)	(0.018)	(0.047)
Pseudo-R^2	0.19	0.12	0.08	0.14	0.08	0.12	0.12	0.16	0.12	0.28	0.13
N	17646	1787	1796	1846	1845	1633	1798	1735	1660	1859	1634
P(DepVar = 1)	0.41	0.26	0.45	0.71	0.28	0.37	0.21	0.65	0.16	0.69	0.28

Note: Cluster standard errors in parentheses. The model for all countries includes country-time fixed effects; the models for individual countries include region-time fixed effects. BG = Bulgaria; HR = Croatia; CZ = Czech Republic; HU = Hungary; PL = Poland; RO = Romania; AL = Albania; BA = Bosnia and Herzegovina; MK = Macedonia, FYR; RS = Serbia.
* $p < 0.1$, ** $p < 0.05$, *** $p < 0.01$.

TABLE G.2 **Determinants of Savings and Saving Instruments**

Dependent variables	All	Respondents with savings					
	Any savings	Formal savings	Cash only	Bank savings	Contractual savings	Capital market savings	>1 formal savings
Bottom 40 percent	−0.098***	−0.049***	0.044***	−0.068***	0.008	0.008	−0.013
	(0.014)	(0.014)	(0.013)	(0.016)	(0.015)	(0.011)	(0.016)
Income no answer	−0.067***	−0.013	−0.012	−0.026	0.020	0.010	−0.004
	(0.015)	(0.017)	(0.015)	(0.018)	(0.019)	(0.011)	(0.016)
House	0.037**	0.014	0.003	0.023	0.015	0.021	0.021
	(0.017)	(0.017)	(0.016)	(0.020)	(0.019)	(0.015)	(0.018)
Other real estate	0.065***	0.011	−0.006	0.004	−0.003	0.039***	0.042***
	(0.012)	(0.014)	(0.013)	(0.015)	(0.015)	(0.008)	(0.013)
Regular income in euros	0.108***	−0.048	0.051*	−0.011	−0.001	0.025	0.041
	(0.034)	(0.032)	(0.029)	(0.035)	(0.037)	(0.020)	(0.032)
Receives remittances	0.133***	0.002	0.003	−0.006	0.015	−0.003	0.009
	(0.020)	(0.022)	(0.019)	(0.025)	(0.023)	(0.016)	(0.022)
Has a loan	0.031**	0.045***	−0.028**	0.008	0.081***	0.013	0.038***
	(0.014)	(0.013)	(0.012)	(0.014)	(0.013)	(0.009)	(0.013)
Plans a loan	0.071***	0.038	−0.021	0.008	0.026	0.009	0.032*
	(0.018)	(0.027)	(0.025)	(0.028)	(0.019)	(0.011)	(0.018)
Medium education	0.051***	0.044***	−0.042***	0.043***	0.020	0.028***	0.038**
	(0.012)	(0.014)	(0.013)	(0.015)	(0.016)	(0.010)	(0.015)
High education	0.141***	0.078***	−0.083***	0.071***	0.071***	0.053***	0.107***
	(0.017)	(0.017)	(0.017)	(0.019)	(0.018)	(0.012)	(0.017)
Employed	0.072***	0.053***	−0.051***	0.063***	0.061***	0.023	0.062***
	(0.015)	(0.018)	(0.016)	(0.021)	(0.021)	(0.015)	(0.020)
Self-employed	0.056***	0.004	0.007	0.005	0.056***	0.030**	0.050***
	(0.017)	(0.018)	(0.016)	(0.021)	(0.019)	(0.013)	(0.016)
Retired	0.044**	0.063**	−0.067***	0.095***	−0.040	0.046**	0.020
	(0.020)	(0.025)	(0.024)	(0.028)	(0.029)	(0.022)	(0.029)
Age	0.004**	0.009***	−0.010***	0.007**	0.012***	0.004**	0.008***
	(0.002)	(0.003)	(0.002)	(0.003)	(0.003)	(0.002)	(0.003)
Age-squared	0.007***	−0.009***	0.011***	−0.008***	−0.011***	−0.004*	−0.007**
	(0.002)	(0.003)	(0.003)	(0.003)	(0.003)	(0.002)	(0.003)
Female	−0.014	−0.012	0.006	−0.010	0.014	−0.023***	−0.006
	(0.009)	(0.012)	(0.013)	(0.014)	(0.013)	(0.008)	(0.011)
Married	0.032**	−0.038**	0.035**	−0.031*	−0.030*	−0.012	−0.024*
	(0.013)	(0.016)	(0.016)	(0.017)	(0.018)	(0.011)	(0.014)
1-person household	−0.012	−0.057**	0.061**	−0.046	−0.074***	−0.007	−0.059**
	(0.020)	(0.025)	(0.026)	(0.028)	(0.027)	(0.020)	(0.028)
2-person household	−0.017	−0.007	0.018	−0.017	−0.012	−0.001	−0.013
	(0.012)	(0.015)	(0.016)	(0.018)	(0.016)	(0.012)	(0.017)
Children in household	0.008	0.009	−0.009	−0.001	0.013	0.001	0.008
	(0.012)	(0.014)	(0.014)	(0.015)	(0.015)	(0.010)	(0.014)
Head of household	0.002	0.013	−0.011	0.004	0.009	0.001	0.010
	(0.011)	(0.014)	(0.015)	(0.015)	(0.014)	(0.009)	(0.013)
Muslim	0.006	−0.053**	0.051***	−0.073***	0.071*	0.042*	0.051
	(0.028)	(0.022)	(0.020)	(0.026)	(0.040)	(0.024)	(0.038)

(Continued)

TABLE G.2 Determinants of Savings and Saving Instruments *(continued)*

Dependent variables	All	Respondents with savings					
	Any savings	Formal savings	Cash only	Bank savings	Contractual savings	Capital market savings	>1 formal savings
Risk averse	0.035**	0.019	−0.016	0.019	−0.001	−0.017	0.001
	(0.017)	(0.018)	(0.018)	(0.020)	(0.020)	(0.012)	(0.020)
Experienced economic growth	0.049***	0.025**	−0.017	0.027**	0.027**	0.013	0.023*
	(0.011)	(0.012)	(0.012)	(0.014)	(0.013)	(0.009)	(0.012)
Trust in government	0.028**	−0.003	0.000	0.008	−0.001	−0.007	−0.007
	(0.014)	(0.014)	(0.013)	(0.016)	(0.016)	(0.012)	(0.015)
Trust in European Union	0.032***	−0.003	0.004	0.008	0.000	0.018**	0.018
	(0.012)	(0.015)	(0.014)	(0.016)	(0.014)	(0.009)	(0.013)
Deposits safe	0.047***	0.041***	−0.033***	0.053***	−0.004	0.008	0.012
	(0.011)	(0.014)	(0.013)	(0.015)	(0.015)	(0.009)	(0.013)
Financial system stable	0.050***	0.016	−0.018	0.025	0.039**	0.018*	0.062***
	(0.011)	(0.016)	(0.015)	(0.018)	(0.016)	(0.011)	(0.015)
Financial loss during transition	0.084***	0.037**	−0.037**	0.037*	0.031**	0.041***	0.059***
	(0.015)	(0.018)	(0.018)	(0.019)	(0.015)	(0.010)	(0.014)
Internet access	0.096***	0.024	−0.009	0.033*	0.043**	0.032**	0.069***
	(0.012)	(0.016)	(0.016)	(0.018)	(0.020)	(0.014)	(0.020)
Distance to nearest bank (log)	−0.008***	0.003	0.000	0.001	0.011***	0.006**	0.007**
	(0.003)	(0.003)	(0.003)	(0.004)	(0.004)	(0.003)	(0.003)
Stable lights	0.001	0.015**	−0.009*	0.019**	0.021**	0.003	0.014*
	(0.007)	(0.006)	(0.006)	(0.008)	(0.010)	(0.006)	(0.008)
Log-L	−5295.1	−1629.7	−1529.8	−1944.8	−1698.2	−929.2	−1541.7
Pseudo-R^2	0.22	0.22	0.19	0.18	0.28	0.19	0.25
N	9893	4241	4241	4241	4241	4178	4241
P(DepVar = 1)	0.43	0.81	0.16	0.75	0.24	0.08	0.19

Note: Cluster standard errors in parentheses.
* $p < 0.1$, ** $p < 0.05$, *** $p < 0.01$.

TABLE G.3 Heterogeneities among Bottom 40 Percent Savers

Dependent variables	All	Respondents with savings					
	Any savings	Formal savings	Cash only	Bank savings	Contractual savings	Capital market savings	>1 formal savings
Bottom 40 percent	−0.097***	−0.055***	0.047***	−0.080***	0.014	0.014	−0.005
	(0.013)	(0.015)	(0.014)	(0.017)	(0.017)	(0.011)	(0.017)
Tertiary education	0.143***	0.072***	−0.080***	0.059***	0.077***	0.057***	0.113***
	(0.016)	(0.018)	(0.017)	(0.020)	(0.018)	(0.013)	(0.017)
Bottom 40 percent × Tertiary education	−0.011	0.045	−0.024	0.094**	−0.046	−0.037	−0.053
	(0.033)	(0.038)	(0.036)	(0.043)	(0.046)	(0.030)	(0.041)
Log-L	−5295.0	−1629.0	−1529.5	−1942.5	−1697.6	−928.4	−1540.9
Bottom 40 percent	−0.102***	−0.044**	0.042**	−0.065***	0.015	0.011	−0.019
	(0.017)	(0.019)	(0.018)	(0.022)	(0.022)	(0.014)	(0.021)
Secondary education	0.048***	0.047***	−0.042***	0.044***	0.024	0.029***	0.035**
	(0.013)	(0.015)	(0.015)	(0.017)	(0.017)	(0.011)	(0.016)
Bottom 40 percent × Secondary education	0.008	−0.009	0.003	−0.005	−0.015	−0.004	0.012
	(0.021)	(0.025)	(0.024)	(0.028)	(0.029)	(0.020)	(0.028)
Log-L	−5295.0	−1629.7	−1529.7	−1944.7	−1698.0	−929.1	−1541.7
Bottom 40 percent	−0.096***	−0.034**	0.028**	−0.051***	0.014	0.010	−0.008
	(0.013)	(0.015)	(0.014)	(0.018)	(0.016)	(0.010)	(0.016)
Self-employed	0.063***	0.030	−0.021	0.034	0.068***	0.033**	0.058***
	(0.019)	(0.020)	(0.019)	(0.022)	(0.020)	(0.013)	(0.018)
Bottom 40 percent × Self-employed	−0.035	−0.118***	0.124***	−0.148***	−0.094	−0.023	−0.067
	(0.038)	(0.037)	(0.036)	(0.044)	(0.058)	(0.033)	(0.051)
Log-L	−5294.7	−1625.4	−1524.4	−1939.7	−1696.8	−928.9	−1540.9
Bottom 40 percent	−0.116***	−0.072***	0.057***	−0.112***	0.058**	0.005	0.012
	(0.017)	(0.020)	(0.019)	(0.024)	(0.024)	(0.016)	(0.026)
Employed	0.060***	0.039**	−0.043**	0.036	0.089***	0.021	0.075***
	(0.017)	(0.020)	(0.018)	(0.023)	(0.023)	(0.016)	(0.023)
Bottom 40 percent × Employed	0.034*	0.043*	−0.025	0.080***	−0.078**	0.005	−0.038
	(0.021)	(0.026)	(0.024)	(0.030)	(0.032)	(0.020)	(0.031)
Log-L	−5293.7	−1628.4	−1529.3	−1941.1	−1694.8	−929.1	−1540.9
Bottom 40 percent	−0.086***	−0.041**	0.036**	−0.047***	−0.017	0.011	−0.026
	(0.014)	(0.016)	(0.015)	(0.018)	(0.018)	(0.011)	(0.017)
Retired	0.060***	0.072***	−0.075***	0.118***	−0.071**	0.048**	0.005
	(0.021)	(0.027)	(0.026)	(0.031)	(0.031)	(0.021)	(0.029)
Bottom 40 percent × Retired	−0.052**	−0.038	0.036	−0.097***	0.134***	−0.013	0.072**
	(0.026)	(0.033)	(0.031)	(0.036)	(0.036)	(0.023)	(0.035)
Log-L	−5292.8	−1629.1	−1529.1	−1941.3	−1691.6	−929.0	−1539.7
Bottom 40 percent	−0.066**	−0.081**	0.074*	−0.122***	−0.021	0.002	−0.067
	(0.031)	(0.040)	(0.039)	(0.043)	(0.041)	(0.035)	(0.046)
Own house	0.047**	0.004	0.012	0.007	0.008	0.019	0.010
	(0.020)	(0.022)	(0.022)	(0.025)	(0.021)	(0.016)	(0.021)
Bottom 40 percent × Own house	−0.037	0.036	−0.034	0.060	0.033	0.007	0.060
	(0.031)	(0.041)	(0.040)	(0.045)	(0.042)	(0.035)	(0.048)
Log-L	−5294.4	−1629.4	−1529.4	−1943.9	−1697.9	−929.1	−1540.8
Bottom 40 percent	−0.083***	−0.030*	0.027*	−0.043**	0.010	0.024**	0.006
	(0.013)	(0.016)	(0.015)	(0.018)	(0.018)	(0.011)	(0.018)
Own other real estate	0.083***	0.026*	−0.020	0.023	−0.001	0.048***	0.053***
	(0.013)	(0.015)	(0.014)	(0.017)	(0.015)	(0.009)	(0.013)
Bottom 40 percent × Own other real estate	−0.075***	−0.069**	0.061**	−0.091***	−0.011	−0.054***	−0.073**
	(0.027)	(0.029)	(0.027)	(0.033)	(0.035)	(0.020)	(0.034)
Log-L	−5290.2	−1626.9	−1527.2	−1940.8	−1698.1	−926.2	−1539.1
N	9893	4241	4241	4241	4241	4178	4241
P(DepVar = 1)	0.43	0.81	0.16	0.75	0.24	0.08	0.19

Note: Cluster standard errors in parentheses.

* p < 0.1, ** p < 0.05, *** p < 0.01.

TABLE G.4 Bottom 40 Percent and Heterogeneities in Trust

	All	Respondents with savings					
Dependent variables	Any savings	Formal savings	Cash only	Bank savings	Contractual savings	Capital market savings	>1 formal savings
Bottom 40 percent	−0.088***	−0.051***	0.048***	−0.072***	0.008	0.008	−0.019
	(0.014)	(0.017)	(0.016)	(0.019)	(0.018)	(0.011)	(0.017)
Trust in government	0.039***	−0.004	0.003	0.005	−0.000	−0.007	−0.011
	(0.014)	(0.016)	(0.015)	(0.018)	(0.016)	(0.011)	(0.016)
Bottom 40 percent × Trust in government	−0.042*	0.006	−0.013	0.012	−0.002	0.001	0.028
	(0.025)	(0.029)	(0.028)	(0.034)	(0.033)	(0.025)	(0.033)
Log-L	−5296.7	−1630.0	−1529.6	−1945.3	−1698.5	−930.2	−1542.1
Bottom 40 percent	−0.076***	−0.029	0.032*	−0.055**	0.003	0.015	−0.023
	(0.015)	(0.019)	(0.019)	(0.021)	(0.019)	(0.012)	(0.020)
Trust in European Union	0.046***	0.007	−0.002	0.015	−0.002	0.021**	0.013
	(0.013)	(0.015)	(0.014)	(0.016)	(0.015)	(0.009)	(0.013)
Bottom 40 percent × Trust in European Union	−0.057**	−0.042	0.026	−0.030	0.014	−0.019	0.030
	(0.022)	(0.026)	(0.025)	(0.030)	(0.030)	(0.021)	(0.030)
Log-L	−5291.0	−1628.4	−1529.2	−1944.2	−1698.0	−928.8	−1541.2
Bottom 40 percent	−0.081***	−0.044**	0.028	−0.078***	0.011	0.004	−0.023
	(0.017)	(0.021)	(0.020)	(0.024)	(0.024)	(0.016)	(0.025)
Trust in deposit safety	0.055***	0.043***	−0.040***	0.049***	−0.003	0.007	0.009
	(0.012)	(0.015)	(0.014)	(0.016)	(0.015)	(0.011)	(0.014)
Bottom 40 percent × Trust in deposit safety	−0.031	−0.008	0.026	0.018	−0.005	0.007	0.015
	(0.021)	(0.025)	(0.023)	(0.028)	(0.029)	(0.019)	(0.029)
Log-L	−5293.8	−1629.7	−1529.2	−1944.6	−1698.1	−929.1	−1541.6
Bottom 40 percent	−0.093***	−0.021	0.017	−0.063**	0.035	0.005	−0.010
	(0.019)	(0.026)	(0.025)	(0.029)	(0.031)	(0.019)	(0.029)
Financial system stable	0.052***	0.025	−0.027	0.026	0.047***	0.017	0.063***
	(0.013)	(0.017)	(0.016)	(0.019)	(0.017)	(0.012)	(0.016)
Bottom 40 percent × Financial system stable	−0.008	−0.038	0.036	−0.006	−0.037	0.004	−0.004
	(0.021)	(0.028)	(0.027)	(0.032)	(0.033)	(0.021)	(0.032)
Log-L	−5295.0	−1628.8	−1528.9	−1944.7	−1697.5	−929.1	−1541.7
Bottom 40 percent	−0.094***	−0.049**	0.046**	−0.076***	0.017	0.017	−0.036*
	(0.015)	(0.020)	(0.019)	(0.022)	(0.021)	(0.013)	(0.021)
Trust in domestic banks	0.080***	0.043***	−0.026*	0.045***	0.009	0.006	0.006
	(0.012)	(0.015)	(0.015)	(0.017)	(0.015)	(0.010)	(0.014)
Bottom 40 percent × Trust in domestic banks	−0.012	−0.004	−0.006	0.011	−0.023	−0.019	0.036
	(0.021)	(0.026)	(0.024)	(0.029)	(0.028)	(0.019)	(0.027)
Log-L	−5381.4	−1657.0	−1557.5	−1972.0	−1715.0	−930.0	−1559.0
Bottom 40 percent	−0.088***	−0.046**	0.036**	−0.063***	−0.002	0.017	−0.034*
	(0.014)	(0.019)	(0.018)	(0.021)	(0.020)	(0.012)	(0.019)
Trust in foreign banks	0.076***	0.032**	−0.037***	0.037**	0.020	0.018*	0.022
	(0.013)	(0.015)	(0.014)	(0.017)	(0.016)	(0.010)	(0.015)
Bottom 40 percent × Trust in foreign banks	−0.034	−0.018	0.019	−0.021	0.010	−0.020	0.031
	(0.022)	(0.025)	(0.024)	(0.028)	(0.027)	(0.019)	(0.026)
Log-L	−5326.0	−1642.9	−1541.0	−1952.4	−1700.2	−917.4	−1543.5
N	10008	4262	4262	4262	4262	4197	4262
P(DepVar = 1)	0.43	0.81	0.16	0.76	0.24	0.08	0.19

Note: Cluster standard errors in parentheses.
* $p < 0.1$, ** $p < 0.05$, *** $p < 0.01$.

TABLE G.5 Internet Access, Social Interaction, and Financial Literacy

	Dependent variables	All	Respondents with savings					
		Any savings	Formal savings	Cash only	Bank savings	Contractual savings	Capital market savings	>1 formal savings
Panel a	Internet	0.083***	0.020	−0.006	0.027	0.040**	0.032**	0.069***
		(0.012)	(0.015)	(0.015)	(0.017)	(0.019)	(0.013)	(0.019)
	Interest rate literacy	0.019**	0.006	0.004	0.004	−0.005	−0.002	−0.003
		(0.009)	(0.012)	(0.012)	(0.014)	(0.014)	(0.010)	(0.013)
	Inflation literacy	0.027***	0.037***	−0.033***	0.052***	0.023	−0.004	0.010
		(0.010)	(0.012)	(0.012)	(0.014)	(0.015)	(0.009)	(0.014)
	Risk literacy	0.010	0.007	0.005	0.007	0.007	−0.005	0.014
		(0.009)	(0.012)	(0.012)	(0.014)	(0.013)	(0.009)	(0.013)
	% of formal savers in PSU	0.478***	0.224***	−0.182***	0.234***	0.106***	0.072***	0.110***
		(0.019)	(0.024)	(0.024)	(0.028)	(0.030)	(0.020)	(0.028)
	Log-L	−4761.3	−1523.1	−1442.8	−1839.3	−1649.5	−911.9	−1499.0
	Pseudo-R^2	0.28	0.25	0.22	0.20	0.28	0.19	0.26
	N	9657	4150	4150	4150	4150	4089	4150
	P(DepVar = 1)	0.43	0.81	0.16	0.76	0.24	0.08	0.19
Panel b	Internet	0.086***	0.025	−0.003	0.032	−0.016	0.011	0.022
		(0.016)	(0.020)	(0.019)	(0.023)	(0.027)	(0.018)	(0.028)
	Interest rate literacy	0.019**	0.006	0.004	0.004	−0.004	−0.001	−0.002
		(0.009)	(0.012)	(0.012)	(0.014)	(0.014)	(0.010)	(0.013)
	Inflation literacy	0.030**	0.044**	−0.030	0.058**	−0.050*	−0.033*	−0.053*
		(0.015)	(0.019)	(0.019)	(0.023)	(0.028)	(0.020)	(0.028)
	Risk literacy	0.010	0.007	0.005	0.008	0.006	−0.006	0.012
		(0.009)	(0.012)	(0.012)	(0.014)	(0.013)	(0.009)	(0.013)
	% of formal savers in PSU	0.478***	0.224***	−0.182***	0.234***	0.105***	0.072***	0.110***
		(0.018)	(0.024)	(0.024)	(0.028)	(0.029)	(0.020)	(0.028)
	Inflation literacy × Internet		−0.010	−0.005	−0.008	0.091***	0.035*	0.078**
			(0.024)	(0.023)	(0.027)	(0.030)	(0.021)	(0.031)
	Log-L	−4761.2	−1523.0	−1442.8	−1839.3	−1645.0	−910.7	−1495.6
	Pseudo-R^2	0.28	0.25	0.22	0.20	0.29	0.19	0.26
	N	9657	4150	4150	4150	4150	4089	4150
	P(DepVar = 1)	0.43	0.81	0.16	0.76	0.24	0.08	0.19

Note: Cluster standard errors in parentheses. PSU = primary sampling unit.
* $p < 0.1$, ** $p < 0.05$, *** $p < 0.01$.

Note

1. Further details on the survey can be found on the Oesterreichische National Bank website, https://www.oenb.at/en/Monetary-Policy/Surveys/OeNB-Euro-Survey.html.

Appendix H
Employed Measures of Financial Inclusion and Stability

This appendix describes the set of empirical indicators used in figure 5.1 from chapter 5 (see figure H.1 below). The complete list of variables used in the analysis, along with the description and data sources, appears in appendix I, table I.1. For individuals, account ownership is captured using the variable "Account at a financial institution." Payments are accounted for by the indicator "Debit card" and a combined measure computed using information on the two waves of Global Findex[1] to compute an indicator for the use of the Internet or other electronic means to make payments. Savings are quantified using the variable "Saved at a financial institution." The provision of credit is measured using the indicators "Credit card" and "Borrowed from a financial institution" from the Global Findex. Both indicators capture formal borrowing. Insurance is measured with the variable "Purchased agriculture insurance." As a robustness measure for insurance, we also use data from the Financial Access Survey (FAS) of the International Monetary Fund (IMF)[2] and include "Life insurance policy holders" and "Nonlife insurance policy holders."

Financial inclusion of firms is measured using information from the Enterprise Survey[3] and Global Findex. Account ownership is measured using the "Percent of firms with a checking or savings account." Payments are quantified with the variable "Used an account at a financial institution for business purposes." Savings for business purposes are captured by the variable "Saved to start, operate, or expand a farm or business." The use of credit is captured through "Percent of firms using banks to finance working capital" and "Percent of firms using banks to finance investments."

FIGURE H.1 Financial stability and inclusion can be measured in many ways

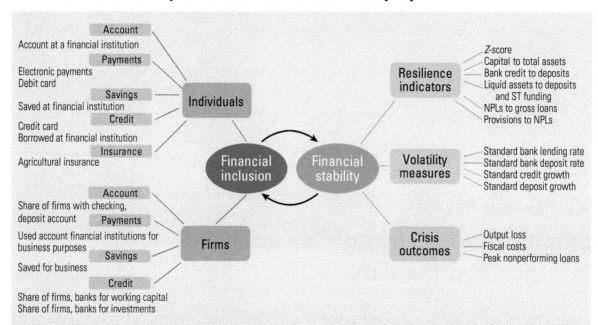

Sources: The use of financial services is measured primarily with data from the World Bank's Global Findex and Enterprise Surveys.
Note: We distinguish between individuals and firms and classify our variables according to the type of financial services. The distinction between firms and individuals can become blurry at the microenterprise level, but for practical purposes, we refer to firms when financial services are used for business purposes. We choose a parsimonious set of indicators that consistently measure our definition of financial inclusion. The variables are selected on the basis of past research (see for instance Beck et al. 2008; Čihák, Demirgüç-Kunt, et al. 2012; and World Bank 2013), and available country coverage. NPLs = nonperforming loans; ST = short-term.

To measure financial stability along the three dimensions discussed in the section, "A More Detailed Look Reveals a Complex Relationship between Inclusion and Stability," in chapter 5—financial resilience, volatility, and crisis outcomes—we retrieve data from the World Bank's Global Financial Development Database (GFDD),[4] the IMF's FAS, and Laeven and Valencia (2013). We choose a parsimonious set of indicators that consistently measure our definition of financial stability. Our selection of the variables reflects the findings of existing research and policy practice as well as an effort to achieve broad country coverage.

The first dimension, financial resilience, is measured using the capitalization of financial institutions, their liquidity positions, and exposure to credit risk. The first subcategory is quantified by using the capital ratio (percentage of capital in total assets) and the z-score. Both measures gauge the solvency of national banking systems. The capital ratio is a well-known measure that, as suggested for example by the Basel Committee on Banking Supervision (2010), is linked negatively to the probability of occurrence and the severity of distress. The z-score is a more comprehensive measure that combines information on leverage (equity to assets) with performance (return on assets) and risk (standard deviation of return on assets) to more fully approximate the likelihood of insolvency in the banking sector (Mare, Moreira, and Rossi 2015). Liquidity standards are also associated with the reduction in the probability of crises (Basel Committee on Banking Supervision 2010). Therefore, in the second subcategory, we quantify the exposure to liquidity risk by examining the risks associated with a mismatch between assets and liabilities. Specifically, to capture the liquidity risk exposure, we use the ratio of credit provisioning to bank deposits and the ratio of the most liquid assets to short-term funding (Bologna 2015). The third subcategory of nonperforming loans (NPLs) accounts for two different aspects. The ratio of NPLs to total loans is widely used as a (lagging) measure of credit risk exposure (Delis, Kokas, and Ongena 2016). The ratio of provisions to NPLs gives an indication on adequate provisioning taking into account past performance and expected losses (Abedifar, Molyneux, and Tarazi 2013).

The second dimension, volatility, is quantified through the standard deviation in credit growth and deposits growth at the country level. We consider both price and volume growth. We first compute the year-on-year growth rate at the country level in the bank lending rate, commercial banks' outstanding loans, deposit interest rate, and commercial banks' outstanding deposits. We then compute the standard deviation of the growth rate at the country level. In this way we are able to quantify the uncertainty and risk deriving from both the variability in the cost and provisioning of credit, and the cost and volume of funding.

The third dimension captures the cost of crises, calculated using data from Laeven and Valencia (2013). We consider measures of banking crises including the output loss (the cumulative loss in income relative to precrisis trends), the costs of government intervention to mitigate and resolve the crises (direct fiscal outlays due to financial sector rescue packages), and the peak level of realized credit risk (the peak ratio of NPLs to total loans).

Notes

1. For more information, see the World Bank website at http://www.worldbank.org/en /programs/globalfindex. The World Bank partners with the Bill & Melinda Gates Foundation and the Gallup World Poll to produce the data set.
2. For more information, see the IMF website at http://data.imf.org/?sk=E5DCAB7E -A5CA-4892-A6EA-598B5463A34C.
3. For more information, see the World Bank website at http://data.worldbank.org/data -catalog/enterprise-surveys.
4. For more information, see the World Bank's website at http://data.worldbank.org/data -catalog/global-financial-development.

References

Abedifar, P., P. Molyneux, and A. Tarazi. 2013. "Risk in Islamic Banking." *Review of Finance* 17 (6): 2035–96.

Basel Committee on Banking Supervision. 2010. "An Assessment of the Long-Term Economic Impact of Stronger Capital and Liquidity Requirements." Bank for International Settlements, Basel, Switzerland.

Bologna, P. 2015. "Structural Funding and Bank Failures." *Journal of Financial Services Research* 47 (1): 81–113.

Delis, M. D., S. Kokas, and S. Ongena. 2016. "Bank Market Power and Firm Performance." *Review of Finance*, February 10.

Laeven, L., and F. Valencia. 2013. "Systemic Banking Crises Database." *IMF Economic Review* 61 (2): 225–70.

Mare, D. S., F. Moreira, and R. Rossi. 2015. "Nonstationary *Z*-score Measures." MPRA Paper 67840, University Library of Munich.

Appendix I
Financial Inclusion and
Stability Tables and Figures

To measure financial inclusion, we use the best available cross-country data from the World Bank Global Findex (for individuals) and Enterprise Survey (for firms) (table I.1). Table I.2 reports the Pearson correlation between overall financial inclusion and financial stability conditional on country characteristics. The sample is split in two using the median value of the conditioning variable. The column "Total number of observations" reports the total number of observations. The column "ρ (low)" shows the Pearson correlation coefficient for inclusion and stability using information on the countries with a value below the median of the conditioning variable. The column "ρ (high)" is the Pearson correlation coefficient for inclusion and stability using information on the countries with a value above the median of the conditioning variable. The column "p-value" reports the p-value of a two-tailed test where the null hypothesis is that both samples of pairs show the same correlation strength, that is, ρ (low) = ρ (high). Appendix K, table K.3, presents a description of the conditioning variables.

TABLE I.1 Financial Inclusion and Financial Stability Variables

Name of variable	Data source	Financial outcome	Category	Subcategory
Borrowed from a financial institution (% age 15+)	Global Findex	Inclusion	Individuals	Credit
Credit card (% age 15+)	Global Findex	Inclusion	Individuals	Credit
Saved at a financial institution (% age 15+)	Global Findex	Inclusion	Individuals	Savings
Account at a financial institution (% age 15+)	Global Findex	Inclusion	Individuals	Account ownership
Purchased agriculture insurance (% working in agriculture, age 15+) [w1]	Global Findex	Inclusion	Individuals	Insurance
Debit card (% age 15+)	Global Findex	Inclusion	Individuals	Payments
Used either the Internet or electronic payments to make payments [w1 & w2]	Global Findex	Inclusion	Individuals	Payments
Percent of firms with a checking or savings account	Enterprise Survey	Inclusion	Firms	Account ownership
Percent of firms using banks to finance investments	Enterprise Survey	Inclusion	Firms	Credit
Percent of firms using banks to finance working capital	Enterprise Survey	Inclusion	Firms	Credit
Saved to start, operate, or expand a farm or business (% age 15+) [w2]	Global Findex	Inclusion	Firms	Savings
Used an account at a financial institution for business purposes (% age 15+) [w1]	Global Findex	Inclusion	Firms	Payments
Bank z-score	GFDD	Stability	Resilience indicators	Capital
Bank capital to total assets (%)	GFDD	Stability	Resilience indicators	Capital
Bank credit to bank deposits (%)	GFDD	Stability	Resilience indicators	Liquidity
Liquid assets to deposits and short-term funding (%)	GFDD	Stability	Resilience indicators	Liquidity
Bank NPLs to gross loans (%)	GFDD	Stability	Resilience indicators	NPLs
Provisions to NPLs (%)	GFDD	Stability	Resilience indicators	NPLs
Standard deviation of the bank lending rate growth	GFDD	Stability	Volatility measures	Credit volatility
Standard deviation of the outstanding loans	Financial Access Survey	Stability	Volatility measures	Credit volatility
Standard deviation of the bank deposit rate growth	GFDD	Stability	Volatility measures	Deposit volatility
Standard deviation of the outstanding deposits	Financial Access Survey	Stability	Volatility measures	Deposit volatility
Cumulative loss in income relative to a precrisis trend	Laeven and Valencia 2013	Stability	Crisis outcomes	Milder/ No crisis
Direct fiscal outlays due to financial sector rescue packages	Laeven and Valencia 2013	Stability	Crisis outcomes	Milder/ No crisis
Peak level of NPLs	Laeven and Valencia 2013	Stability	Crisis outcomes	Milder/ No crisis

Sources: World Bank Global Findex, Enterprise Survey, and Global Financial Development Database (GFDD).
Note: NPLs = nonperforming loans; w1 = wave 1 of the survey in 2007; w2 = wave 2 of the survey in 2013.

TABLE I.2 Pairwise Pearson Correlation Coefficients between Overall Financial Inclusion and Stability Conditioning on Individual Country Characteristics

Conditioning variable	Total number of observations	ρ (low)	ρ (high)	p-value
GDP per capita growth (annual %)	157	−0.395	−0.252	0.323
Population density (people per km² of land area)	157	−0.400	−0.360	0.774
Asset share of foreign-controlled banks	124	−0.378	−0.395	0.917
Asset share of government-controlled banks	111	−0.455	−0.422	0.834
Domestic credit to private sector (% of GDP)	152	−0.264	−0.144	0.451
Average loan annual growth	154	−0.334	−0.142	0.215
Barro–Lee: Average years of total schooling, age 25+, total	132	−0.217	−0.238	0.901
School enrollment, secondary (% gross)	146	−0.092	−0.173	0.623
Age dependency ratio (% of working-age population)	157	−0.177	−0.398	0.137
Percent of firms competing against unregistered or informal firms	116	−0.394	−0.174	0.207
Percent of firms formally registered when they started operations in the country	116	−0.141	−0.380	0.175
Number of years firm operated without formal registration	116	−0.409	−0.065	**0.054**
Percent of firms identifying practices of competitors in the informal sector as a major constraint	117	−0.286	−0.162	0.493
Proportion of private domestic ownership in a firm (%)	118	−0.391	−0.124	0.128
Proportion of private foreign ownership in a firm (%)	118	−0.132	−0.407	0.113
Proportion of government/state ownership in a firm (%)	118	−0.427	−0.208	0.202
Chinn and Ito Financial Openness Index	150	−0.118	−0.414	**0.053**
Quality of supervision	117	−0.392	−0.375	0.918
Fiscal freedom	155	−0.508	−0.118	**0.007**
Investment freedom	154	−0.049	−0.436	**0.011**
Financial freedom	151	−0.141	−0.362	0.153
Strength of investor protection index (0–10)	156	−0.314	−0.345	0.831
Strength of insolvency framework index (0–16)	145	−0.173	−0.337	0.309
Credit: Strength of legal rights index (0 = weak to 10 = strong)	156	−0.391	−0.307	0.558
Depth of credit information index (0 = low to 6 = high)	156	−0.368	−0.329	0.786
Strength of governance structure index (0–10.5)	156	−0.456	−0.237	0.126
Mobile cellular subscriptions (per 100 people)	156	−0.197	−0.229	0.836
Control of corruption (estimate)	157	−0.057	−0.259	0.202
Government effectiveness (estimate)	157	−0.048	−0.279	0.143
Regulatory quality (estimate)	157	−0.093	−0.308	0.166
Rule of law (estimate)	157	−0.071	−0.254	0.248

	Total number of observations	ρ (0)	ρ (1)	p-value
Developing ECA dummy	157	−0.446	−0.092	**0.082**
Strategies	157	−0.402	−0.285	0.489

Note: Boldface entries indicate significant conditioning variables at the 5 percent level.

Table I.3 reports the results of the analysis of a proxy for covariance between overall financial stability and financial inclusion conditioning on multiple country characteristics. The dependent variable is constructed using equation (J.7). Column 1 presents the estimates obtained using equation (J.6) and including the variables significant in the univariate analysis (table I.2). Column 2 presents the estimates obtained using equation (J.6) and maximizing the number of countries included in the estimation. In column 2, standard errors are corrected for heteroscedasticity.

The next two figures report the distribution of the indicators employed in the analysis, arranged by country income-group. Figure I.1 highlights the median, the minimum, and the maximum of the distribution by income group; and figure I.2

TABLE I.3 Covariance between Overall Financial Inclusion and Stability Conditioning on Multivariate Country Characteristics

Variable	1	2
Number of years firm operated without formal registration	−0.006 (0.005)	
Chinn and Ito Financial Openness Index	−0.009** (0.004)	−0.002 (0.004)
Fiscal freedom	0.014 (0.009)	0.016** (0.007)
Investment freedom	0.005 (0.008)	−0.011 (0.010)
Developing ECA dummy	0.002 (0.003)	0.003 (0.002)
Firms formally registered when they started operations in the country (%)	−0.013* (0.008)	
Population density	0.047 (0.032)	0.013* (0.007)
School enrollment, secondary (% gross)	0.017** (0.007)	
Domestic credit to private sector (% of GDP)	−0.004 (0.009)	−0.012 (0.008)
Depth of credit information index	0.002 (0.004)	0.008** (0.004)
Rule of law (estimate)	−0.006 (0.009)	0.000 (0.007)
Constant	−0.006 (0.008)	−0.011 (0.008)
Observations	99	144
R-squared	0.207	0.188

Note: Column 1 presents the estimates obtained using equation (J.6) and including the variables significant in the univariate analysis (table I.2). Column 2 presents the estimates obtained using equation (J.6) and maximizing the number of countries included in the estimation. In column 2, standard errors are corrected for heteroscedasticity. Standard errors in parentheses.
*$p < 0.1$, **$p < 0.05$.

reports the median value of each financial inclusion indicator by World Bank region.

Figures I.3 and I.4 report the distribution of the various indicators used to measure financial stability. Figure I.3 highlights the median, the minimum, and the maximum of the distribution by income group, and figure I.4 shows the median financial inclusion indicators across World Bank regions.

Figure I.5 presents the distribution of the pairwise correlation coefficients between financial stability and financial inclusion for individuals reported in table 5.1 in chapter 5. It includes the values for the linear dependence of each individual financial stability indicator and each individual financial inclusion indicator; pairwise correlations among financial inclusion for individuals or among financial stability indicators are not included in the graph below.

FIGURE I.1 Individual distributions of the financial inclusion indicators by income group

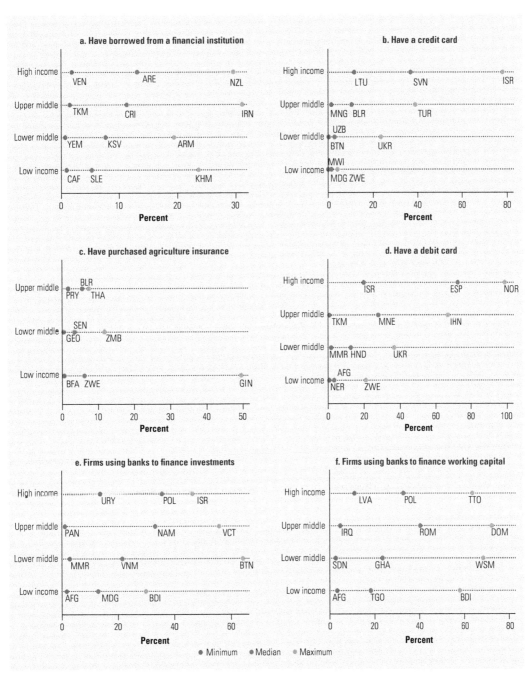

(Continued)

FIGURE I.1 Individual distributions of the financial inclusion indicators by income group *(continued)*

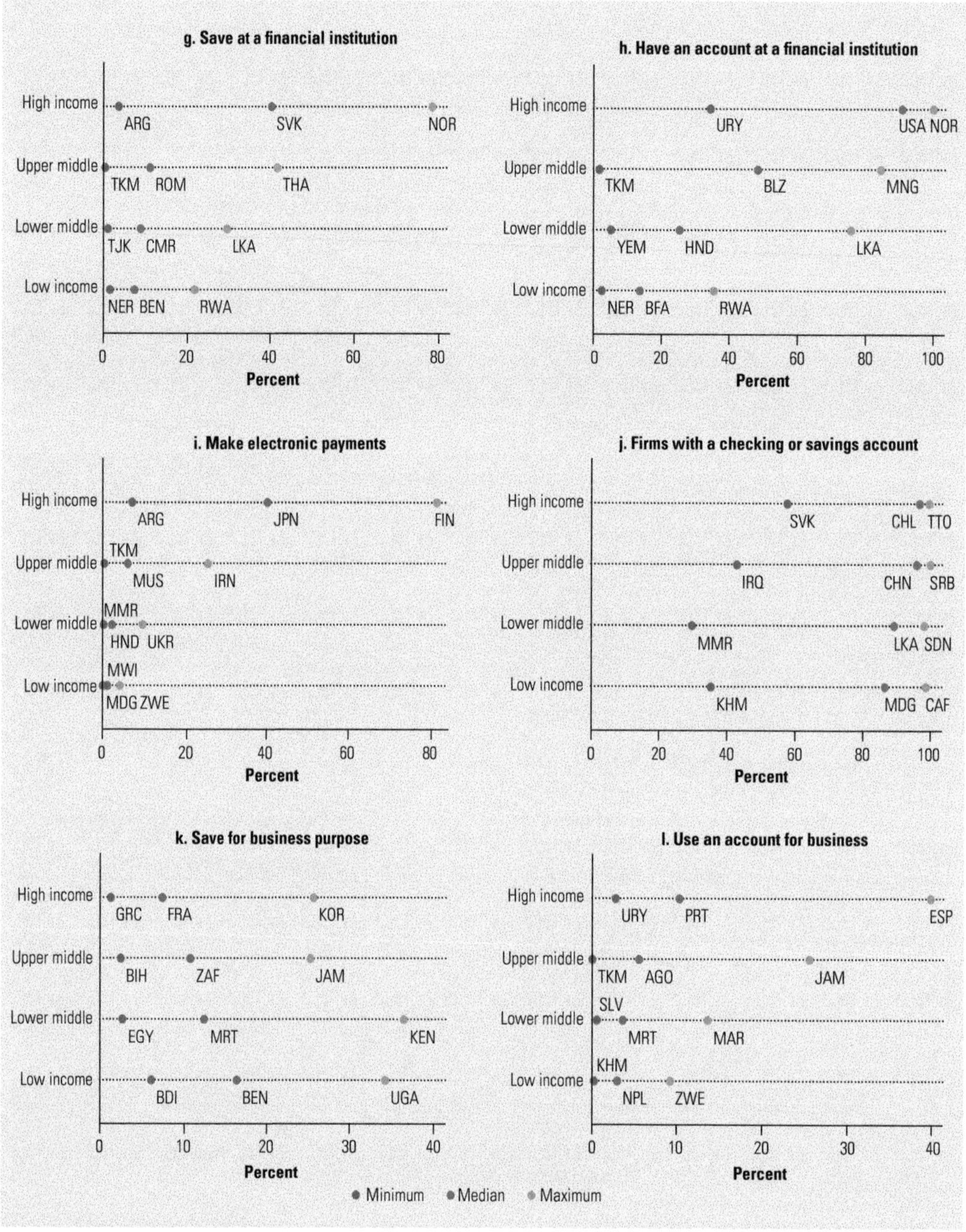

g. Save at a financial institution

h. Have an account at a financial institution

i. Make electronic payments

j. Firms with a checking or savings account

k. Save for business purpose

l. Use an account for business

● Minimum ● Median ● Maximum

Sources: Data averaged from two rounds of Global Findex (2011 and 2014) and over the period 2007–14 for Enterprise Surveys data.
Note: The distribution of each financial inclusion indicator is given, along with the country code for the minimum, maximum, and median value.

FIGURE I.2 Median value of each financial inclusion indicator by World Bank region

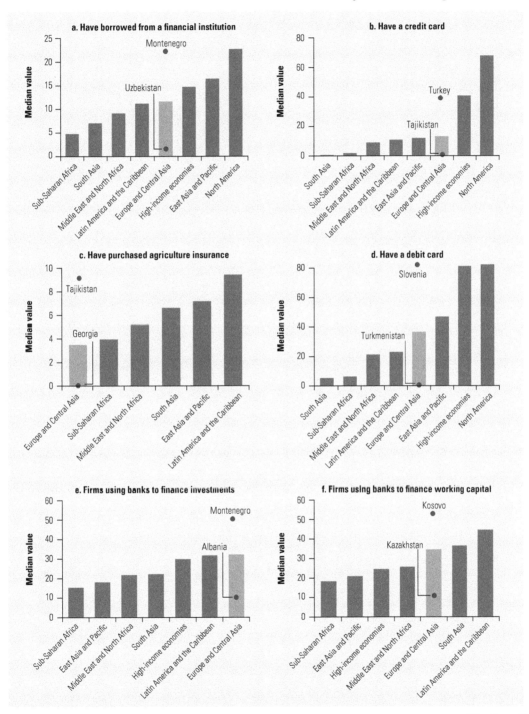

(Continued)

FIGURE I.2 Median value of each financial inclusion indicator by World Bank region *(continued)*

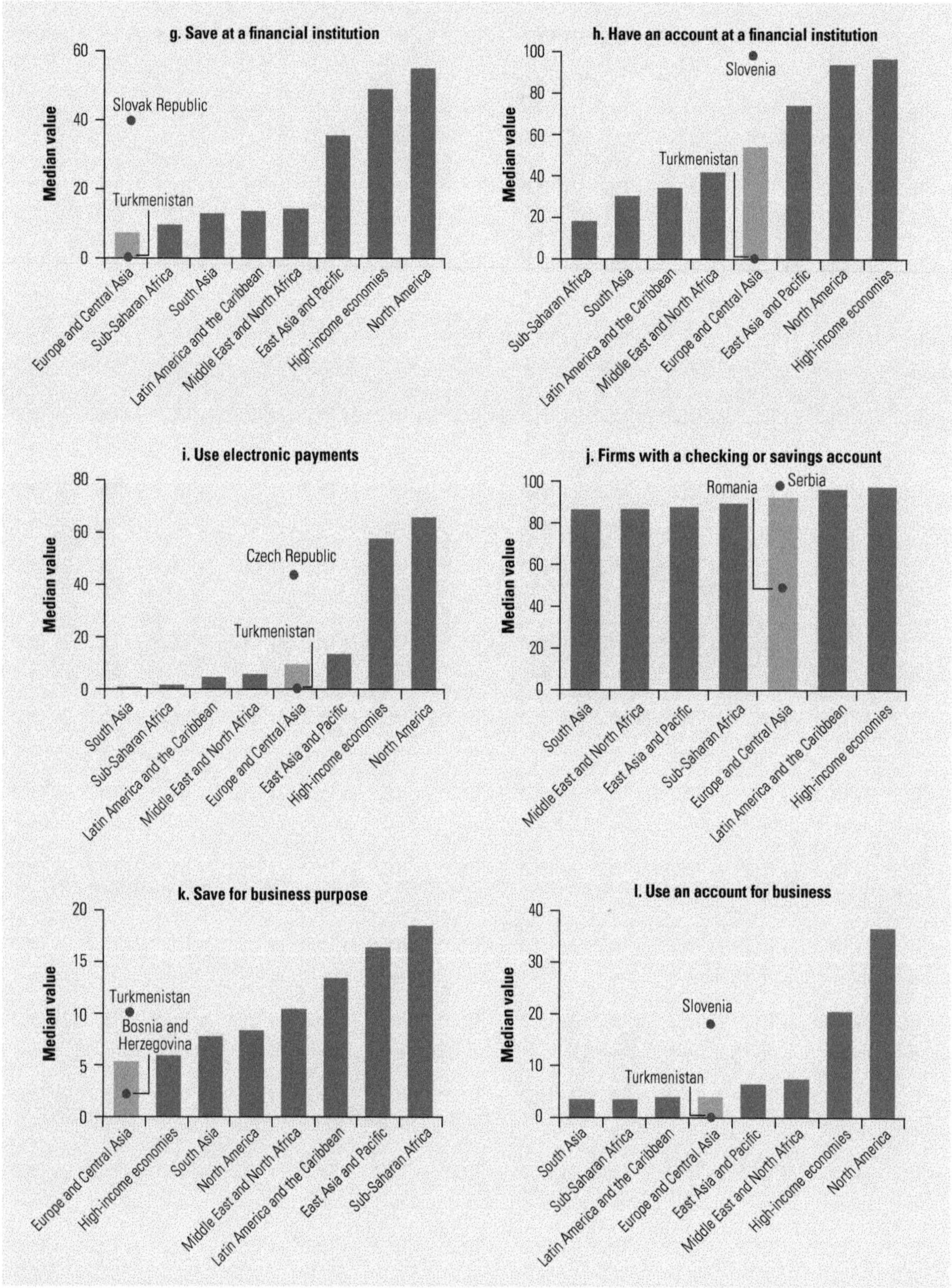

g. Save at a financial institution

h. Have an account at a financial institution

i. Use electronic payments

j. Firms with a checking or savings account

k. Save for business purpose

l. Use an account for business

Source: Global Findex.

FIGURE I.3 Individual distributions of the financial stability indicators by income group

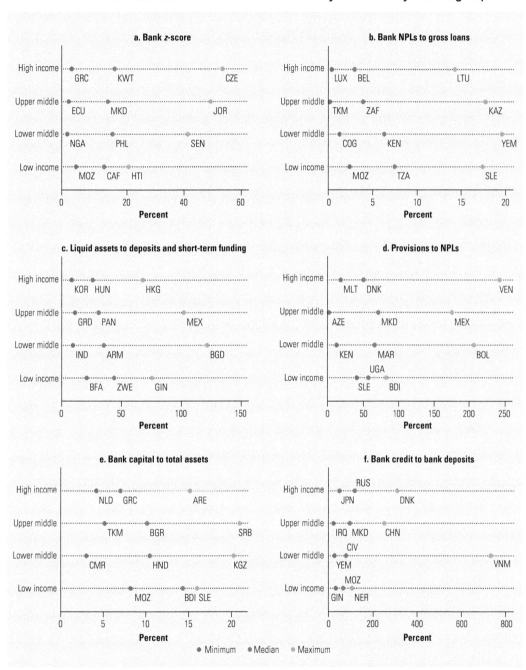

(Continued)

FIGURE I.3 Individual distributions of the financial stability indicators by income group *(continued)*

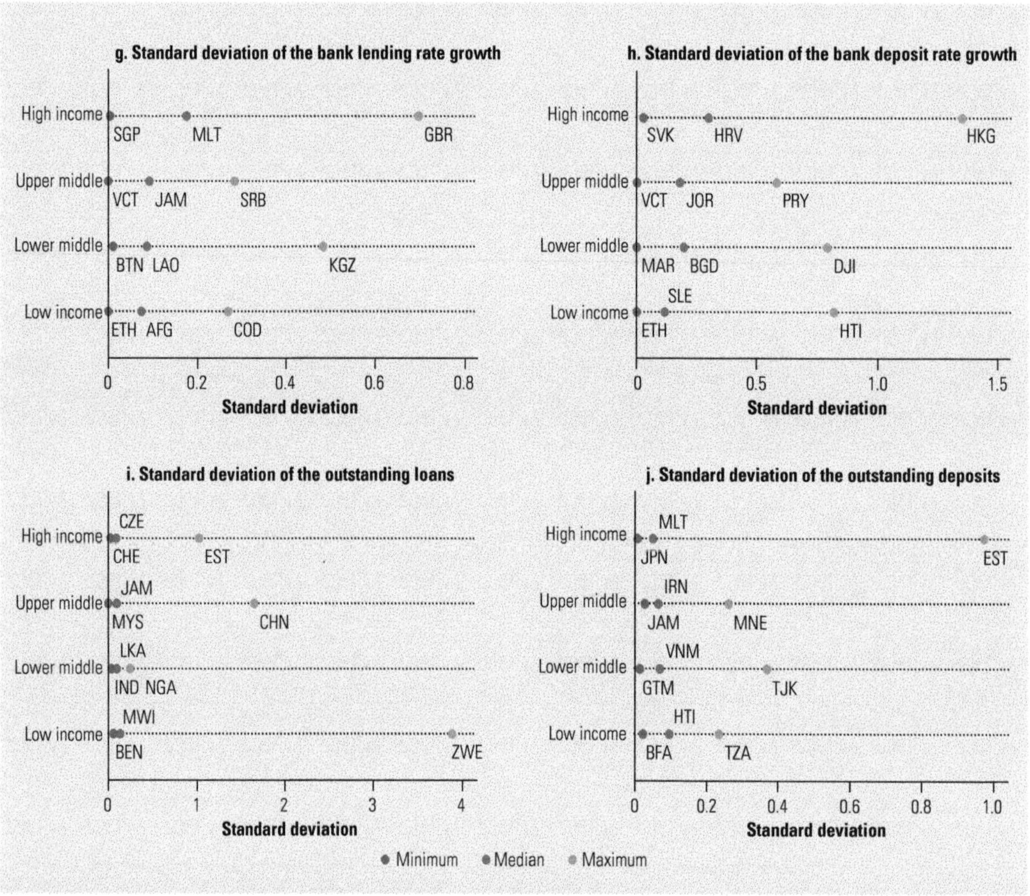

g. Standard deviation of the bank lending rate growth

h. Standard deviation of the bank deposit rate growth

i. Standard deviation of the outstanding loans

j. Standard deviation of the outstanding deposits

● Minimum   ● Median   ● Maximum

Sources: Data averaged over the period 2007–14 for the Global Financial Development Database (GFDD), Financial Access Survey (International Monetary Fund), and Laeven and Valencia (2013).
Note: The distribution of each financial stability indicator is given, along with the country code for the minimum, maximum, and median value. NPL = nonperforming loans.

FIGURE I.4 Individual distributions of the financial stability indicators by World Bank region

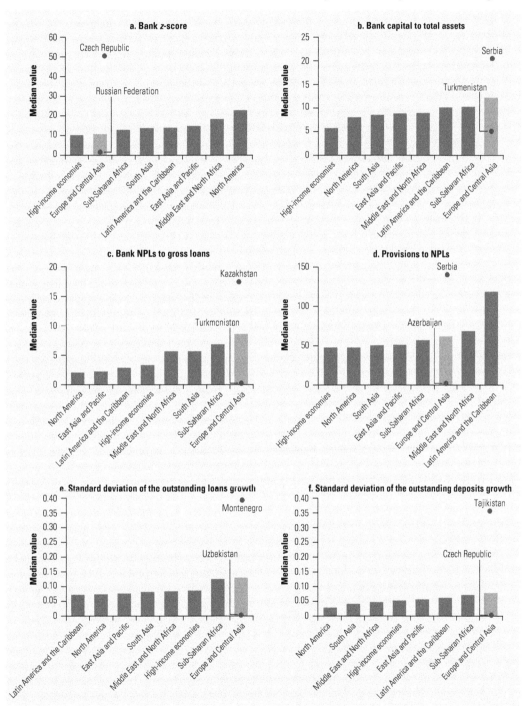

(Continued)

FIGURE I.4 Individual distributions of the financial stability indicators by World Bank region (*continued*)

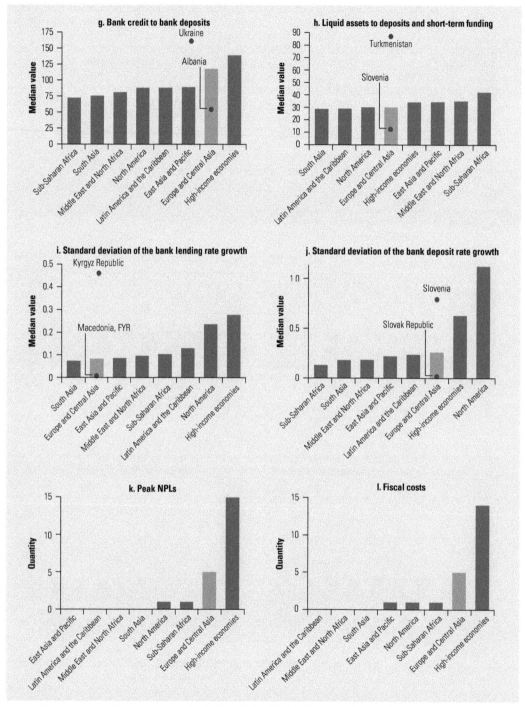

Sources: Data are averaged over the two rounds of Global Findex (2011, 2014) or over the period 2007–14 for Enterprise Survey data. We then compute the median value for the countries included in a specific World Bank region.
Note: NPLs = nonperforming loans.

FIGURE I.5 Histogram of the distribution of the pairwise correlation coefficients between financial inclusion of individuals and financial stability

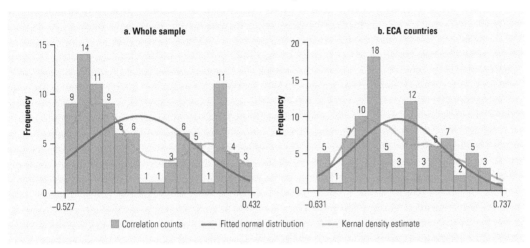

Note: The test for normality refers to the *p*-value for the overall test statistic where the null hypothesis is normality. Pr(Skewness) is the *p*-value for the test for normality based on skewness while Pr(Kurtosis) is based on kurtosis. The *p*-value of the test for unimodality refers to the dip statistic test, where the null hypothesis is unimodality. For panel a, the test for normality (prob. > χ^2) = 0.000; Pr(Skewness) = 0.058; Pr(Kurtosis) = 0.000; test for unimodality = 0.288. For panel b, the test for normality (prob. > χ^2) = 0.071; Pr(Skewness) = 0.094; Pr(Kurtosis) = 0.106; test for unimodality = 0.427.

Confirming the Assumption of a Linear Relationship between Inclusion and Stability

Chapter 5 discusses the average correlations between aggregate indexes of inclusion and stability, although these relationships may differ significantly at different levels of financial stability. Measuring the correlation between financial inclusion and stability at different deciles of financial stability can determine whether this relationship is usefully summarized by the average correlation. We compute the quantile mean of financial inclusion for each decile of the distribution of the financial stability index. The results of this analysis are shown in figure I.6, which reports the quantile mean indexes for overall inclusion (panel a), individuals (panel b), and firms (panel c) for each decile of the distribution of financial stability. The figure presents the quantile conditional mean of the overall financial inclusion index and the confidence interval around it, given the decile of the distribution of the financial stability index.

The mean values of the correlation between overall inclusion per decile of stability suggest a fairly linear negative relationship, where increases in overall stability are associated with decreases in overall inclusion—confirming the earlier finding of a potential trade-off between inclusion and stability at all levels. As revealed by panels b and c, the negative linear relationship reflects the relationship for individual inclusion. The relationship between stability and individual inclusion is stronger than that between stability and the overall inclusion index. In contrast, the average value of inclusion of firms per decile of the stability index is fairly flat, suggesting no significant correlation across the entire range of the stability deciles.[1]

FIGURE I.6 Mean of financial inclusion index conditional on the overall stability index

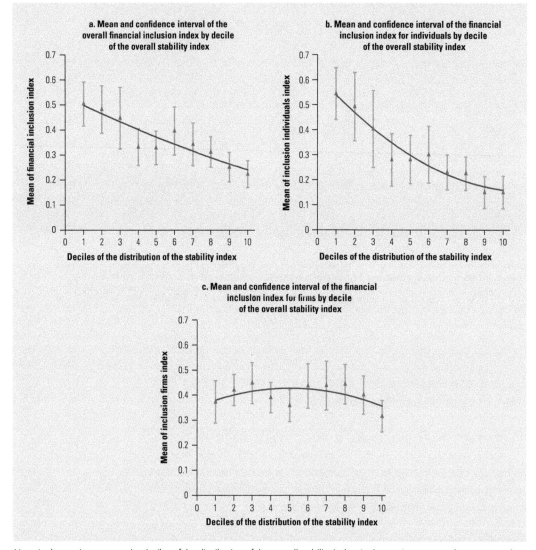

Note: In the *x*-axis we report the deciles of the distribution of the overall stability index. In the *y*-axis we report the average value of the inclusion index for countries included in a specific decile of the stability index. The yellow bars represent the length of the 95 percent confidence interval around the mean value. The fitted red line is obtained from a linear regression of the overall inclusion index on the overall stability index.

Note

1. If anything, the chart suggests a hump-shaped relationship, indicating that an optimal level of financial stability could exist to maximize inclusion for firms. The hump-shaped relationship is more visible for the aggregate indices constructed using alternative methods, in particular using the weights of inverse standard deviation.

Reference

Laeven, L., and F. Valencia. 2013. "Systemic Banking Crises Database." *IMF Economic Review* 61 (2): 225–70.

Appendix J
Modeling the Dependence between Financial Inclusion and Stability

We use the Spearman's rank correlation as the normalized and robust measure of the covariance between inclusion and stability [equation (J.1)]—that is, to estimate the degree of interdependence between the two concepts. The correlation is computed as follows:

$$\rho = 1 - \frac{6\sum d_i^2}{n(n^2 - 1)},$$ (J.1)

where n is the sample size and d represents the difference between ranks of two variables. The correlation coefficient estimates the cross-country, linear interdependence between financial inclusion and financial stability—in other words the association between the changes in inclusion and stability. In general, the correlation coefficients between financial inclusion and stability that we can estimate from our data set can be expressed as follows:

$$\rho_{ijk} = (FI_{ij}; FS_{ik}),$$ (J.2)

where the subscripts i, j, and k denote the country, the financial inclusion indicator, and the stability indicator, respectively.

We use this general notation to clearly delineate our four pieces of analysis. First, we take a disaggregated perspective to study the distributional properties of the linear dependency, considering individual measures organized by type of product/service, agent (individuals and firms), and stability dimensions. The Spearman's correlation coefficients are computed as follows:

$$\rho_{jk}(FI_j; FS_k) = \frac{1}{i}\sum_1^i (FI_j - \overline{FI_j})(FS_k - \overline{FS_k}).$$ (J.3)

Using these results, we explore the distribution of the pairwise correlation coefficients for all considered measures of financial stability and inclusion to broadly characterize the shape of the association between the concepts of inclusion and stability. We examine the modes, central tendency, dispersion, and skewness of this distribution. Moreover, to gain a better understanding of the association by type of economic agent, we examine separately the distributions for the inclusion of individuals and firms.

Second, we look into how the correlations between inclusion and stability vary across types of economic agent, financial services, and dimensions of financial stability, by averaging the correlation coefficients for the relevant pair. For instance, the use of credit could be positively correlated with financial crises, but the use of savings could be negatively correlated with financial volatility. In doing so, we are interested in finding whether promoting financial inclusion in certain financial services could be associated with more systemic risk (World Bank 2014). Further, we would like to know whether promoting financial inclusion in these services would risk a higher volatility of the financial cycle or occurrence of banking crises. Similarly, we are interested in observing whether greater stability could bear negative associations with certain dimensions of financial inclusion and which ones in particular. Moreover, we are interested in finding out whether financial inclusion in some services could help generate synergies with financial stability and vice versa (World Bank 2014).

Third, to estimate the macro association between financial inclusion and stability, we construct aggregate indexes measuring financial inclusion and financial stability, and calculate their correlation. Recognizing the challenges of coming up with a weighting scheme for a mash-up index, our baseline approach is to calculate the index using an average of equally weighted rescaled indicators; we follow this baseline approach by a range of robustness checks. The baseline index is computed as follows:

$$[y = min(Y)] / [max(Y) - min(Y)], \tag{J.4}$$

where y is a realization of the indicator Y, $max(Y)$ is its maximum value, and $min(Y)$ is its minimum value. This way, we rescale each variable to the 0–1 range. We then take the average of the indicators included in a specific subcategory—for instance, the average of all the stability indicators for the overall stability index. Moreover, using the aggregate indexes, we dissect the average correlation based on increasing levels of financial stability by deciles.

Fourth, given that individual country characteristics may be important for shaping the interaction between financial inclusion and stability, we condition the aggregate correlation between the overall stability index and inclusion index on individual country characteristics,[1] including the conditions of different financial sector architectures (Allen et al. 2012). This can be expressed as follows:

$$\rho_i = (FI; FS | X), \tag{J.5}$$

where X is a set of country characteristics that affect how inclusion and stability interplay with each other (see appendix K for a description of the conditioning variables). We perform the conditioning one country characteristic at a time by formally comparing the difference between the average aggregate correlation calculated for the lower 50 percent and upper 50 percent of a given country characteristic—for instance, the 50 percent of countries in our sample that have their value of GDP per capita lower than the median versus the 50 percent that have the value higher than the median. We also include two binary variables for developing countries in Europe and Central Asia and for the country adoption of financial strategies.[2] This univariate conditioning is employed to maximize the number of available observations for our conditional estimations. Later, we also condition the correlation between inclusion and stability on a multivariate set of country characteristics. We select a parsimonious subset of the most pertinent country characteristics in the multivariate conditioning using forward-stepwise selection (Berk 1978). For the multivariate conditioning, we fit the following regression (parametric) model. We use the *cov(.)* notation to refer back to equation (J.1) in more general terms:

$$cov(FI;FS)_i = \alpha + \sum_{w=1}^{w} \beta_w X_i^w + \varepsilon_i. \tag{J.6}$$

where the subscript *i* denotes the country, $w = 1, \ldots, W$ is the number of conditioning variables that potentially affect the covariance between inclusion and stability. The covariance is approximated by the product of the deviations from the cross-sectional mean for overall inclusion and stability:

$$cov(FI;FS)_i = (FI_i = \overline{FI}) \times (FS_i - \overline{FS}). \tag{J.7}$$

Note that there is no need to standardize the *FI* and *FS* indicators at this point because they have been standardized during their construction. The complete list of country characteristics appears in appendix K, table K.3.

Notes

1. Recall that, from the literature review, we do not have any strong priors on how inclusion in individual financial services affects stability and vice versa. Estimating the covariance of aggregated inclusion and stability across different measures of inclusion and stability can help wash away arbitrary idiosyncrasies due to measurement errors in individual data series and be more representative of the underlying relationship between inclusion and stability at the country level.
2. See Melecky and Podpiera (forthcoming) for a detailed explanation of the construction of this variable.

References

Allen, F., A. Demirgüç-Kunt, L. F. Klapper, and M. S. Martinez Peria. 2012. "The Foundations of Financial Inclusion: Understanding Ownership and Use of Formal Accounts." Policy Research Working Paper 6290, World Bank, Washington, DC.

Berk, K. N. 1978. "Comparing Subset Regression Procedures." *Technometrics* 20 (1): 1–6.

Melecky, M., and A. Podpiera. Forthcoming. "Financial Sector Strategies and Financial Sector Outcomes: Do the Strategies Perform?" Unpublished manuscript.

World Bank. 2014. *Global Financial Development Report 2014: Financial Inclusion*. Washington, DC: World Bank.

Appendix K
The Nexus between Financial Inclusion and Stability: Additional Results

TABLE K.1 Correlation between Individual Indicators of Financial Inclusion

Indicator	1	2	3	4	5	6	7	8	9	10	11	12
1. Borrowed from a financial institution	1											
2. Credit card	0.600	1										
3. Saved at a financial institution	0.538	0.692	1									
4. Account at a financial institution	0.629	0.878	0.856	1								
5. Purchased agriculture insurance	0.075	0.127	0.220	0.043	1							
6. Debit card	0.577	0.892	0.779	0.950	0.096	1						
7. Used either Internet or electronic payments	0.555	0.922	0.743	0.906	0.126	0.935	1					
8. Percent of firms with a checking or savings account	0.145	0.458	0.318	0.479	−0.242	0.460	0.420	1				
9. Percent of firms using banks to finance investments	0.429	0.582	0.372	0.635	−0.157	0.602	0.509	0.557	1			
10. Percent of firms using banks to finance working capital	0.395	0.406	0.312	0.459	−0.193	0.399	0.355	0.537	0.748	1		
11. Saved to start, operate, or expand a farm or business	−0.187	−0.339	0.035	−0.338	0.130	−0.332	−0.325	−0.141	−0.350	−0.197	1	
12. Used an account at a financial institution for business purposes	0.549	0.672	0.724	0.797	0.100	0.746	0.721	0.363	0.469	0.385	−0.174	1

Note: Spearman correlation coefficients for the individual indicators are included in the financial inclusion category for individuals and firms. We highlight in red and green the coefficients that are included in the left tail and right tail of the distribution of the Spearman coefficients: lighter green in the highest 5 percent; darker green in the highest 10 percent; darker red in the lowest 10 percent; and lighter red in the lowest 5 percent.

TABLE K.2 Correlation between Individual Indicators of Financial Stability

Indicator	1	2	3	4	5	6	7	8	9	10	11	12	13
1. Bank z–score	1												
2. Bank NPLs to gross loans	−0.092	1											
3. Bank capital to total assets	−0.118	0.288	1										
4. Bank credit to bank deposits	−0.062	−0.067	−0.025	1									
5. Liquid assets to deposits & short-term funding	−0.186	0.043	−0.003	−0.404	1								
6. Provisions to NPLs	−0.001	−0.099	0.225	−0.134	0.049	1							
7. Bank lending rate growth, SD	−0.126	−0.197	−0.178	0.305	0.003	0.018	1						
8. Bank deposit rate growth, SD	0.039	−0.186	−0.081	0.213	0.012	0.037	0.552	1					
9. Domestic credit growth, SD	−0.314	0.309	0.437	−0.108	0.251	0.058	0.076	0.098	1				
10. Deposit growth, SD	−0.279	0.186	0.390	−0.167	0.358	0.120	0.068	0.049	0.653	1			
11. Cumulative loss in income	0.065	0.041	−0.434	0.318	−0.028	−0.194	0.263	0.238	−0.147	−0.223	1		
12. Direct fiscal outlays	0.061	0.077	−0.343	0.332	−0.016	−0.162	0.236	0.241	−0.052	−0.114	0.811	1	
13. Peak level of NPLs	−0.014	0.130	−0.327	0.360	−0.015	−0.155	0.243	0.284	−0.071	−0.152	0.853	0.942	1

Note: Spearman correlation coefficients for the individual indicators are included in the financial stability category. We highlight in red and green the coefficients that are included in the left tail and right tail of the distribution of the Spearman coefficients: lighter green in the highest 5 percent; darker green in the highest 10 percent; darker red in the lowest 10 percent; and lighter red in the lowest 5 percent. NPLs = nonperforming loans; SD = standard deviation.

TABLE K.3 Definition and Data Source of Indicators Included as Conditioning Variables

Conditioning variable	Description
GDP per capita growth (annual %)	Annual percentage growth rate of GDP per capita based on constant local currency. Source: World Development Indicators.
Population density (people per km² of land area)	Midyear population divided by land area in square kilometers. Source: World Development Indicators.
Asset share of foreign-controlled banks	Percentage of foreign bank assets among total bank assets. Source: Global Financial Development.
Asset share of government-controlled banks	Percentage of the banking system's assets in banks that were government controlled. Source: Bank Regulation and Supervision Survey.
Domestic credit to private sector (% of GDP)	Financial resources provided to the private sector by financial intermediaries. Source: World Development Indicators.
Average loan annual growth	The 2007–14 average of the annual growth in commercial bank loans. Source: World Bank calculation using IMF Financial Access Survey.
Barro-Lee: Average years of total schooling, age 25+, total	Average years of total schooling for people older than 25. Source: Robert J. Barro and Jong-Wha Lee, http://www.barrolee.com/.
School enrollment, secondary (% gross)	Total enrollment in secondary education, regardless of age, expressed as a percentage of the population of official secondary education age. Source: World Development Indicators.
Age dependency ratio (% of working-age population)	Ratio of dependents (people younger than 15 or older than 64) to the working-age population (those ages 15–64). Source: World Development Indicators.
Percent of firms competing against unregistered or informal firms	Percentage of firms competing against unregistered or informal firms. Source: Enterprise Surveys.
Percent of firms formally registered when they started operations in the country	Percentage of firms formally registered when they started operations in the country. Source: Enterprise Surveys.
Number of years firm operated without formal registration	Number of years firm operated without formal registration. Source: Enterprise Surveys.
Percent of firms identifying practices of competitors in the informal sector as a major constraint	Percentage of firms identifying practices of competitors in the informal sector as a major constraint. Source: Enterprise Surveys.
Proportion of private domestic ownership in a firm (%)	Proportion of private domestic ownership in a firm (%). Source: Enterprise Surveys.
Proportion of private foreign ownership in a firm (%)	Proportion of private foreign ownership in a firm (%). Source: Enterprise Surveys.
Proportion of government/state ownership in a firm (%)	Proportion of government/state ownership in a firm (%). Source: Enterprise Surveys.
Chinn and Ito Financial Openness Index	Index measuring a country's degree of capital account openness. Source: http://web.pdx.edu/~ito/Chinn-Ito_website.htm
Quality of supervision	Index built by aggregating the answers to 14 selected questions regarding supervisory powers that were collected in the 2003, 2007, and 2011 surveys. Source: World Bank calculation using Bank Regulation and Supervision Survey.
Fiscal freedom	Measure of the tax burden imposed by government. Source: Heritage Foundation Index of Economic Freedom.
Investment freedom	Measure of the constraints on the flow of investment capital. Source: Heritage Foundation Index of Economic Freedom.
Financial freedom	Measure of banking efficiency and independence from government control and interference in the financial sector. Source: Heritage Foundation Index of Economic Freedom.

(Continued)

TABLE K.3 Definition and Data Source of Indicators Included as Conditioning Variables *(continued)*

Conditioning variable	Description
Strength of investor protection index (0–10)	Average of three indexes: the extent of disclosure index, the extent of director liability index, and the ease of shareholder suit index, 10 being greater investor protection. Source: World Bank, Doing Business Project.
Strength of insolvency framework index (0–16)	Measures whether insolvency legislation is designed for rehabilitating viable firms and liquidating nonviable ones. Source: World Bank, Doing Business Project.
Credit: Strength of legal rights index (0 = weak to 10 = strong)	Measures the degree to which collateral and bankruptcy laws protect the rights of borrowers and lenders and thus facilitate lending. Source: World Bank, Doing Business Project.
Depth of credit information index (0 = low to 6 = high)	Measures rules affecting the scope, accessibility, and quality of credit information available through public or private credit registries. Source: World Bank, Doing Business Project.
Strength of governance structure index (0–10.5)	Governance safeguards protecting shareholders from undue board control and entrenchment based on seven components of corporate governance. Source: World Bank, Doing Business Project.
Mobile cellular subscriptions (per 100 people)	Subscriptions to a public mobile telephone service that provides access to the PSTN using cellular technology. Source: World Development Indicators.
Control of corruption (estimate)	Reflects perceptions of the extent to which public power is exercised for private gain. Source: Worldwide Governance Indicators.
Government effectiveness (estimate)	Reflects perceptions of the degree of effectiveness of public services and public policies. Source: Worldwide Governance Indicators.
Regulatory quality (estimate)	Reflects perceptions of the ability of the government to formulate and implement sound policies and regulations. Source: Worldwide Governance Indicators.
Rule of law (estimate)	Reflects perceptions of the degree of confidence in the rule of law. Source: Worldwide Governance Indicators.

Note: IMF = International Monetary Fund; PSTN = public switched telephone network.

TABLE K.4 Countries Included or Excluded from Estimation

Income group	Excluded	Included	Total
Low	7	18	25
Lower-middle	7	35	42
Upper-middle	10	31	41
High	34	15	49
Total	58	99	157

Note: Number by income group of countries was excluded from the estimation in table I.3, column 1, because of missing information for one or more independent variables ("Excluded"), countries included in the estimation in table I.3, column 1 ("Included"), and the total number of countries per income group included in the analysis ("Total").

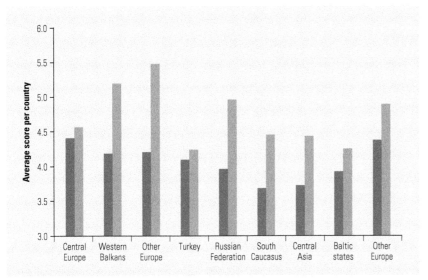

FIGURE K.1
Risk-taking appetite and informality

■ Informal
▨ Formal

Source: World Bank estimates based on Life in Transition Survey (LITS) II.
Note: The risk-taking indicator is based on the question: "Rate your willingness to take risks, in general, on a scale from 1 to 10, where 1 means that you are not willing to take risks at all, and 10 means that you are very much willing to take risks." Sample includes individuals aged 18–64. Informal = those in firms with 0–5 employees or in an unskilled occupation.

Appendix L
The Nexus between Financial Inclusion and Stability: Multivariate Regression Results

TABLE L.1 Additional Estimation Results for Stability

	Explanatory variables	Dependent variable: average output loss			
		1	2	3	4
Strategy variables	Index strategy impulse variable	ns			
	Index strategy shift variable		−1.011* (0.582)		
	Dummy strategy impulse variable			−6.113** (3.090)	
	Dummy strategy shift variable				−8.071** (3.337)
Institutional and macroeconomic variables	GDP per capita	0.000917*** (0.000274)	0.000915*** (0.000296)	0.000923*** (0.000283)	0.000946*** (0.000322)
	Financial openness	ns	ns	ns	ns
	Governance	ns	ns	ns	ns
	Interest rate	0.238** (0.100)	0.234** (0.0999)	0.234** (0.0991)	0.200** (0.0991)
	Exchange rate	ns	ns	ns	ns
	Inflation	ns	ns	ns	ns
	Constant	−60.07*** (14.08)	−57.98*** (15.44)	−59.42*** (14.71)	−57.86*** (16.30)
	Observations	1,642	1,642	1,642	1,642
	Number of individuals	121	121	121	121

Note: Standard errors in parentheses. ns = not statistically significant.
* $p < 0.1$, ** $p < 0.05$, *** $p < 0.01$.

TABLE L.2 Additional Estimation Results for Inclusion

	Explanatory variables	Dependent variable							
		Growth of number of deposit accounts per 1,000 adults				Growth of number of borrowers per 1,000 adults			
		1	2	3	4	5	6	7	8
Strategy variables	Index strategy impulse variable	4.982* (2.875)				ns			
	Index strategy shift variable		5.381* (3.248)				ns		
	Dummy strategy impulse variable			ns				ns	
	Dummy strategy shift variable				59.02* (36.55)				ns
Institutional and macroeconomic variables	GDP per capita	ns	ns	ns	ns	ns	ns	ns	ns
	Financial openness	ns	ns	ns	ns	ns	ns	ns	ns
	Governance	ns	ns	ns	ns	ns	ns	ns	ns
	GDP growth	ns	ns	ns	ns	0.962** (0.448)	0.864** (0.436)	0.942** (0.438)	0.900** (0.438)
	Interest rate	ns	ns	ns	ns	−3.880** (1.585)	−3.952** (1.668)	−4.089** (1.727)	−4.423** (1.993)
	Exchange rate	ns	ns	ns	ns	−0.0228* (0.0122)	−0.026** (0.0126)	−0.0219* (0.0118)	−0.023** (0.011)
	Inflation	ns	ns	ns	ns	ns	ns	ns	ns
Social variables	Age dependency ratio	ns	ns	ns	ns	3.016*** (1.117)	3.389** (1.331)	3.036*** (1.127)	3.988** (1.833)
	Population density	ns	ns	ns	ns	ns	ns	ns	ns
	Constant	ns	ns	ns	ns	−139.3** (63.49)	−168.5** (71.94)	−139.5** (63.3)	−235.6* (125.4)
	Observations	556	556	556	556	444	444	444	444
	R-squared	0.156	0.155	0.156	0.158	0.266	0.272	0.263	0.274

Note: Standard errors in parentheses. ns = not statistically significant.
* $p < 0.1$, ** $p < 0.05$, *** $p < 0.01$.